15

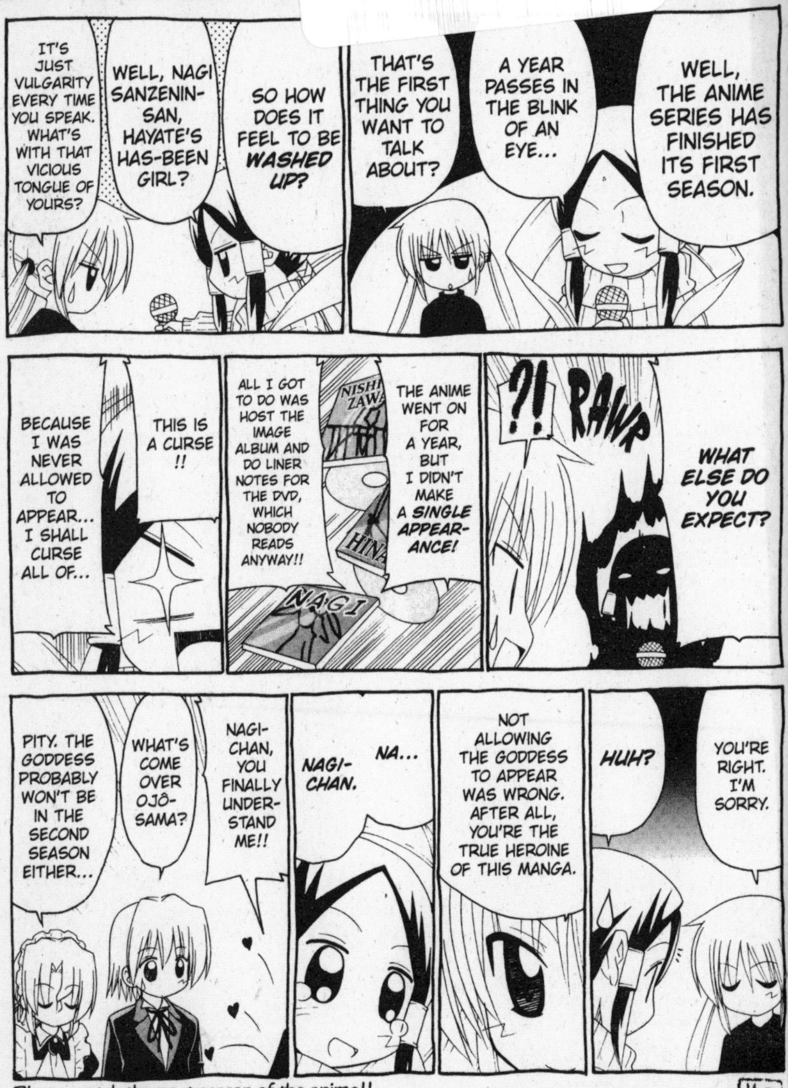
WELL, THE ANIME SERIES HAS FINISHED ITS FIRST SEASON.
A YEAR PASSES IN THE BLINK OF AN EYE...
THAT'S THE FIRST THING YOU WANT TO TALK ABOUT?
SO HOW DOES IT FEEL TO BE *WASHED UP?*
WELL, NAGI SANZENIN-SAN, HAYATE'S HAS-BEEN GIRL?
IT'S JUST VULGARITY EVERY TIME YOU SPEAK. WHAT'S WITH THAT VICIOUS TONGUE OF YOURS?
WHAT ELSE DO YOU EXPECT?
?!
RAWR
THE ANIME WENT ON FOR A YEAR, BUT I DIDN'T MAKE A *SINGLE APPEARANCE!*
NISHIZAWA
HINA
NAGI
ALL I GOT TO DO WAS HOST THE IMAGE ALBUM AND DO LINER NOTES FOR THE DVD, WHICH NOBODY READS ANYWAY!!
THIS IS A CURSE!!
BECAUSE I WAS NEVER ALLOWED TO APPEAR... I SHALL CURSE ALL OF...
YOU'RE RIGHT. I'M SORRY.
HUH?
NOT ALLOWING THE GODDESS TO APPEAR WAS WRONG. AFTER ALL, YOU'RE THE TRUE HEROINE OF THIS MANGA.
NA...
NAGI-CHAN.
NAGI-CHAN, YOU FINALLY UNDERSTAND ME!!
WHAT'S COME OVER OJÔ-SAMA?
PITY. THE GODDESS PROBABLY WON'T BE IN THE SECOND SEASON EITHER...

Please watch the next season of the anime!!

HAYATE THE COMBAT BUTLER
VOL. 15
Shonen Sunday Edition

STORY AND ART BY
KENJIRO HATA

© 2005 Kenjiro HATA/Shogakukan
All rights reserved.
Original Japanese edition "HAYATE NO GOTOKU!" published by SHOGAKUKAN Inc.

English Adaptation/Mark Giambruno
Translation/Yuki Yoshioka and Cindy H. Yamauchi
Touch-up Art & Lettering/Hudson Yards
Design/Yukiko Whitley
Editor/Shaenon K. Garrity

VP, Production/Alvin Lu
VP, Sales & Product Marketing/Gonzalo Ferreyra
VP, Creative/Linda Espinosa
Publisher/Hyoe Narita

Printed in Canada

Published by VIZ Media, LLC
P.O. Box 77010
San Francisco, CA 94107

10 9 8 7 6 5 4 3 2 1
First printing, June 2010

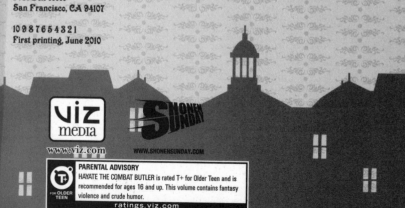

VIZ MEDIA
www.viz.com

SHONEN SUNDAY
WWW.SHONENSUNDAY.COM

Hayate the Combat Butler

15

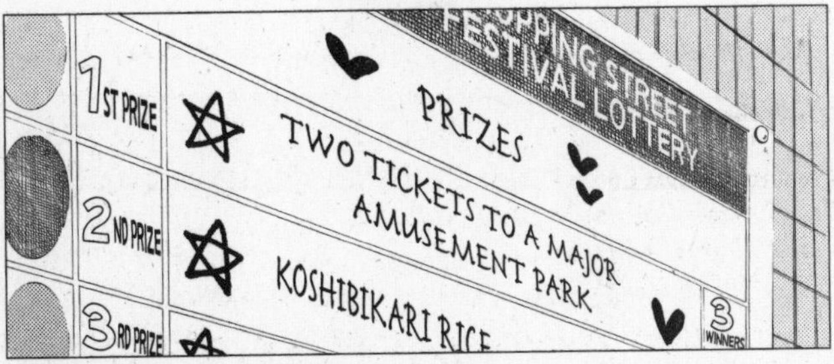
PPING STREET
FESTIVAL LOTTERY
PRIZES
1ST PRIZE
TWO TICKETS TO A MAJOR AMUSEMENT PARK
2ND PRIZE
KOSHIBIKARI RICE
3RD PRIZE
3 WINNERS

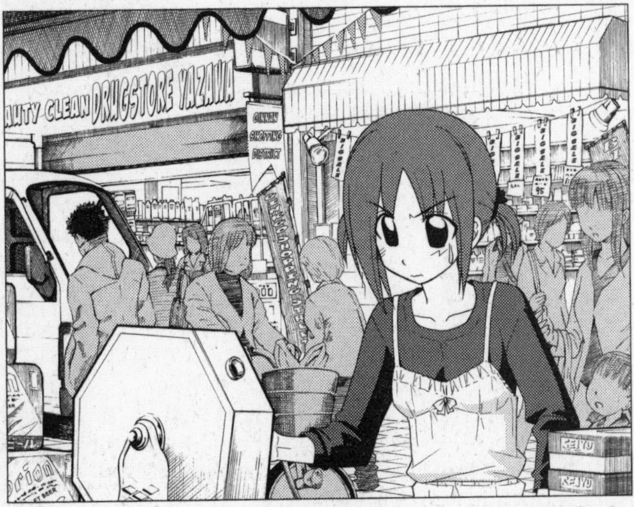
DRUGSTORE YAZAWA

KENJIRO HATA

*The birds spell out "Table of Contents."

Episode 1:
"Unnecessary *Moe* and Necessary Courage"

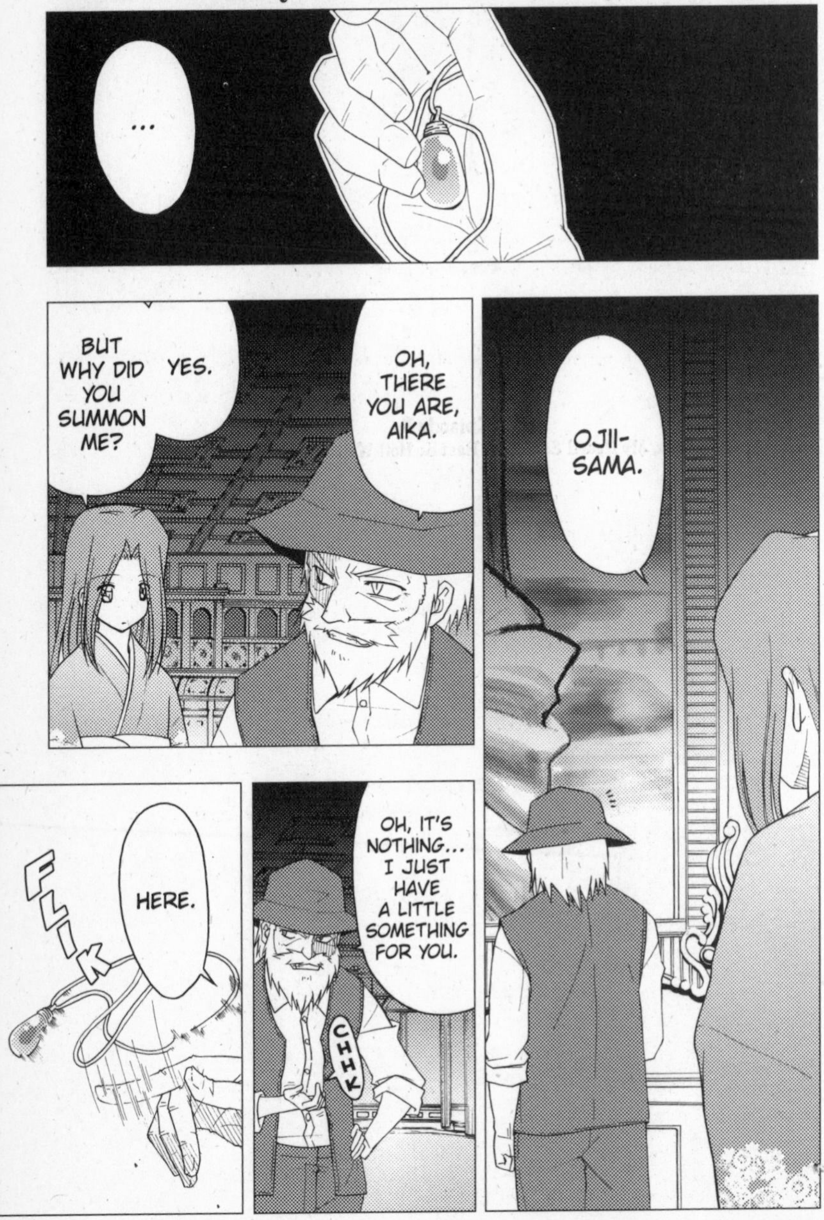
...
OJII-SAMA.
OH, THERE YOU ARE, AIKA.
YES.
BUT WHY DID YOU SUMMON ME?
OH, IT'S NOTHING... I JUST HAVE A LITTLE SOMETHING FOR YOU.
CHHK
HERE.
FLIK

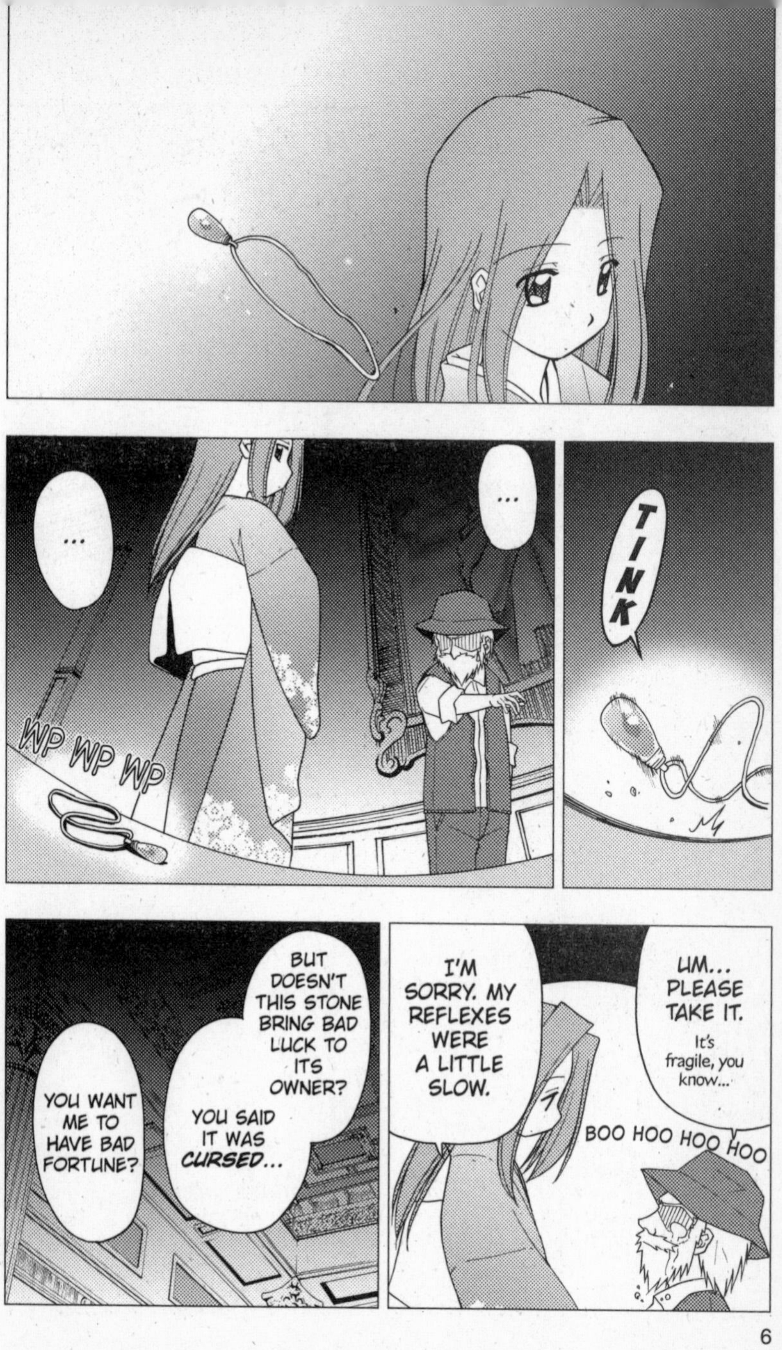
TINK
...
...
WP WP WP
UM... PLEASE TAKE IT.
It's fragile, you know...
BOO HOO HOO HOO
I'M SORRY. MY REFLEXES WERE A LITTLE SLOW.
BUT DOESN'T THIS STONE BRING BAD LUCK TO ITS OWNER?
YOU SAID IT WAS CURSED...
YOU WANT ME TO HAVE BAD FORTUNE?

Episode 1:
"Unnecessary *Moe* and Necessary Courage"

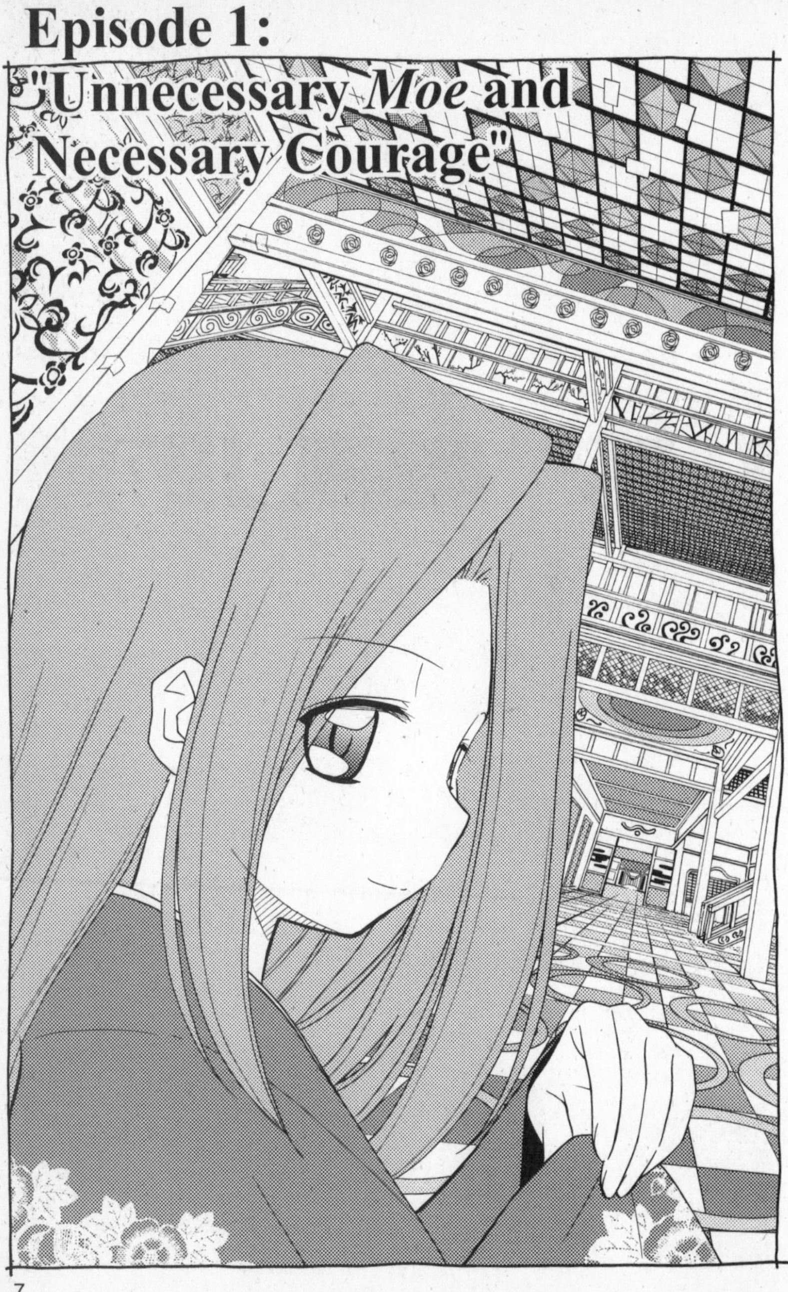

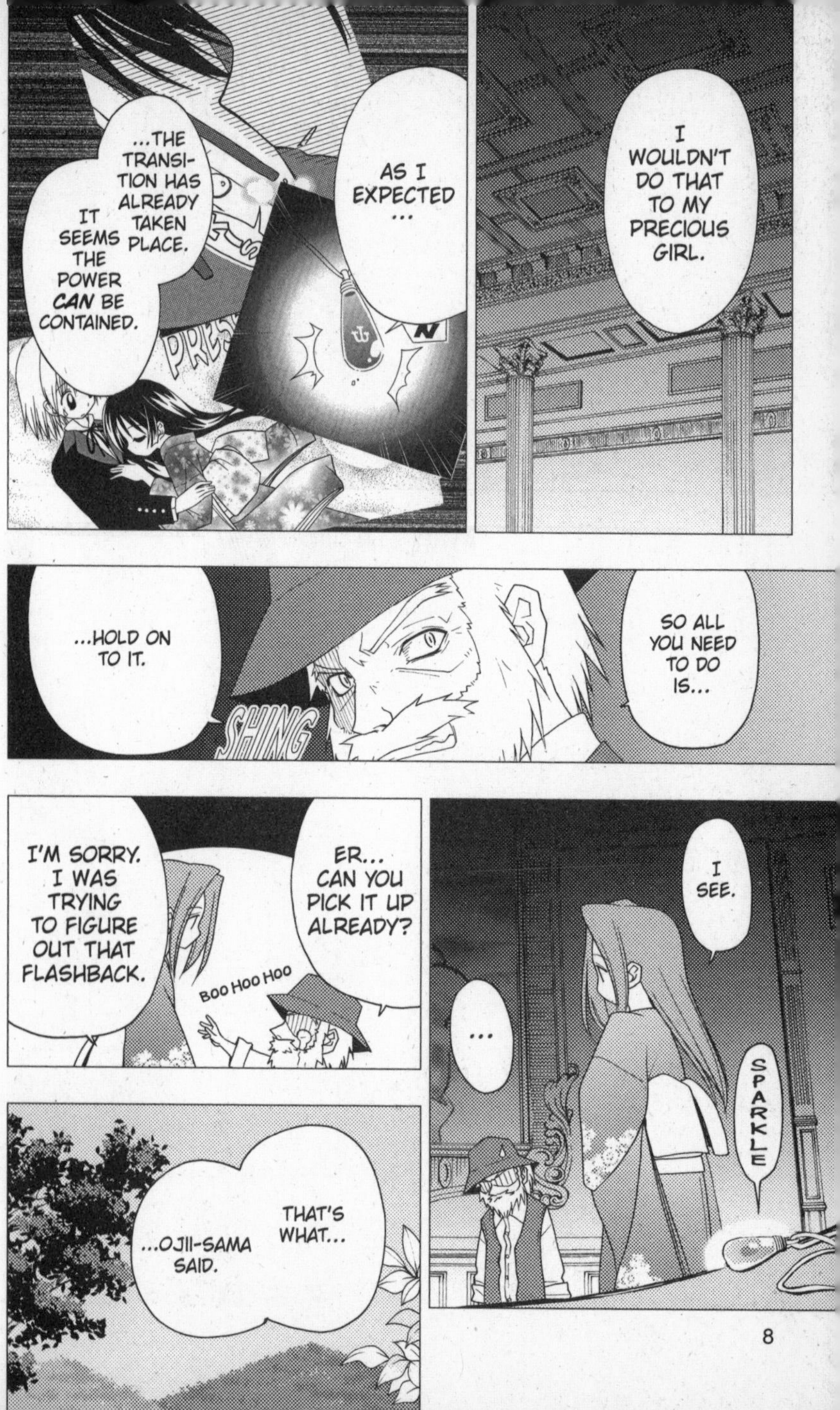
I WOULDN'T DO THAT TO MY PRECIOUS GIRL.
AS I EXPECTED...
...THE TRANSITION HAS ALREADY TAKEN PLACE.
IT SEEMS THE POWER *CAN* BE CONTAINED.
SO ALL YOU NEED TO DO IS...
SHING
...HOLD ON TO IT.
I SEE.
...
SPARKLE
ER... CAN YOU PICK IT UP ALREADY?
I'M SORRY. I WAS TRYING TO FIGURE OUT THAT FLASHBACK.
BOO HOO HOO
THAT'S WHAT...
...OJII-SAMA SAID.

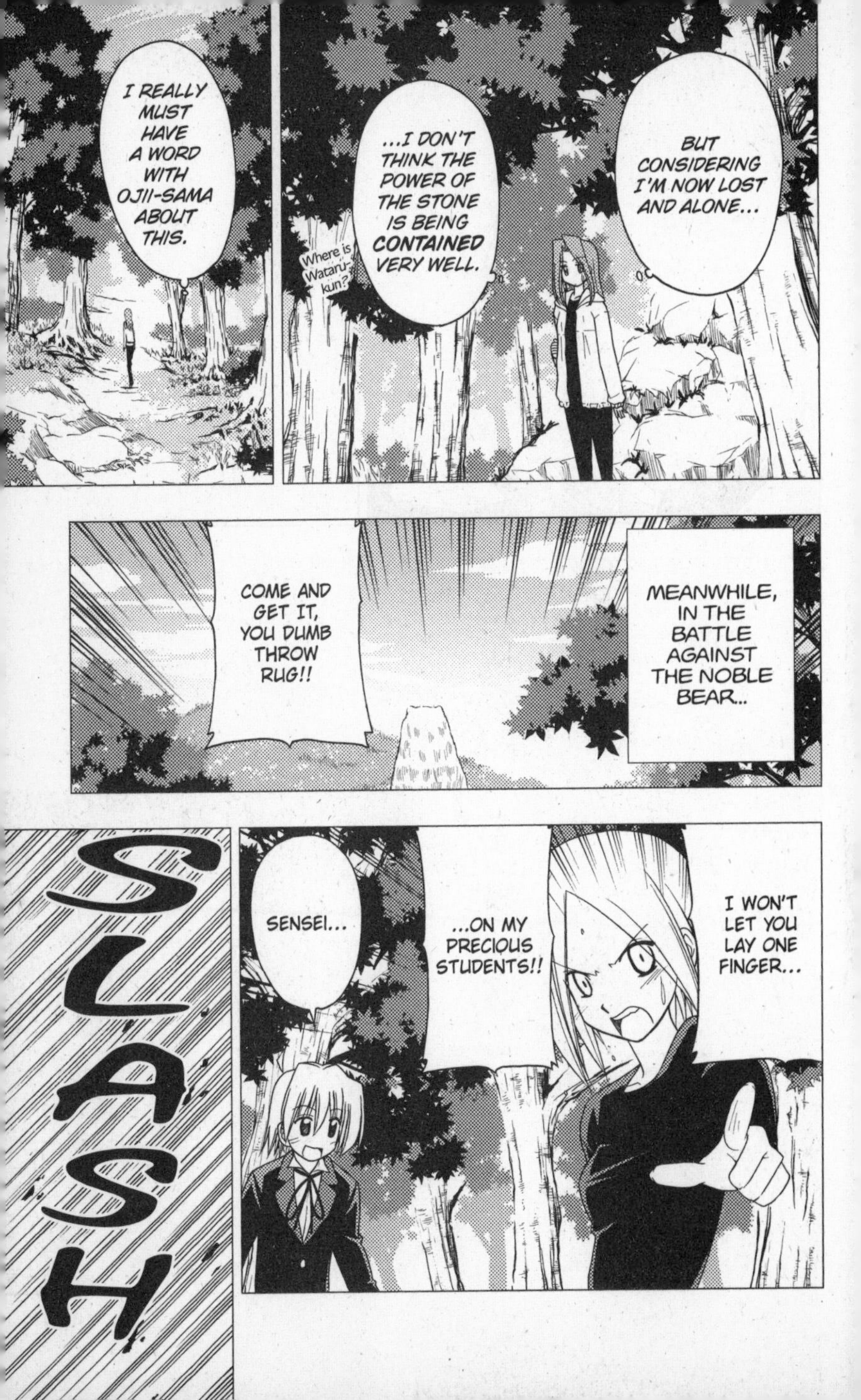
BUT CONSIDERING I'M NOW LOST AND ALONE...
...I DON'T THINK THE POWER OF THE STONE IS BEING CONTAINED VERY WELL.
Where is Wataru-kun?
I REALLY MUST HAVE A WORD WITH OJII-SAMA ABOUT THIS.
MEANWHILE, IN THE BATTLE AGAINST THE NOBLE BEAR...
COME AND GET IT, YOU DUMB THROW RUG!!
I WON'T LET YOU LAY ONE FINGER...
...ON MY PRECIOUS STUDENTS!!
SENSEI...
SLASH

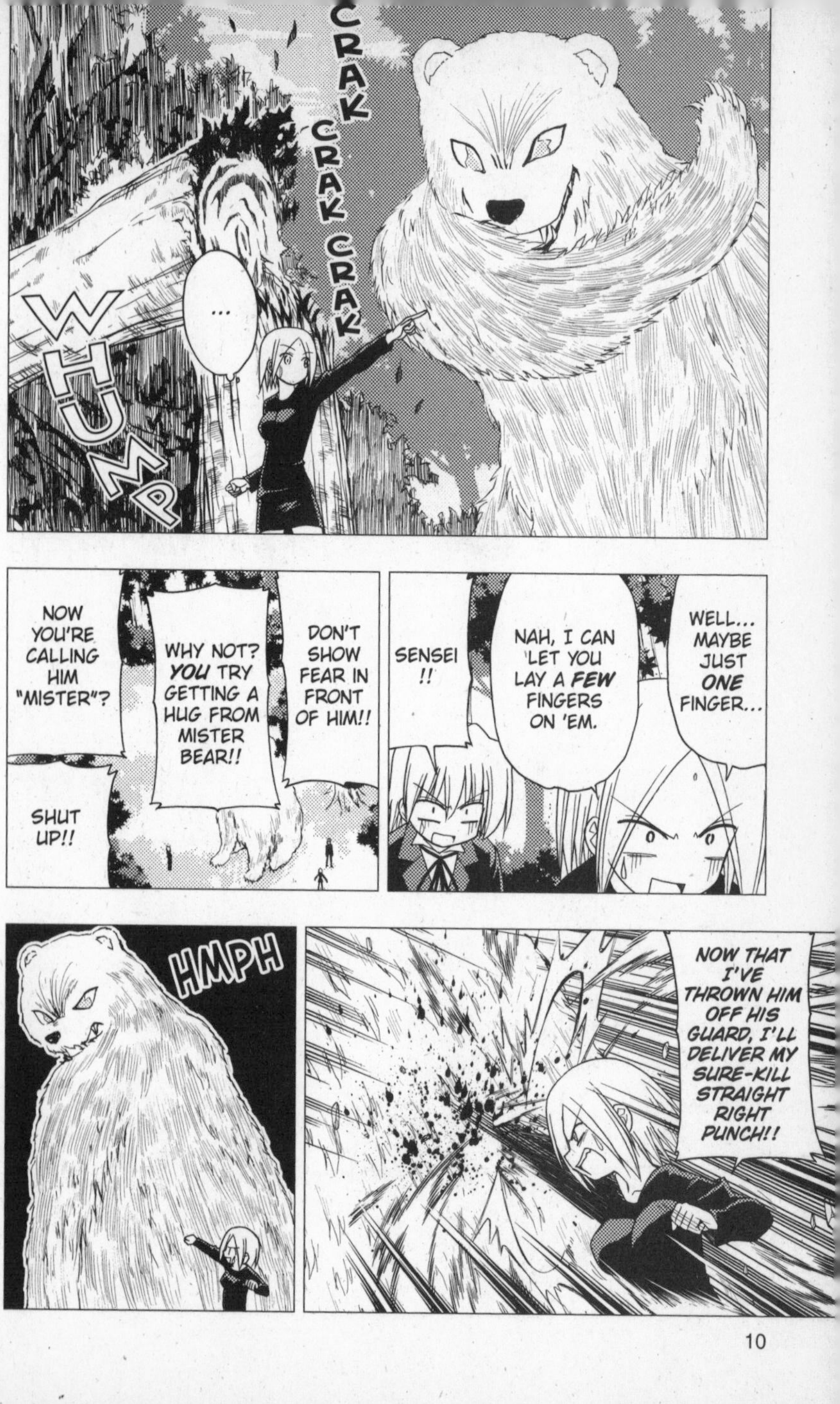
CRAK CRAK CRAK
...
WHUMP
WELL... MAYBE JUST ONE FINGER...
NAH, I CAN LET YOU LAY A FEW FINGERS ON 'EM.
SENSEI!!
DON'T SHOW FEAR IN FRONT OF HIM!!
WHY NOT? YOU TRY GETTING A HUG FROM MISTER BEAR!!
NOW YOU'RE CALLING HIM "MISTER"?
SHUT UP!!
NOW THAT I'VE THROWN HIM OFF HIS GUARD, I'LL DELIVER MY SURE-KILL STRAIGHT RIGHT PUNCH!!
HMPH

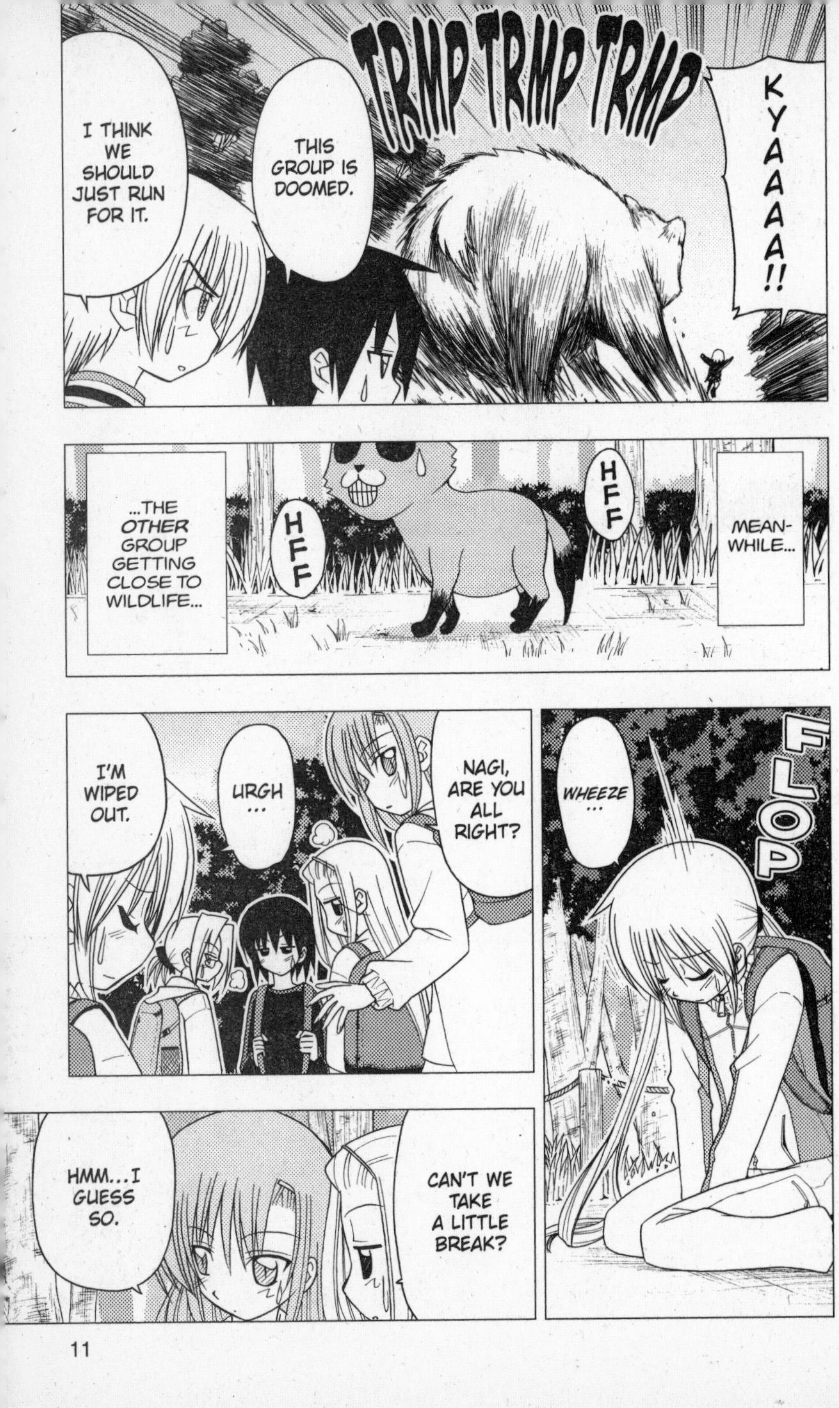

KYAAAAA!!
TRMP TRMP TRMP
THIS GROUP IS DOOMED.
I THINK WE SHOULD JUST RUN FOR IT.
MEAN-WHILE...
HFF
HFF
...THE OTHER GROUP GETTING CLOSE TO WILDLIFE...
FLOP
WHEEZE...
NAGI, ARE YOU ALL RIGHT?
URGH...
I'M WIPED OUT.
CAN'T WE TAKE A LITTLE BREAK?
HMM...I GUESS SO.

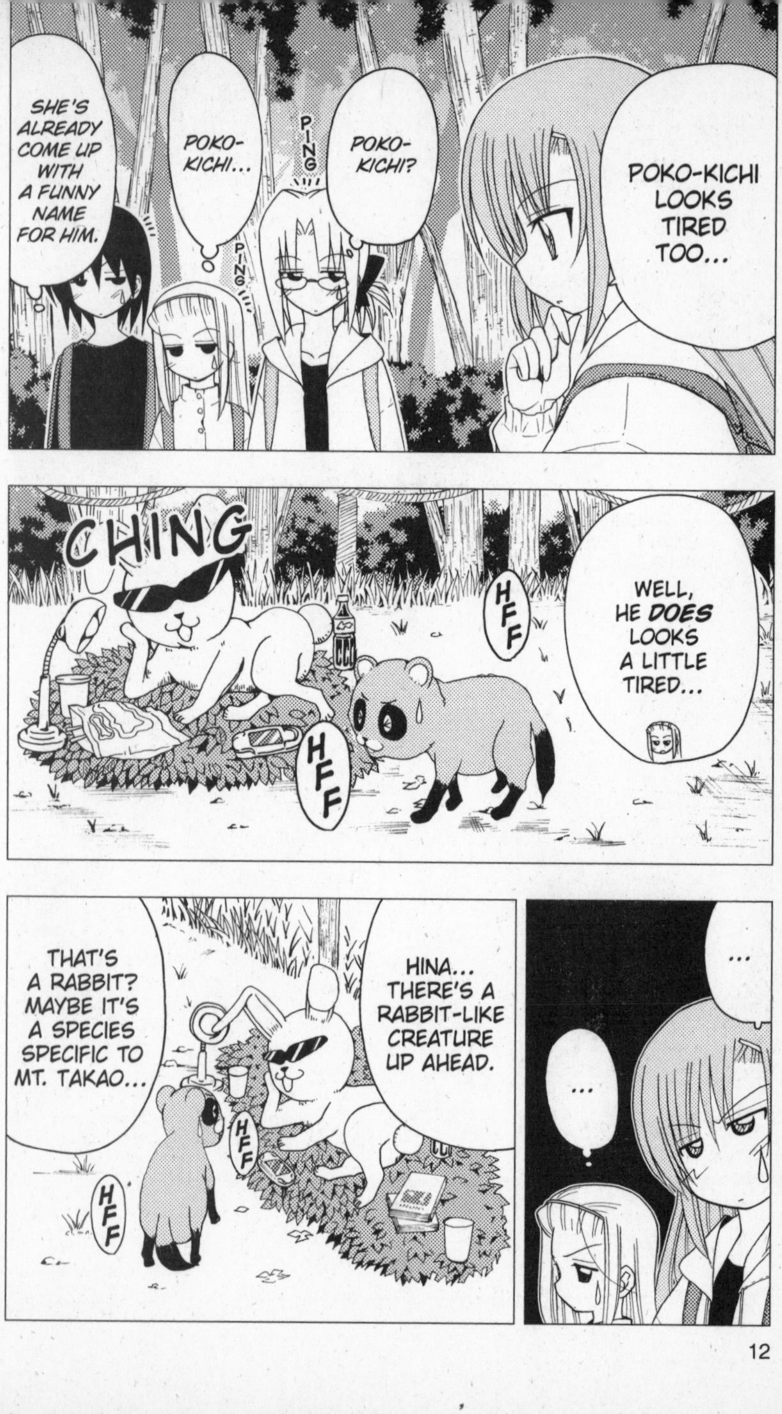
POKO-KICHI LOOKS TIRED TOO...
POKO-KICHI?
PING
PING
POKO-KICHI...
SHE'S ALREADY COME UP WITH A FUNNY NAME FOR HIM.
WELL, HE DOES LOOKS A LITTLE TIRED...
HFF
HFF
CHING
...
...
HINA... THERE'S A RABBIT-LIKE CREATURE UP AHEAD.
HFF
THAT'S A RABBIT? MAYBE IT'S A SPECIES SPECIFIC TO MT. TAKAO...
HFF

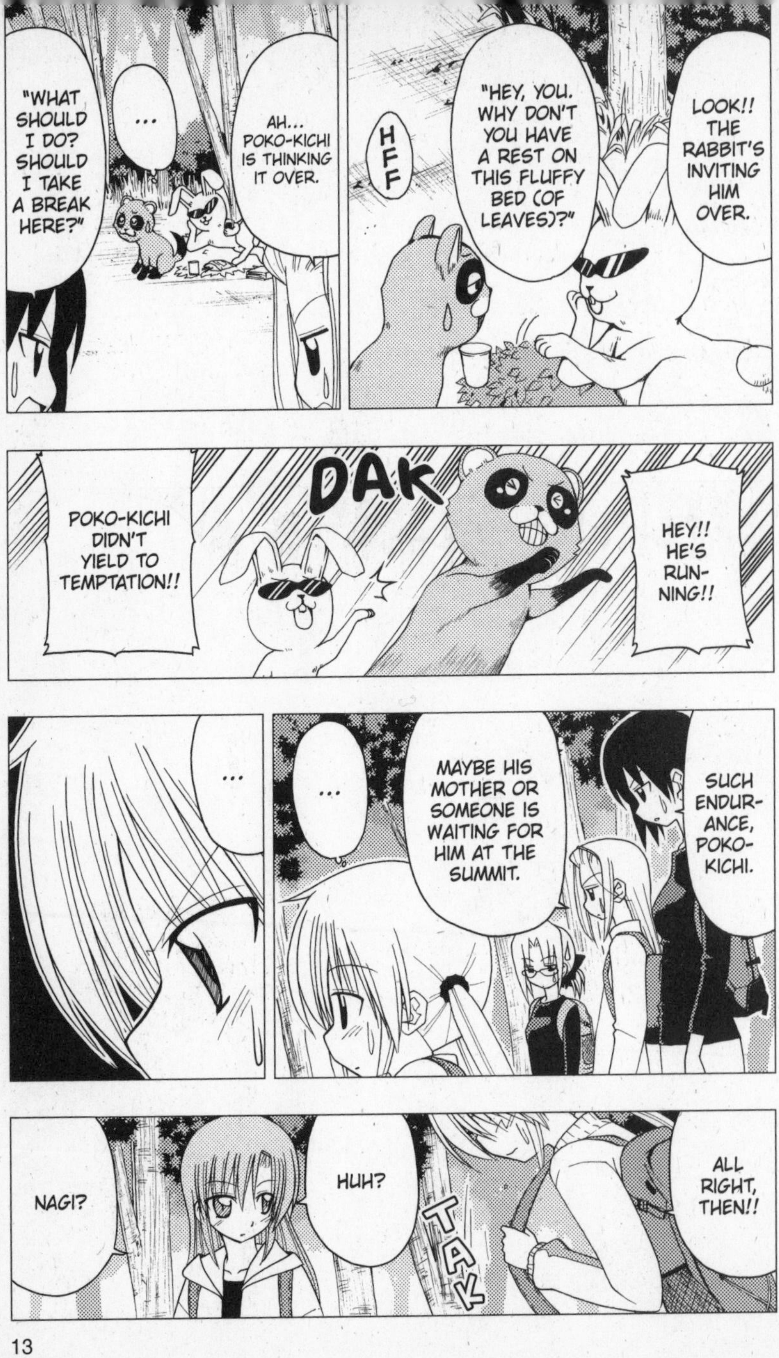
LOOK!! THE RABBIT'S INVITING HIM OVER.
"HEY, YOU. WHY DON'T YOU HAVE A REST ON THIS FLUFFY BED (OF LEAVES)?"
HFF
AH... POKO-KICHI IS THINKING IT OVER.
...
"WHAT SHOULD I DO? SHOULD I TAKE A BREAK HERE?"
HEY!! HE'S RUN-NING!!
DAK
POKO-KICHI DIDN'T YIELD TO TEMPTATION!!
SUCH ENDUR-ANCE, POKO-KICHI.
MAYBE HIS MOTHER OR SOMEONE IS WAITING FOR HIM AT THE SUMMIT.
...
...
ALL RIGHT, THEN!!
TAK
HUH?
NAGI?

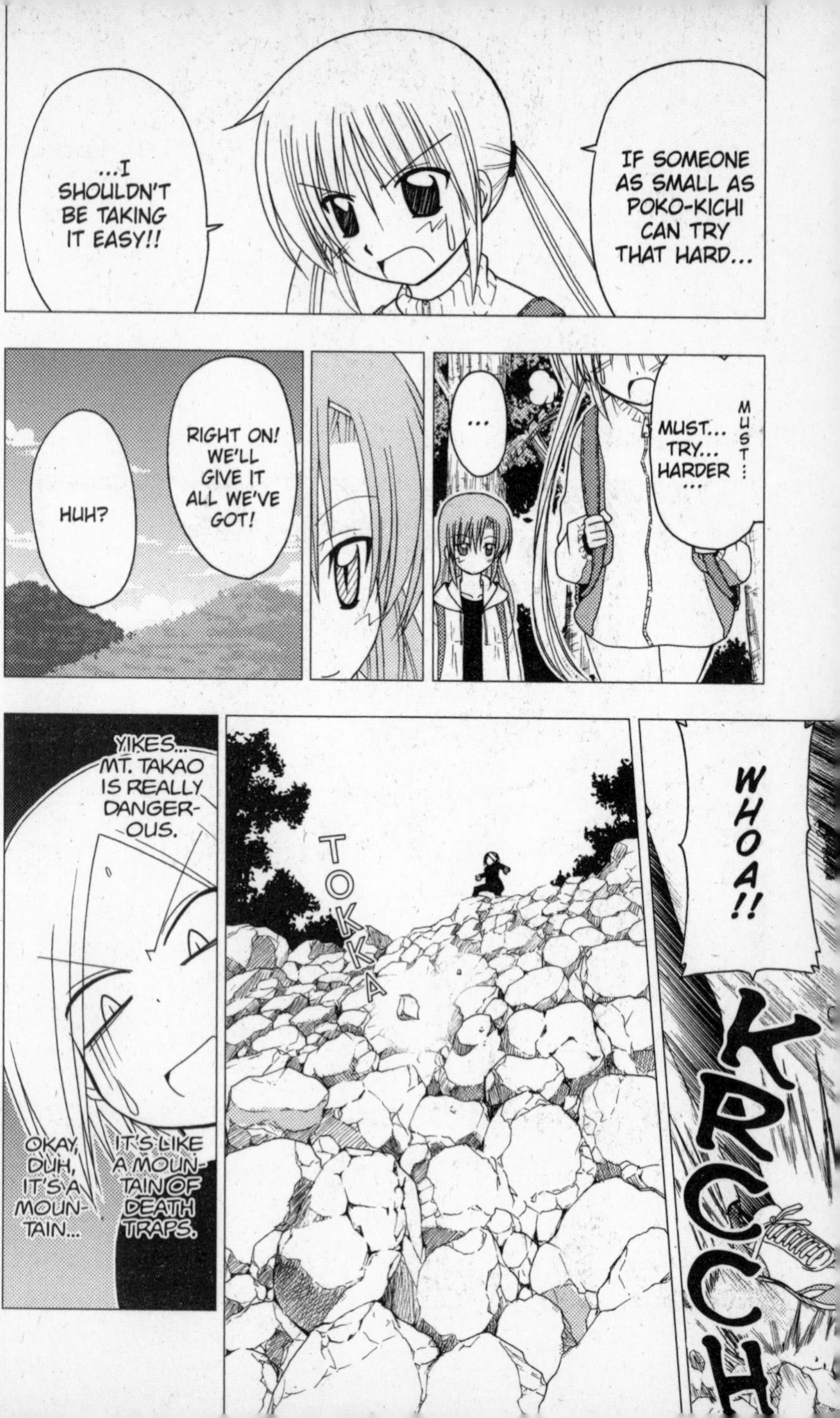
IF SOMEONE AS SMALL AS POKO-KICHI CAN TRY THAT HARD...
...I SHOULDN'T BE TAKING IT EASY!!
MUST... TRY... HARDER ...
MUST...
...
RIGHT ON! WE'LL GIVE IT ALL WE'VE GOT!
HUH?
WHOA!!
KRCCH
TOKA
YIKES... MT. TAKAO IS REALLY DANGER-OUS.
IT'S LIKE A MOUN-TAIN OF DEATH TRAPS.
OKAY, DUH, IT'S A MOUN-TAIN...

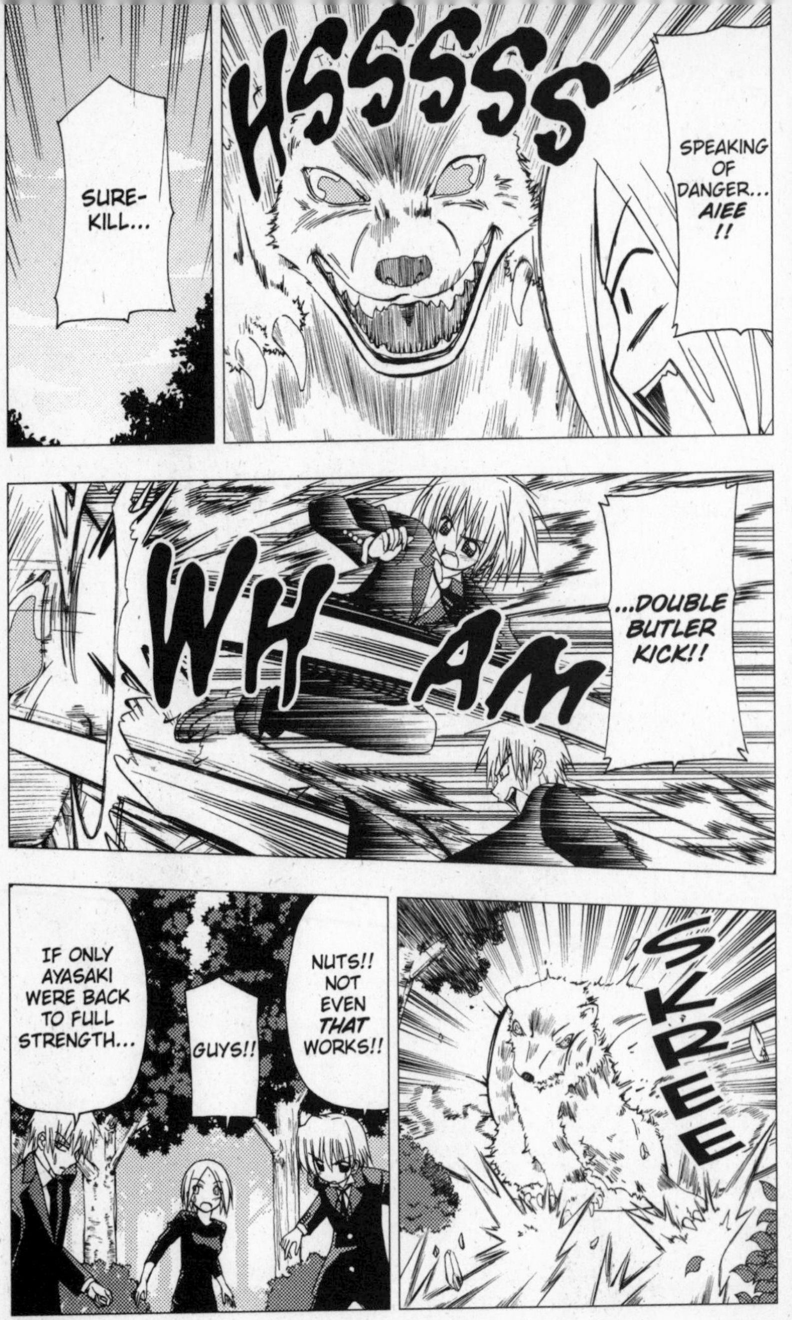
SPEAKING OF DANGER... AIEE!!
HSSSSS
SURE-KILL...
...DOUBLE BUTLER KICK!!
WHAM
SKREE
NUTS!! NOT EVEN *THAT* WORKS!!
GUYS!!
IF ONLY AYASAKI WERE BACK TO FULL STRENGTH...

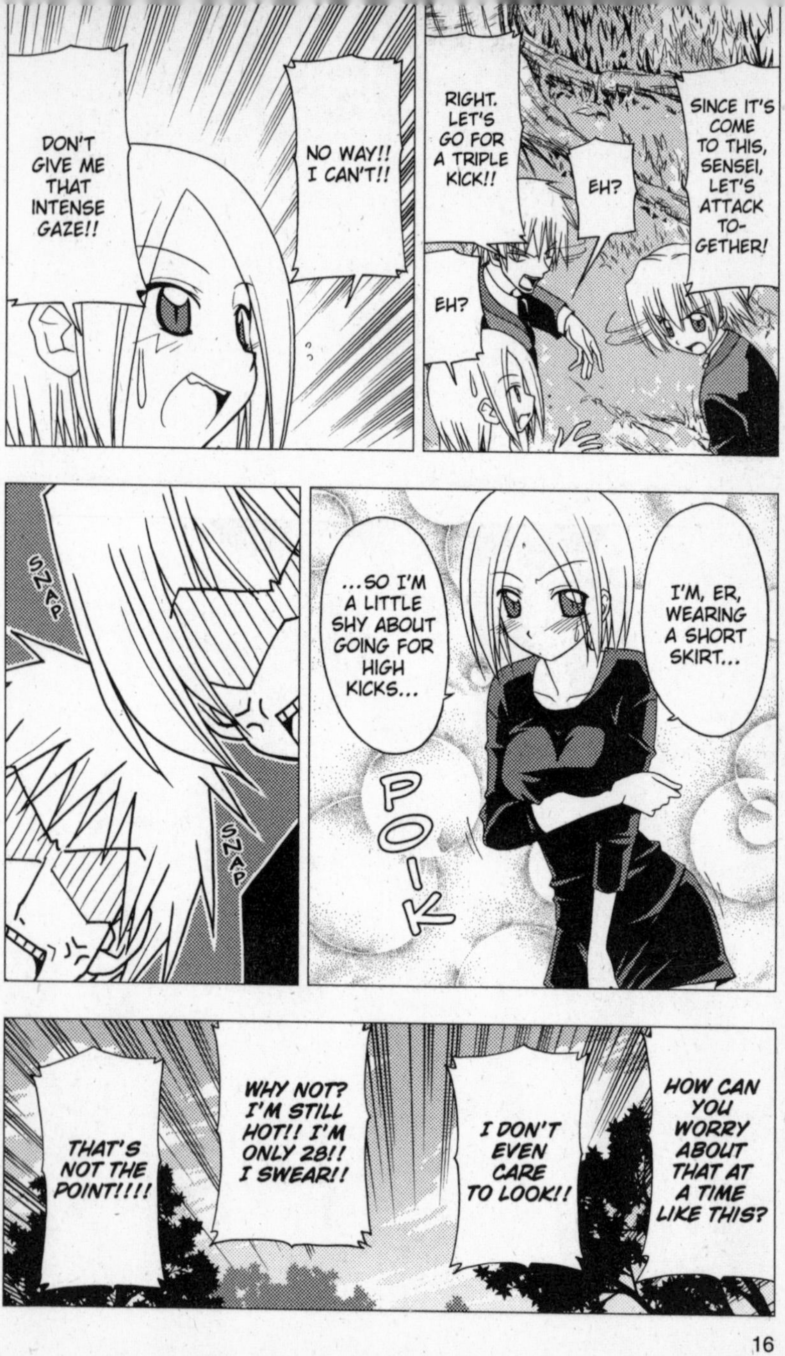
SINCE IT'S COME TO THIS, SENSEI, LET'S ATTACK TO-GETHER!
EH?
RIGHT. LET'S GO FOR A TRIPLE KICK!!
EH?
NO WAY!! I CAN'T!!
DON'T GIVE ME THAT INTENSE GAZE!!
I'M, ER, WEARING A SHORT SKIRT...
...SO I'M A LITTLE SHY ABOUT GOING FOR HIGH KICKS...
POIK
SNAP
SNAP
HOW CAN YOU WORRY ABOUT THAT AT A TIME LIKE THIS?
I DON'T EVEN CARE TO LOOK!!
WHY NOT? I'M STILL HOT!! I'M ONLY 28!! I SWEAR!!
THAT'S NOT THE POINT!!!!

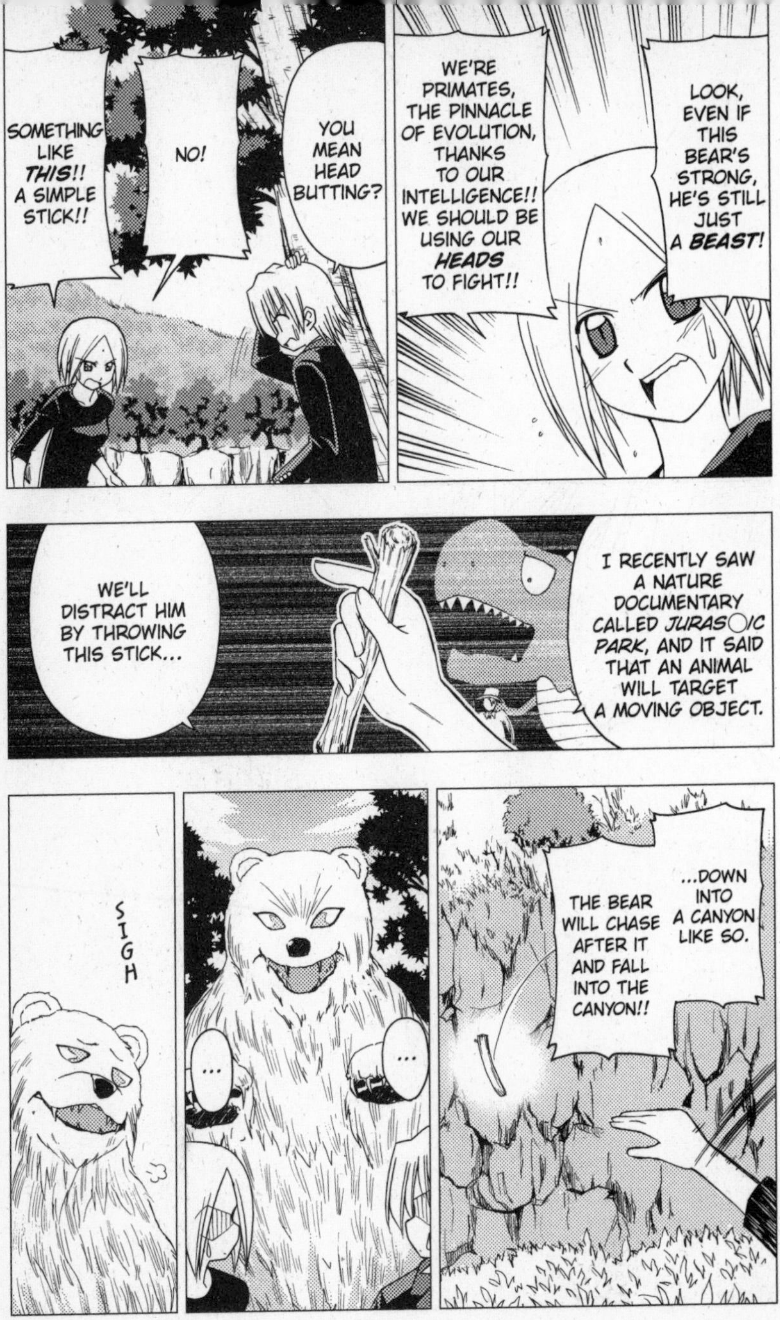
LOOK, EVEN IF THIS BEAR'S STRONG, HE'S STILL JUST A BEAST!
WE'RE PRIMATES, THE PINNACLE OF EVOLUTION, THANKS TO OUR INTELLIGENCE!! WE SHOULD BE USING OUR HEADS TO FIGHT!!
YOU MEAN HEAD BUTTING?
NO!
SOMETHING LIKE THIS!! A SIMPLE STICK!!
I RECENTLY SAW A NATURE DOCUMENTARY CALLED JURAS◯IC PARK, AND IT SAID THAT AN ANIMAL WILL TARGET A MOVING OBJECT.
WE'LL DISTRACT HIM BY THROWING THIS STICK...
...DOWN INTO A CANYON LIKE SO.
THE BEAR WILL CHASE AFTER IT AND FALL INTO THE CANYON!!
...
...
SIGH

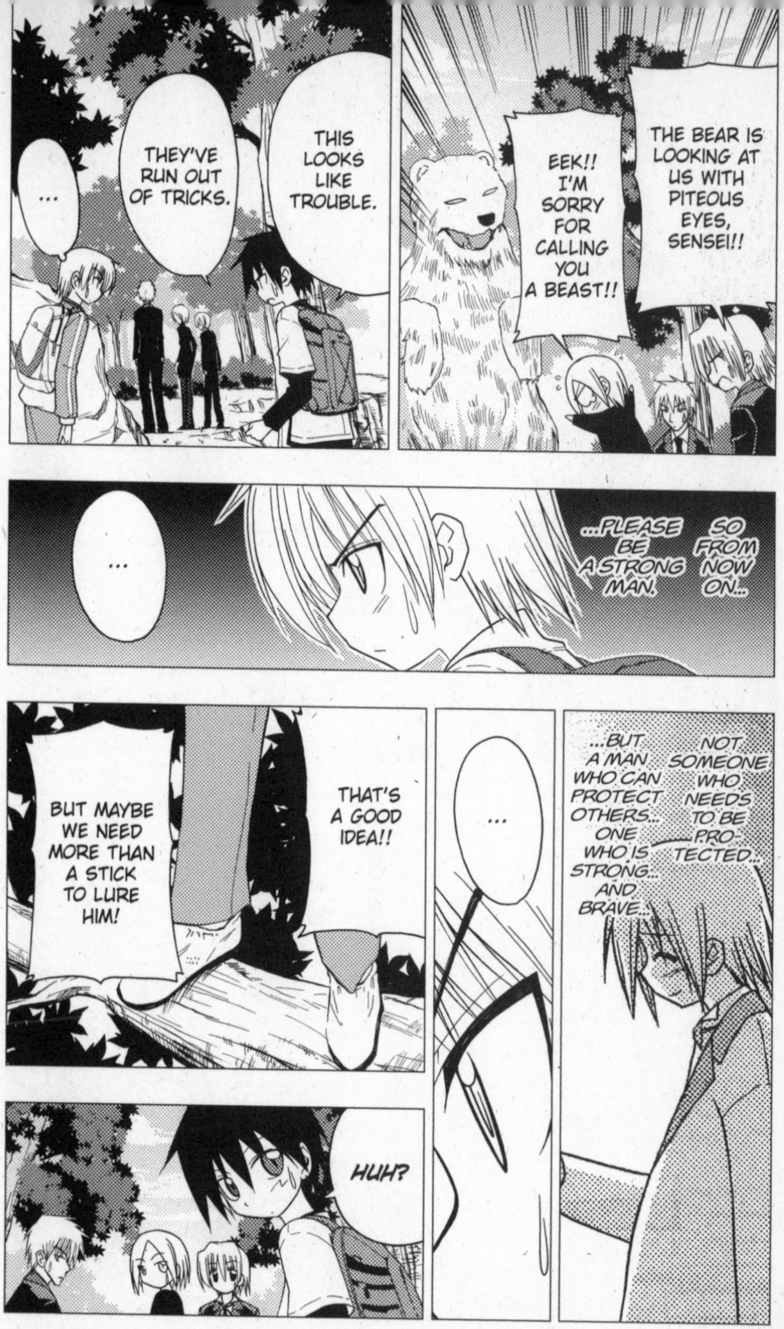
THE BEAR IS LOOKING AT US WITH PITEOUS EYES, SENSEI!!
EEK!! I'M SORRY FOR CALLING YOU A BEAST!!
THIS LOOKS LIKE TROUBLE.
THEY'VE RUN OUT OF TRICKS.
...
SO FROM NOW ON...
...PLEASE BE A STRONG MAN.
...
NOT SOMEONE WHO NEEDS TO BE PROTECTED...
...BUT A MAN WHO CAN PROTECT OTHERS... ONE WHO IS STRONG... AND BRAVE...
...
THAT'S A GOOD IDEA!!
BUT MAYBE WE NEED MORE THAN A STICK TO LURE HIM!
HUH?

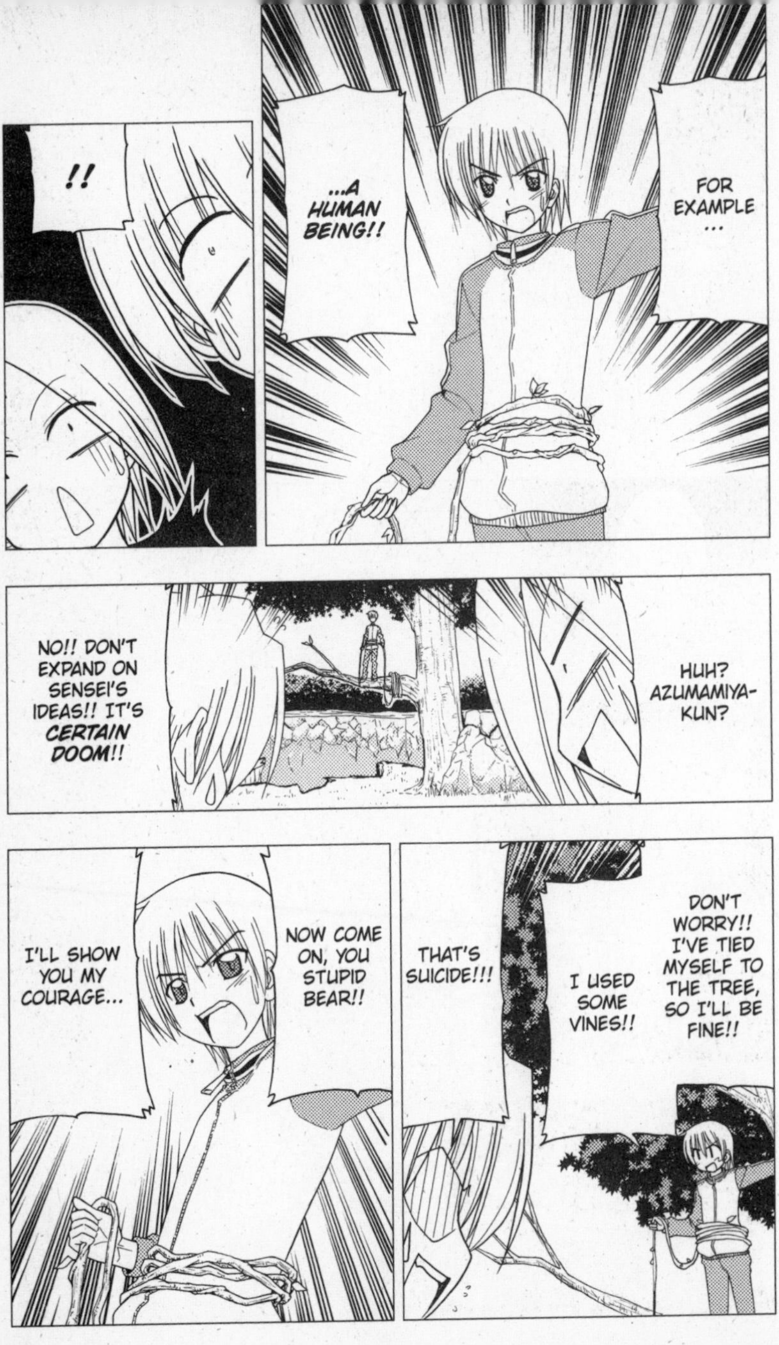
FOR EXAMPLE...
...A HUMAN BEING!!
!!
HUH? AZUMAMIYA-KUN?
NO!! DON'T EXPAND ON SENSEI'S IDEAS!! IT'S *CERTAIN DOOM*!!
DON'T WORRY!! I'VE TIED MYSELF TO THE TREE, SO I'LL BE FINE!!
I USED SOME VINES!!
THAT'S SUICIDE!!!
NOW COME ON, YOU STUPID BEAR!!
I'LL SHOW YOU MY COURAGE...

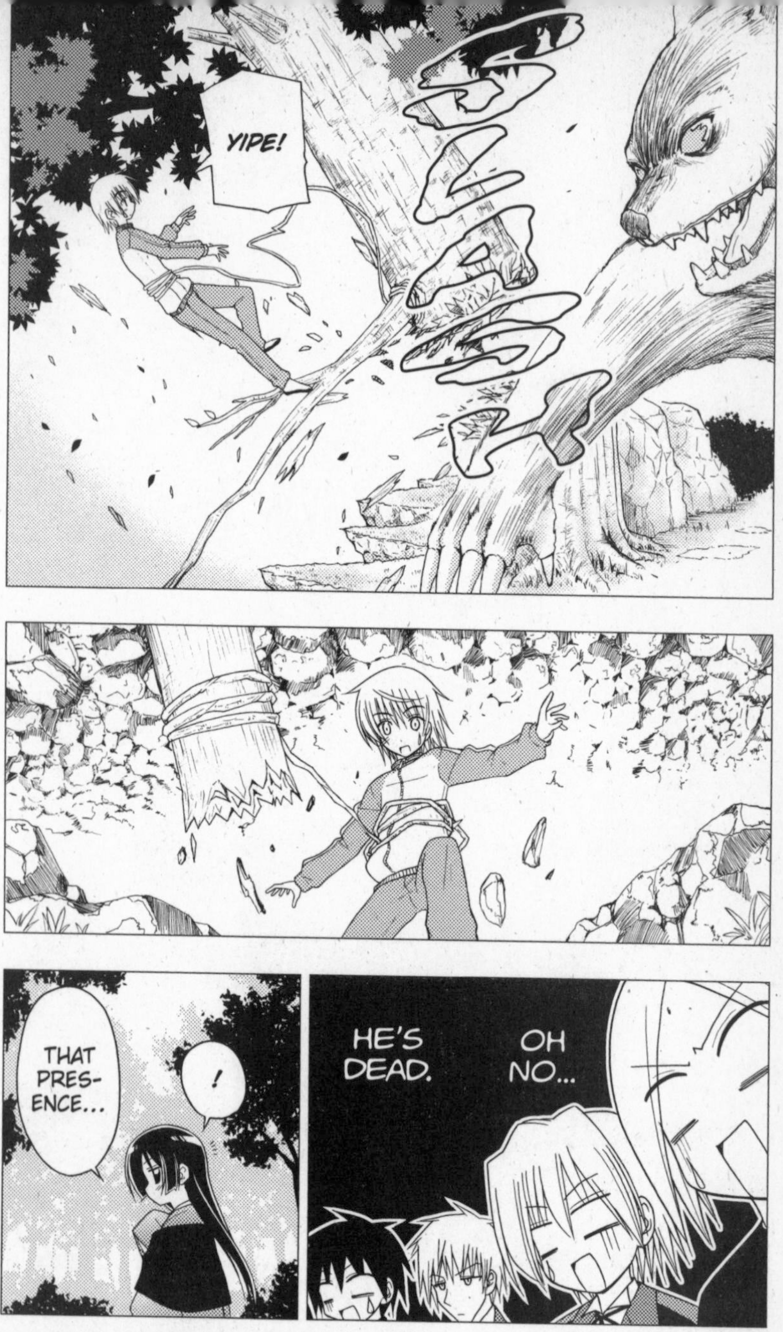
YIPE!
OH NO...
HE'S DEAD.
!
THAT PRES-ENCE...

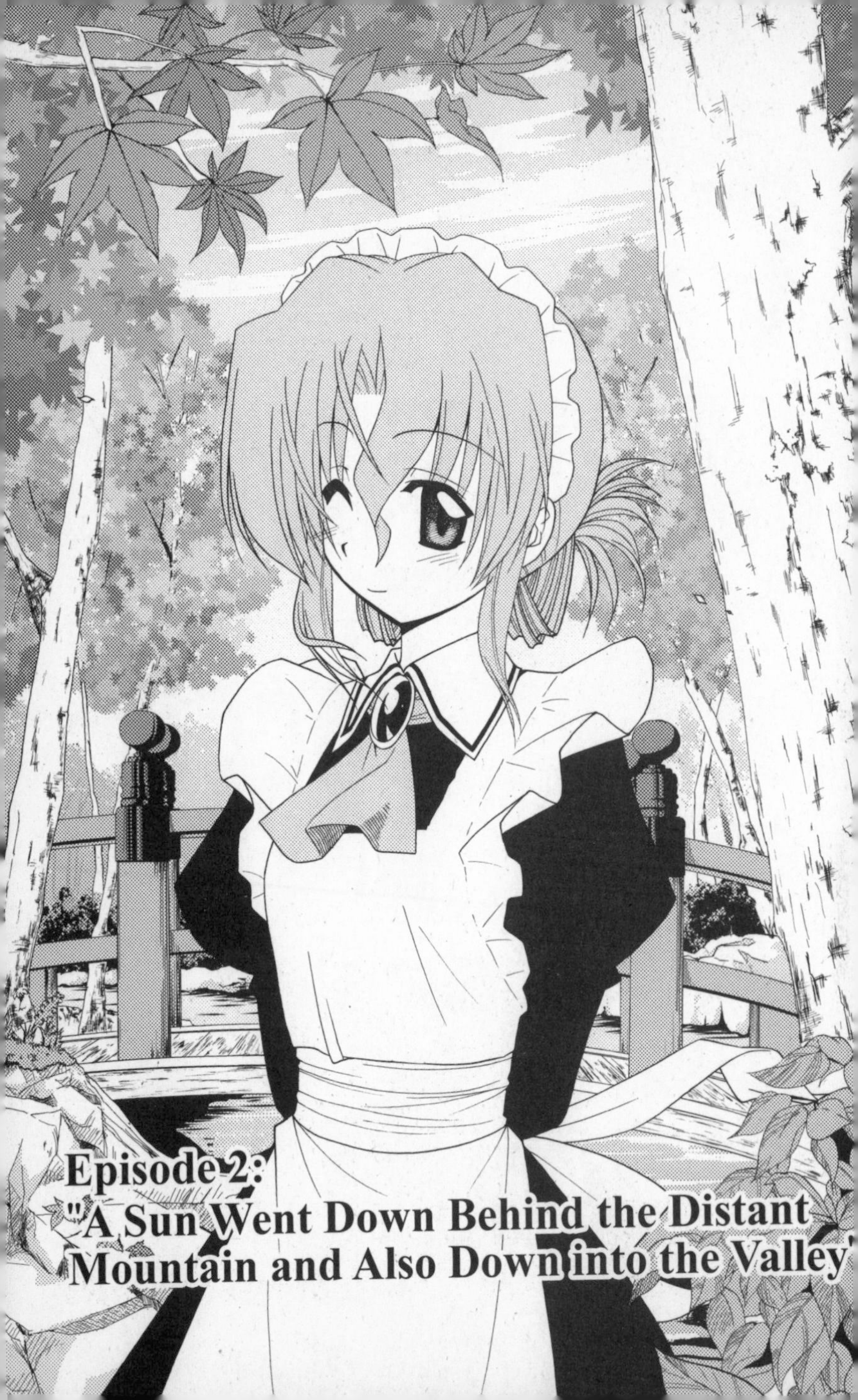
Episode 2:
"A Sun Went Down Behind the Distant Mountain and Also Down into the Valley"

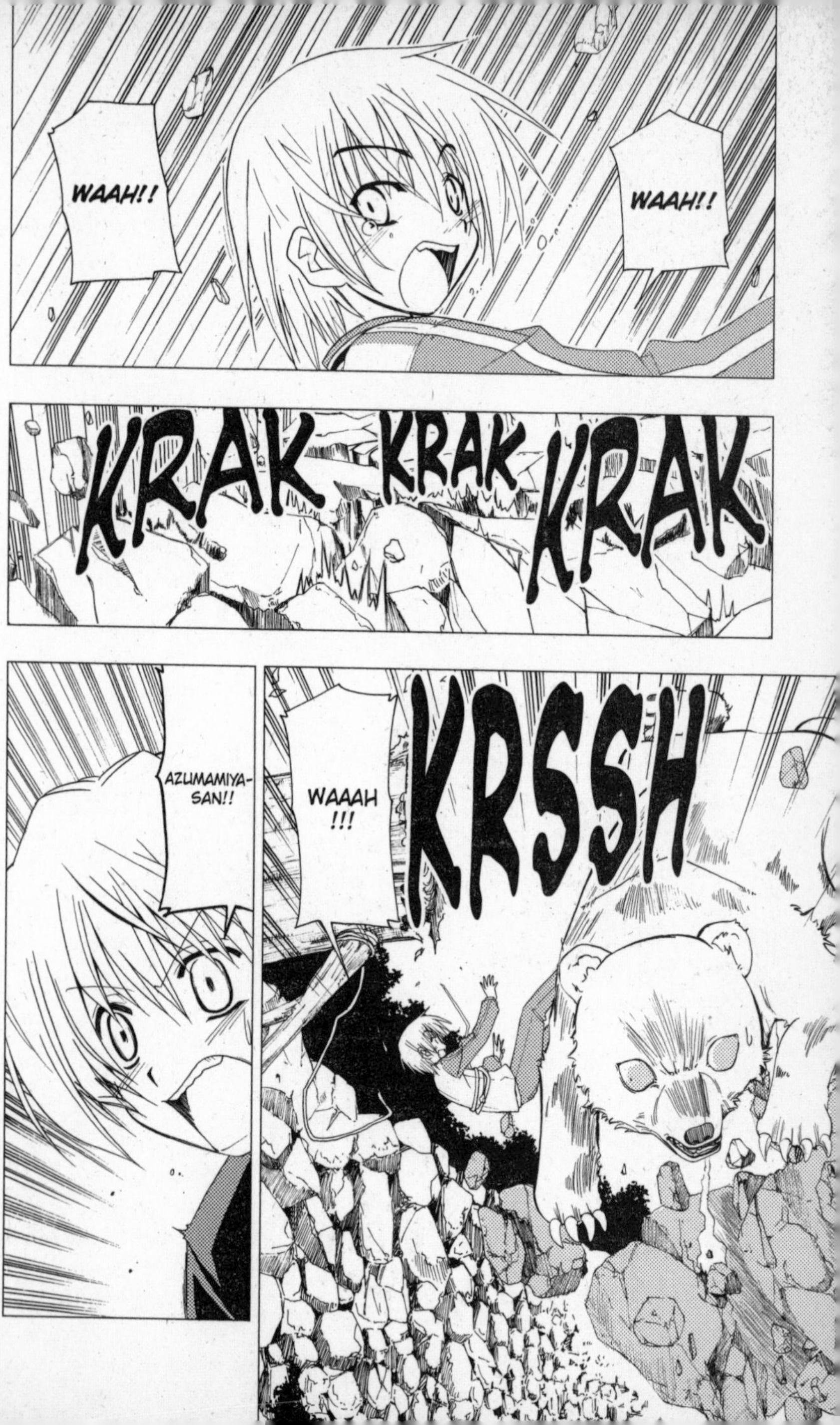
WAAH!!
WAAH!!
KRAK KRAK KRAK
KRSSH
WAAAH!!!
AZUMAMIYA-SAN!!

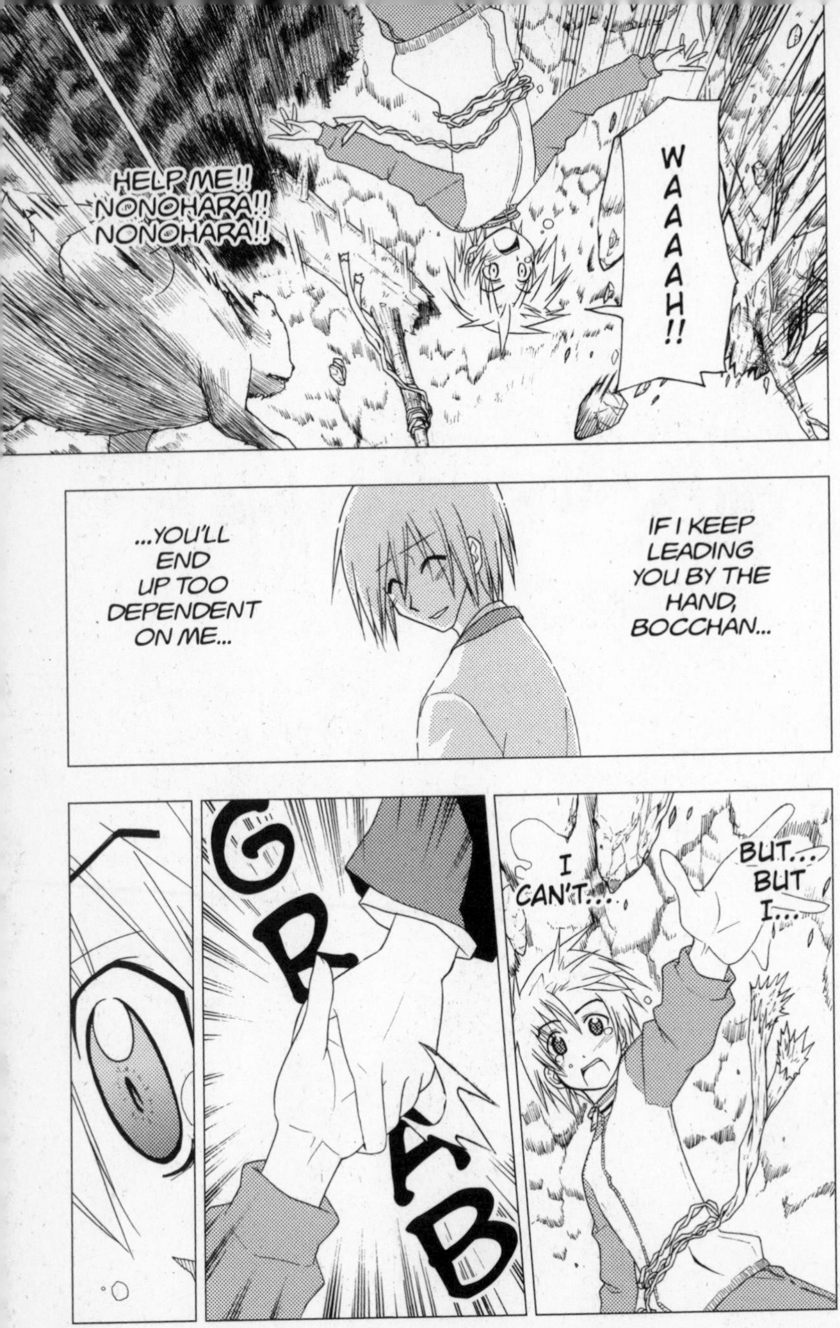
WAAAAAH!!
HELP ME!! NONOHARA!! NONOHARA!!
IF I KEEP LEADING YOU BY THE HAND, BOCCHAN...
...YOU'LL END UP TOO DEPENDENT ON ME...
BUT... BUT I...
I CAN'T...
GRAB

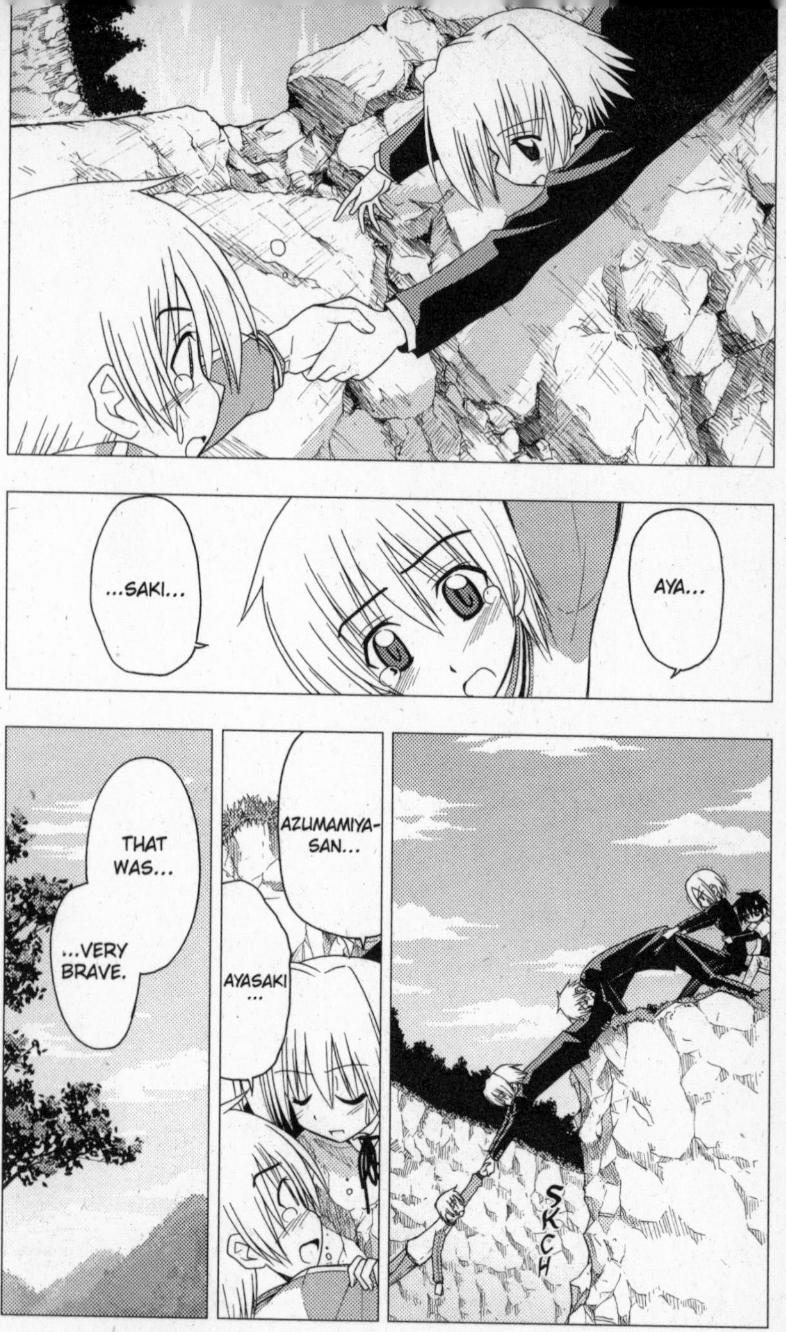
AYA...
...SAKI...
SKCH
AZUMAMIYA-SAN...
AYASAKI ...
THAT WAS...
...VERY BRAVE.

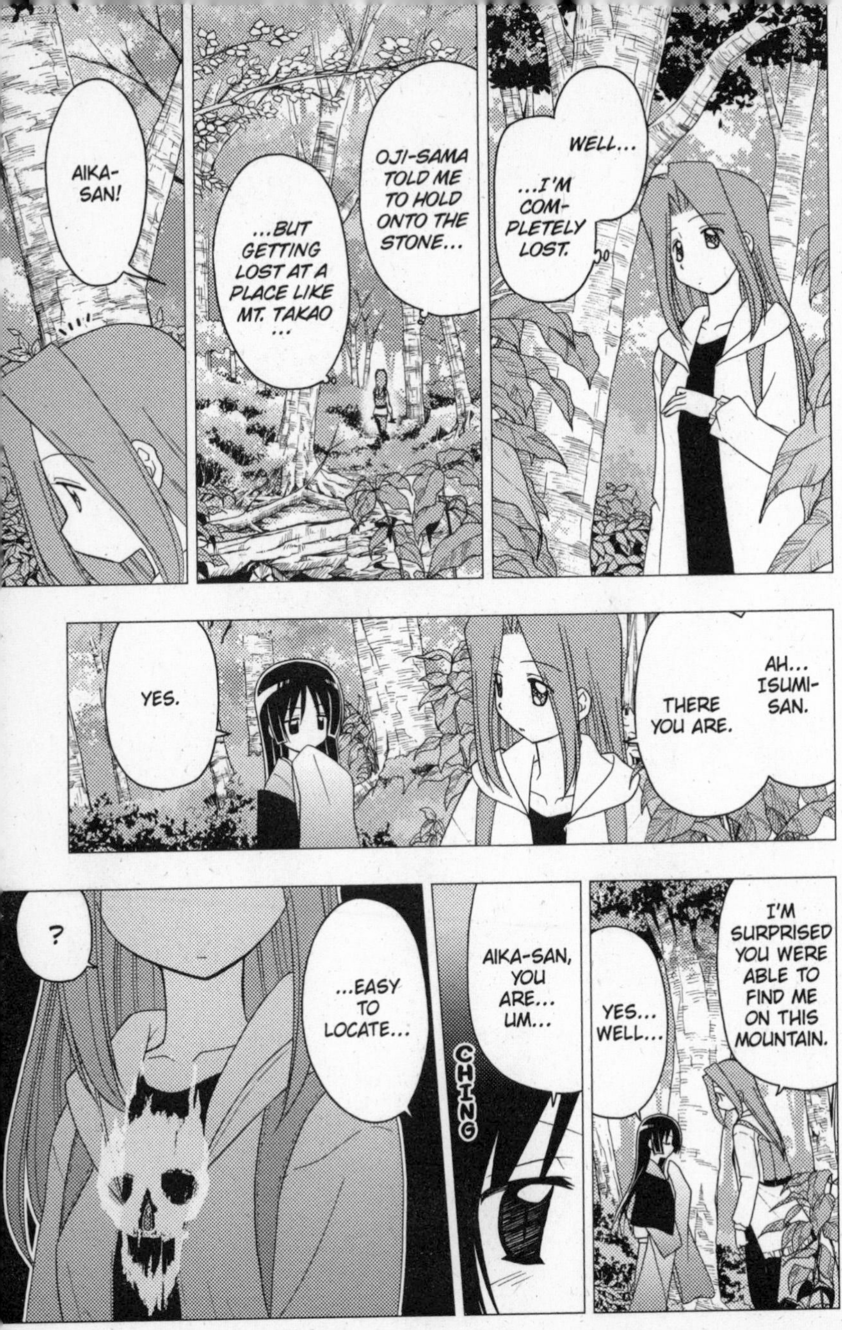
WELL...
...I'M COM-PLETELY LOST.
OJI-SAMA TOLD ME TO HOLD ONTO THE STONE...
...BUT GETTING LOST AT A PLACE LIKE MT. TAKAO ...
AIKA-SAN!
AH... ISUMI-SAN.
THERE YOU ARE.
YES.
I'M SURPRISED YOU WERE ABLE TO FIND ME ON THIS MOUNTAIN.
YES... WELL...
AIKA-SAN, YOU ARE... UM...
CHING
...EASY TO LOCATE...
?

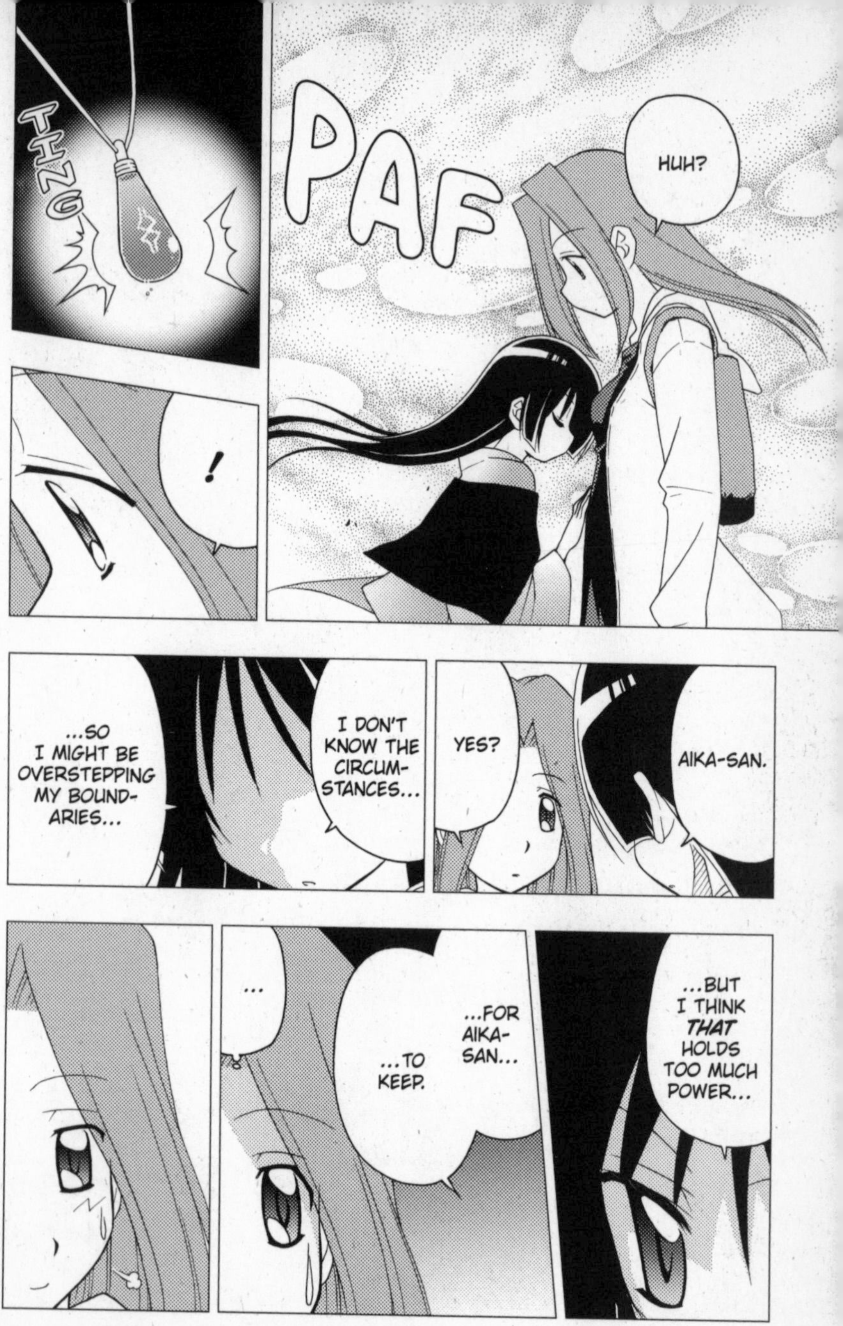
PAF
HUH?
TING
!
AIKA-SAN.
YES?
I DON'T KNOW THE CIRCUMSTANCES...
...SO I MIGHT BE OVERSTEPPING MY BOUNDARIES...
...BUT I THINK *THAT* HOLDS TOO MUCH POWER...
...FOR AIKA-SAN...
...TO KEEP.
...

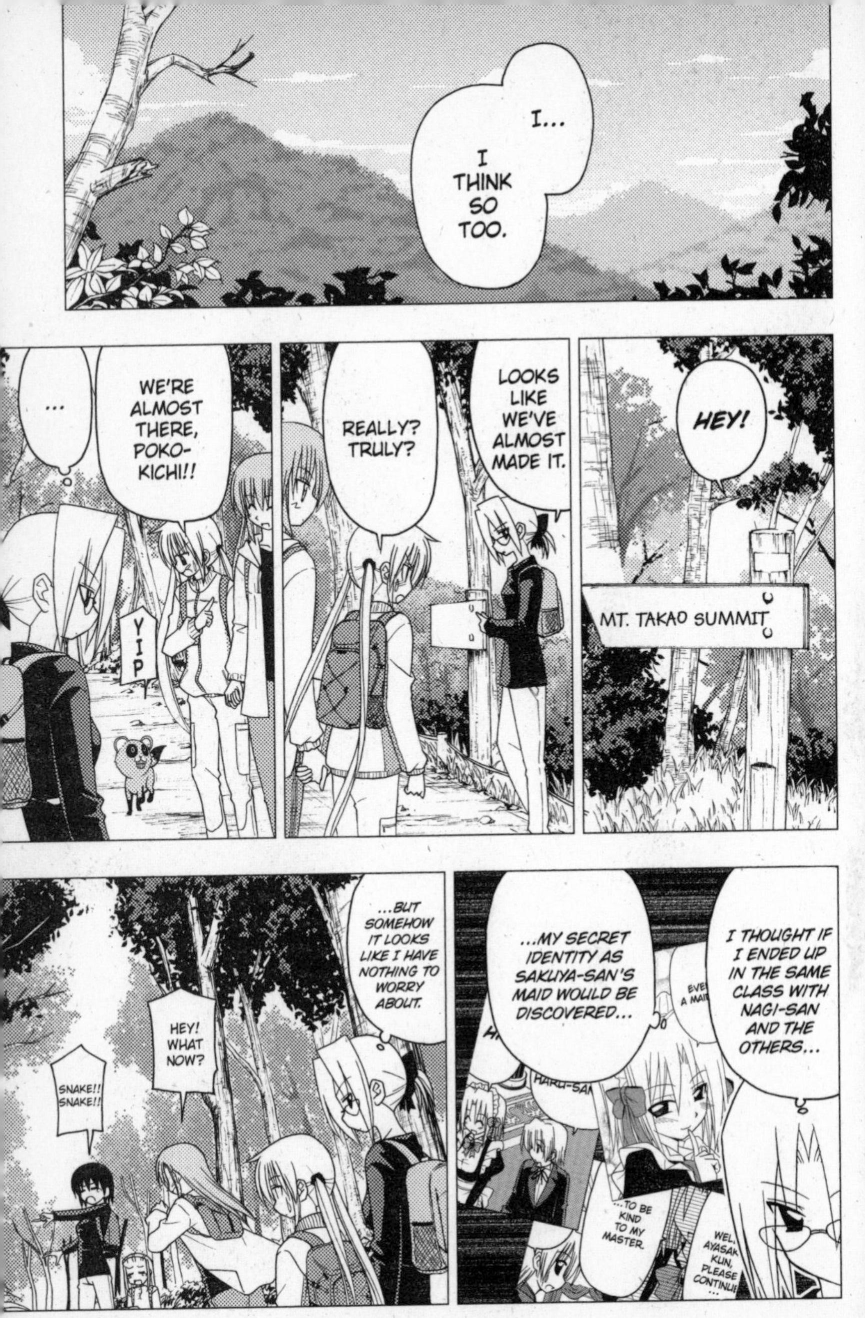
I...
I THINK SO TOO.
HEY!
MT. TAKAO SUMMIT
LOOKS LIKE WE'VE ALMOST MADE IT.
REALLY? TRULY?
WE'RE ALMOST THERE, POKO-KICHI!!
...
YIP
I THOUGHT IF I ENDED UP IN THE SAME CLASS WITH NAGI-SAN AND THE OTHERS...
...MY SECRET IDENTITY AS SAKUYA-SAN'S MAID WOULD BE DISCOVERED...
...TO BE KIND TO MY MASTER.
...BUT SOMEHOW IT LOOKS LIKE I HAVE NOTHING TO WORRY ABOUT.
HEY! WHAT NOW?
SNAKE!! SNAKE!!

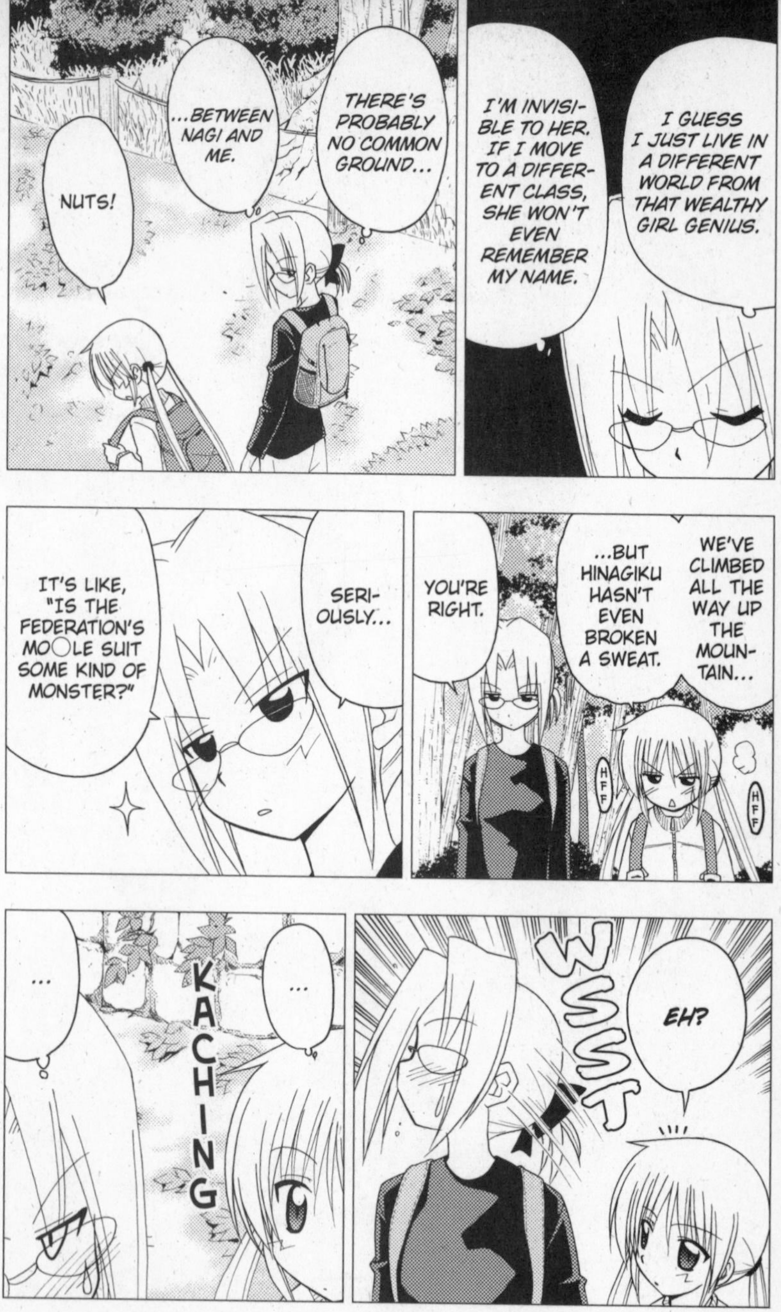
I GUESS I JUST LIVE IN A DIFFERENT WORLD FROM THAT WEALTHY GIRL GENIUS.
I'M INVISIBLE TO HER. IF I MOVE TO A DIFFERENT CLASS, SHE WON'T EVEN REMEMBER MY NAME.
THERE'S PROBABLY NO COMMON GROUND...
...BETWEEN NAGI AND ME.
NUTS!
WE'VE CLIMBED ALL THE WAY UP THE MOUNTAIN...
...BUT HINAGIKU HASN'T EVEN BROKEN A SWEAT.
HFF
HFF
YOU'RE RIGHT.
SERIOUSLY...
IT'S LIKE, "IS THE FEDERATION'S MO◯LE SUIT SOME KIND OF MONSTER?"
EH?
WSST
...
KACHING
...

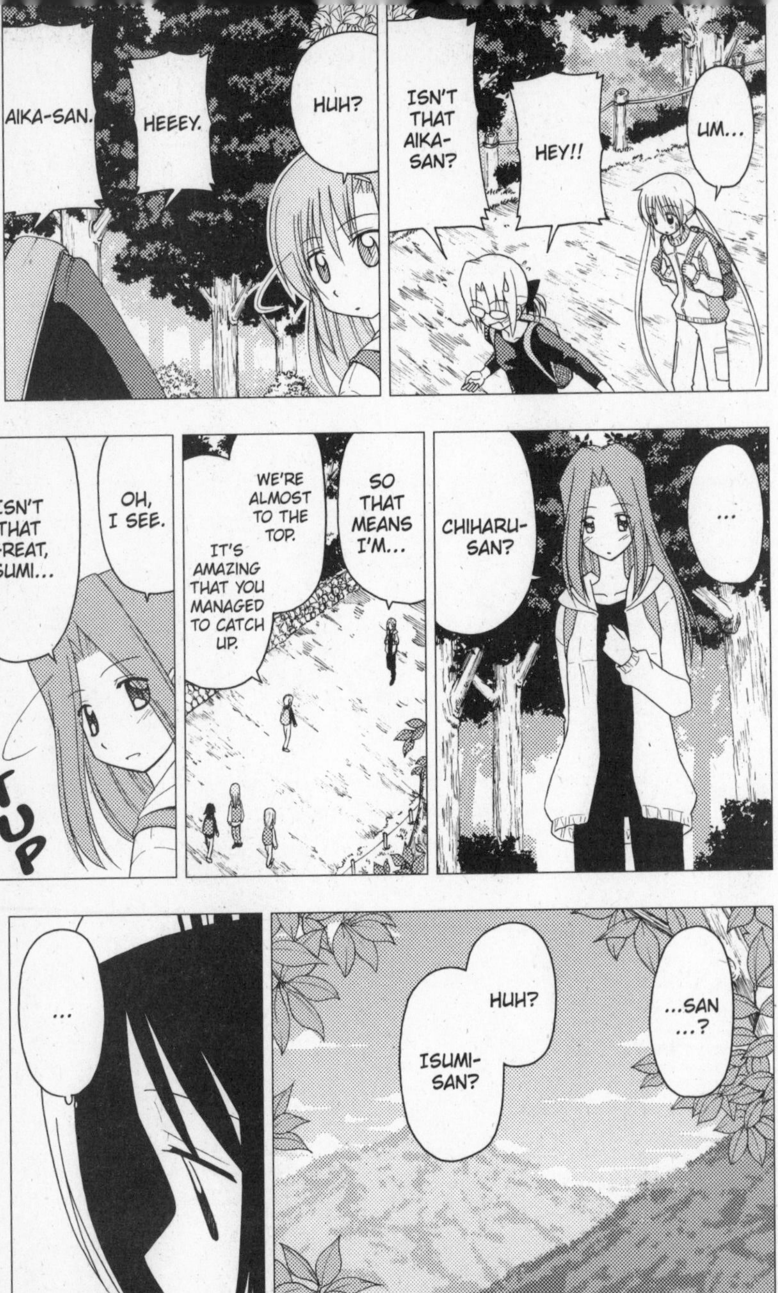
UM...
HEY!!
ISN'T THAT AIKA-SAN?
HUH?
HEEEY.
AIKA-SAN.
...
CHIHARU-SAN?
SO THAT MEANS I'M...
WE'RE ALMOST TO THE TOP.
IT'S AMAZING THAT YOU MANAGED TO CATCH UP.
OH, I SEE.
ISN'T THAT GREAT, ISUMI...
TUP
...SAN ...?
HUH?
ISUMI-SAN?
...

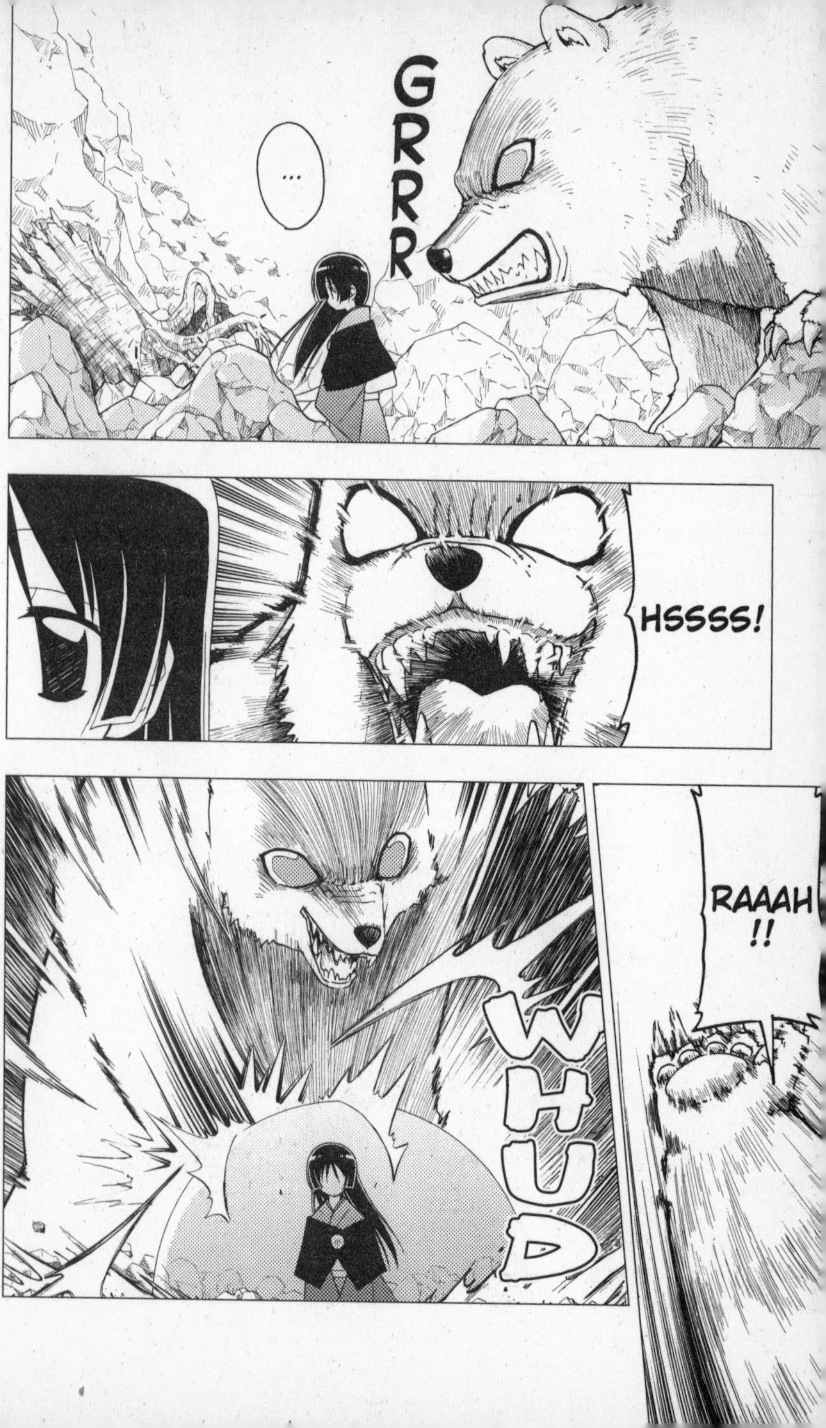
GRRR
...
HSSSS!
RAAAH !!
WHUD

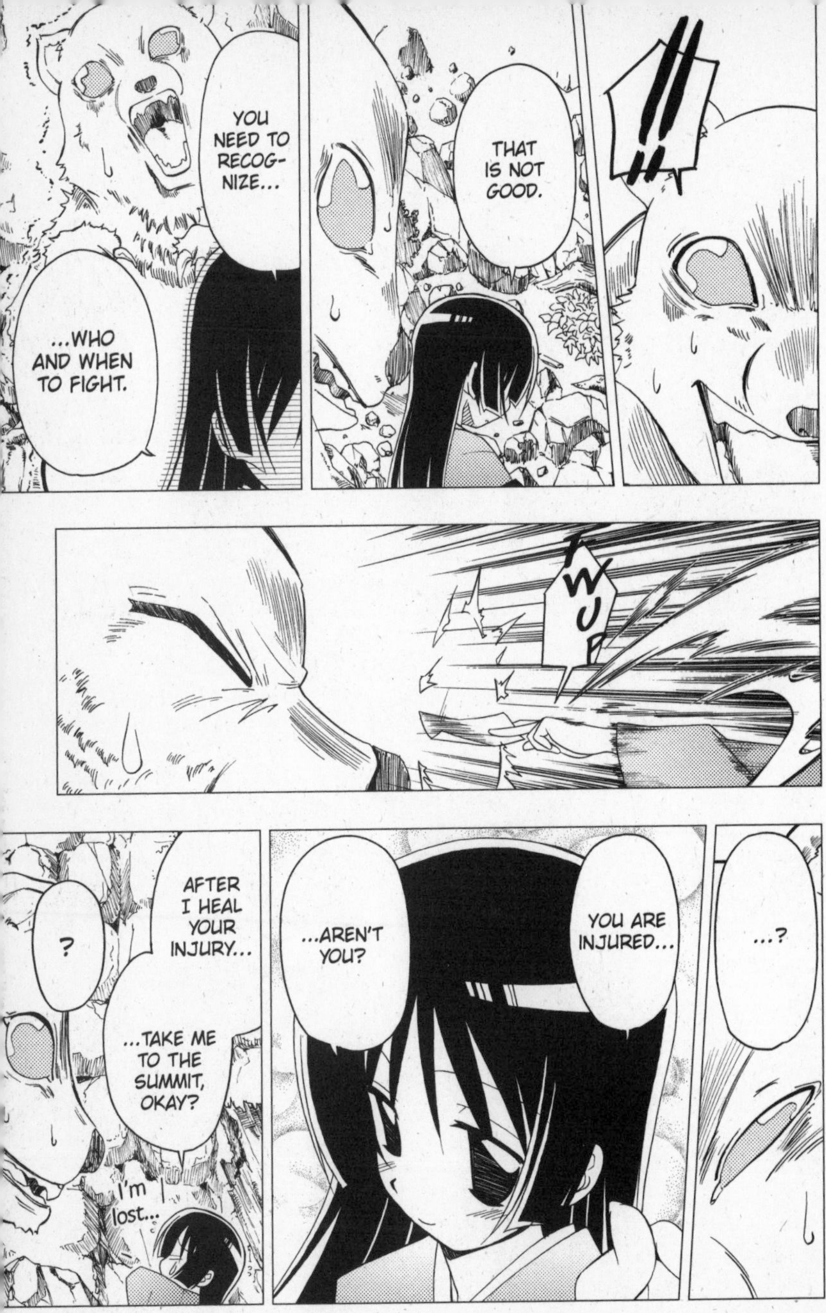
THAT IS NOT GOOD.
YOU NEED TO RECOG-NIZE...
...WHO AND WHEN TO FIGHT.
FWUP
...?
YOU ARE INJURED...
...AREN'T YOU?
AFTER I HEAL YOUR INJURY...
?
...TAKE ME TO THE SUMMIT, OKAY?
I'm lost...

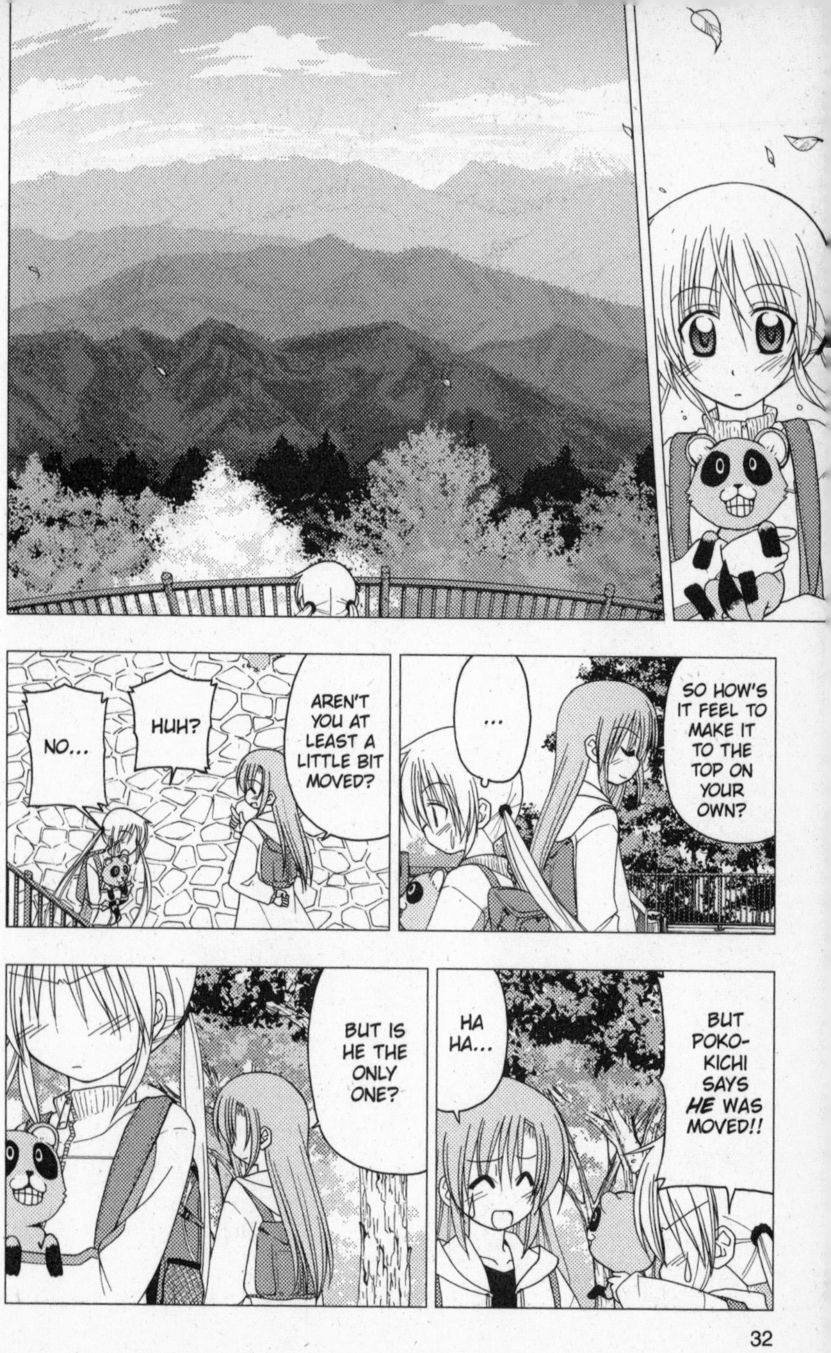
SO HOW'S IT FEEL TO MAKE IT TO THE TOP ON YOUR OWN?
...
AREN'T YOU AT LEAST A LITTLE BIT MOVED?
HUH?
NO...
BUT POKO-KICHI SAYS **HE** WAS MOVED!!
HA HA...
BUT IS HE THE ONLY ONE?

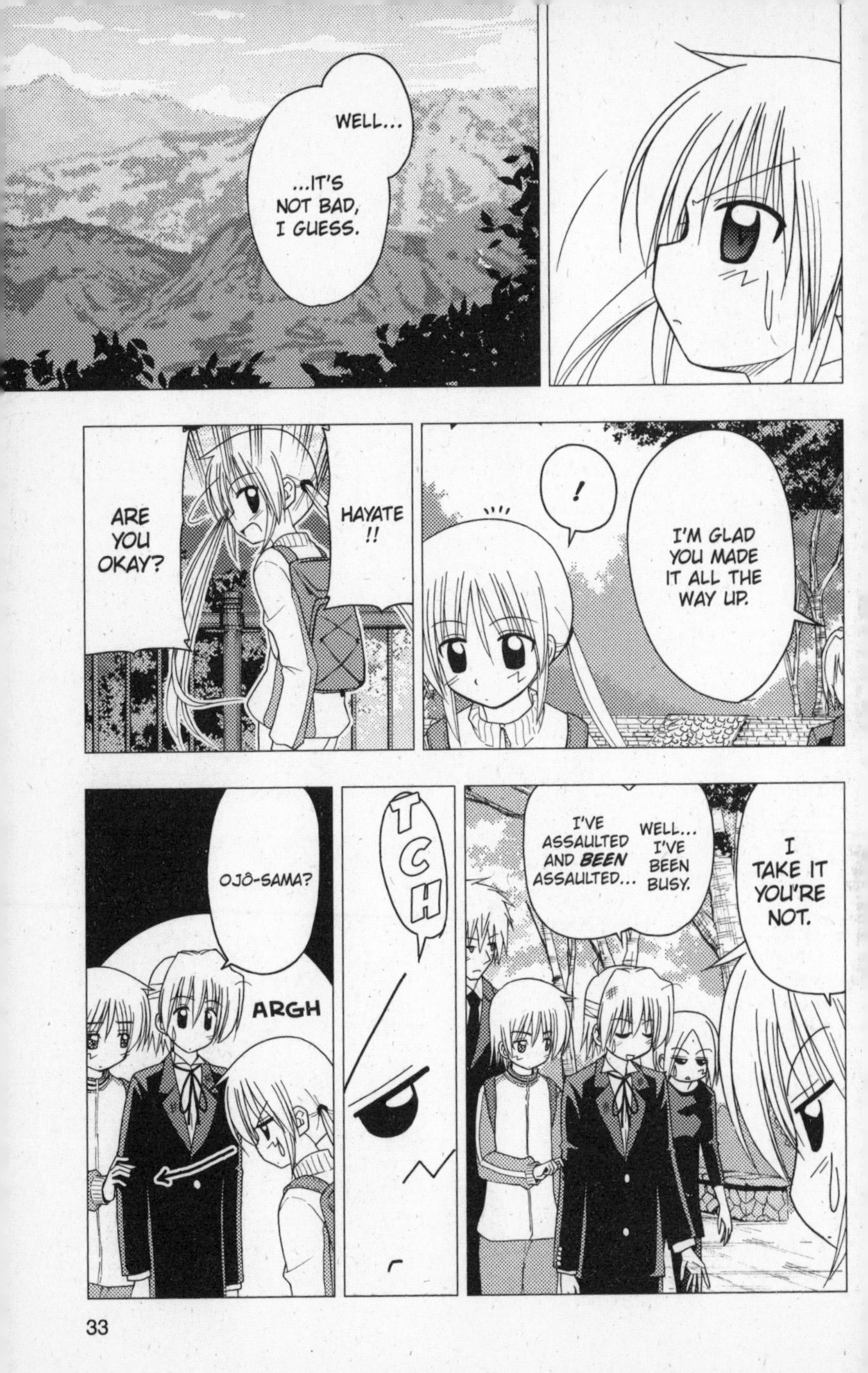

WELL...
...IT'S NOT BAD, I GUESS.
!
I'M GLAD YOU MADE IT ALL THE WAY UP.
HAYATE!!
ARE YOU OKAY?
I TAKE IT YOU'RE NOT.
WELL... I'VE BEEN BUSY.
I'VE ASSAULTED AND ***BEEN*** ASSAULTED...
TCH
OJÔ-SAMA?
ARGH

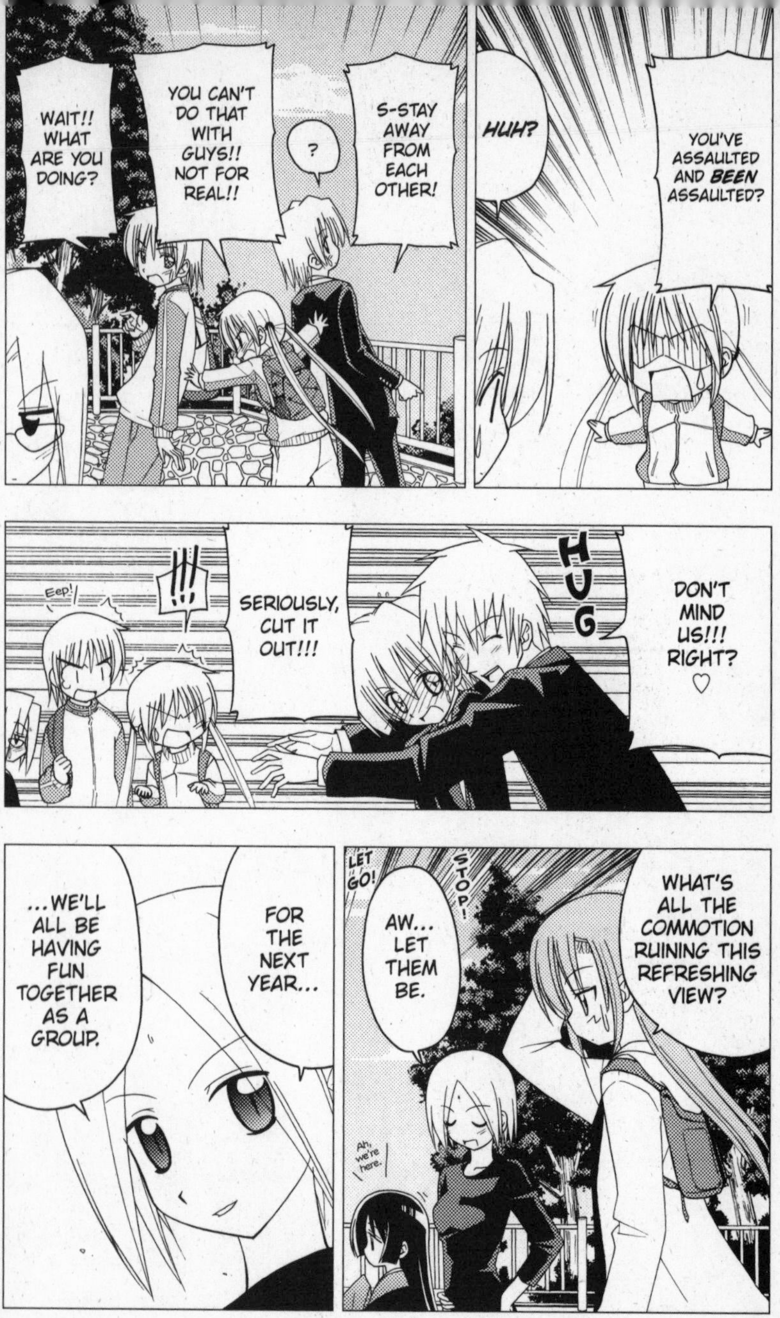
YOU'VE ASSAULTED AND BEEN ASSAULTED?
HUH?
S-STAY AWAY FROM EACH OTHER!
?
YOU CAN'T DO THAT WITH GUYS!! NOT FOR REAL!!
WAIT!! WHAT ARE YOU DOING?
DON'T MIND US!!! RIGHT? ♡
HUG
SERIOUSLY, CUT IT OUT!!!
!!!
Eep!
WHAT'S ALL THE COMMOTION RUINING THIS REFRESHING VIEW?
STOP!
AW... LET THEM BE.
LET GO!
Ah, we're here.
FOR THE NEXT YEAR...
...WE'LL ALL BE HAVING FUN TOGETHER AS A GROUP.

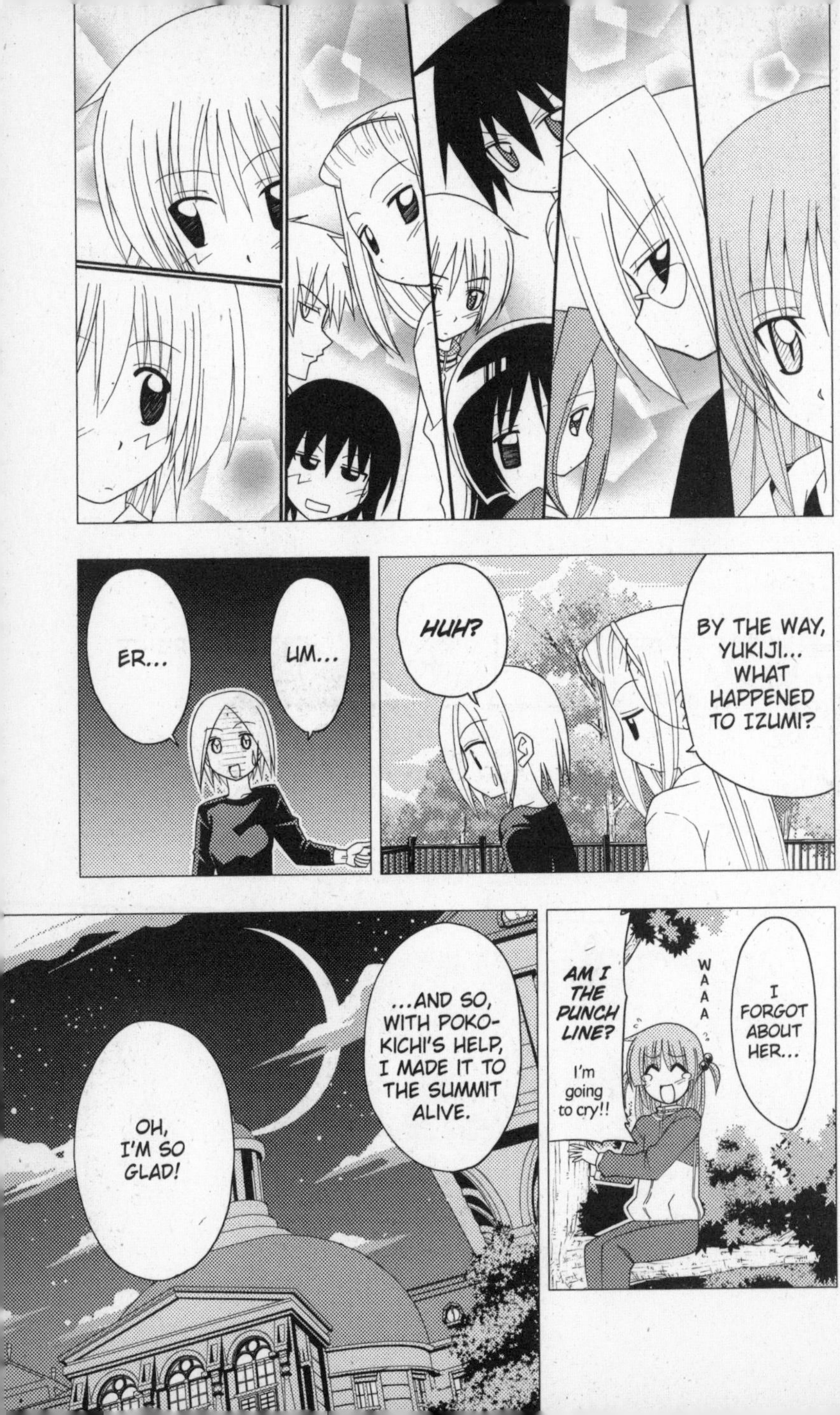
BY THE WAY, YUKIJI... WHAT HAPPENED TO IZUMI?
HUH?
UM...
ER...
I FORGOT ABOUT HER...
WAAA
AM I THE PUNCH LINE?
I'm going to cry!!
...AND SO, WITH POKO-KICHI'S HELP, I MADE IT TO THE SUMMIT ALIVE.
OH, I'M SO GLAD!

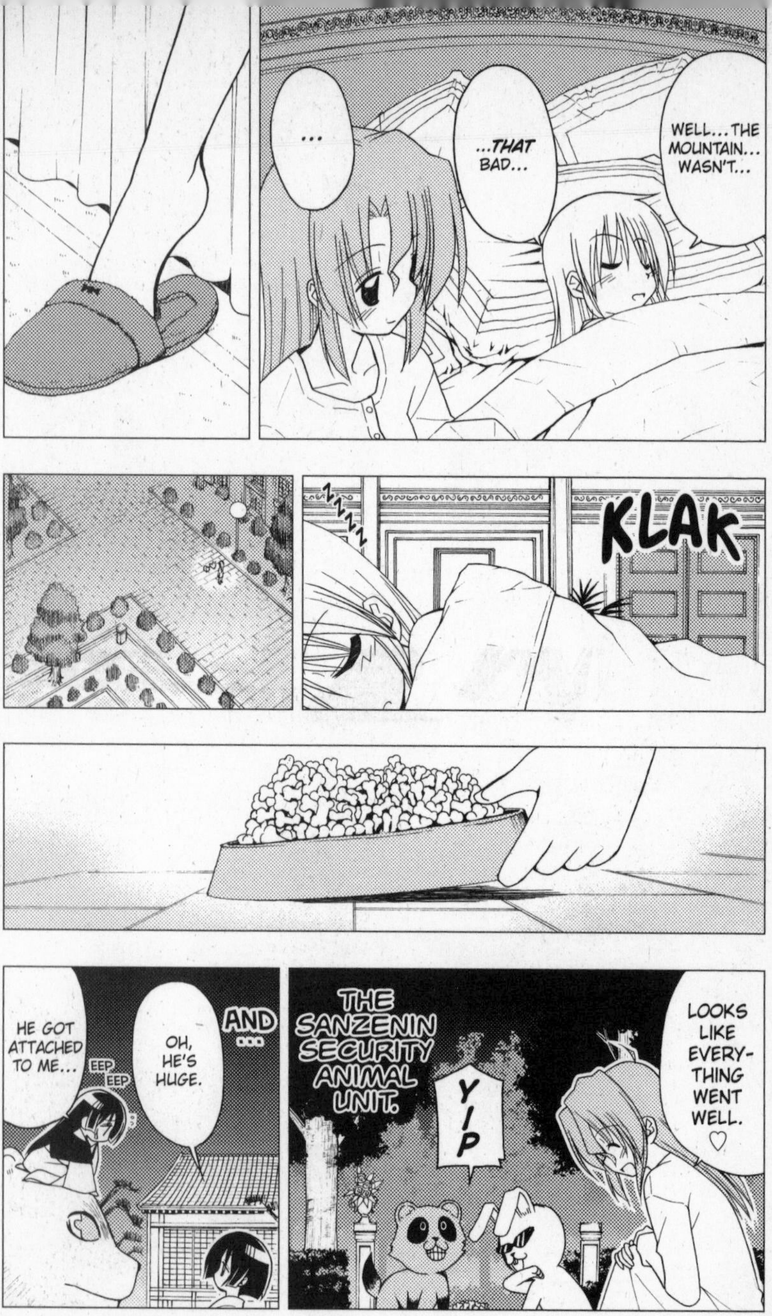
WELL...THE MOUNTAIN... WASN'T...
...THAT BAD...
...
ZZZZ
KLAK
LOOKS LIKE EVERY-THING WENT WELL. ♡
THE SANZENIN SECURITY ANIMAL UNIT.
YIP
AND...
OH, HE'S HUGE.
HE GOT ATTACHED TO ME...
EEP EEP

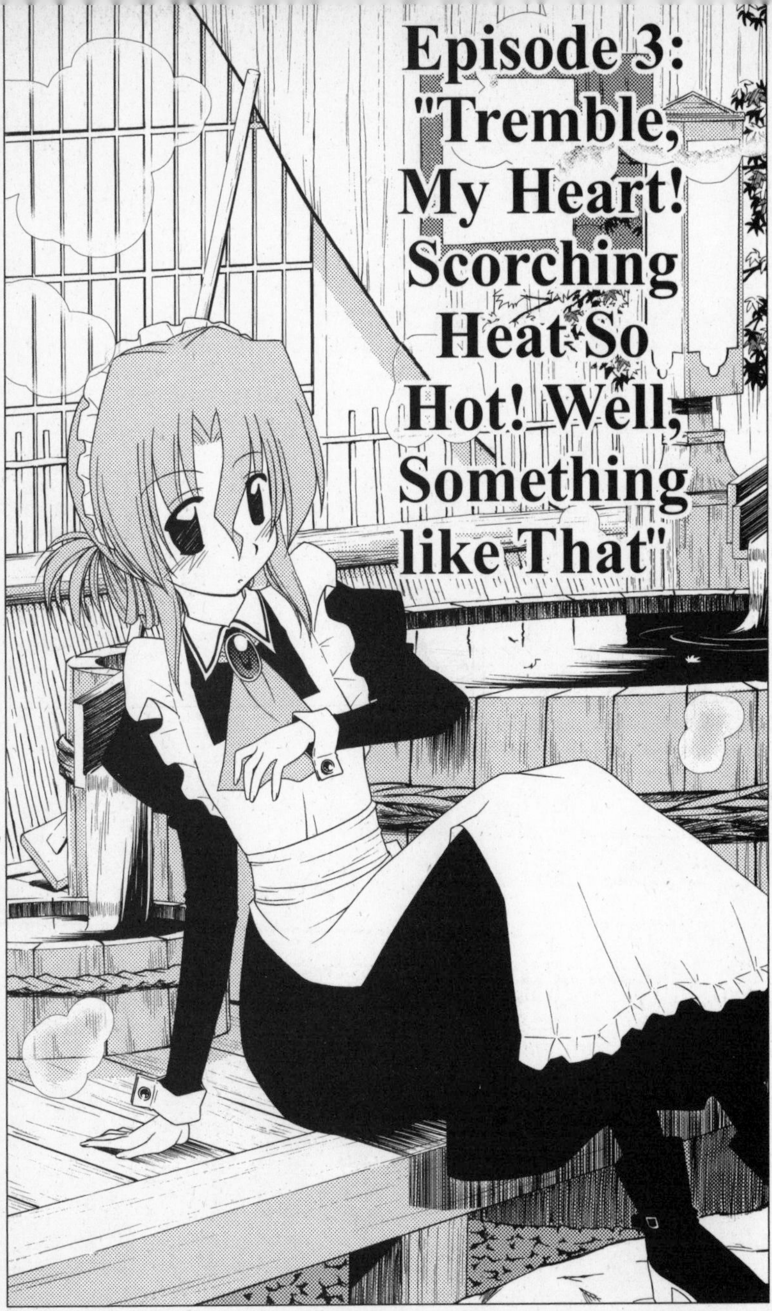
Episode 3: "Tremble, My Heart! Scorching Heat So Hot! Well, Something like That"

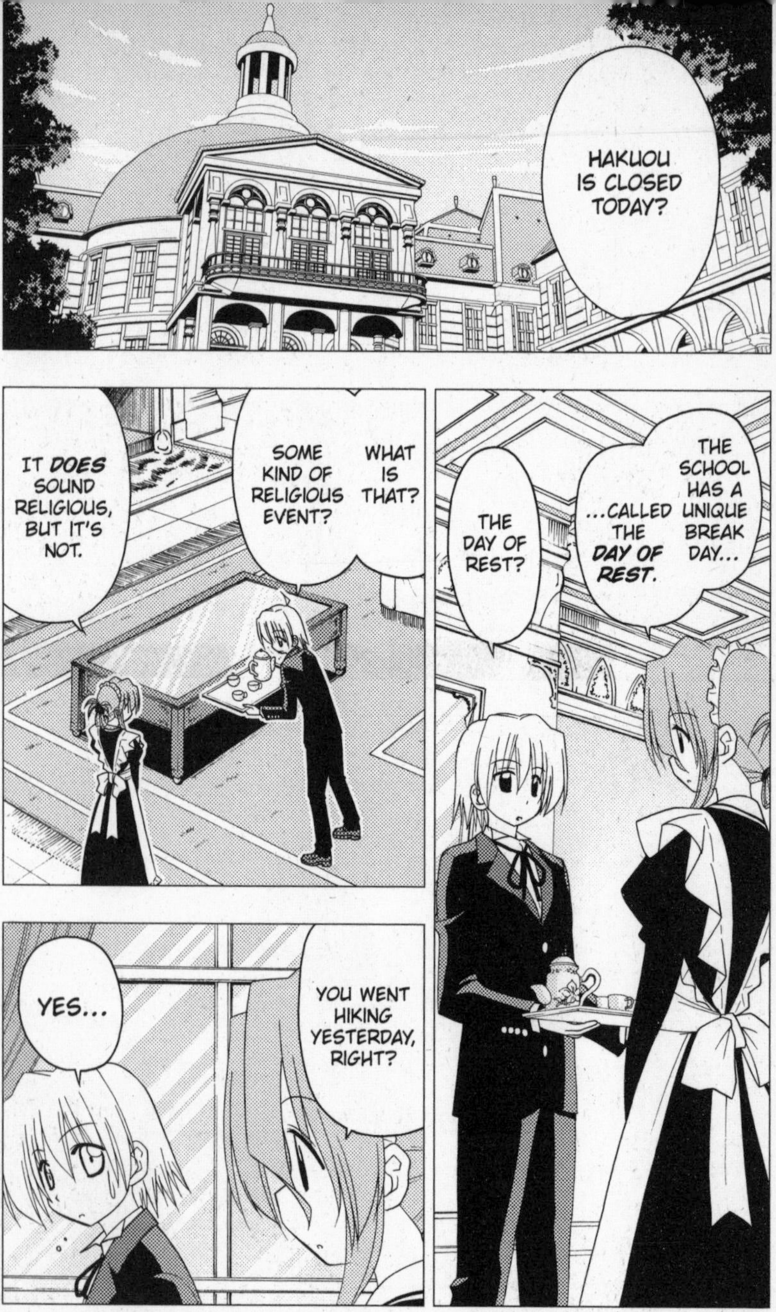
HAKUOU IS CLOSED TODAY?
THE SCHOOL HAS A UNIQUE BREAK DAY...
...CALLED THE **DAY OF REST**.
THE DAY OF REST?
WHAT IS THAT? SOME KIND OF RELIGIOUS EVENT?
IT **DOES** SOUND RELIGIOUS, BUT IT'S NOT.
YOU WENT HIKING YESTERDAY, RIGHT?
YES...

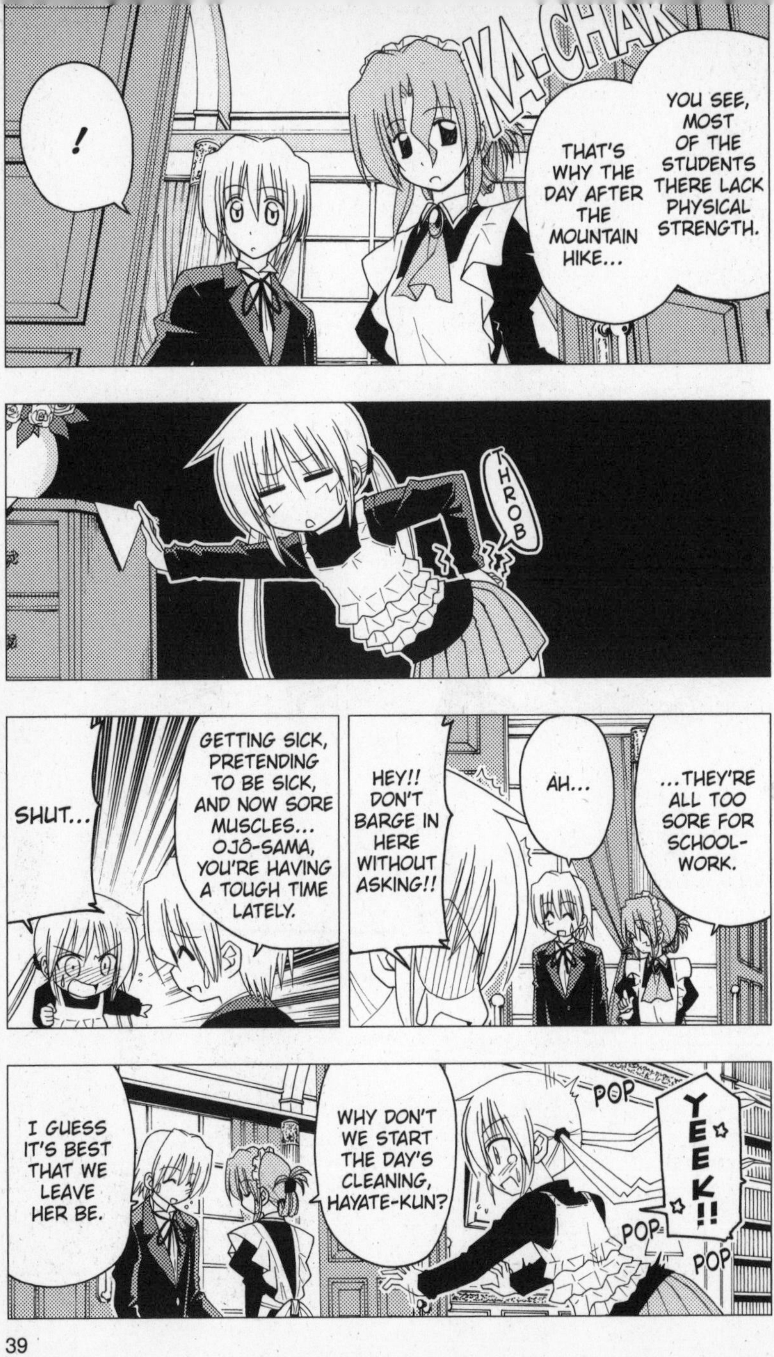
KA-CHAK
YOU SEE, MOST OF THE STUDENTS THERE LACK PHYSICAL STRENGTH.
THAT'S WHY THE DAY AFTER THE MOUNTAIN HIKE...
!
THROB
...THEY'RE ALL TOO SORE FOR SCHOOL-WORK.
AH...
HEY!! DON'T BARGE IN HERE WITHOUT ASKING!!
GETTING SICK, PRETENDING TO BE SICK, AND NOW SORE MUSCLES... OJÔ-SAMA, YOU'RE HAVING A TOUGH TIME LATELY.
SHUT...
YEEK!!
POP
POP
POP
WHY DON'T WE START THE DAY'S CLEANING, HAYATE-KUN?
I GUESS IT'S BEST THAT WE LEAVE HER BE.

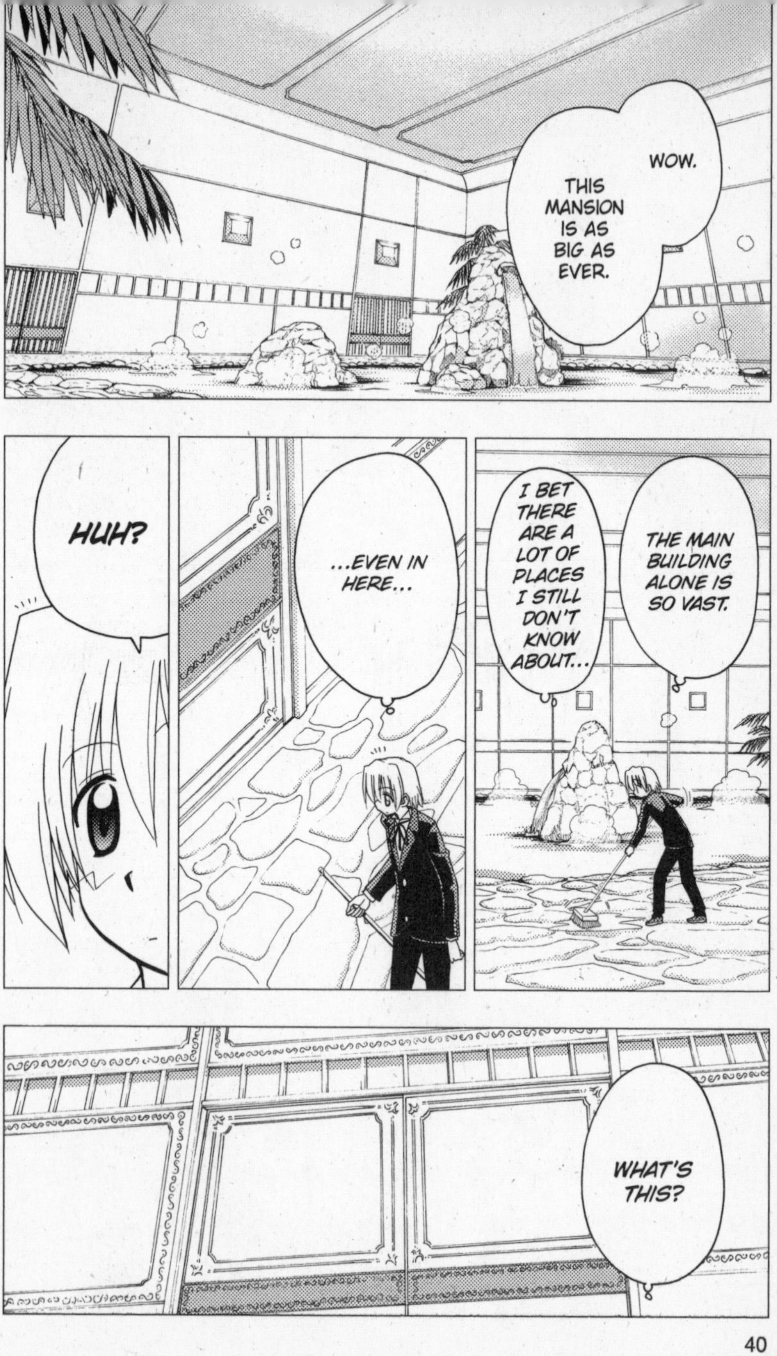
WOW.
THIS MANSION IS AS BIG AS EVER.
THE MAIN BUILDING ALONE IS SO VAST.
I BET THERE ARE A LOT OF PLACES I STILL DON'T KNOW ABOUT...
...EVEN IN HERE...
HUH?
WHAT'S THIS?

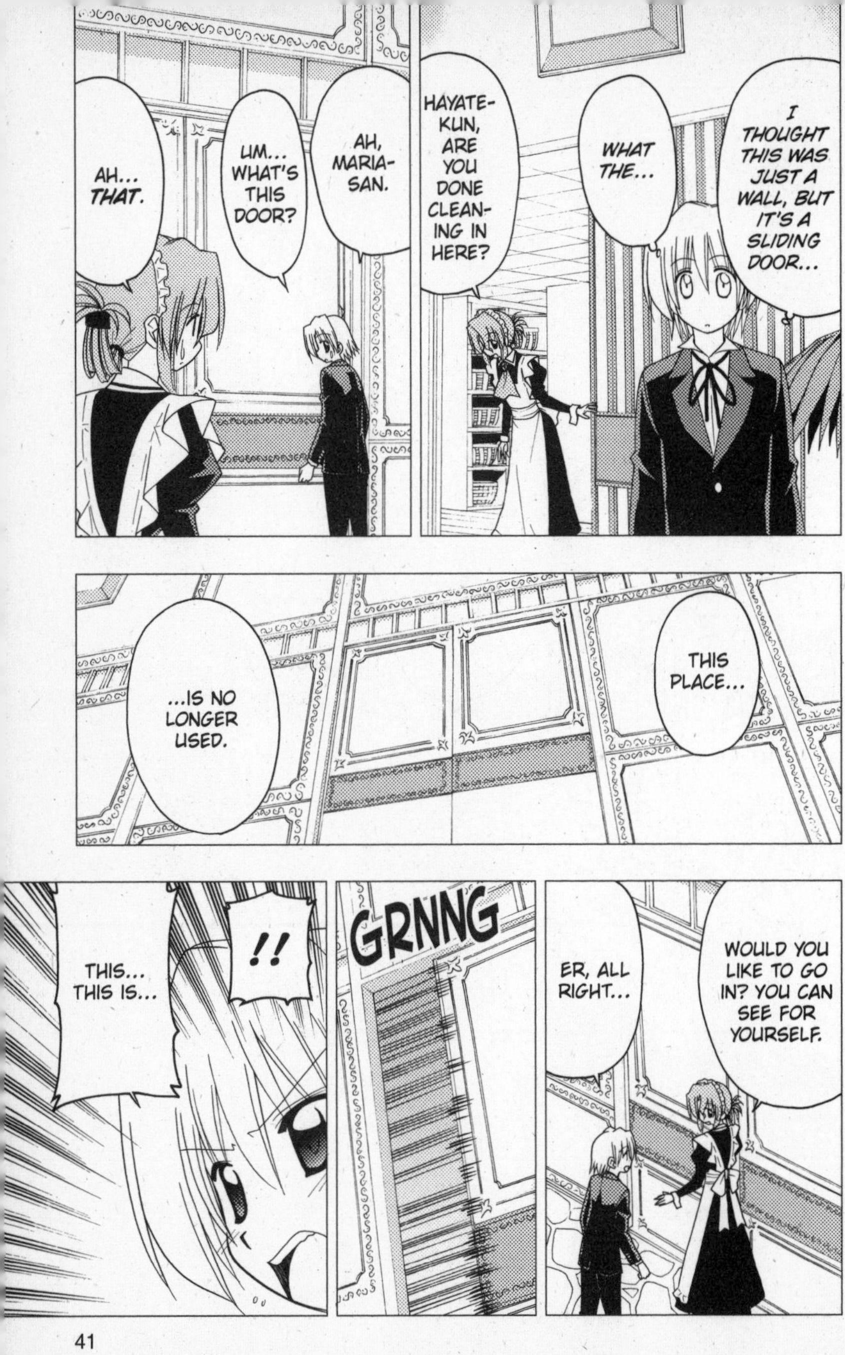
I THOUGHT THIS WAS JUST A WALL, BUT IT'S A SLIDING DOOR...
WHAT THE...
HAYATE-KUN, ARE YOU DONE CLEANING IN HERE?
AH, MARIA-SAN.
UM... WHAT'S THIS DOOR?
AH... THAT.
THIS PLACE...
...IS NO LONGER USED.
WOULD YOU LIKE TO GO IN? YOU CAN SEE FOR YOURSELF.
ER, ALL RIGHT...
GRNNG
!!
THIS... THIS IS...

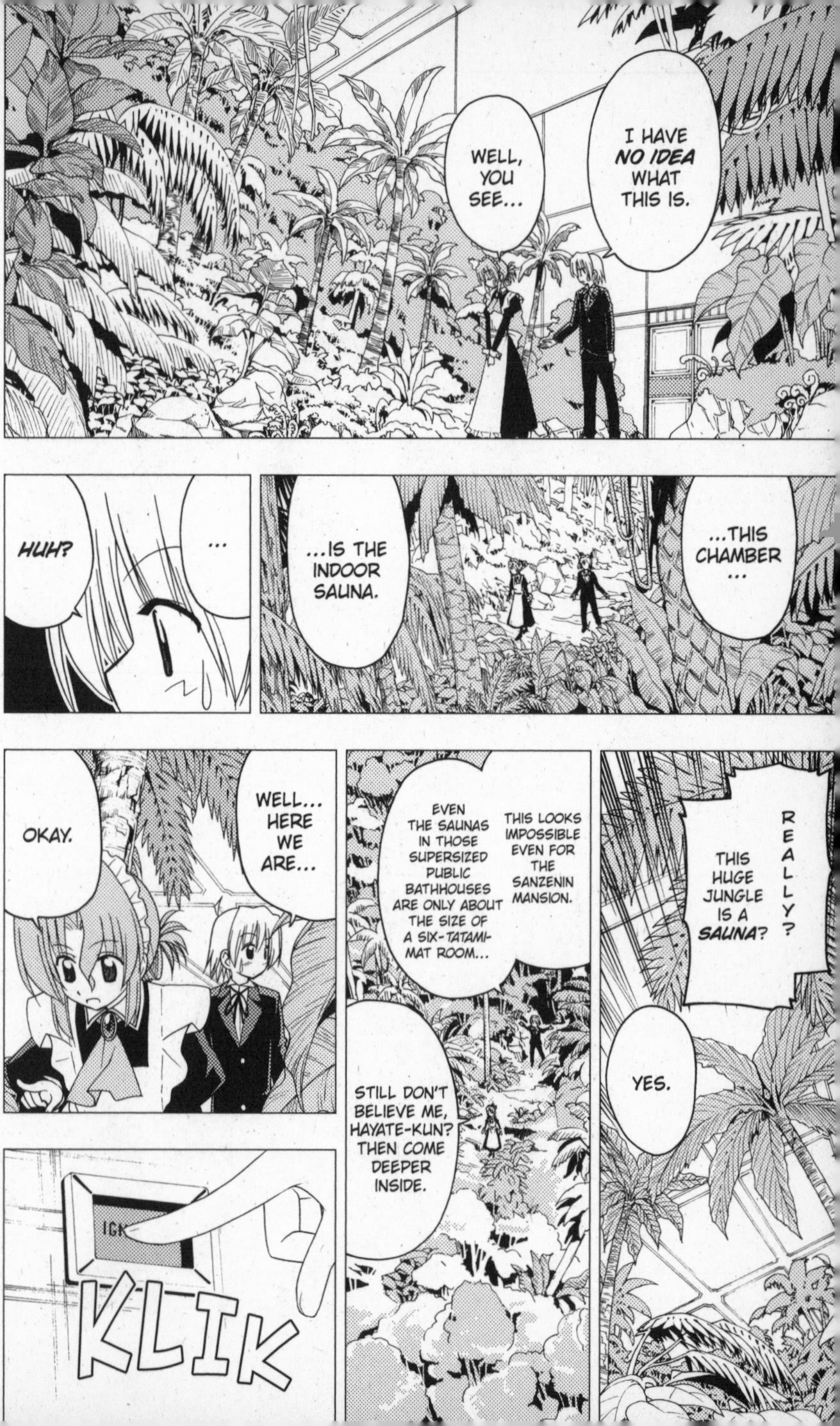
I HAVE NO IDEA WHAT THIS IS.
WELL, YOU SEE...
...THIS CHAMBER...
...IS THE INDOOR SAUNA.
...
HUH?
REALLY?
THIS HUGE JUNGLE IS A SAUNA?
YES.
THIS LOOKS IMPOSSIBLE EVEN FOR THE SANZENIN MANSION.
EVEN THE SAUNAS IN THOSE SUPERSIZED PUBLIC BATHHOUSES ARE ONLY ABOUT THE SIZE OF A SIX-TATAMI-MAT ROOM...
STILL DON'T BELIEVE ME, HAYATE-KUN? THEN COME DEEPER INSIDE.
WELL... HERE WE ARE...
OKAY.
KLIK

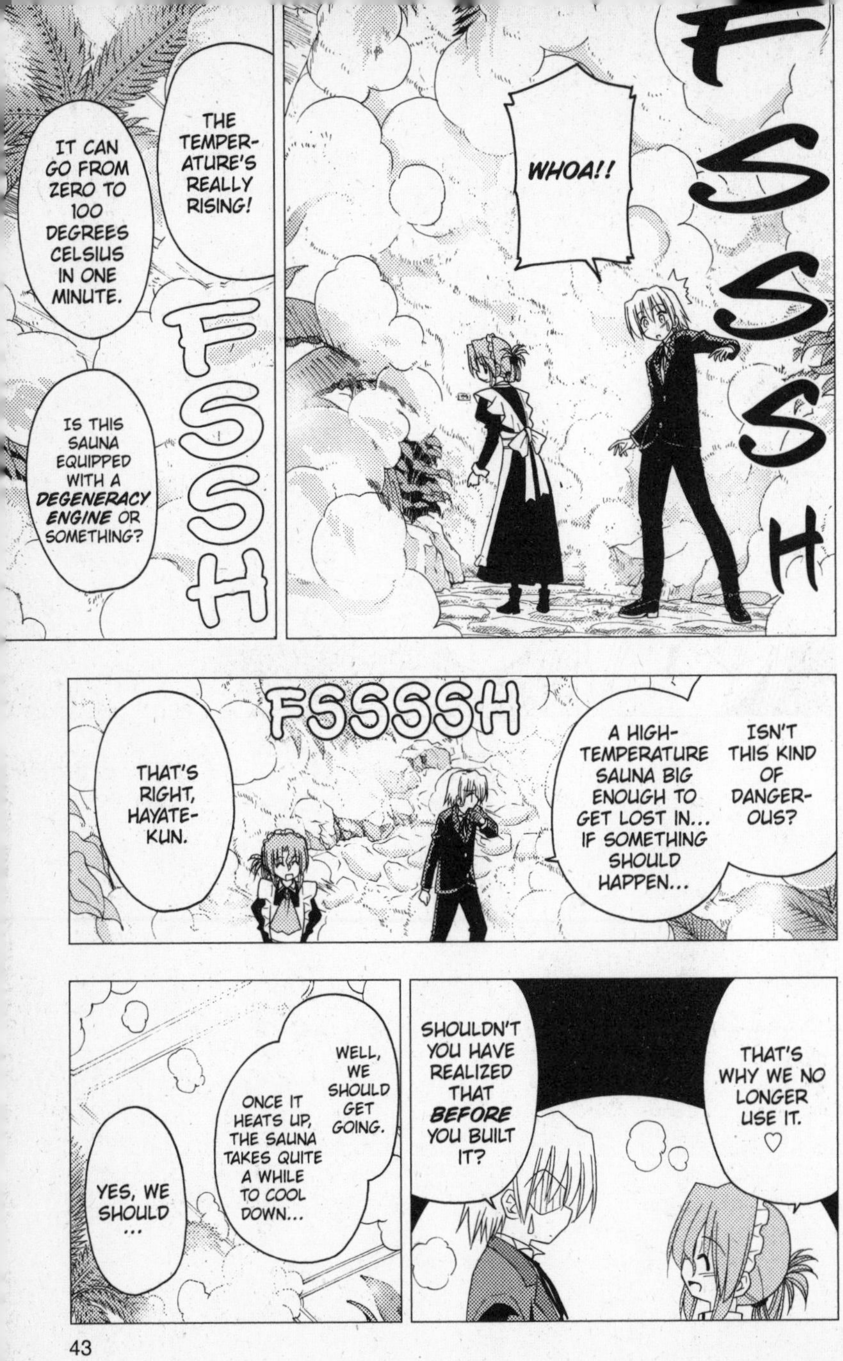
FSSSH
WHOA!!
THE TEMPERATURE'S REALLY RISING!
IT CAN GO FROM ZERO TO 100 DEGREES CELSIUS IN ONE MINUTE.
FSSH
IS THIS SAUNA EQUIPPED WITH A ***DEGENERACY ENGINE*** OR SOMETHING?
FSSSSH
ISN'T THIS KIND OF DANGEROUS?
A HIGH-TEMPERATURE SAUNA BIG ENOUGH TO GET LOST IN... IF SOMETHING SHOULD HAPPEN...
THAT'S RIGHT, HAYATE-KUN.
THAT'S WHY WE NO LONGER USE IT. ♡
SHOULDN'T YOU HAVE REALIZED THAT ***BEFORE*** YOU BUILT IT?
WELL, WE SHOULD GET GOING.
ONCE IT HEATS UP, THE SAUNA TAKES QUITE A WHILE TO COOL DOWN...
YES, WE SHOULD...

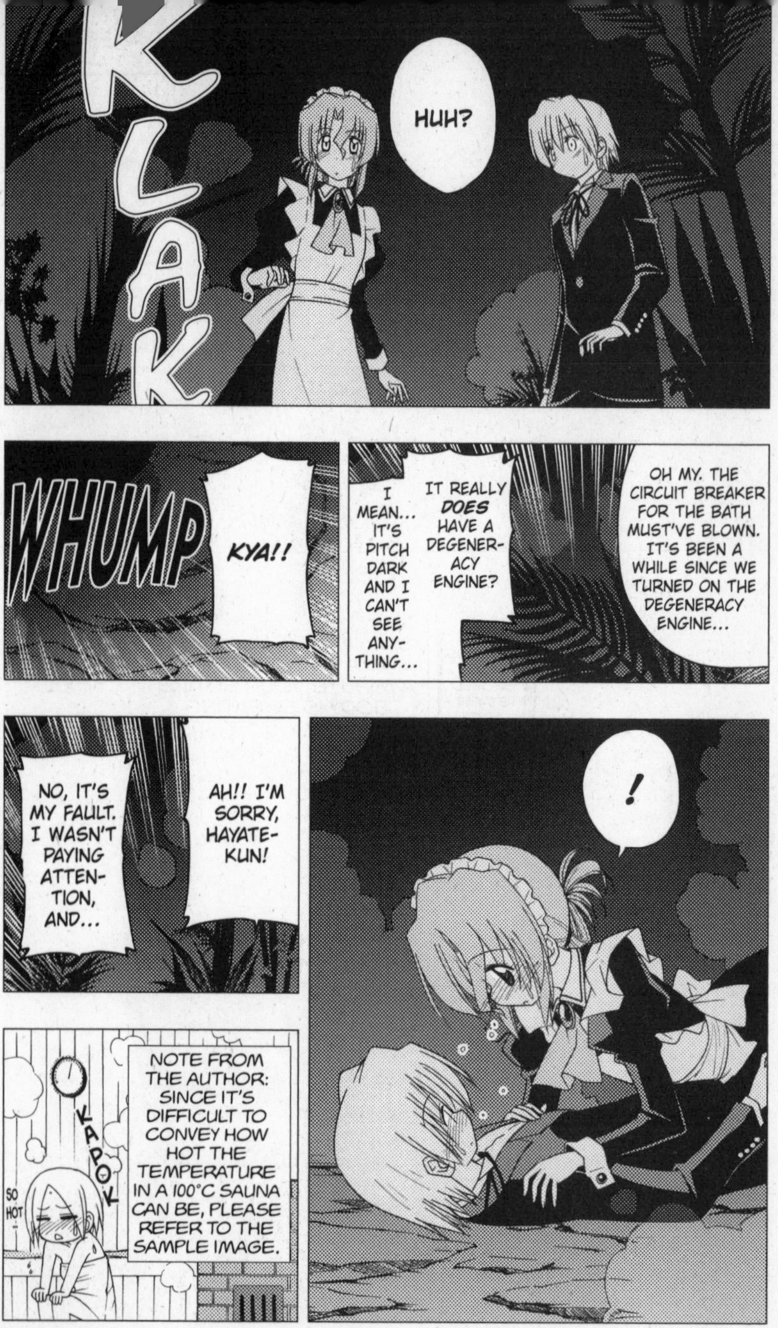
HUH?
KLAK
OH MY. THE CIRCUIT BREAKER FOR THE BATH MUST'VE BLOWN. IT'S BEEN A WHILE SINCE WE TURNED ON THE DEGENERACY ENGINE...
IT REALLY DOES HAVE A DEGENERACY ENGINE?
I MEAN... IT'S PITCH DARK AND I CAN'T SEE ANYTHING...
KYA!!
WHUMP
!
AH!! I'M SORRY, HAYATE-KUN!
NO, IT'S MY FAULT. I WASN'T PAYING ATTENTION, AND...
NOTE FROM THE AUTHOR: SINCE IT'S DIFFICULT TO CONVEY HOW HOT THE TEMPERATURE IN A 100°C SAUNA CAN BE, PLEASE REFER TO THE SAMPLE IMAGE.
KAPOK
SO HOT ...

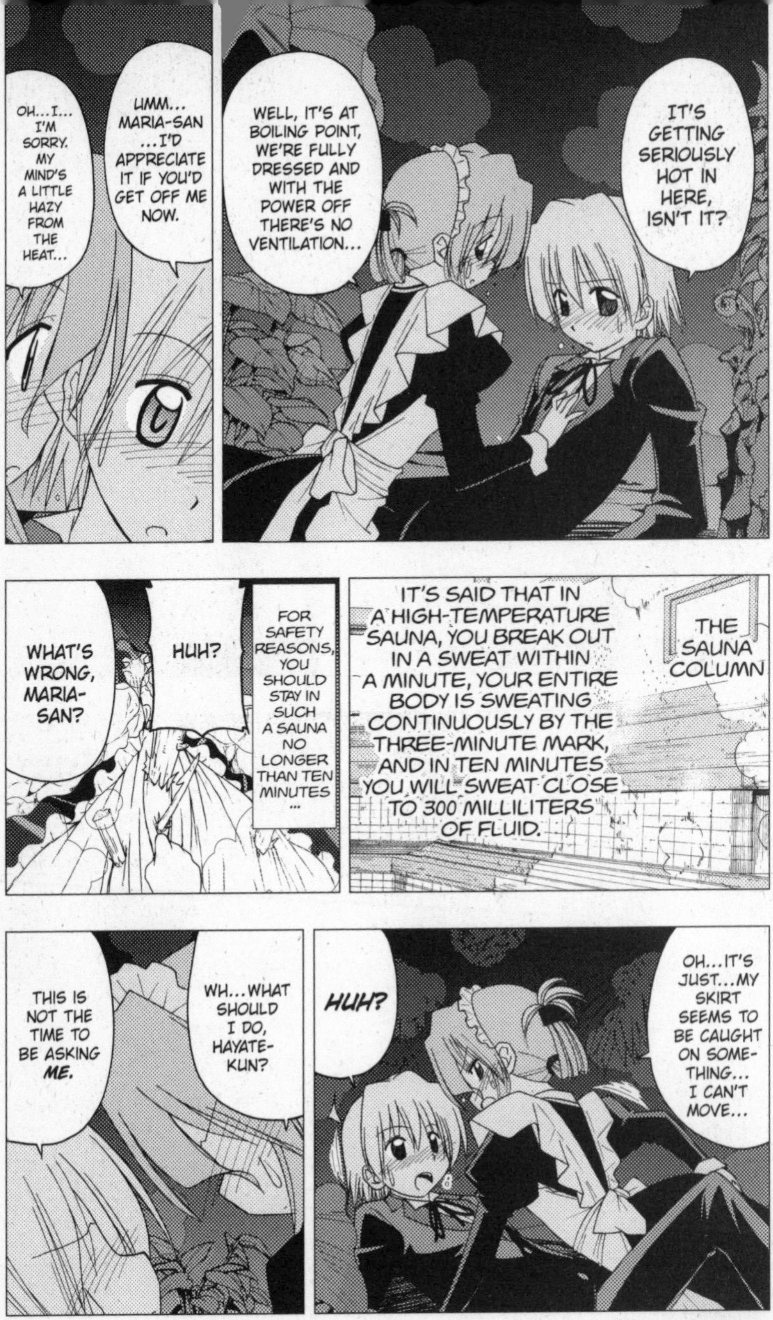
IT'S GETTING SERIOUSLY HOT IN HERE, ISN'T IT?
WELL, IT'S AT BOILING POINT, WE'RE FULLY DRESSED AND WITH THE POWER OFF THERE'S NO VENTILATION...
UMM... MARIA-SAN ...I'D APPRECIATE IT IF YOU'D GET OFF ME NOW.
OH...I... I'M SORRY. MY MIND'S A LITTLE HAZY FROM THE HEAT...
THE SAUNA COLUMN
IT'S SAID THAT IN A HIGH-TEMPERATURE SAUNA, YOU BREAK OUT IN A SWEAT WITHIN A MINUTE, YOUR ENTIRE BODY IS SWEATING CONTINUOUSLY BY THE THREE-MINUTE MARK, AND IN TEN MINUTES YOU WILL SWEAT CLOSE TO 300 MILLILITERS OF FLUID.
FOR SAFETY REASONS, YOU SHOULD STAY IN SUCH A SAUNA NO LONGER THAN TEN MINUTES ...
HUH?
WHAT'S WRONG, MARIA-SAN?
OH...IT'S JUST...MY SKIRT SEEMS TO BE CAUGHT ON SOME-THING... I CAN'T MOVE...
HUH?
WH...WHAT SHOULD I DO, HAYATE-KUN?
THIS IS NOT THE TIME TO BE ASKING ME.

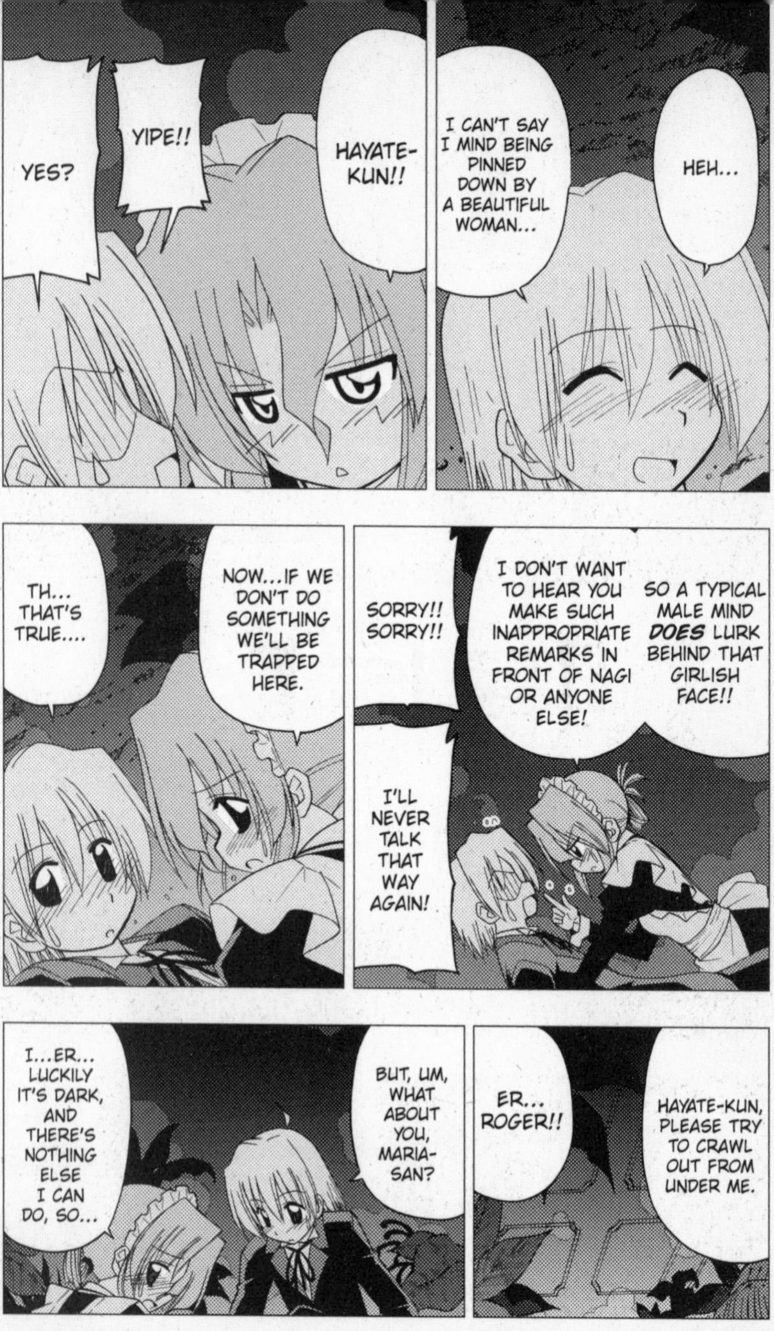
HEH...
I CAN'T SAY I MIND BEING PINNED DOWN BY A BEAUTIFUL WOMAN...
HAYATE-KUN!!
YIPE!!
YES?
SO A TYPICAL MALE MIND **DOES** LURK BEHIND THAT GIRLISH FACE!!
I DON'T WANT TO HEAR YOU MAKE SUCH INAPPROPRIATE REMARKS IN FRONT OF NAGI OR ANYONE ELSE!
SORRY!! SORRY!!
I'LL NEVER TALK THAT WAY AGAIN!
NOW...IF WE DON'T DO SOMETHING WE'LL BE TRAPPED HERE.
TH... THAT'S TRUE....
HAYATE-KUN, PLEASE TRY TO CRAWL OUT FROM UNDER ME.
ER... ROGER!!
BUT, UM, WHAT ABOUT YOU, MARIA-SAN?
I...ER... LUCKILY IT'S DARK, AND THERE'S NOTHING ELSE I CAN DO, SO...

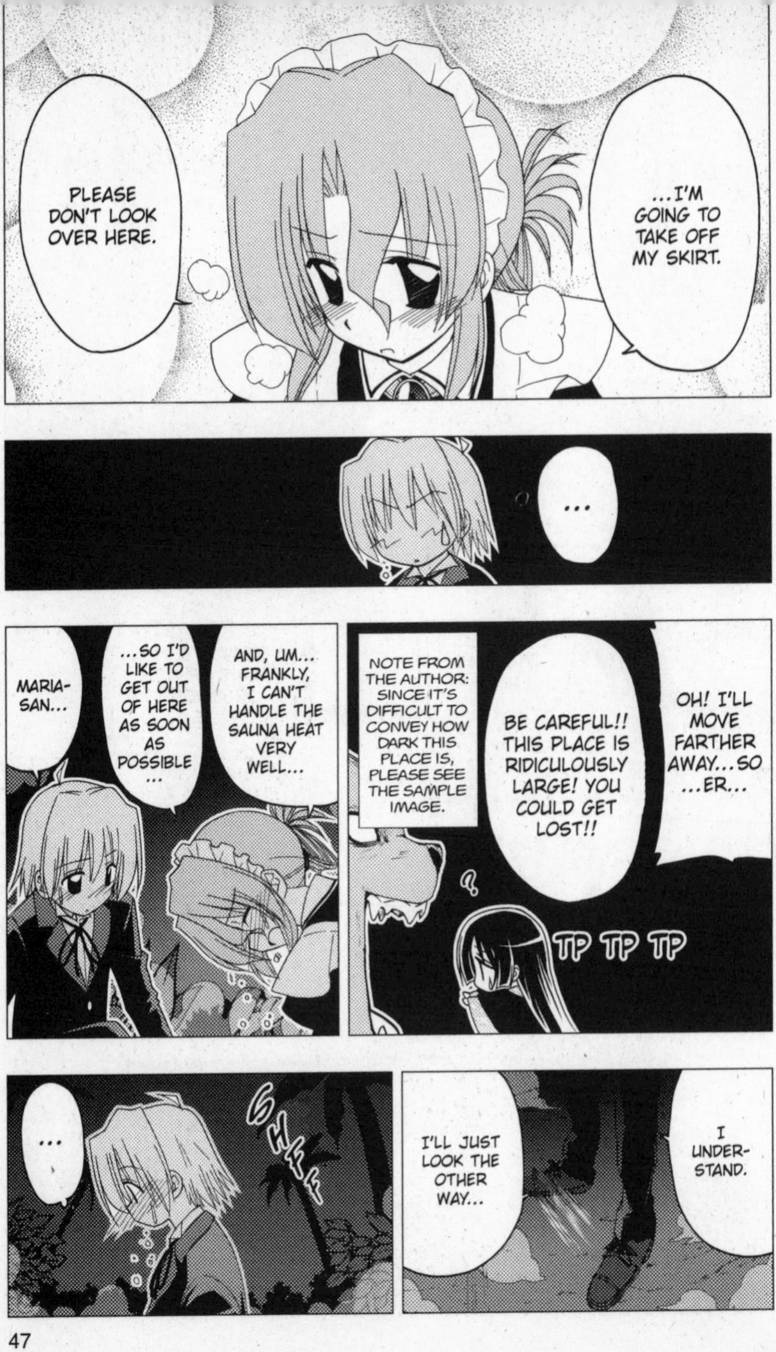

...I'M GOING TO TAKE OFF MY SKIRT.
PLEASE DON'T LOOK OVER HERE.
...
OH! I'LL MOVE FARTHER AWAY...SO ...ER...
BE CAREFUL!! THIS PLACE IS RIDICULOUSLY LARGE! YOU COULD GET LOST!!
NOTE FROM THE AUTHOR: SINCE IT'S DIFFICULT TO CONVEY HOW DARK THIS PLACE IS, PLEASE SEE THE SAMPLE IMAGE.
TP TP TP
AND, UM... FRANKLY, I CAN'T HANDLE THE SAUNA HEAT VERY WELL...
...SO I'D LIKE TO GET OUT OF HERE AS SOON AS POSSIBLE...
MARIA-SAN...
I UNDER-STAND.
I'LL JUST LOOK THE OTHER WAY...
SHFF
...

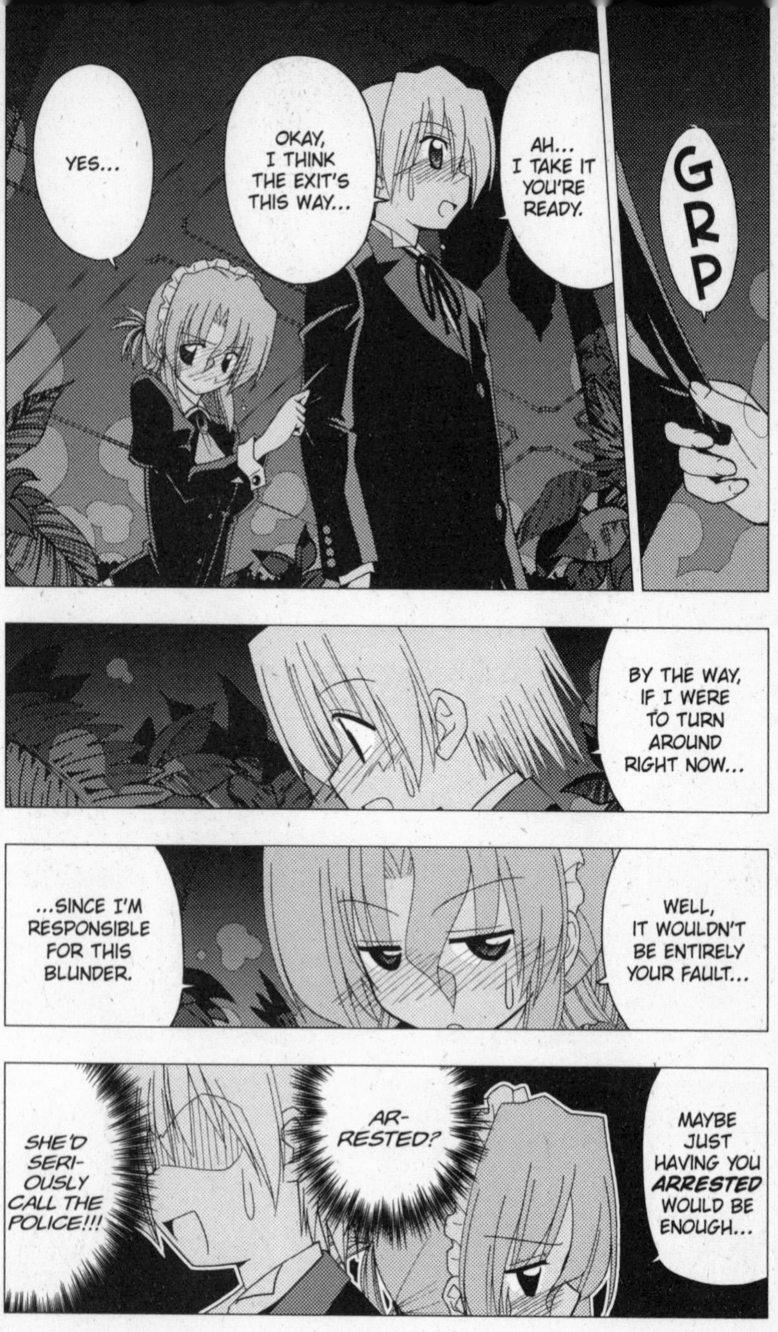
GRP
AH... I TAKE IT YOU'RE READY.
OKAY, I THINK THE EXIT'S THIS WAY...
YES...
BY THE WAY, IF I WERE TO TURN AROUND RIGHT NOW...
WELL, IT WOULDN'T BE ENTIRELY YOUR FAULT...
...SINCE I'M RESPONSIBLE FOR THIS BLUNDER.
MAYBE JUST HAVING YOU ARRESTED WOULD BE ENOUGH...
AR-RESTED?
SHE'D SERI-OUSLY CALL THE POLICE!!!

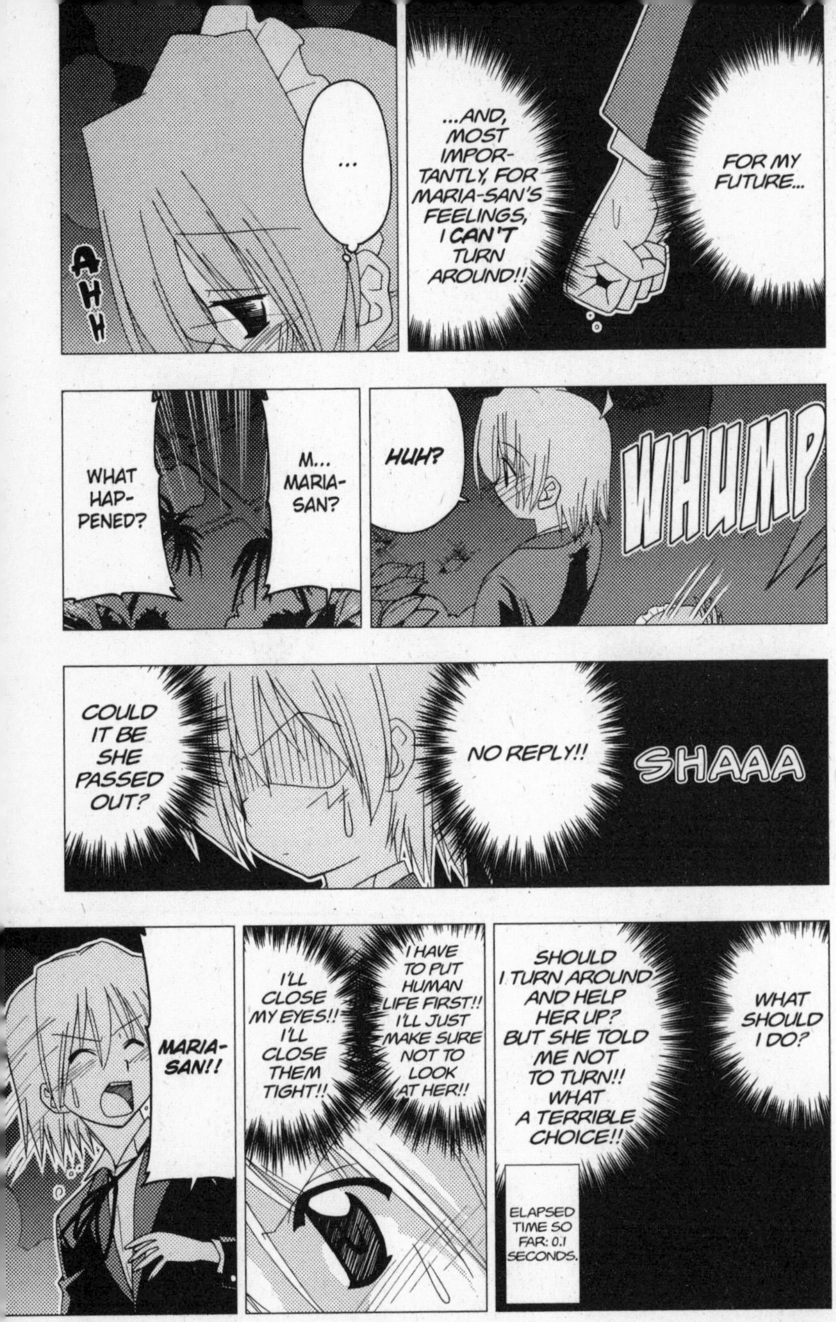
FOR MY FUTURE...
...AND, MOST IMPORTANTLY, FOR MARIA-SAN'S FEELINGS, I CAN'T TURN AROUND!!
...
AHH
WHUMP
HUH?
M... MARIA-SAN?
WHAT HAPPENED?
SHAAA
NO REPLY!!
COULD IT BE SHE PASSED OUT?
WHAT SHOULD I DO?
SHOULD I TURN AROUND AND HELP HER UP? BUT SHE TOLD ME NOT TO TURN!! WHAT A TERRIBLE CHOICE!!
ELAPSED TIME SO FAR: 0.1 SECONDS.
I HAVE TO PUT HUMAN LIFE FIRST!! I'LL JUST MAKE SURE NOT TO LOOK AT HER!!
I'LL CLOSE MY EYES!! I'LL CLOSE THEM TIGHT!!
MARIA-SAN!!

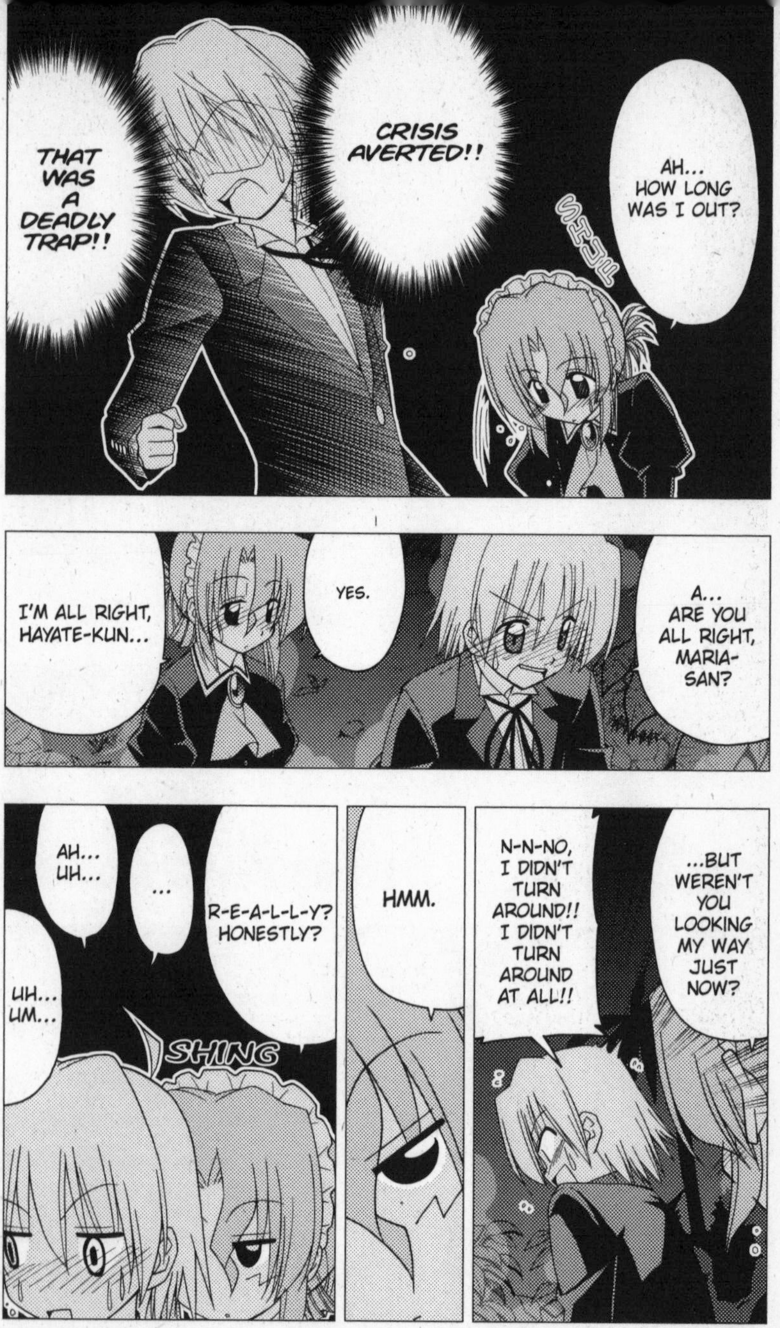
AH... HOW LONG WAS I OUT?
CRISIS AVERTED!!
THAT WAS A DEADLY TRAP!!
A... ARE YOU ALL RIGHT, MARIA-SAN?
YES.
I'M ALL RIGHT, HAYATE-KUN...
...BUT WEREN'T YOU LOOKING MY WAY JUST NOW?
N-N-NO, I DIDN'T TURN AROUND!! I DIDN'T TURN AROUND AT ALL!!
HMM.
R-E-A-L-L-Y? HONESTLY?
...
AH... UH...
SHING
UH... UM...

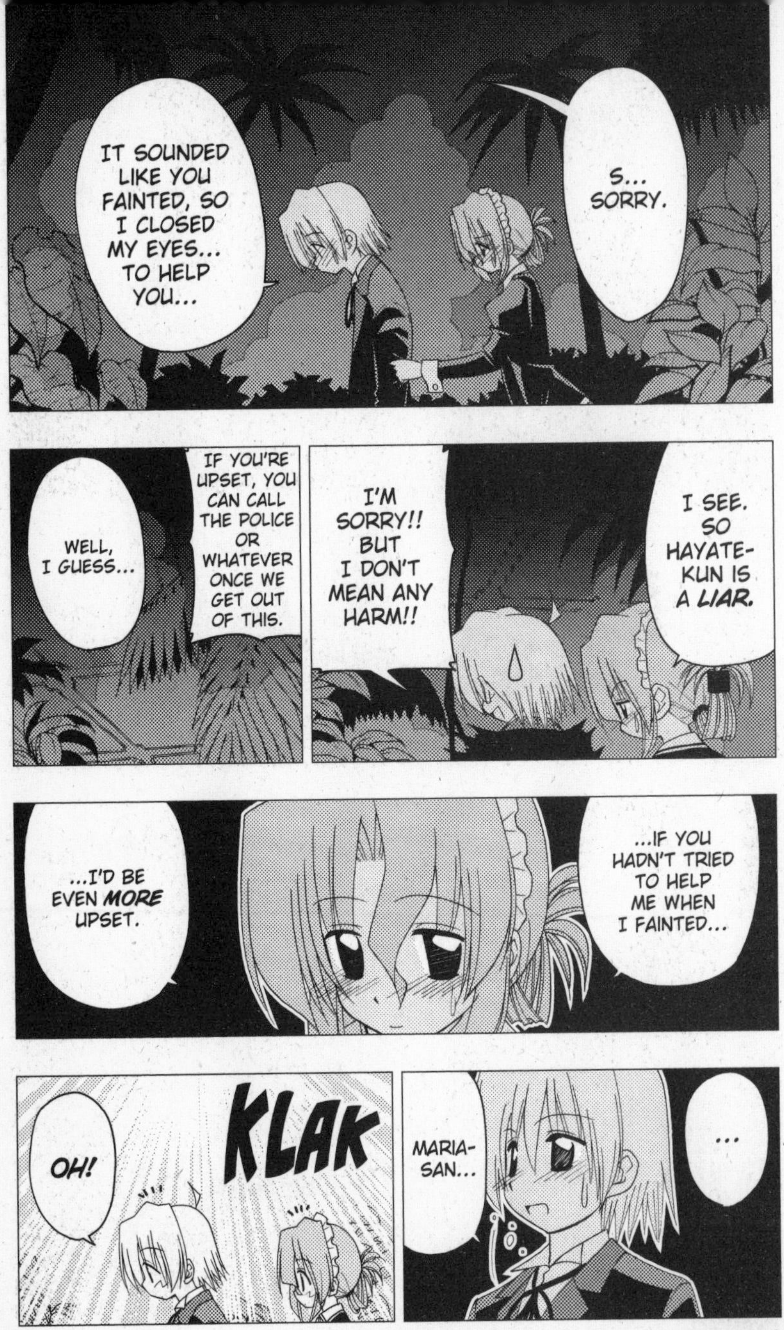
S... SORRY.
IT SOUNDED LIKE YOU FAINTED, SO I CLOSED MY EYES... TO HELP YOU...
I SEE. SO HAYATE-KUN IS A *LIAR.*
I'M SORRY!! BUT I DON'T MEAN ANY HARM!!
IF YOU'RE UPSET, YOU CAN CALL THE POLICE OR WHATEVER ONCE WE GET OUT OF THIS.
WELL, I GUESS...
...IF YOU HADN'T TRIED TO HELP ME WHEN I FAINTED...
...I'D BE EVEN *MORE* UPSET.
...
MARIA-SAN...
KLAK
OH!

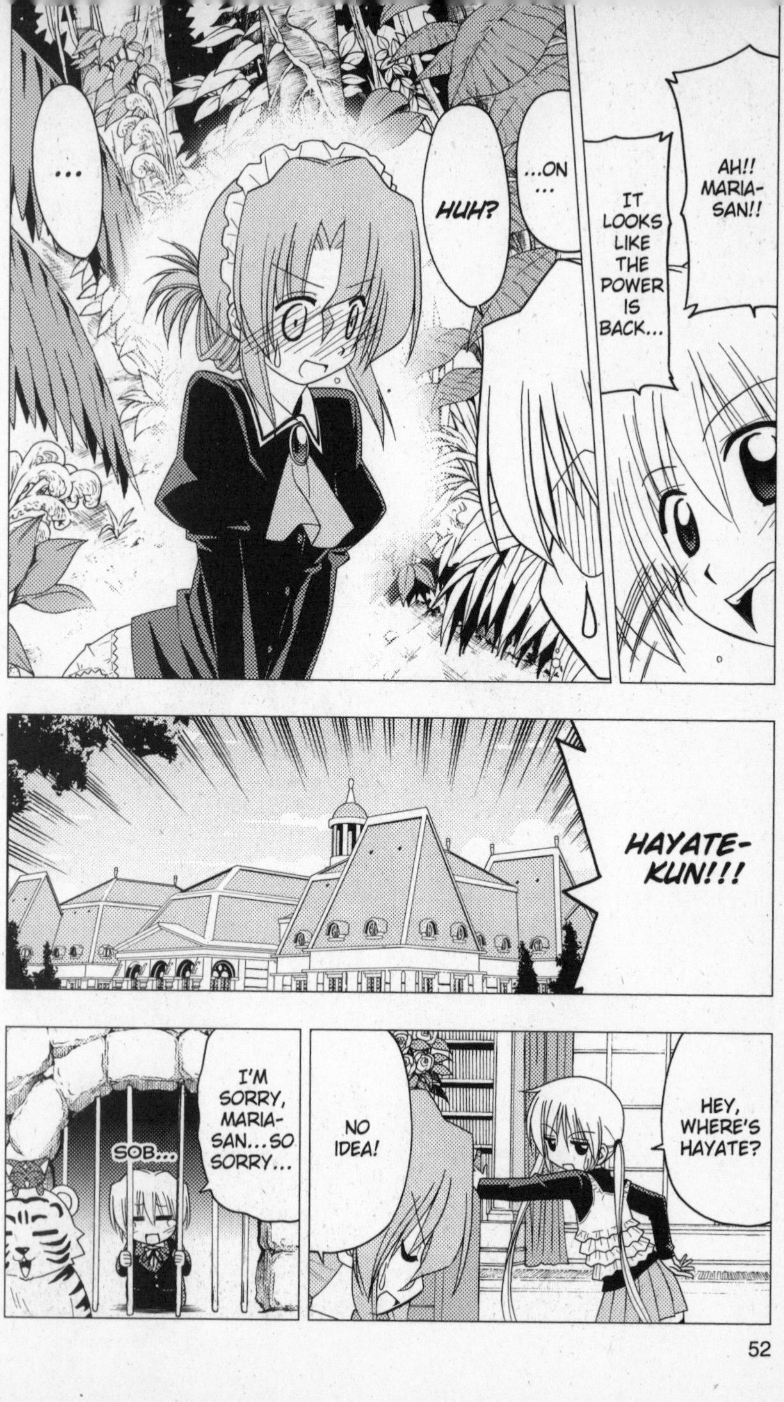
AH!! MARIA-SAN!!
IT LOOKS LIKE THE POWER IS BACK...
...ON ...
HUH?
...
HAYATE-KUN!!!
HEY, WHERE'S HAYATE?
NO IDEA!
I'M SORRY, MARIA-SAN...SO SORRY...
SOB...

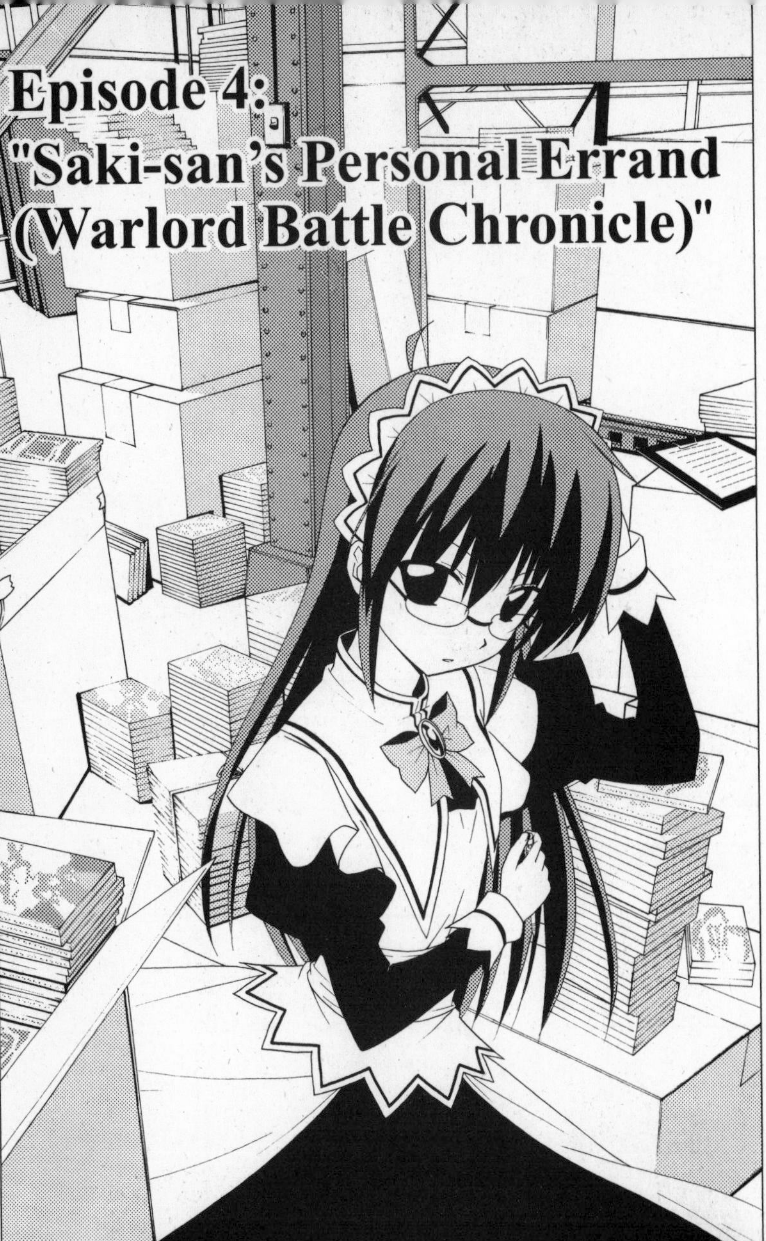
Episode 4:
"Saki-san's Personal Errand
(Warlord Battle Chronicle)"

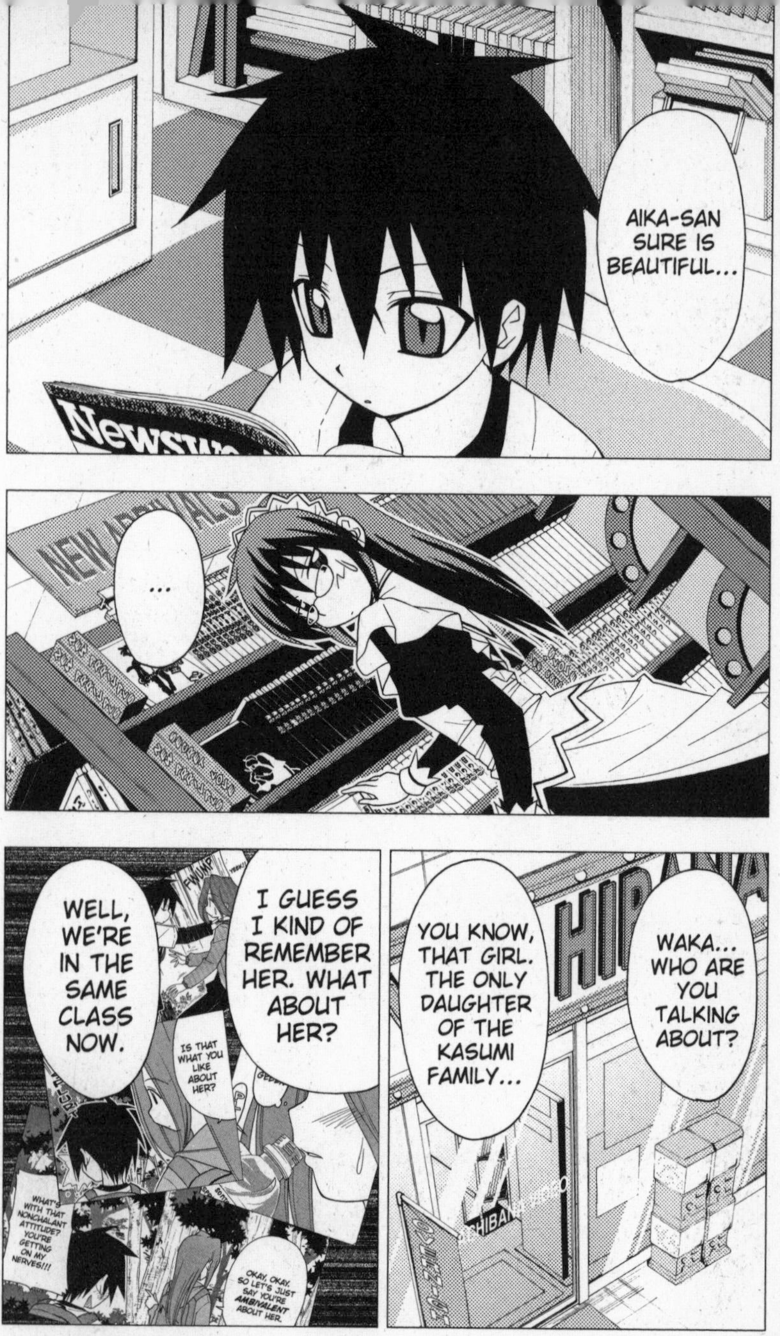
AIKA-SAN SURE IS BEAUTIFUL...
...
WAKA... WHO ARE YOU TALKING ABOUT?
YOU KNOW, THAT GIRL. THE ONLY DAUGHTER OF THE KASUMI FAMILY...
I GUESS I KIND OF REMEMBER HER. WHAT ABOUT HER?
WELL, WE'RE IN THE SAME CLASS NOW.
YEEK!!
FWUMP
IS THAT WHAT YOU LIKE ABOUT HER?
WHAT'S WITH THAT NONCHALANT ATTITUDE? YOU'RE GETTING ON MY NERVES!!!
OKAY, OKAY. SO LET'S JUST SAY YOU'RE AMBIVALENT ABOUT HER.

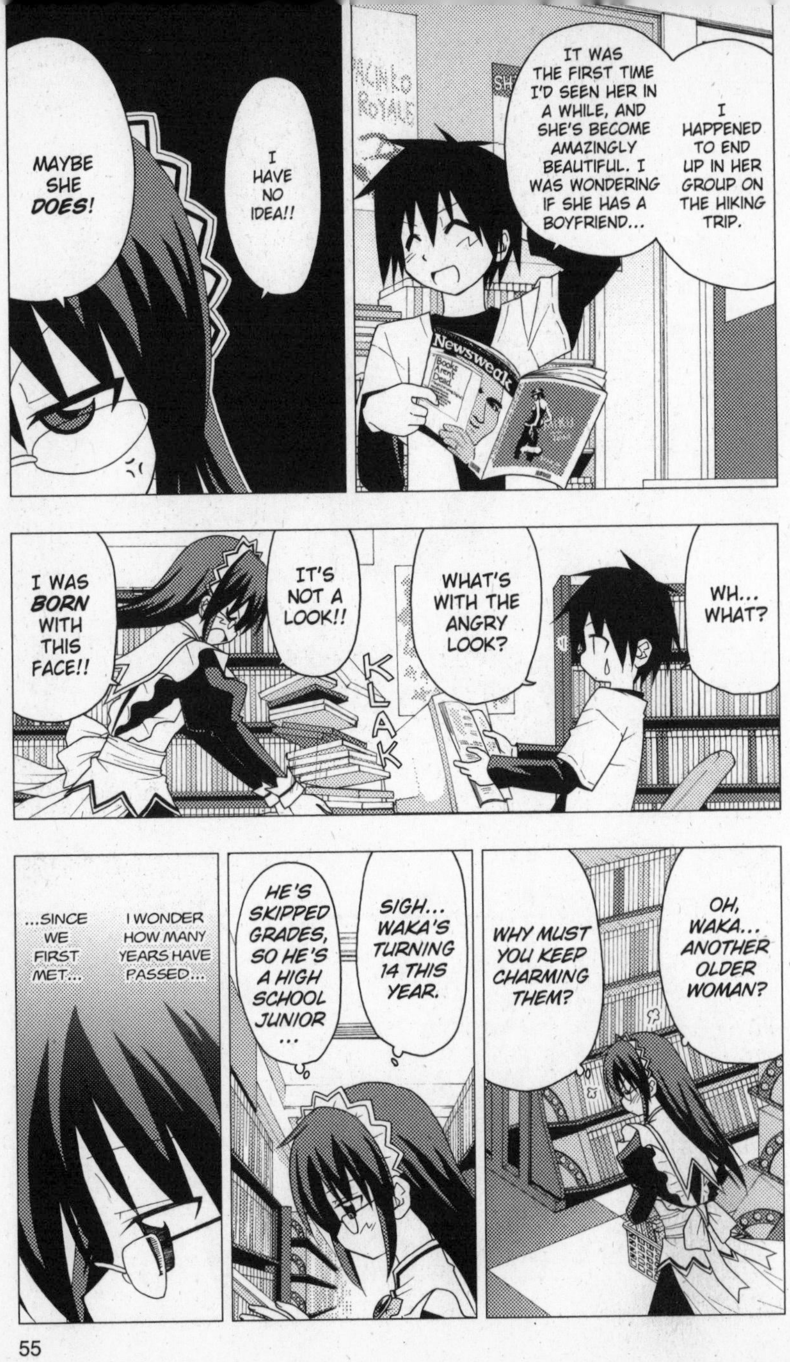
I HAPPENED TO END UP IN HER GROUP ON THE HIKING TRIP.
IT WAS THE FIRST TIME I'D SEEN HER IN A WHILE, AND SHE'S BECOME AMAZINGLY BEAUTIFUL. I WAS WONDERING IF SHE HAS A BOYFRIEND...
Newsweek
Books Arent Dead.
I HAVE NO IDEA!!
MAYBE SHE *DOES!*
WH... WHAT?
WHAT'S WITH THE ANGRY LOOK?
KLAK
IT'S NOT A LOOK!!
I WAS *BORN* WITH THIS FACE!!
OH, WAKA... ANOTHER OLDER WOMAN?
WHY MUST YOU KEEP CHARMING THEM?
SIGH... WAKA'S TURNING 14 THIS YEAR.
HE'S SKIPPED GRADES, SO HE'S A HIGH SCHOOL JUNIOR...
I WONDER HOW MANY YEARS HAVE PASSED...
...SINCE WE FIRST MET...

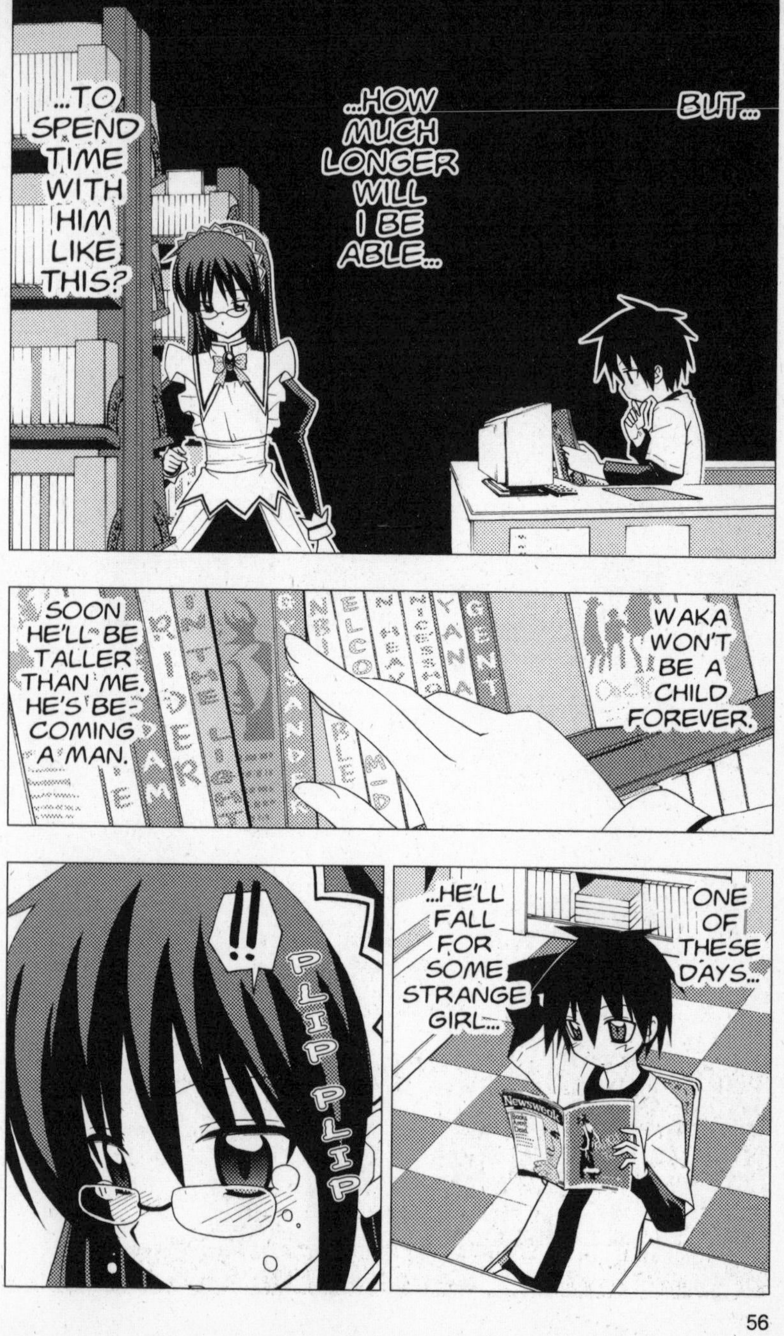
BUT...
...HOW MUCH LONGER WILL I BE ABLE...
...TO SPEND TIME WITH HIM LIKE THIS?
WAKA WON'T BE A CHILD FOREVER.
SOON HE'LL BE TALLER THAN ME. HE'S BE-COMING A MAN.
ONE OF THESE DAYS...
...HE'LL FALL FOR SOME STRANGE GIRL...
Newsweek
!!
PLIP PLIP PLIP

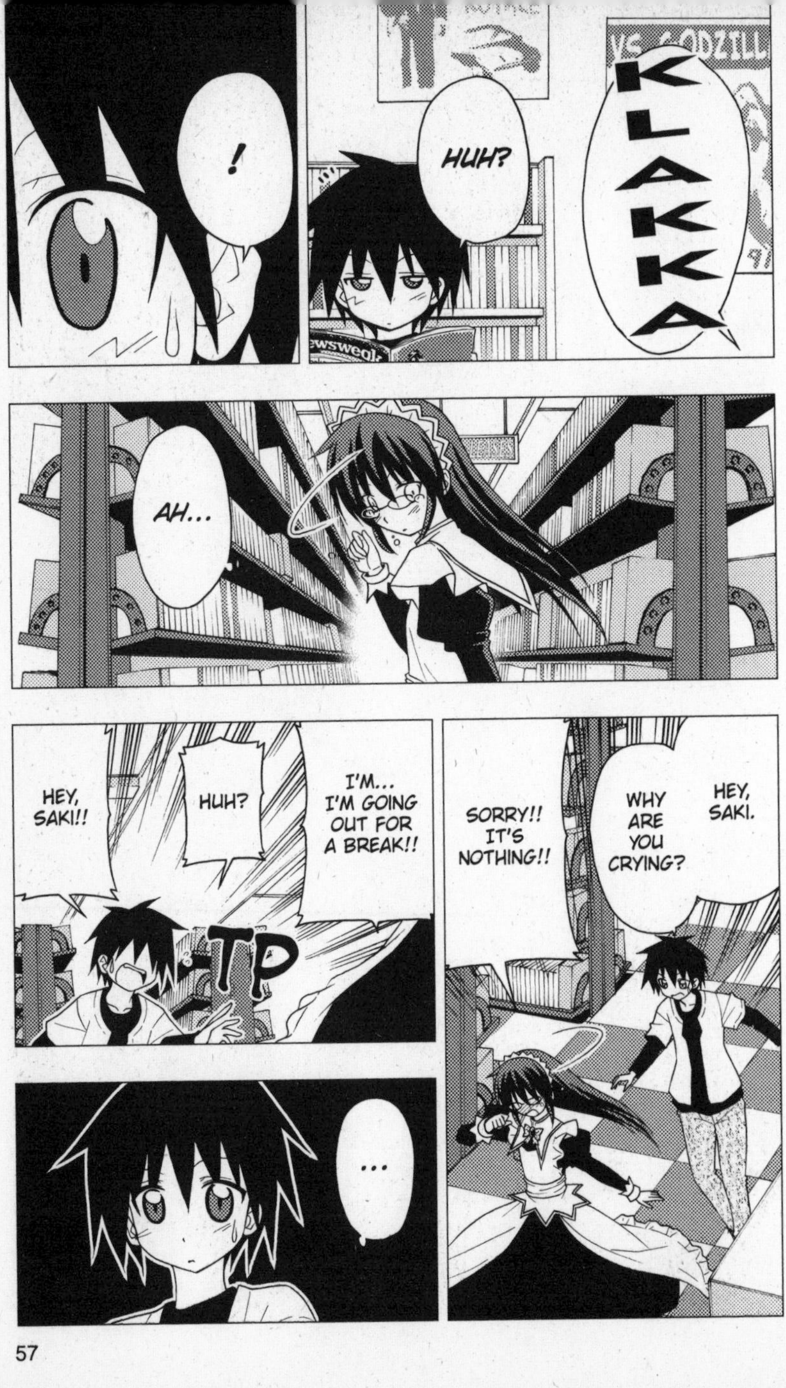
KLAKA
HUH?
!
AH...
HEY, SAKI.
WHY ARE YOU CRYING?
SORRY!! IT'S NOTHING!!
I'M... I'M GOING OUT FOR A BREAK!!
HUH?
HEY, SAKI!!
TP
...

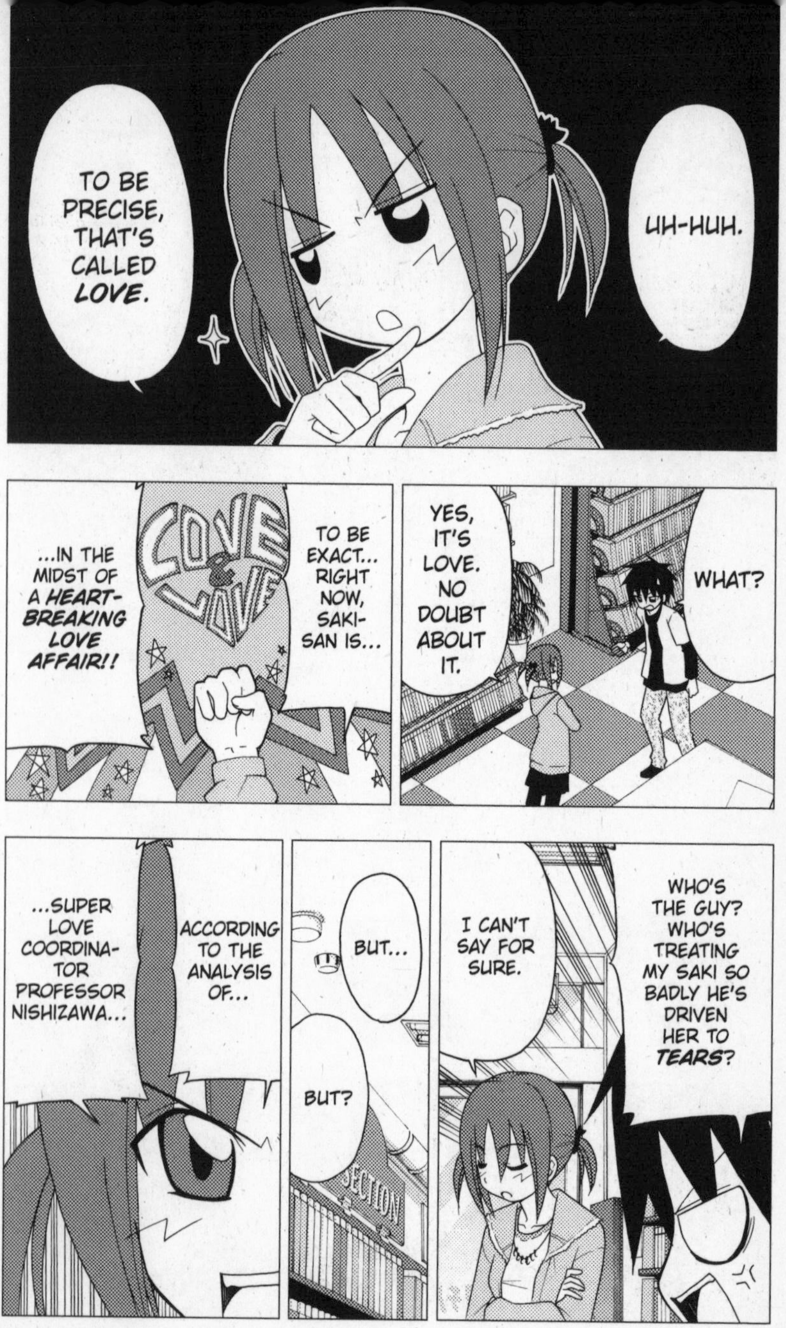
UH-HUH.
TO BE PRECISE, THAT'S CALLED LOVE.
WHAT?
YES, IT'S LOVE. NO DOUBT ABOUT IT.
TO BE EXACT... RIGHT NOW, SAKI-SAN IS...
LOVE & LOVE
...IN THE MIDST OF A HEART-BREAKING LOVE AFFAIR!!
WHO'S THE GUY? WHO'S TREATING MY SAKI SO BADLY HE'S DRIVEN HER TO TEARS?
I CAN'T SAY FOR SURE.
BUT...
BUT?
SECTION
ACCORDING TO THE ANALYSIS OF...
...SUPER LOVE COORDINATOR PROFESSOR NISHIZAWA...

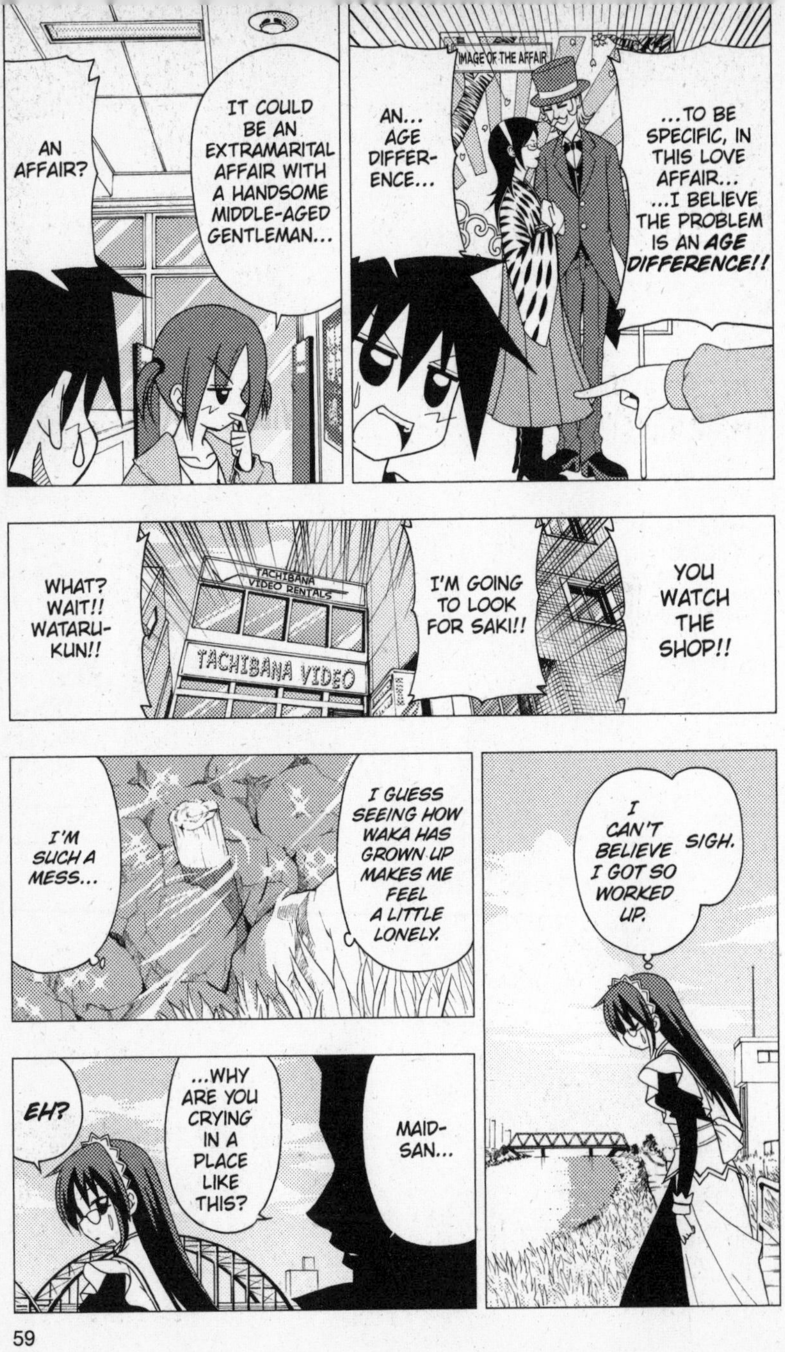
...TO BE SPECIFIC, IN THIS LOVE AFFAIR... ...I BELIEVE THE PROBLEM IS AN AGE DIFFERENCE!!
IMAGE OF THE AFFAIR
AN... AGE DIFFER-ENCE...
IT COULD BE AN EXTRAMARITAL AFFAIR WITH A HANDSOME MIDDLE-AGED GENTLEMAN...
AN AFFAIR?
YOU WATCH THE SHOP!!
I'M GOING TO LOOK FOR SAKI!!
TACHIBANA VIDEO RENTALS
TACHIBANA VIDEO
WHAT? WAIT!! WATARU-KUN!!
SIGH.
I CAN'T BELIEVE I GOT SO WORKED UP.
I GUESS SEEING HOW WAKA HAS GROWN UP MAKES ME FEEL A LITTLE LONELY.
I'M SUCH A MESS...
MAID-SAN...
...WHY ARE YOU CRYING IN A PLACE LIKE THIS?
EH?

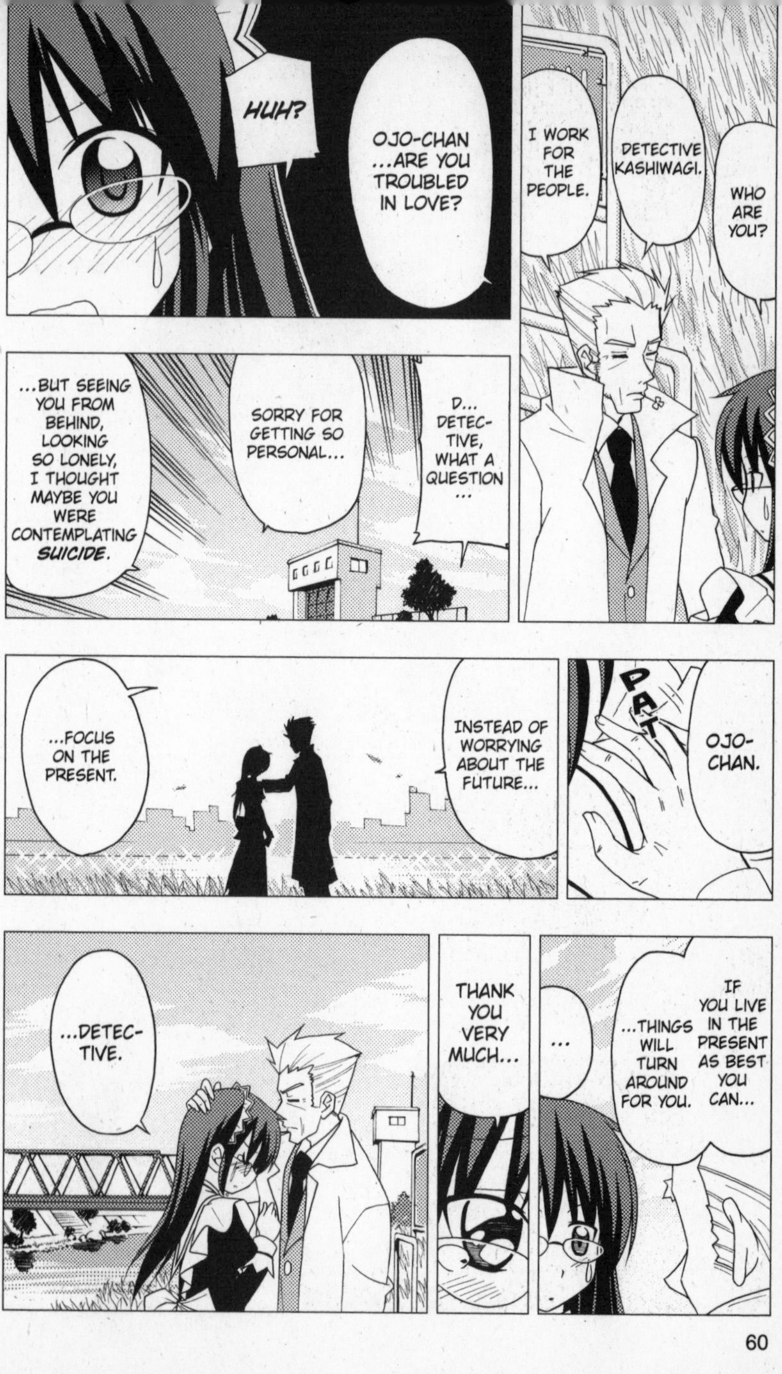
WHO ARE YOU?
DETECTIVE KASHIWAGI.
I WORK FOR THE PEOPLE.
OJO-CHAN ...ARE YOU TROUBLED IN LOVE?
HUH?
D... DETEC-TIVE, WHAT A QUESTION ...
SORRY FOR GETTING SO PERSONAL...
...BUT SEEING YOU FROM BEHIND, LOOKING SO LONELY, I THOUGHT MAYBE YOU WERE CONTEMPLATING SUICIDE.
PAT
OJO-CHAN.
INSTEAD OF WORRYING ABOUT THE FUTURE...
...FOCUS ON THE PRESENT.
IF YOU LIVE IN THE PRESENT AS BEST YOU CAN...
...THINGS WILL TURN AROUND FOR YOU.
...
THANK YOU VERY MUCH...
...DETEC-TIVE.

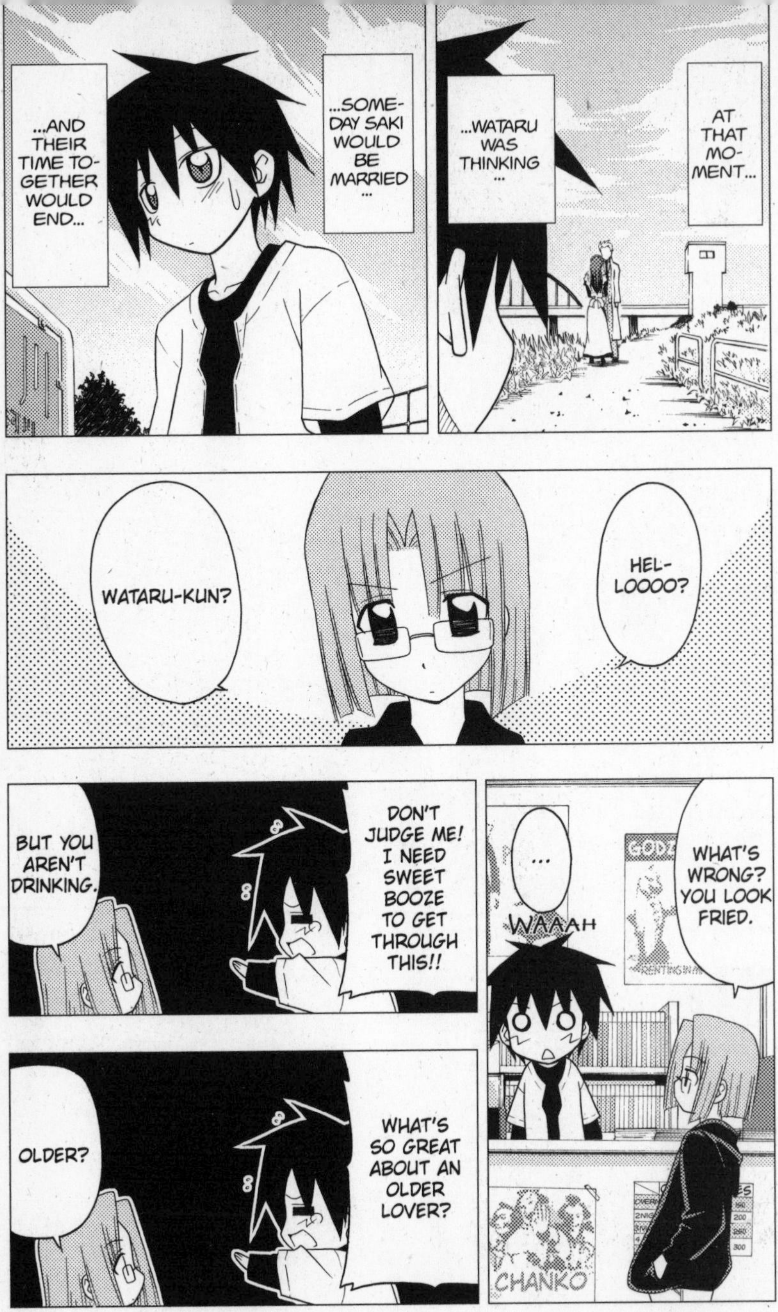
AT THAT MO-MENT...
...WATARU WAS THINKING...
...SOME-DAY SAKI WOULD BE MARRIED...
...AND THEIR TIME TO-GETHER WOULD END...
HEL-LOOOO?
WATARU-KUN?
WHAT'S WRONG? YOU LOOK FRIED.
...
WAAAH
CHANKO
DON'T JUDGE ME! I NEED SWEET BOOZE TO GET THROUGH THIS!!
BUT YOU AREN'T DRINKING.
WHAT'S SO GREAT ABOUT AN OLDER LOVER?
OLDER?

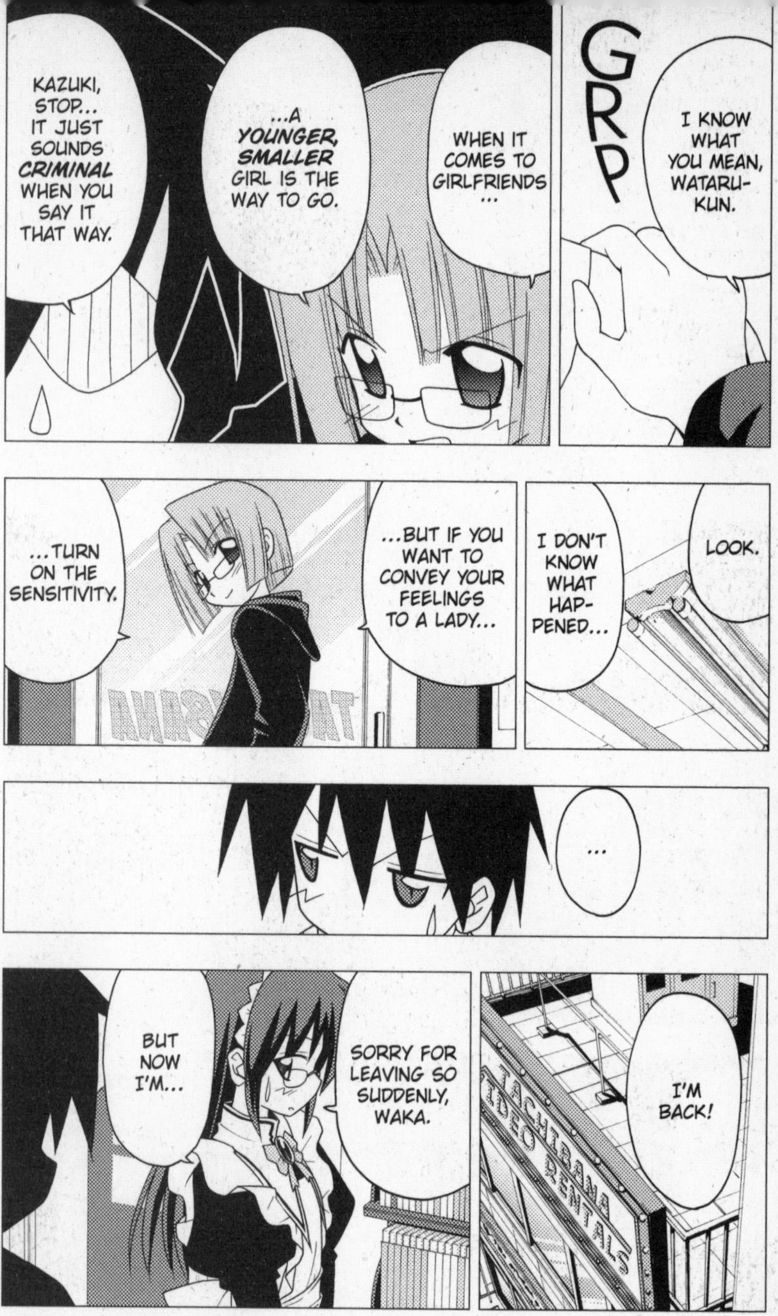
GRP
I KNOW WHAT YOU MEAN, WATARU-KUN.
WHEN IT COMES TO GIRLFRIENDS...
...A *YOUNGER, SMALLER* GIRL IS THE WAY TO GO.
KAZUKI, STOP... IT JUST SOUNDS *CRIMINAL* WHEN YOU SAY IT THAT WAY.
LOOK.
I DON'T KNOW WHAT HAP-PENED...
...BUT IF YOU WANT TO CONVEY YOUR FEELINGS TO A LADY...
...TURN ON THE SENSITIVITY.
...
TACHIBANA VIDEO RENTALS
I'M BACK!
SORRY FOR LEAVING SO SUDDENLY, WAKA.
BUT NOW I'M...

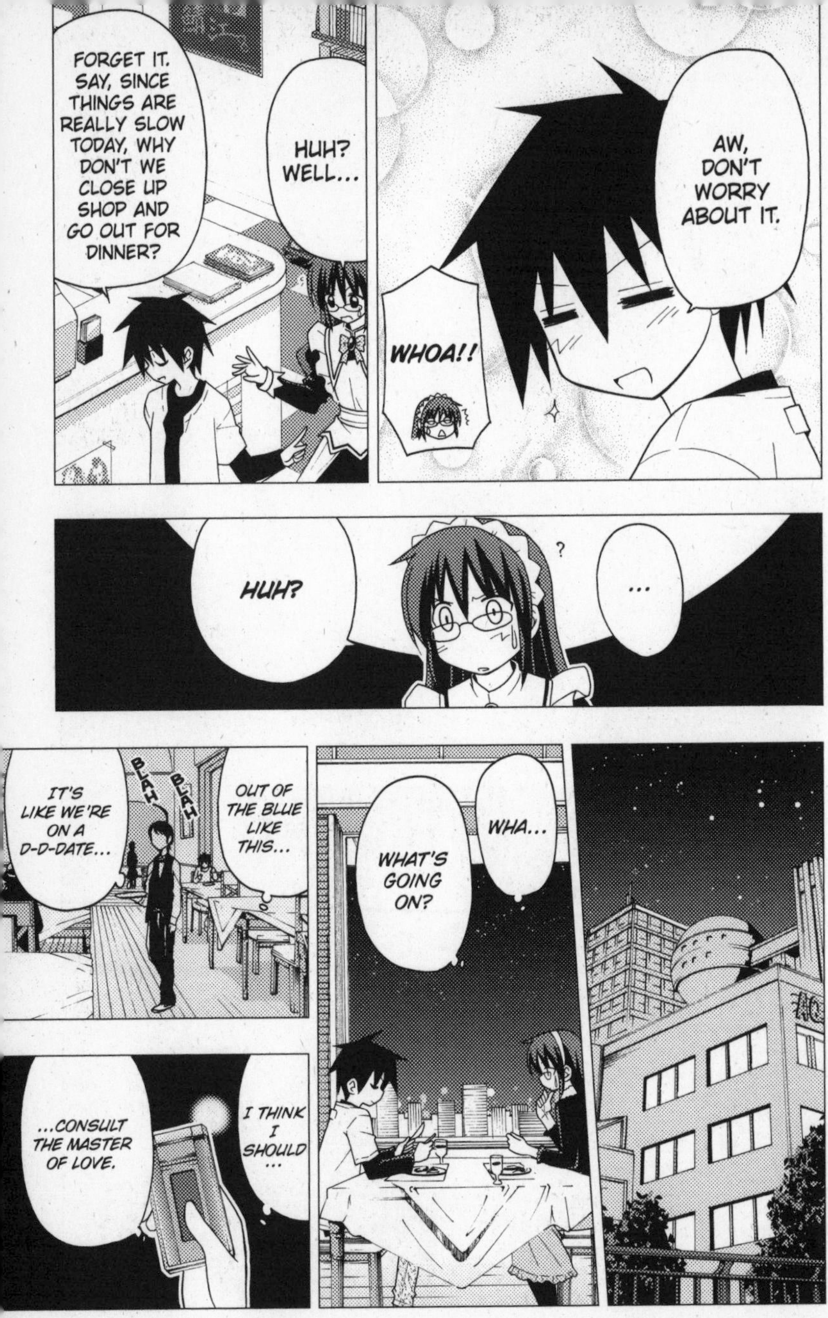
AW, DON'T WORRY ABOUT IT.
WHOA!!
HUH? WELL...
FORGET IT. SAY, SINCE THINGS ARE REALLY SLOW TODAY, WHY DON'T WE CLOSE UP SHOP AND GO OUT FOR DINNER?
...
?
HUH?
WHA...
WHAT'S GOING ON?
OUT OF THE BLUE LIKE THIS...
BLAH BLAH
IT'S LIKE WE'RE ON A D-D-DATE...
I THINK I SHOULD...
...CONSULT THE MASTER OF LOVE.

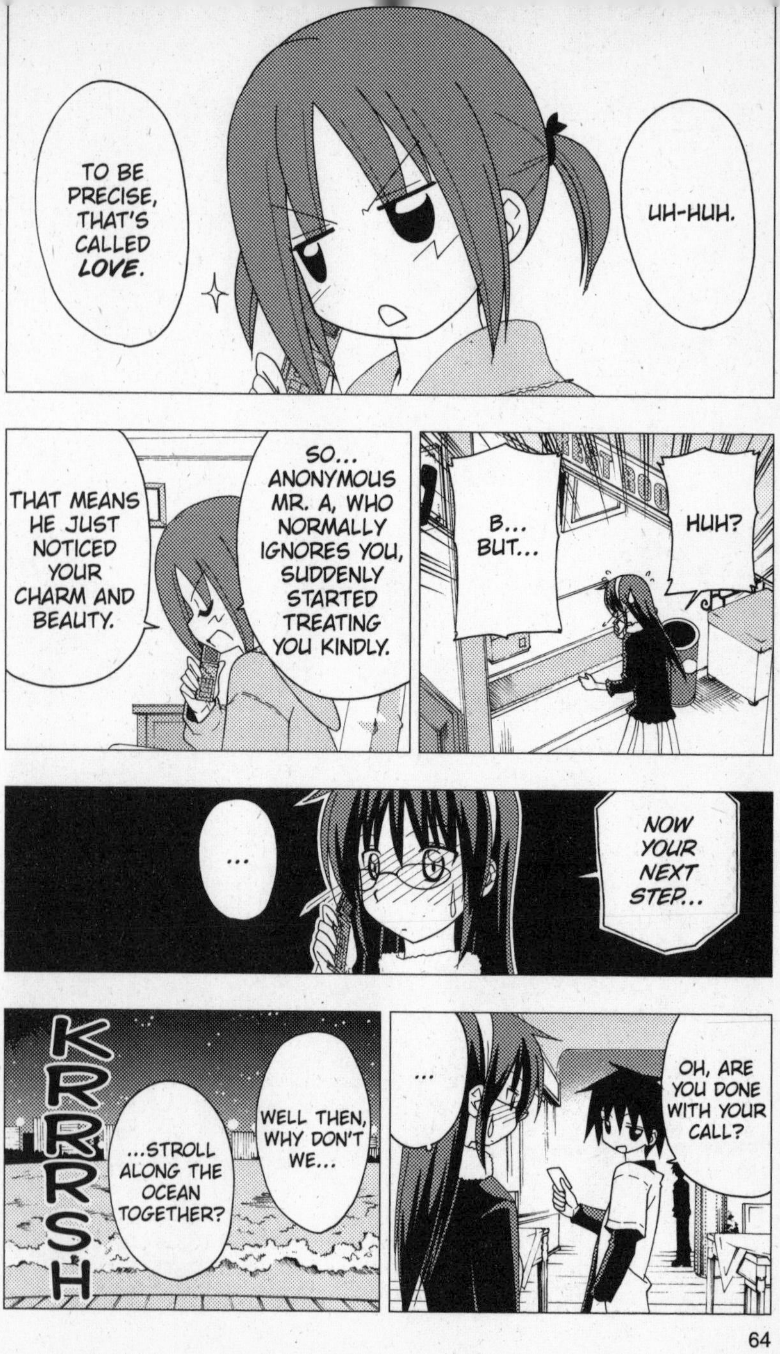
UH-HUH.
TO BE PRECISE, THAT'S CALLED ***LOVE***.
HUH?
B... BUT...
SO... ANONYMOUS MR. A, WHO NORMALLY IGNORES YOU, SUDDENLY STARTED TREATING YOU KINDLY.
THAT MEANS HE JUST NOTICED YOUR CHARM AND BEAUTY.
NOW YOUR NEXT STEP...
...
OH, ARE YOU DONE WITH YOUR CALL?
...
WELL THEN, WHY DON'T WE...
...STROLL ALONG THE OCEAN TOGETHER?
KRRRSH

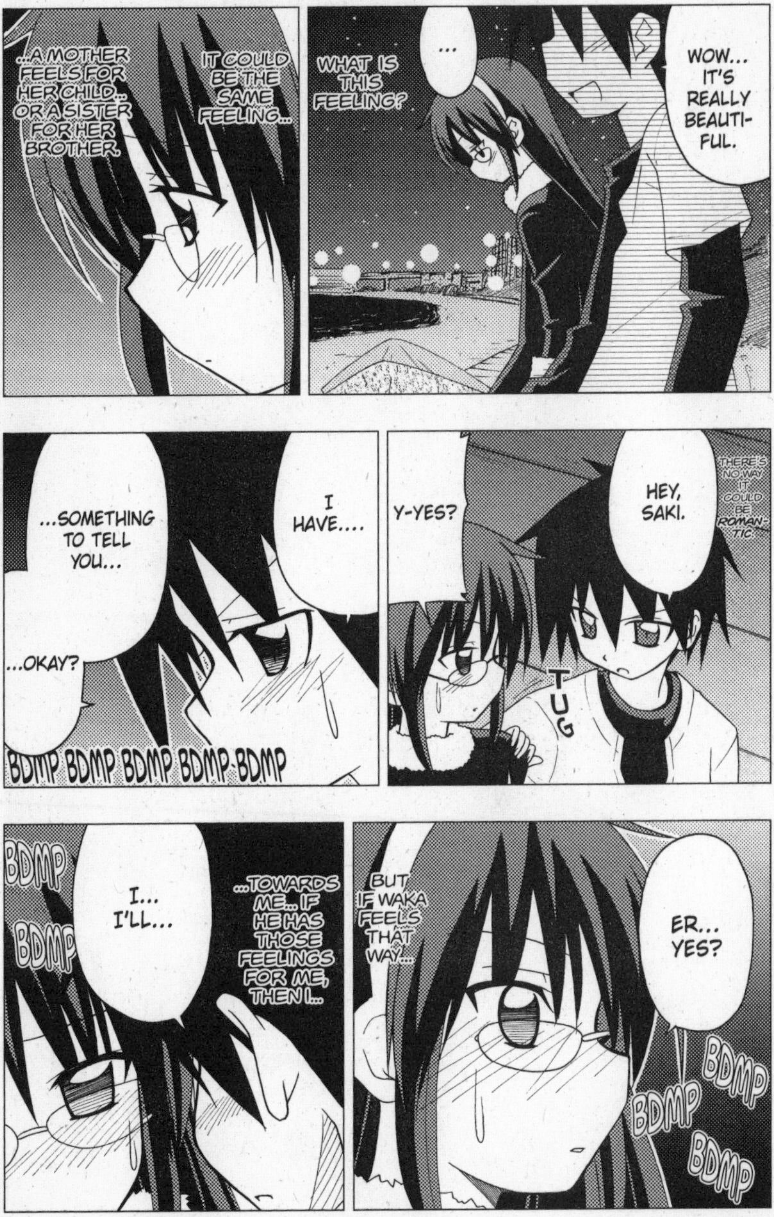
WOW... IT'S REALLY BEAUTIFUL.
...
WHAT IS THIS FEELING?
IT COULD BE THE SAME FEELING...
...A MOTHER FEELS FOR HER CHILD... OR A SISTER FOR HER BROTHER.
HEY, SAKI.
THERE'S NO WAY IT COULD BE ROMANTIC.
TUG
Y-YES?
I HAVE....
...SOMETHING TO TELL YOU...
...OKAY?
BDMP BDMP BDMP BDMP BDMP
ER... YES?
BDMP BDMP BDMP
BUT IF WAKA FEELS THAT WAY...
...TOWARDS ME... IF HE HAS THOSE FEELINGS FOR ME, THEN I...
I... I'LL...
BDMP BDMP

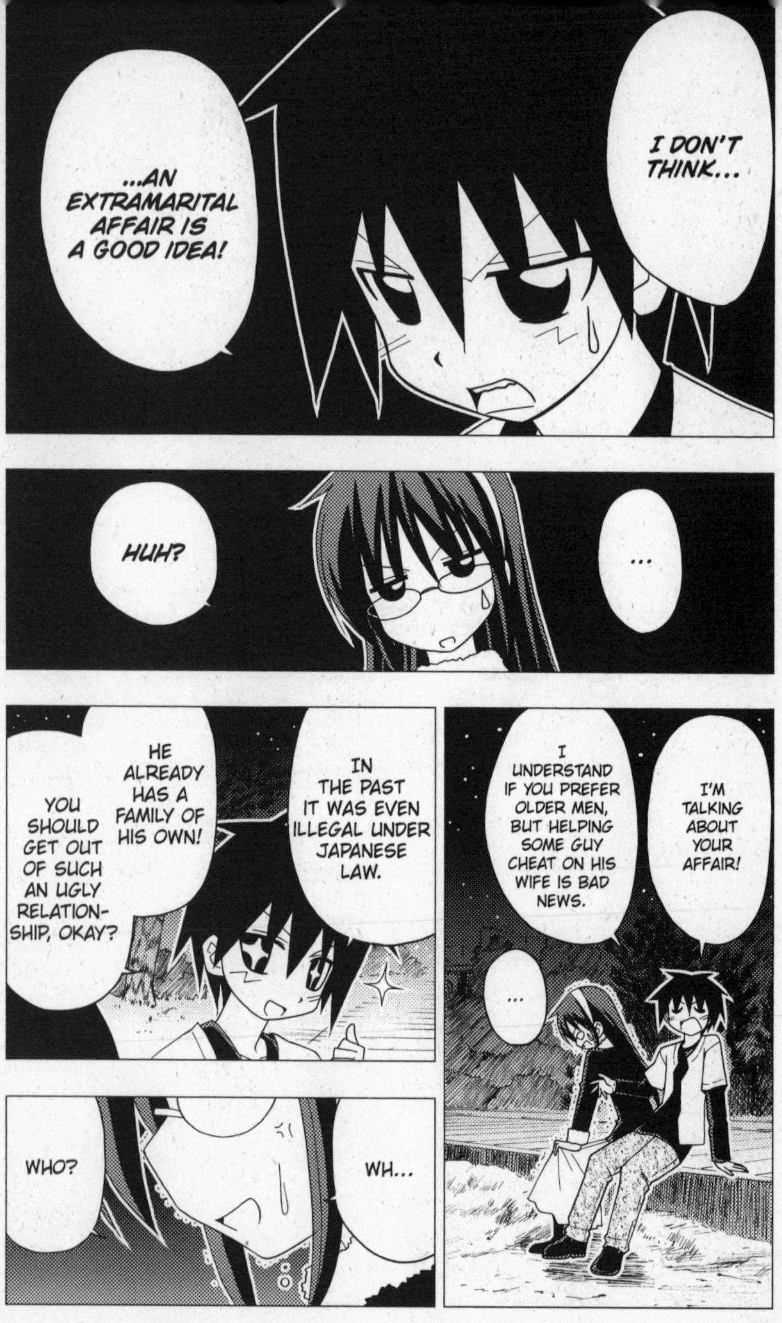
I DON'T THINK...
...AN EXTRAMARITAL AFFAIR IS A GOOD IDEA!
...
HUH?
I'M TALKING ABOUT YOUR AFFAIR!
I UNDERSTAND IF YOU PREFER OLDER MEN, BUT HELPING SOME GUY CHEAT ON HIS WIFE IS BAD NEWS.
...
IN THE PAST IT WAS EVEN ILLEGAL UNDER JAPANESE LAW.
HE ALREADY HAS A FAMILY OF HIS OWN!
YOU SHOULD GET OUT OF SUCH AN UGLY RELATION-SHIP, OKAY?
WH...
WHO?

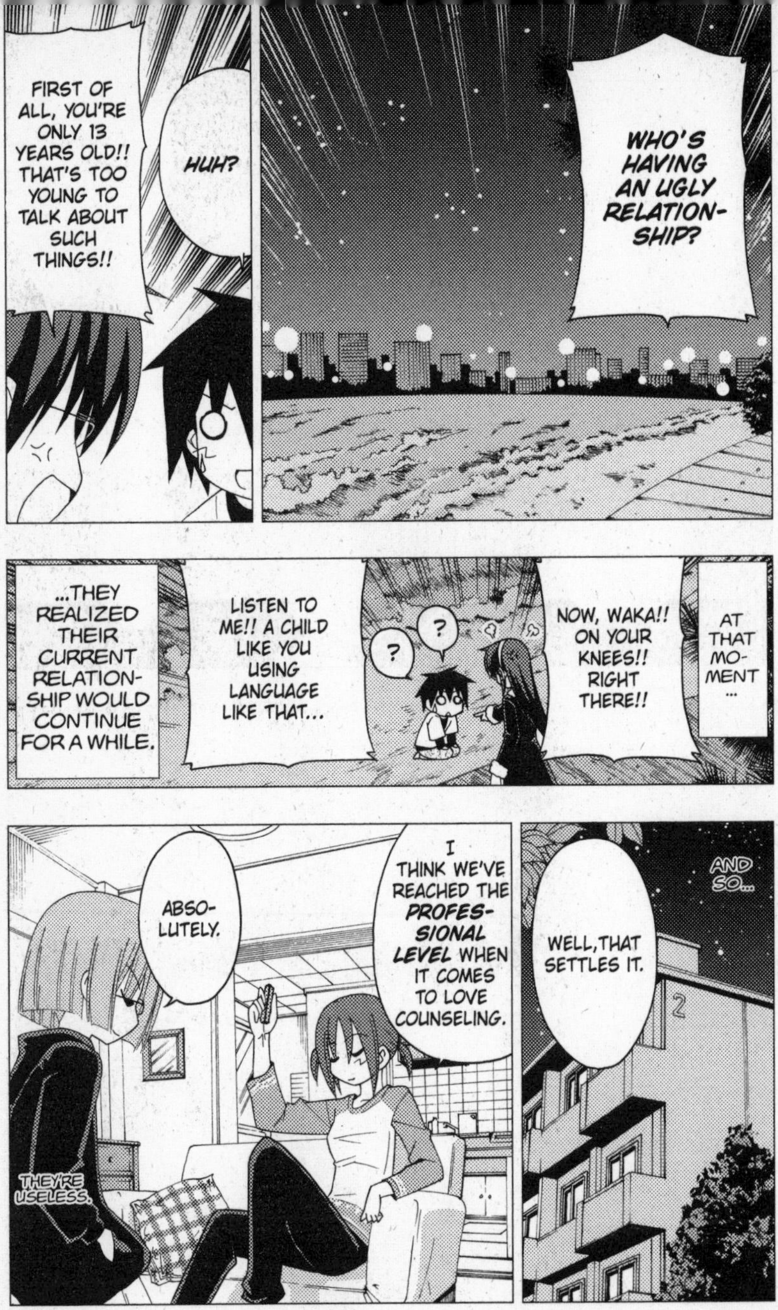
WHO'S HAVING AN UGLY RELATION-SHIP?
HUH?
FIRST OF ALL, YOU'RE ONLY 13 YEARS OLD!! THAT'S TOO YOUNG TO TALK ABOUT SUCH THINGS!!
AT THAT MO-MENT ...
NOW, WAKA!! ON YOUR KNEES!! RIGHT THERE!!
?
?
LISTEN TO ME!! A CHILD LIKE YOU USING LANGUAGE LIKE THAT...
...THEY REALIZED THEIR CURRENT RELATION-SHIP WOULD CONTINUE FOR A WHILE.
AND SO...
WELL, THAT SETTLES IT.
I THINK WE'VE REACHED THE PROFES-SIONAL LEVEL WHEN IT COMES TO LOVE COUNSELING.
ABSO-LUTELY.
THEY'RE USELESS.

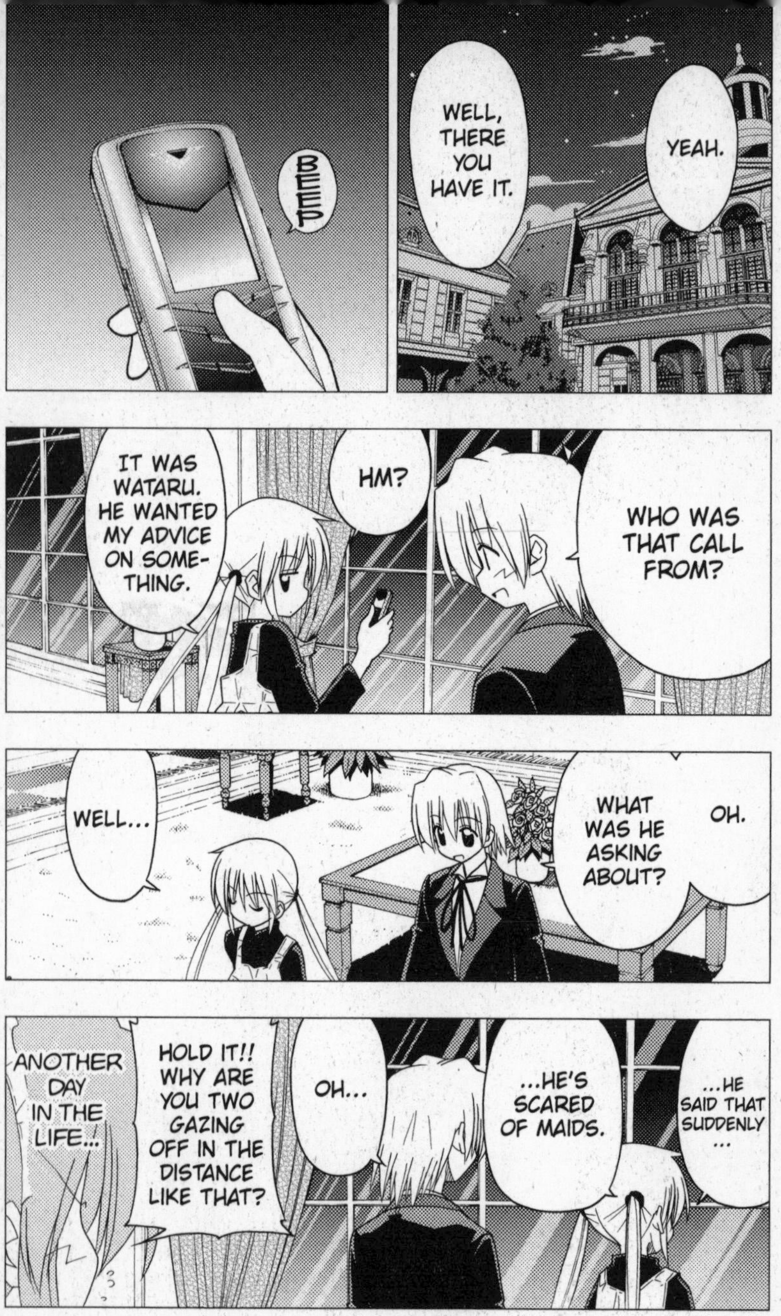
YEAH.
WELL, THERE YOU HAVE IT.
BEEP
WHO WAS THAT CALL FROM?
HM?
IT WAS WATARU. HE WANTED MY ADVICE ON SOME-THING.
OH.
WHAT WAS HE ASKING ABOUT?
WELL...
...HE SAID THAT SUDDENLY ...
...HE'S SCARED OF MAIDS.
OH...
HOLD IT!! WHY ARE YOU TWO GAZING OFF IN THE DISTANCE LIKE THAT?
ANOTHER DAY IN THE LIFE...

Episode 5: "Sleepless at 2:00 A.M., Broke the Door in Irritation"

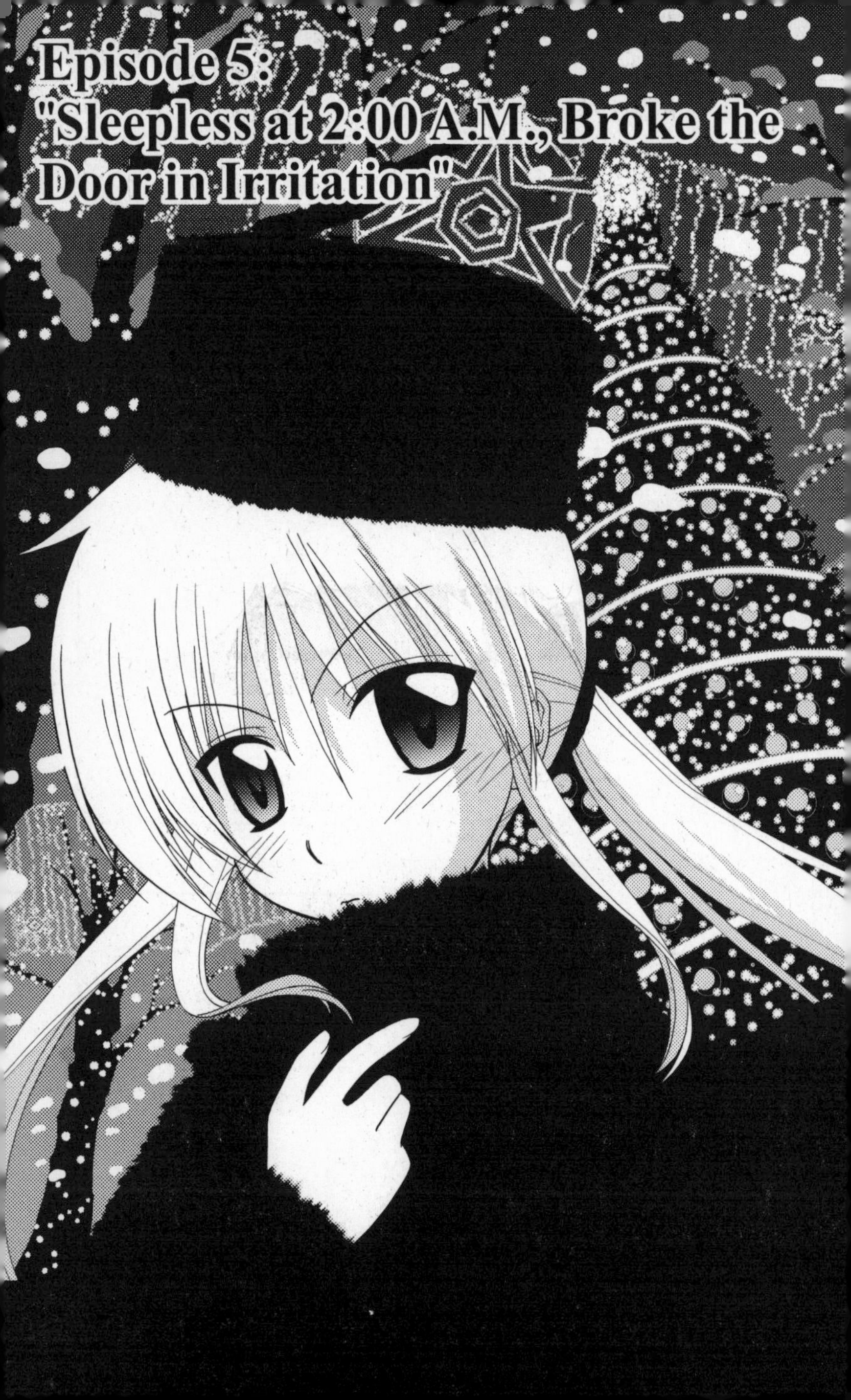

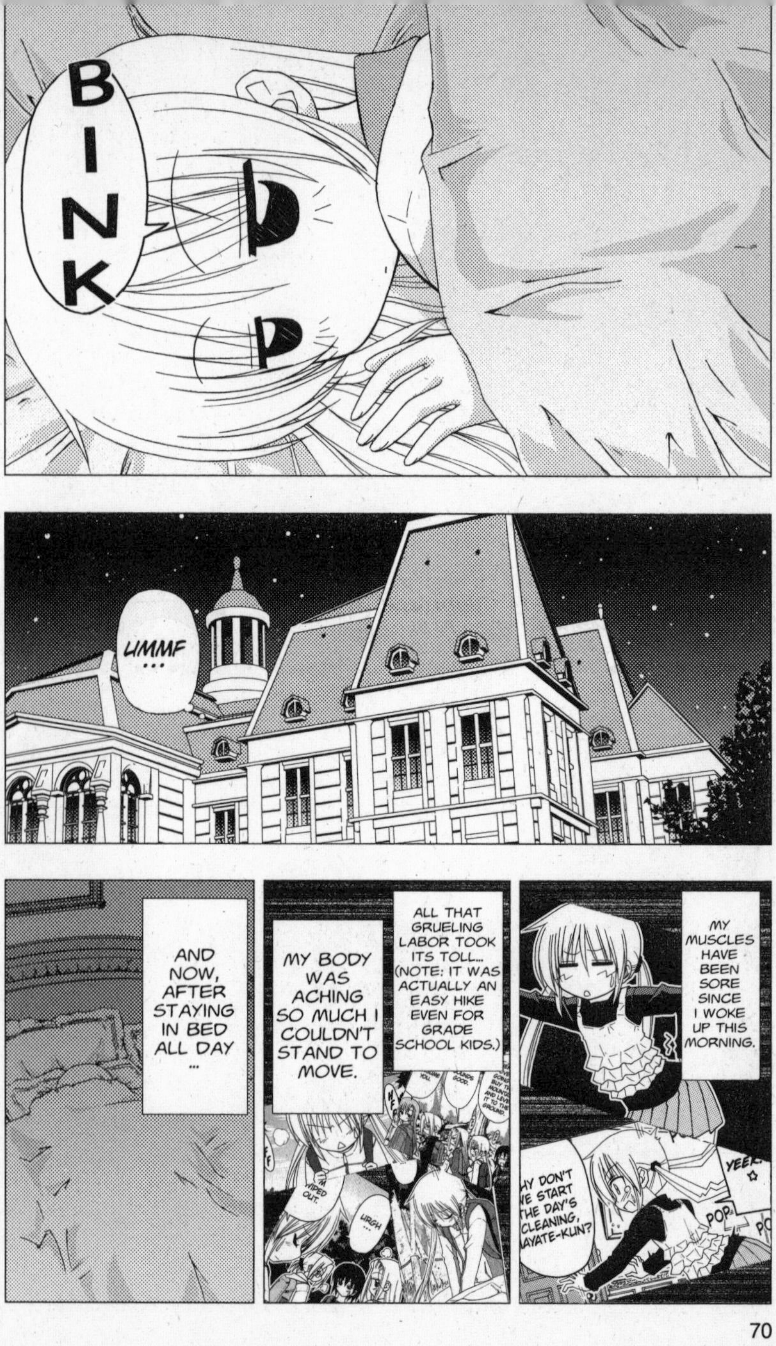
BINK
UMMF ...
MY MUSCLES HAVE BEEN SORE SINCE I WOKE UP THIS MORNING.
YEEK.
POP
HY DON'T E START THE DAY'S CLEANING, AYATE-KUN?
ALL THAT GRUELING LABOR TOOK ITS TOLL... (NOTE: IT WAS ACTUALLY AN EASY HIKE EVEN FOR GRADE SCHOOL KIDS.)
MY BODY WAS ACHING SO MUCH I COULDN'T STAND TO MOVE.
SOUNDS GOOD.
WIPED OUT.
URGH ...
AND NOW, AFTER STAYING IN BED ALL DAY ...

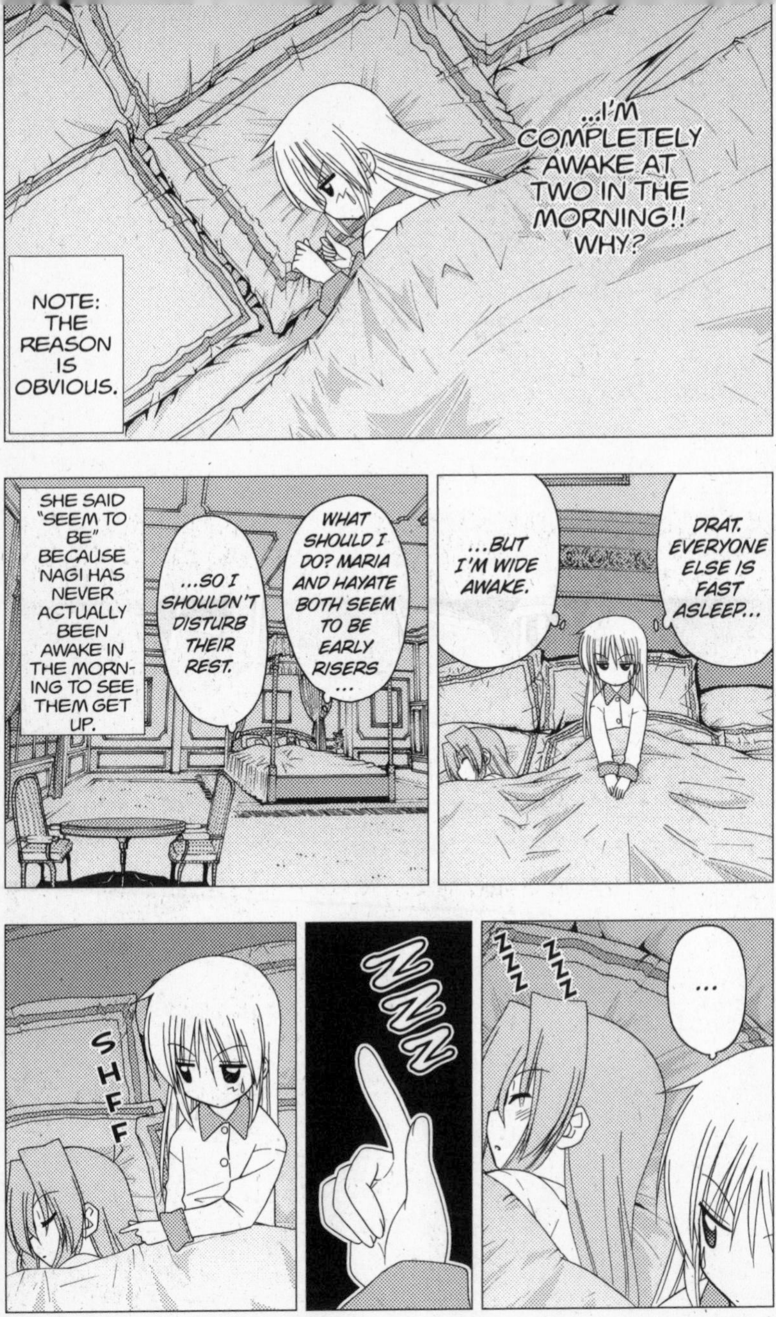
...I'M COMPLETELY AWAKE AT TWO IN THE MORNING!! WHY?
NOTE: THE REASON IS OBVIOUS.
DRAT. EVERYONE ELSE IS FAST ASLEEP...
...BUT I'M WIDE AWAKE.
WHAT SHOULD I DO? MARIA AND HAYATE BOTH SEEM TO BE EARLY RISERS...
...SO I SHOULDN'T DISTURB THEIR REST.
SHE SAID "SEEM TO BE" BECAUSE NAGI HAS NEVER ACTUALLY BEEN AWAKE IN THE MORNING TO SEE THEM GET UP.
ZZZ
ZZZ
...
NNN
SHFF

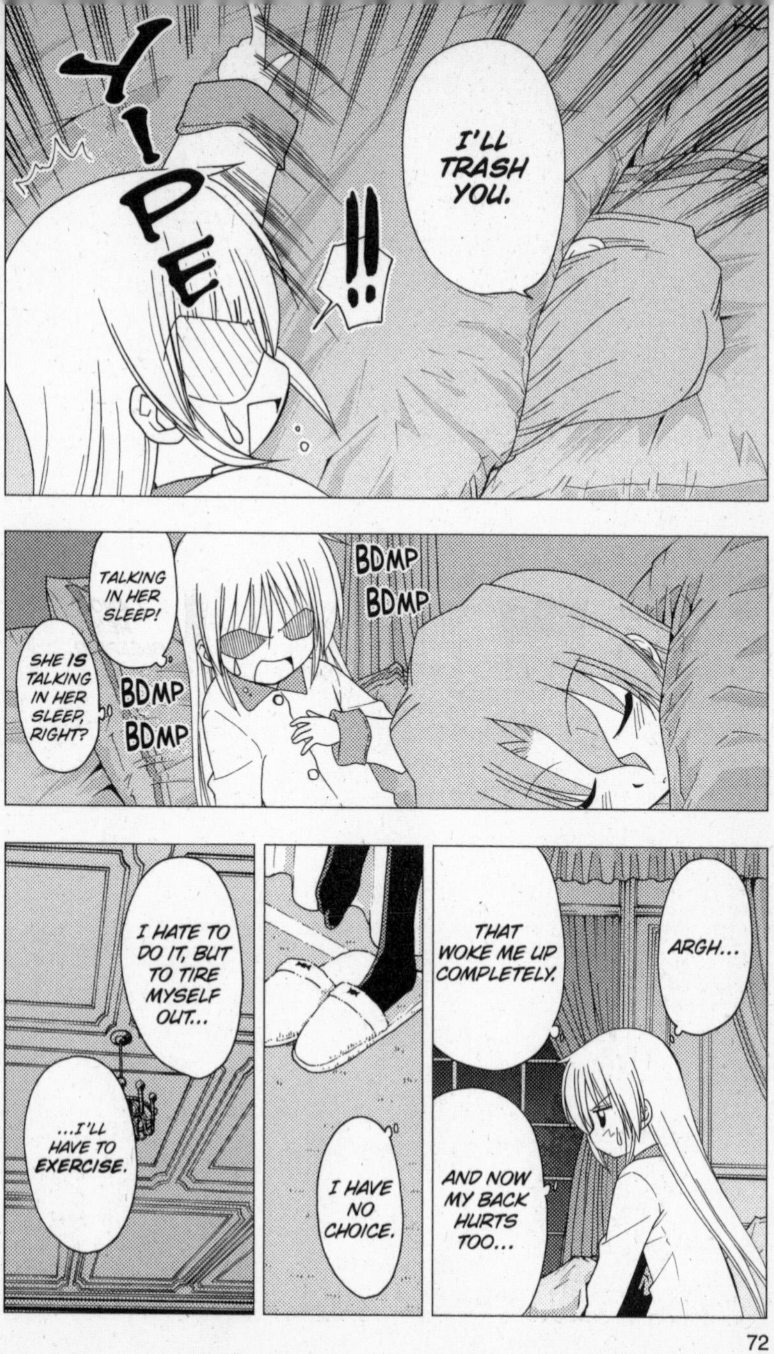
I'LL TRASH YOU.
!!
YIPE
BDMP BDMP
TALKING IN HER SLEEP!
SHE IS TALKING IN HER SLEEP, RIGHT?
BDMP BDMP
ARGH...
THAT WOKE ME UP COMPLETELY.
AND NOW MY BACK HURTS TOO...
I HAVE NO CHOICE.
I HATE TO DO IT, BUT TO TIRE MYSELF OUT...
...I'LL HAVE TO EXERCISE.

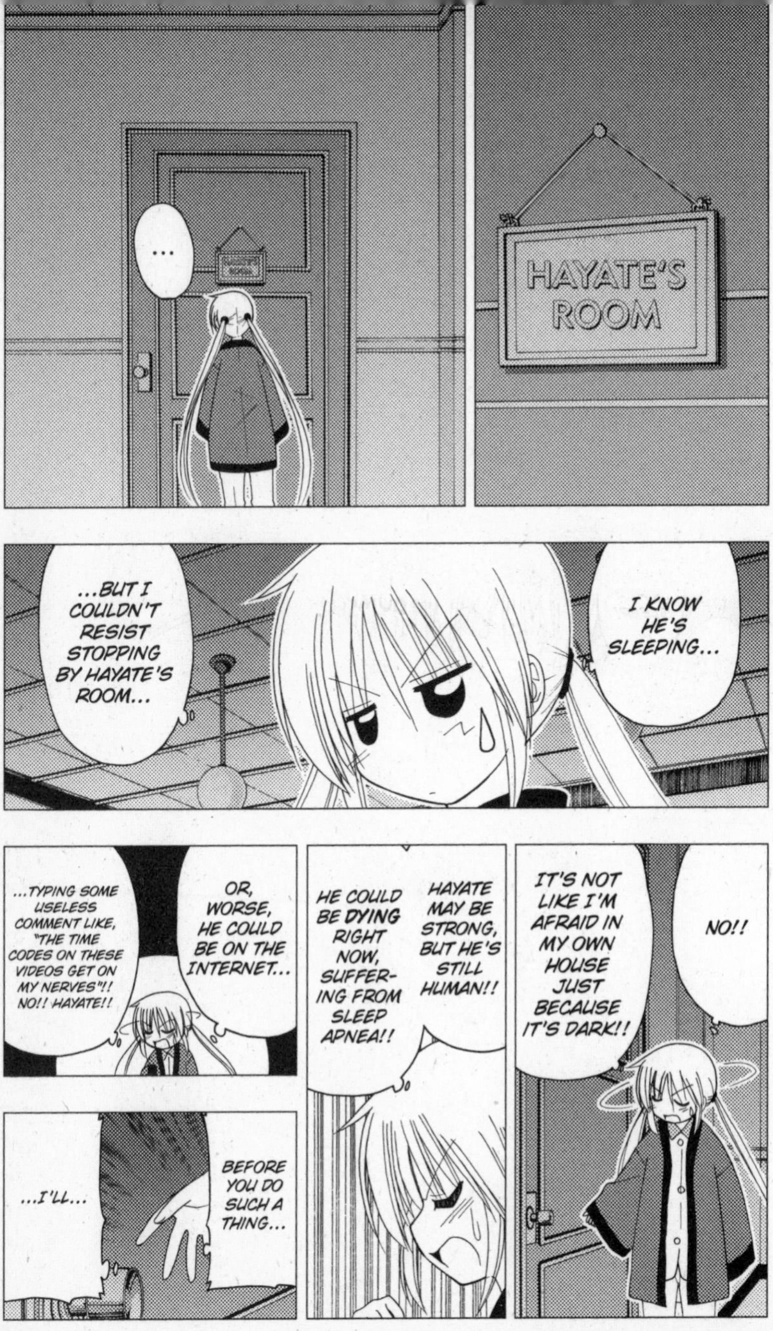
HAYATE'S ROOM
...
I KNOW HE'S SLEEPING...
...BUT I COULDN'T RESIST STOPPING BY HAYATE'S ROOM...
NO!!
IT'S NOT LIKE I'M AFRAID IN MY OWN HOUSE JUST BECAUSE IT'S DARK!!
HAYATE MAY BE STRONG, BUT HE'S STILL HUMAN!!
HE COULD BE DYING RIGHT NOW, SUFFERING FROM SLEEP APNEA!!
OR, WORSE, HE COULD BE ON THE INTERNET...
...TYPING SOME USELESS COMMENT LIKE, "THE TIME CODES ON THESE VIDEOS GET ON MY NERVES"!! NO!! HAYATE!!
BEFORE YOU DO SUCH A THING...
...I'LL...

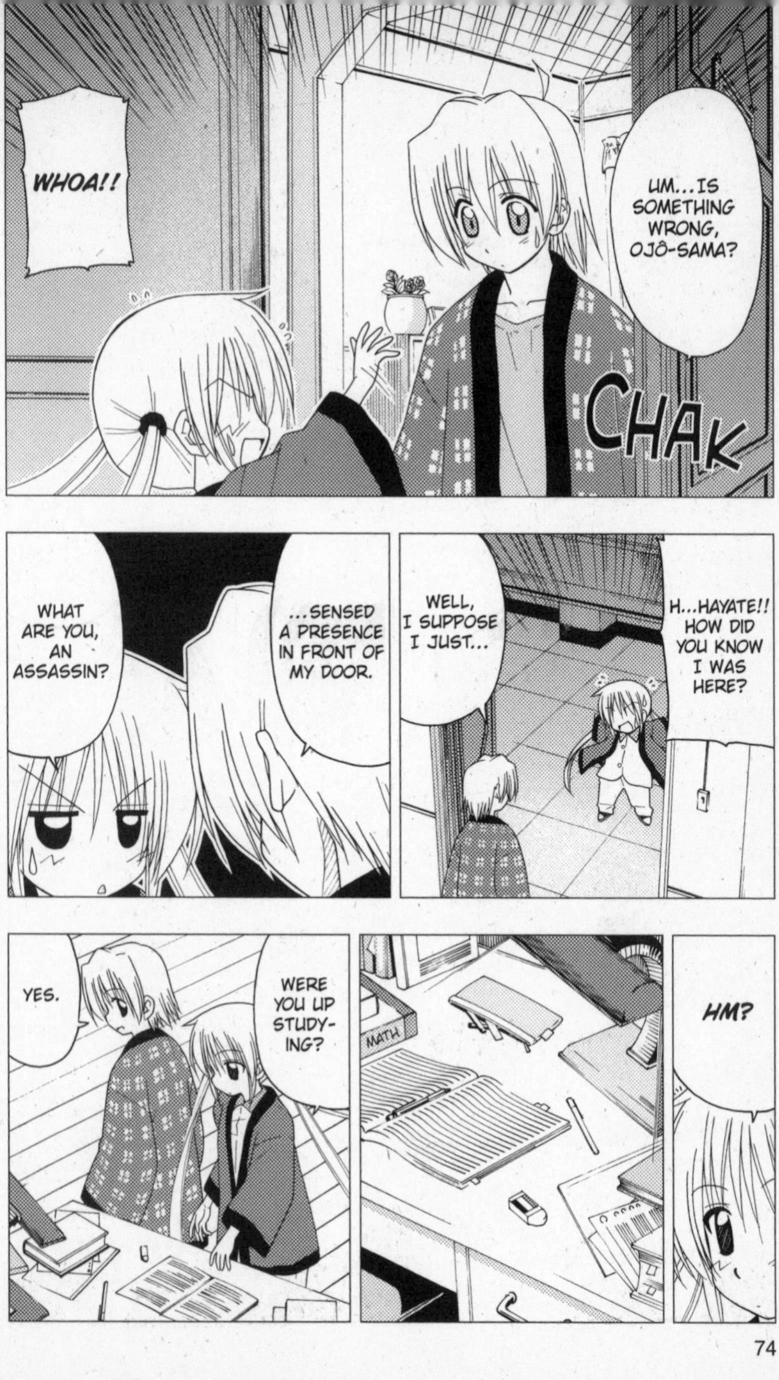
UM...IS SOMETHING WRONG, OJÔ-SAMA?
WHOA!!
CHAK
H...HAYATE!! HOW DID YOU KNOW I WAS HERE?
WELL, I SUPPOSE I JUST...
...SENSED A PRESENCE IN FRONT OF MY DOOR.
WHAT ARE YOU, AN ASSASSIN?
HM?
MATH
WERE YOU UP STUDYING?
YES.

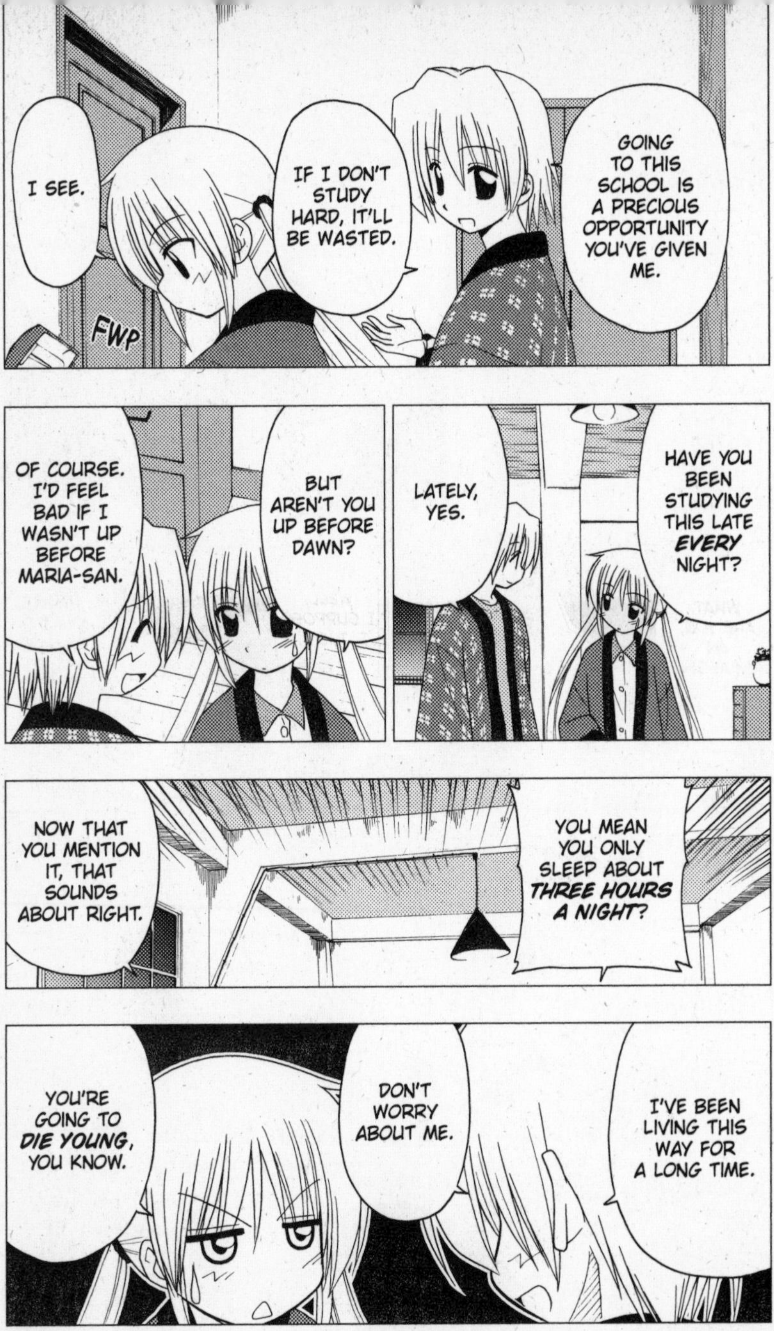
GOING TO THIS SCHOOL IS A PRECIOUS OPPORTUNITY YOU'VE GIVEN ME.
IF I DON'T STUDY HARD, IT'LL BE WASTED.
I SEE.
FWP
HAVE YOU BEEN STUDYING THIS LATE EVERY NIGHT?
LATELY, YES.
BUT AREN'T YOU UP BEFORE DAWN?
OF COURSE. I'D FEEL BAD IF I WASN'T UP BEFORE MARIA-SAN.
YOU MEAN YOU ONLY SLEEP ABOUT THREE HOURS A NIGHT?
NOW THAT YOU MENTION IT, THAT SOUNDS ABOUT RIGHT.
I'VE BEEN LIVING THIS WAY FOR A LONG TIME.
DON'T WORRY ABOUT ME.
YOU'RE GOING TO DIE YOUNG, YOU KNOW.

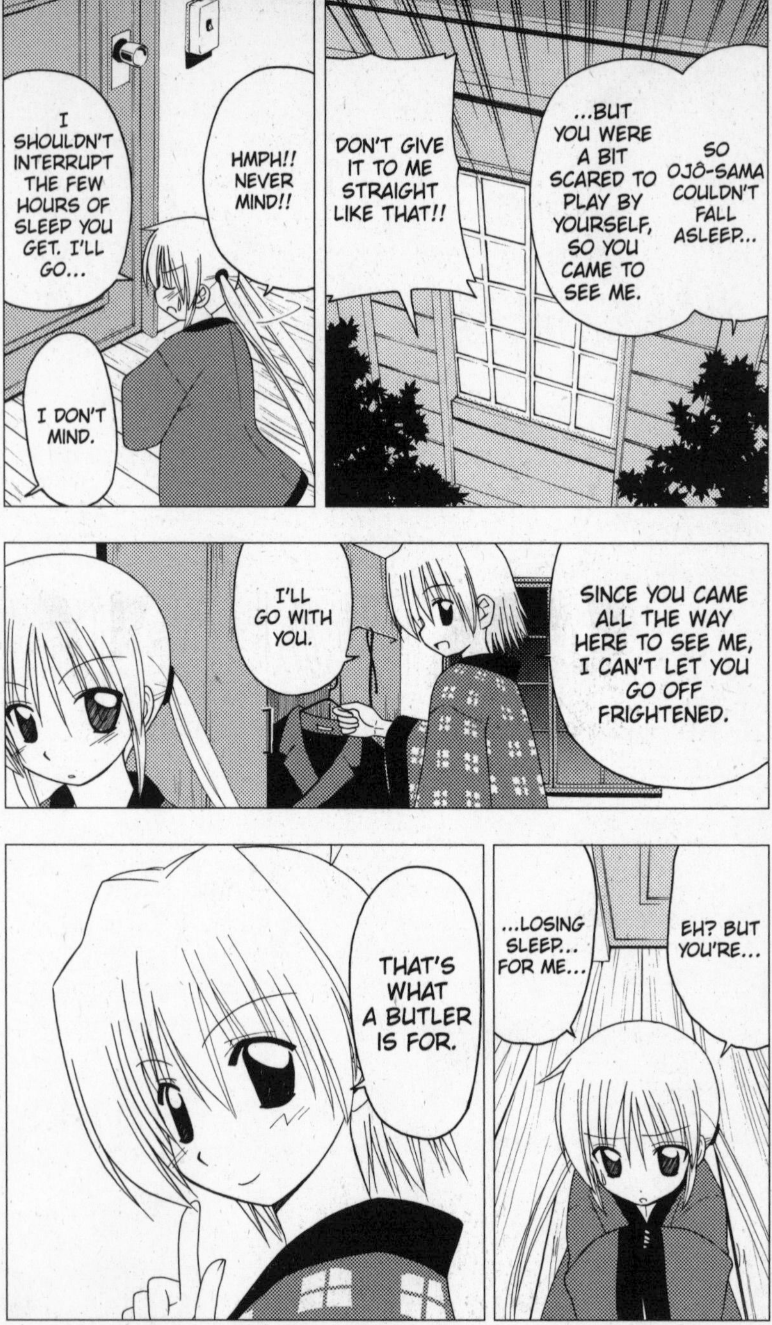
SO OJÔ-SAMA COULDN'T FALL ASLEEP...
...BUT YOU WERE A BIT SCARED TO PLAY BY YOURSELF, SO YOU CAME TO SEE ME.
DON'T GIVE IT TO ME STRAIGHT LIKE THAT!!
HMPH!! NEVER MIND!!
I SHOULDN'T INTERRUPT THE FEW HOURS OF SLEEP YOU GET. I'LL GO...
I DON'T MIND.
SINCE YOU CAME ALL THE WAY HERE TO SEE ME, I CAN'T LET YOU GO OFF FRIGHTENED.
I'LL GO WITH YOU.
EH? BUT YOU'RE...
...LOSING SLEEP... FOR ME...
THAT'S WHAT A BUTLER IS FOR.

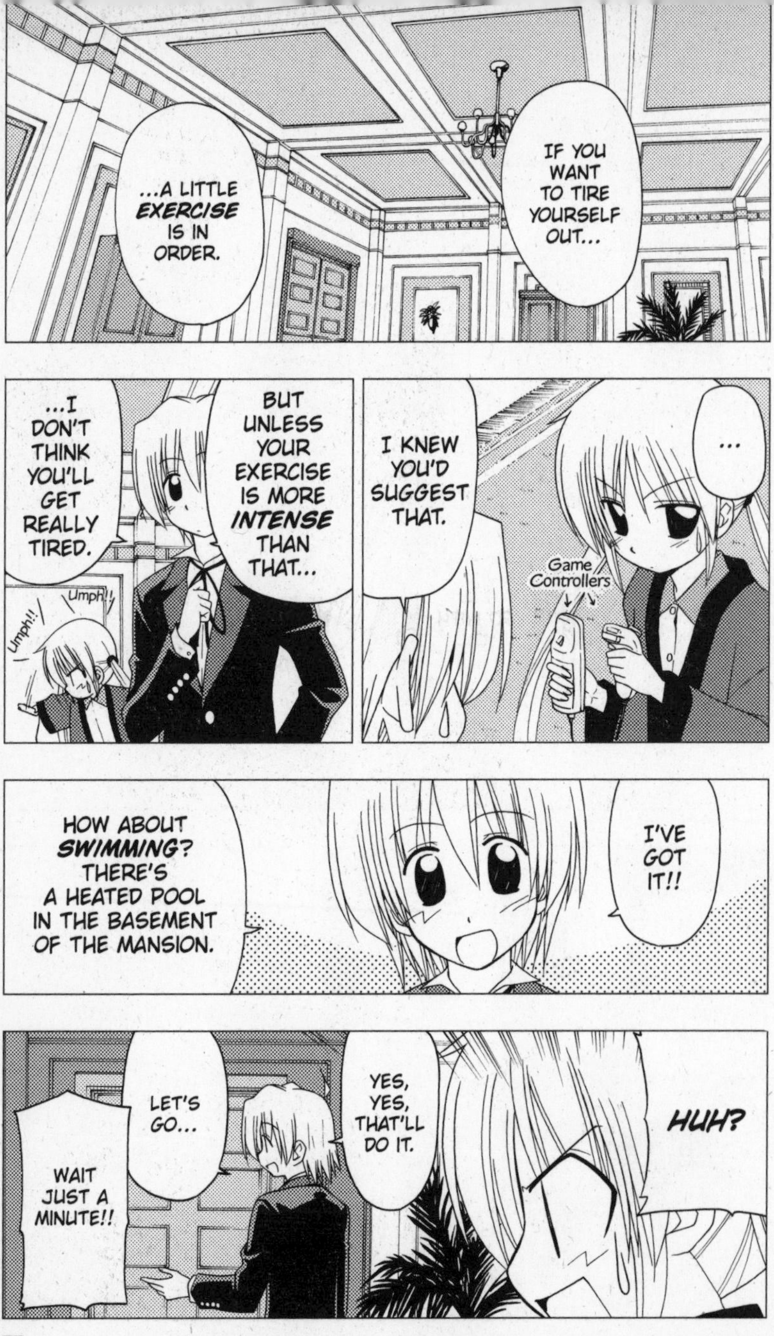
IF YOU WANT TO TIRE YOURSELF OUT...
...A LITTLE EXERCISE IS IN ORDER.
...
I KNEW YOU'D SUGGEST THAT.
Game Controllers
BUT UNLESS YOUR EXERCISE IS MORE INTENSE THAN THAT...
...I DON'T THINK YOU'LL GET REALLY TIRED.
Umph!!
Umph!!
I'VE GOT IT!!
HOW ABOUT SWIMMING? THERE'S A HEATED POOL IN THE BASEMENT OF THE MANSION.
HUH?
YES, YES, THAT'LL DO IT.
LET'S GO...
WAIT JUST A MINUTE!!

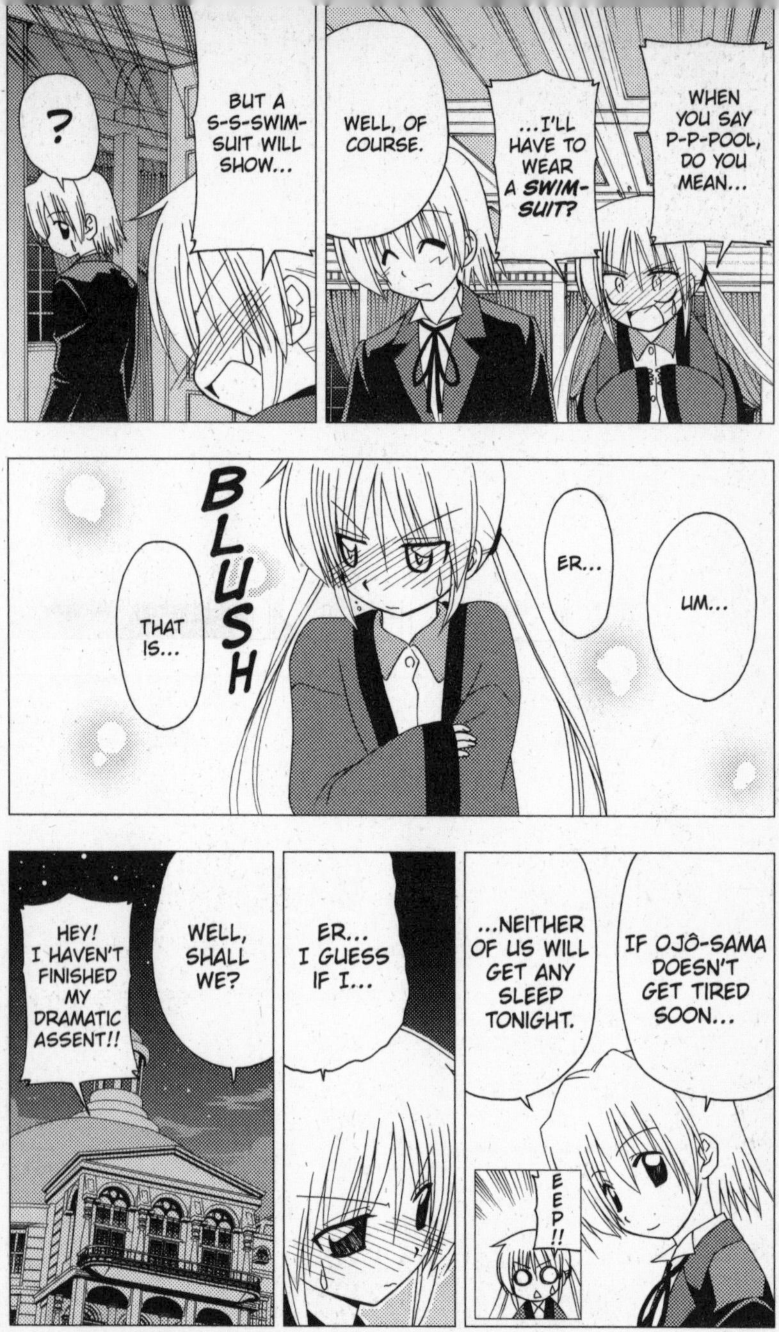
WHEN YOU SAY P-P-POOL, DO YOU MEAN...
...I'LL HAVE TO WEAR A *SWIM-SUIT?*
WELL, OF COURSE.
BUT A S-S-SWIM-SUIT WILL SHOW...
?
UM...
ER...
BLUSH
THAT IS...
IF OJÔ-SAMA DOESN'T GET TIRED SOON...
...NEITHER OF US WILL GET ANY SLEEP TONIGHT.
EEP!!
ER... I GUESS IF I...
WELL, SHALL WE?
HEY! I HAVEN'T FINISHED MY DRAMATIC ASSENT!!

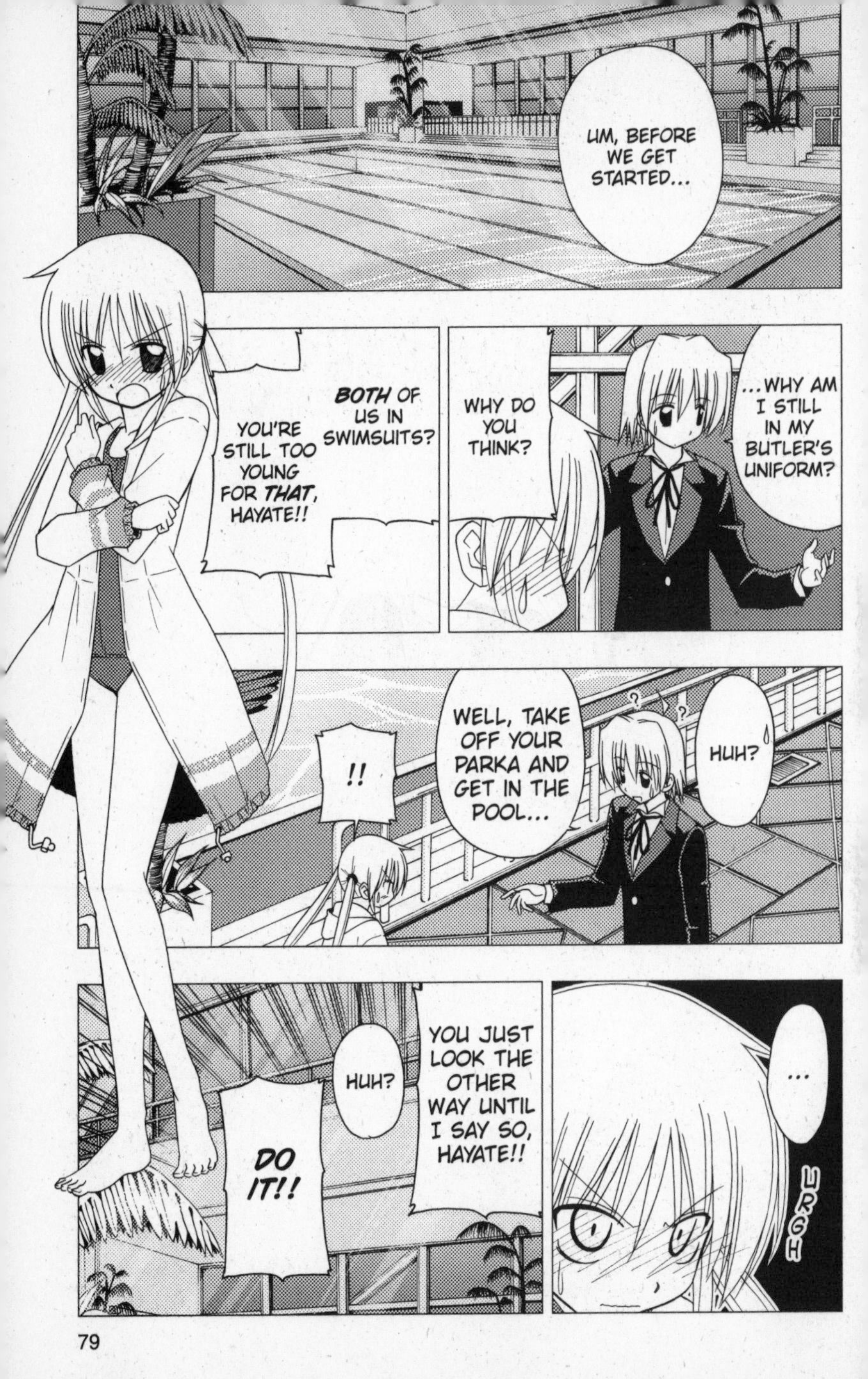
UM, BEFORE WE GET STARTED...
...WHY AM I STILL IN MY BUTLER'S UNIFORM?
WHY DO YOU THINK?
BOTH OF US IN SWIMSUITS?
YOU'RE STILL TOO YOUNG FOR *THAT*, HAYATE!!
HUH?
WELL, TAKE OFF YOUR PARKA AND GET IN THE POOL...
!!
...
URGH
YOU JUST LOOK THE OTHER WAY UNTIL I SAY SO, HAYATE!!
HUH?
DO IT!!

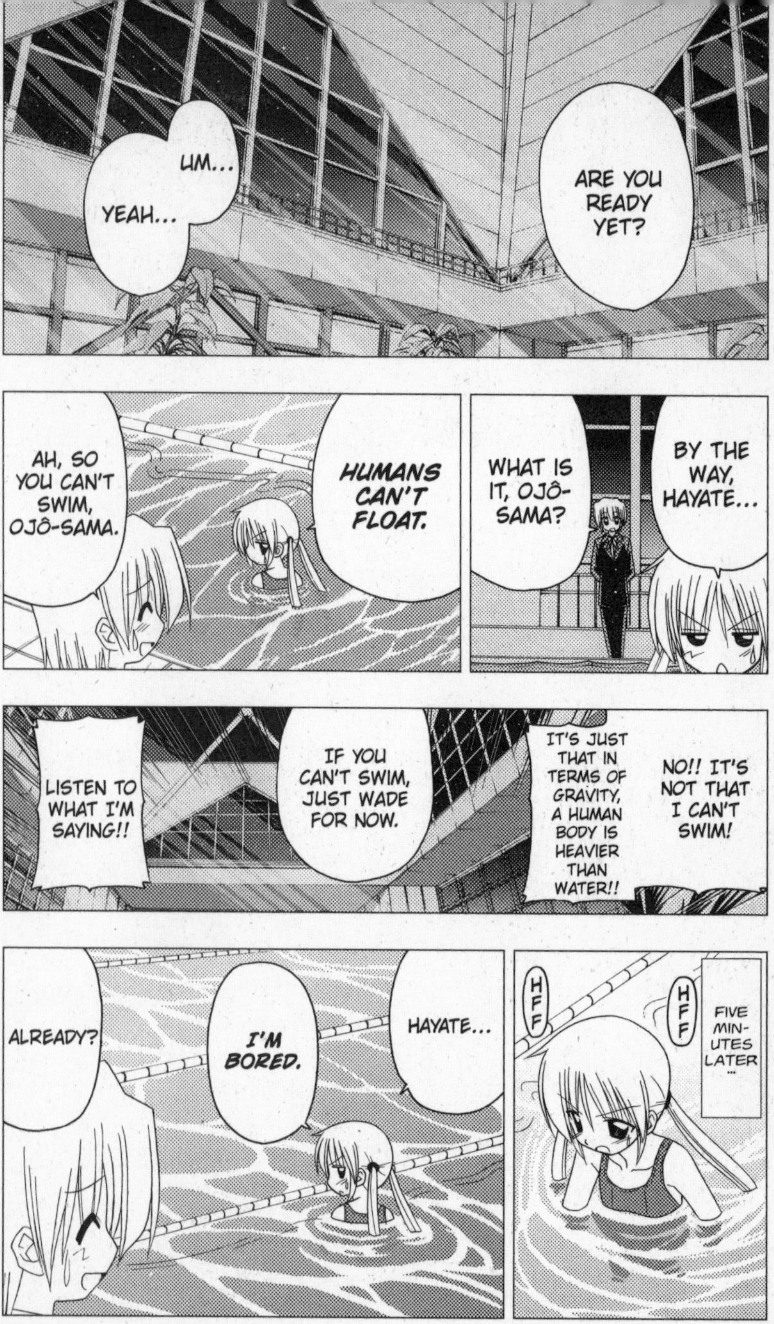
ARE YOU READY YET?
UM...
YEAH...
BY THE WAY, HAYATE...
WHAT IS IT, OJÔ-SAMA?
HUMANS CAN'T FLOAT.
AH, SO YOU CAN'T SWIM, OJÔ-SAMA.
NO!! IT'S NOT THAT I CAN'T SWIM!
IT'S JUST THAT IN TERMS OF GRAVITY, A HUMAN BODY IS HEAVIER THAN WATER!!
IF YOU CAN'T SWIM, JUST WADE FOR NOW.
LISTEN TO WHAT I'M SAYING!!
FIVE MIN-UTES LATER...
HFF
HFF
HAYATE...
I'M BORED.
ALREADY?

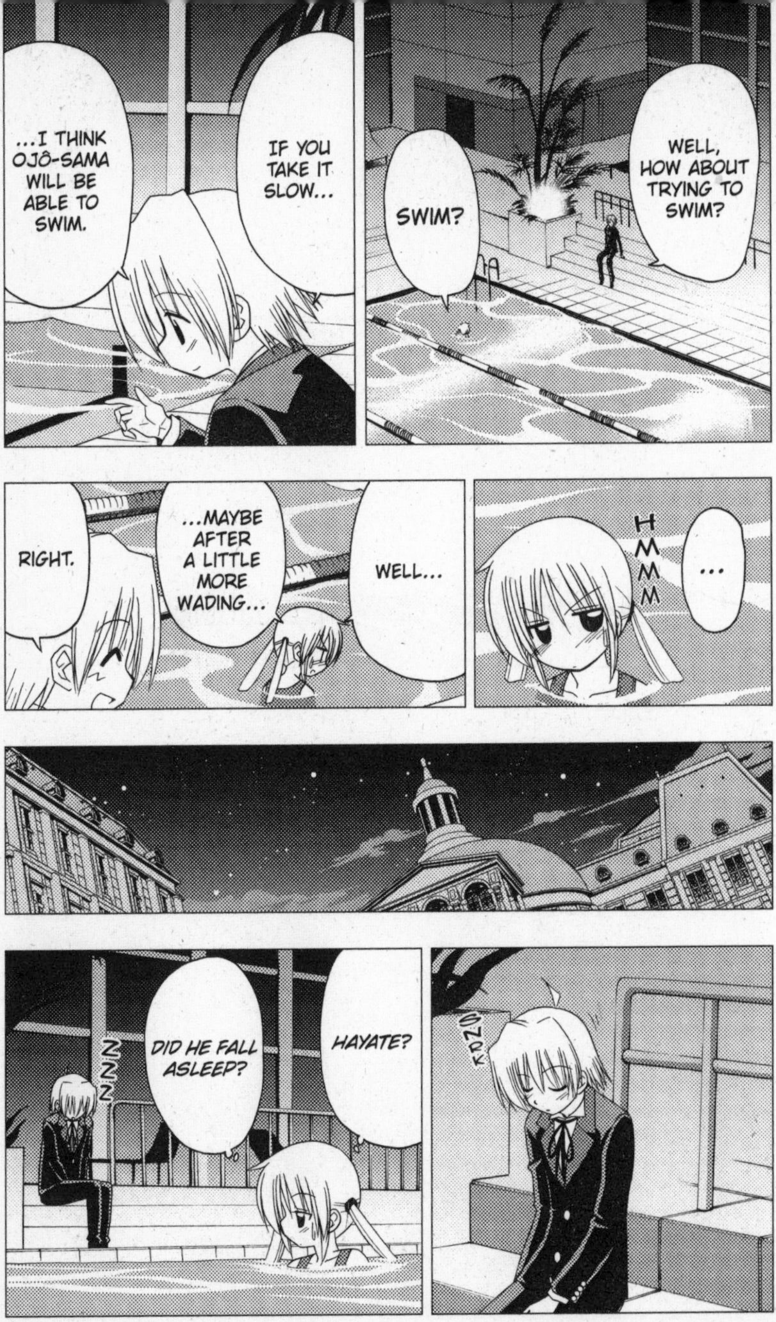
WELL, HOW ABOUT TRYING TO SWIM?
SWIM?
IF YOU TAKE IT SLOW...
...I THINK OJÔ-SAMA WILL BE ABLE TO SWIM.
...
HMMMM
WELL...
...MAYBE AFTER A LITTLE MORE WADING...
RIGHT.
SNRK
HAYATE?
DID HE FALL ASLEEP?
ZZZ

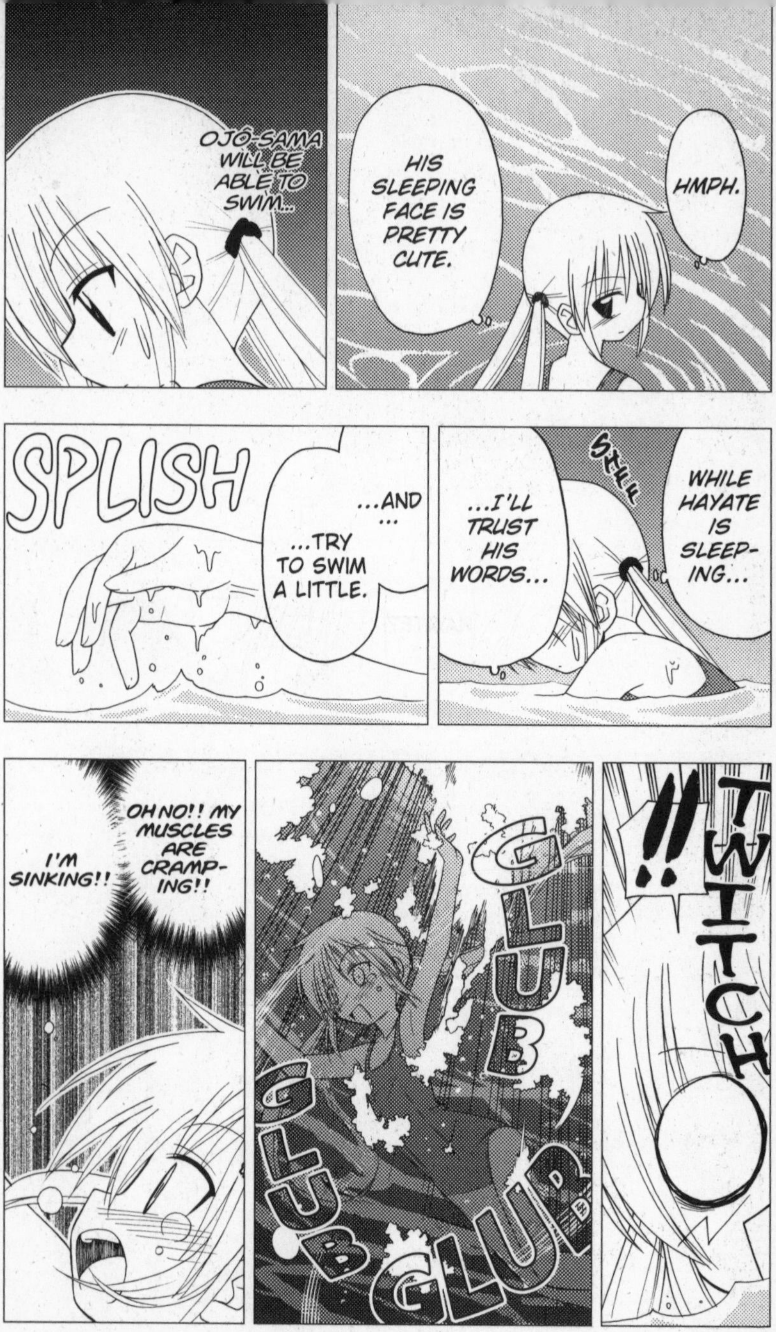
HMPH.
HIS SLEEPING FACE IS PRETTY CUTE.
OJÔ-SAMA WILL BE ABLE TO SWIM...
WHILE HAYATE IS SLEEP-ING...
SHFF
...I'LL TRUST HIS WORDS...
...AND ...
...TRY TO SWIM A LITTLE.
SPLISH
TWITCH
!!
GLUB
GLUB
GLUB
GLUB
OH NO!! MY MUSCLES ARE CRAMP-ING!!
I'M SINKING!!

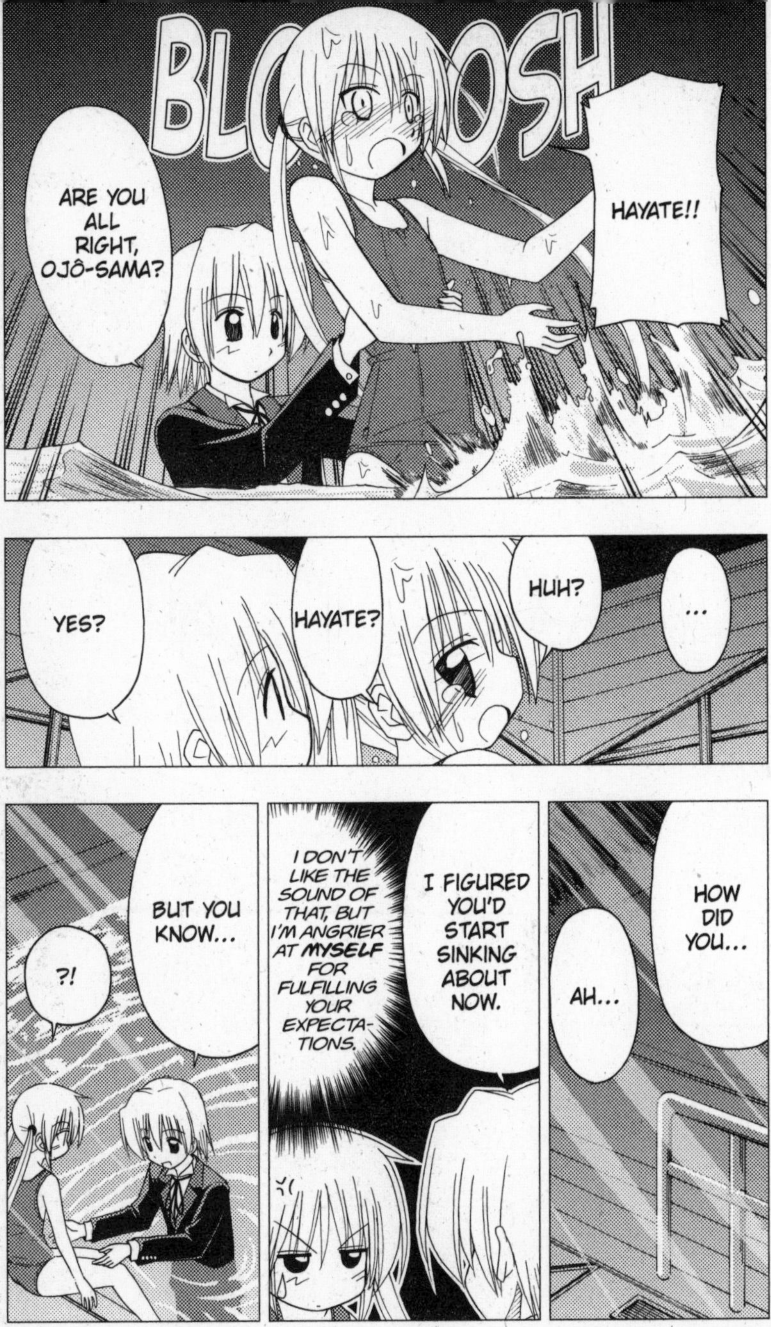
HAYATE!!
ARE YOU ALL RIGHT, OJÔ-SAMA?
...
HUH?
HAYATE?
YES?
HOW DID YOU...
AH...
I FIGURED YOU'D START SINKING ABOUT NOW.
I DON'T LIKE THE SOUND OF THAT, BUT I'M ANGRIER AT **MYSELF** FOR FULFILLING YOUR EXPECTATIONS.
BUT YOU KNOW...
?!

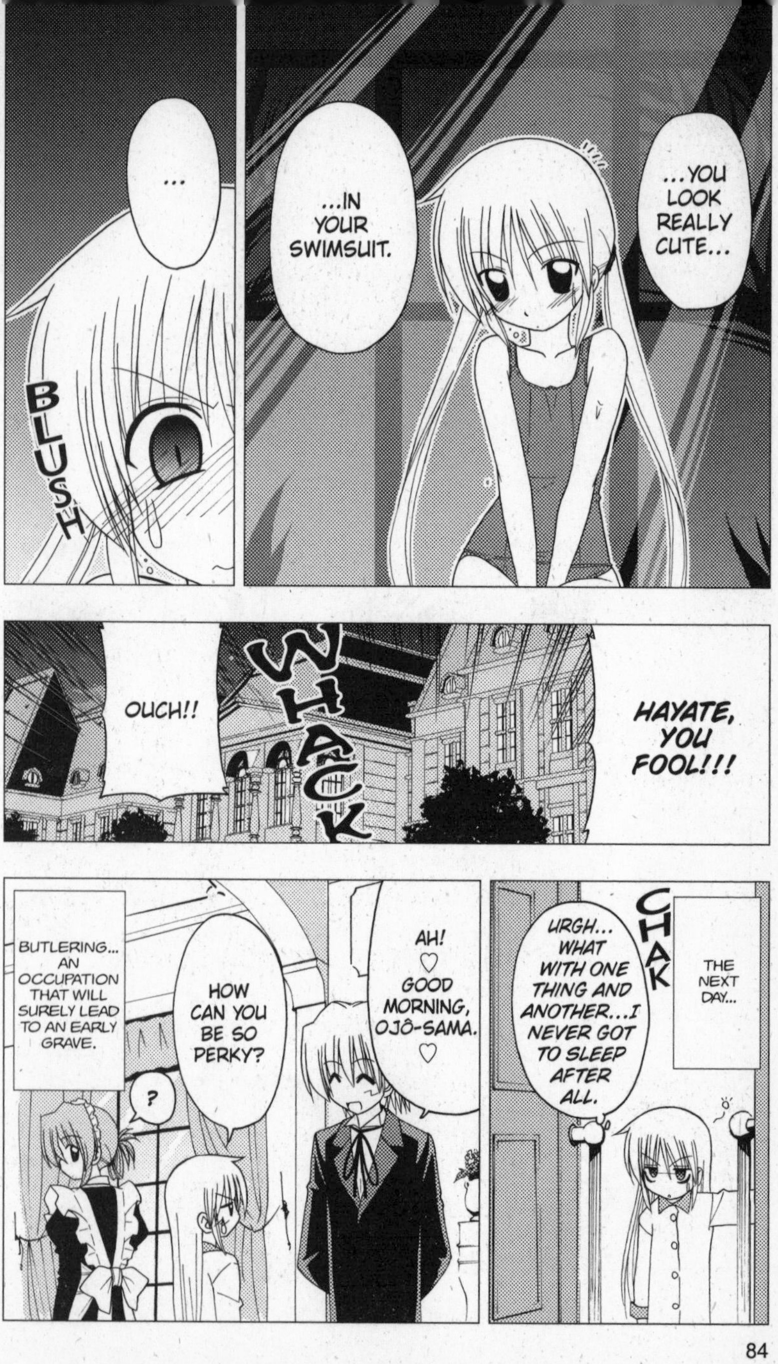
...YOU LOOK REALLY CUTE...
...IN YOUR SWIMSUIT.
...
BLUSH
HAYATE, YOU FOOL!!!
WHACK
OUCH!!
THE NEXT DAY...
CHAK
URGH... WHAT WITH ONE THING AND ANOTHER...I NEVER GOT TO SLEEP AFTER ALL.
AH! ♡ GOOD MORNING, OJÔ-SAMA. ♡
HOW CAN YOU BE SO PERKY?
?
BUTLERING... AN OCCUPATION THAT WILL SURELY LEAD TO AN EARLY GRAVE.

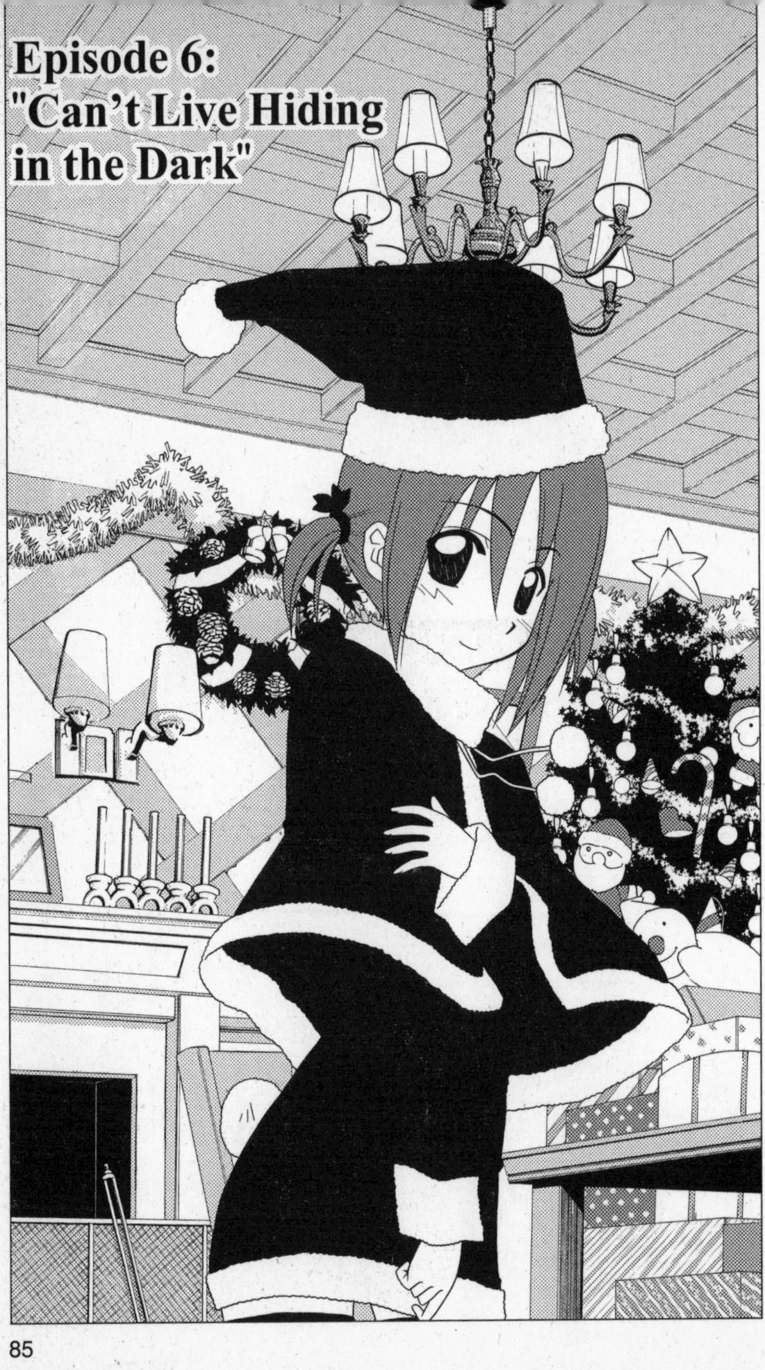
Episode 6:
"Can't Live Hiding in the Dark"

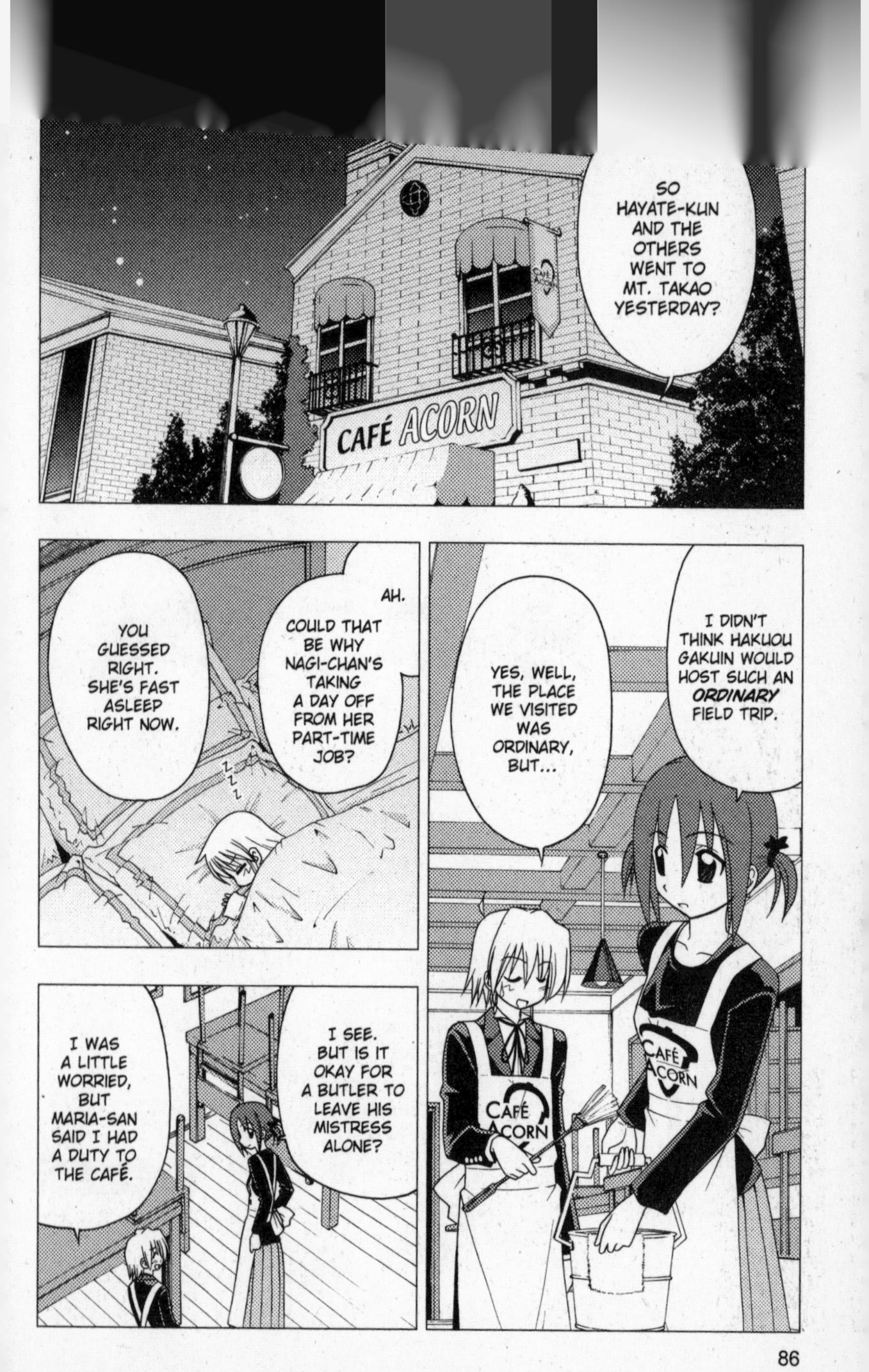
SO HAYATE-KUN AND THE OTHERS WENT TO MT. TAKAO YESTERDAY?
CAFÉ ACORN
I DIDN'T THINK HAKUOU GAKUIN WOULD HOST SUCH AN ***ORDINARY*** FIELD TRIP.
YES, WELL, THE PLACE WE VISITED WAS ORDINARY, BUT...
CAFÉ ACORN
CAFÉ ACORN
AH.
COULD THAT BE WHY NAGI-CHAN'S TAKING A DAY OFF FROM HER PART-TIME JOB?
YOU GUESSED RIGHT. SHE'S FAST ASLEEP RIGHT NOW.
Z Z Z
I SEE. BUT IS IT OKAY FOR A BUTLER TO LEAVE HIS MISTRESS ALONE?
I WAS A LITTLE WORRIED, BUT MARIA-SAN SAID I HAD A DUTY TO THE CAFÉ.

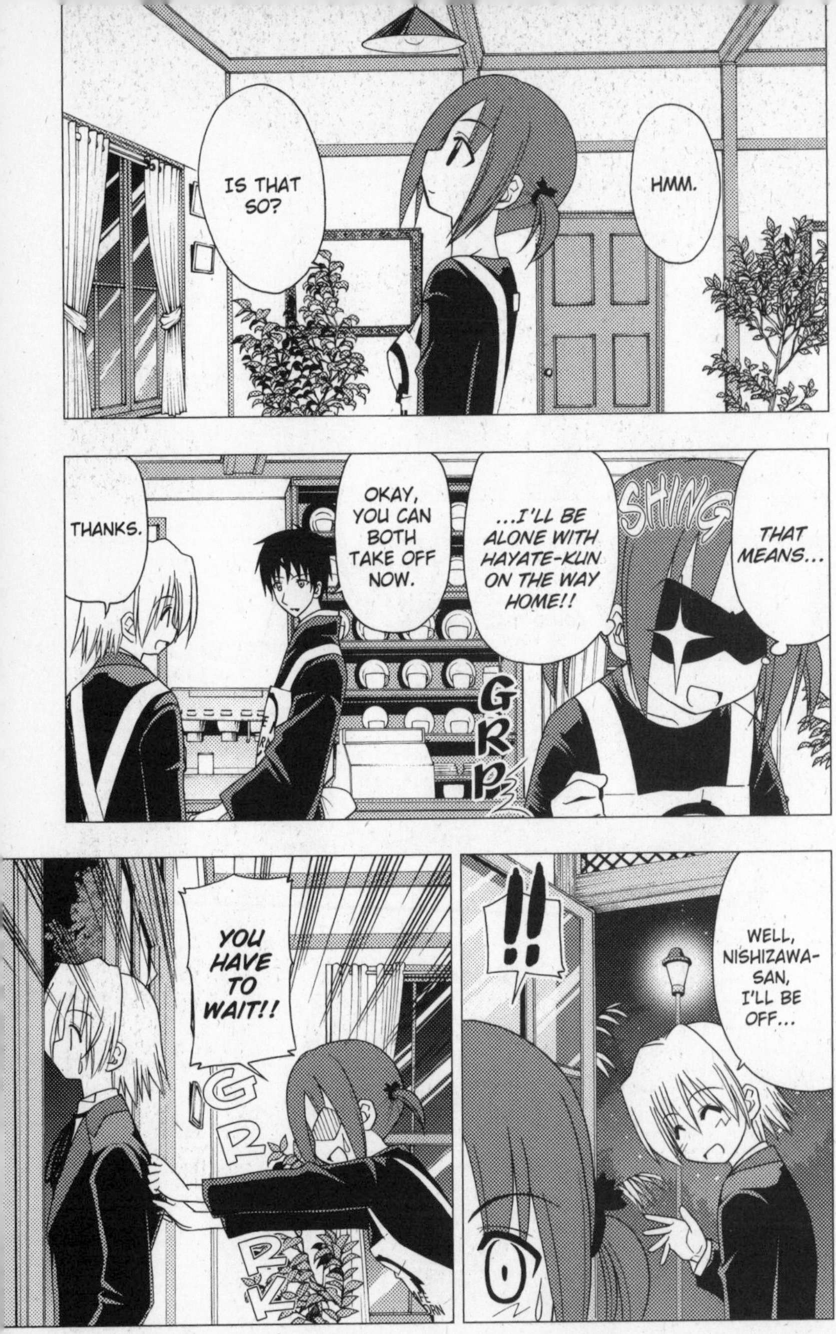
HMM.
IS THAT SO?
THAT MEANS...
SHING
...I'LL BE ALONE WITH HAYATE-KUN ON THE WAY HOME!!
OKAY, YOU CAN BOTH TAKE OFF NOW.
THANKS.
GRP
WELL, NISHIZAWA-SAN, I'LL BE OFF...
!!
YOU HAVE TO WAIT!!
GRRK

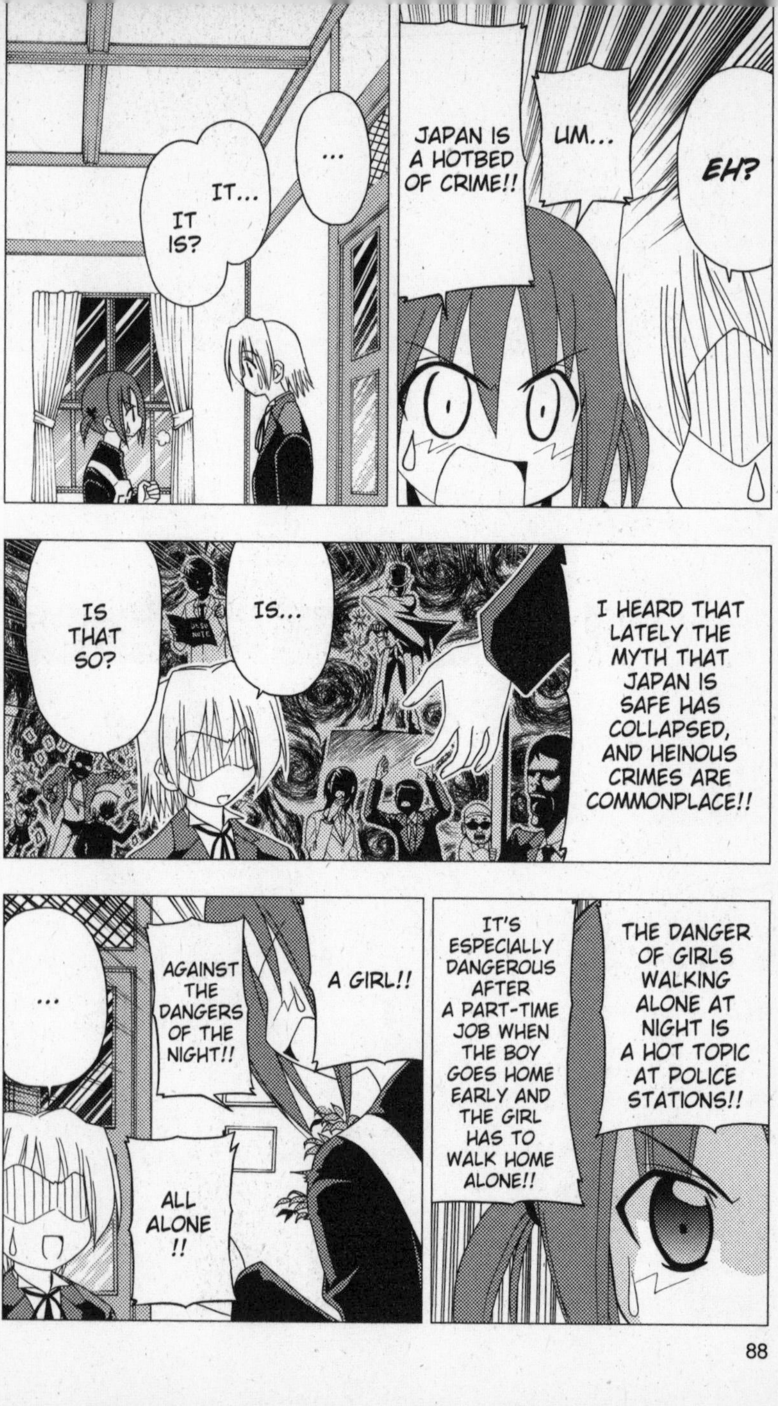
EH?
UM...
JAPAN IS A HOTBED OF CRIME!!
...
IT...
IT IS?
I HEARD THAT LATELY THE MYTH THAT JAPAN IS SAFE HAS COLLAPSED, AND HEINOUS CRIMES ARE COMMONPLACE!!
IS...
IS THAT SO?
THE DANGER OF GIRLS WALKING ALONE AT NIGHT IS A HOT TOPIC AT POLICE STATIONS!!
IT'S ESPECIALLY DANGEROUS AFTER A PART-TIME JOB WHEN THE BOY GOES HOME EARLY AND THE GIRL HAS TO WALK HOME ALONE!!
A GIRL!!
AGAINST THE DANGERS OF THE NIGHT!!
...
ALL ALONE !!

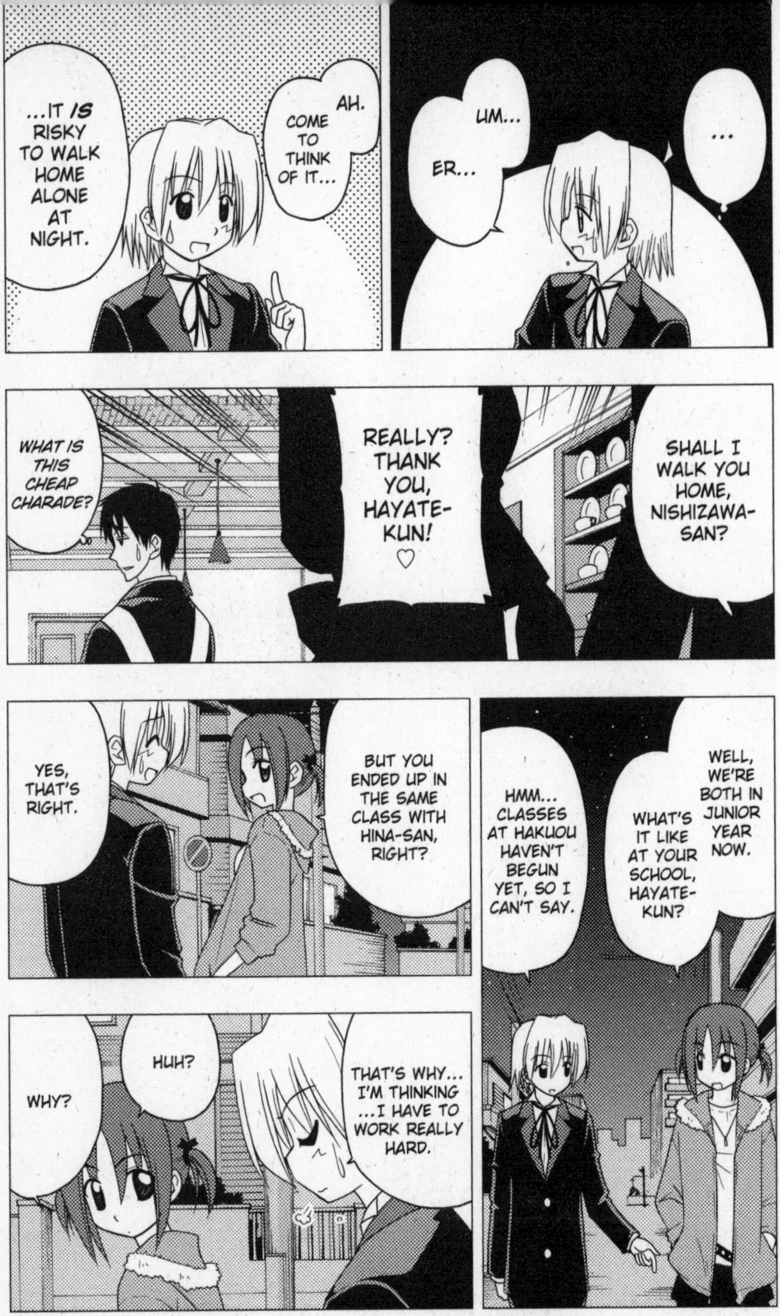
...
UM...
ER...
AH. COME TO THINK OF IT...
...IT *IS* RISKY TO WALK HOME ALONE AT NIGHT.
SHALL I WALK YOU HOME, NISHIZAWA-SAN?
REALLY? THANK YOU, HAYATE-KUN! ♡
WHAT IS THIS CHEAP CHARADE?
WELL, WE'RE BOTH IN JUNIOR YEAR NOW.
WHAT'S IT LIKE AT YOUR SCHOOL, HAYATE-KUN?
HMM... CLASSES AT HAKUOU HAVEN'T BEGUN YET, SO I CAN'T SAY.
BUT YOU ENDED UP IN THE SAME CLASS WITH HINA-SAN, RIGHT?
YES, THAT'S RIGHT.
THAT'S WHY... I'M THINKING ...I HAVE TO WORK REALLY HARD.
HUH?
WHY?

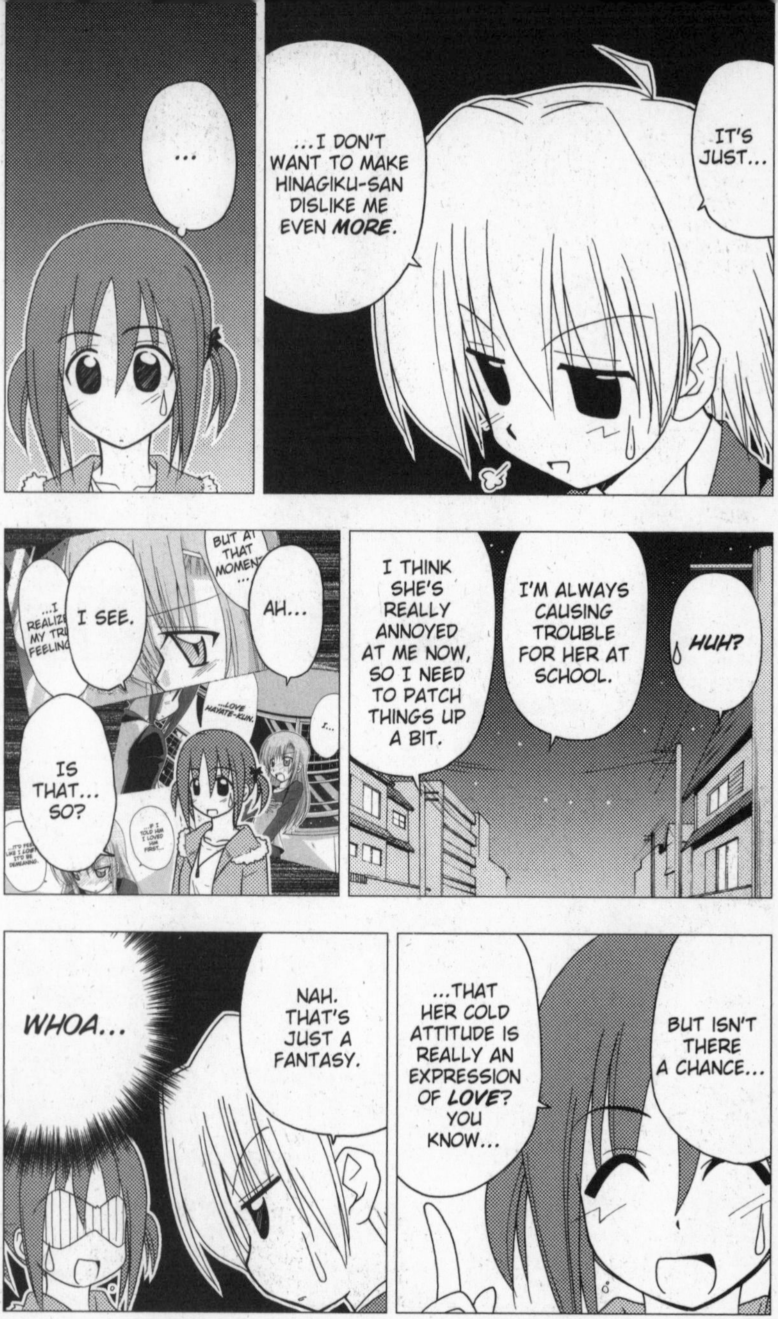
IT'S JUST...
...I DON'T WANT TO MAKE HINAGIKU-SAN DISLIKE ME EVEN **MORE**.
...
HUH?
I'M ALWAYS CAUSING TROUBLE FOR HER AT SCHOOL.
I THINK SHE'S REALLY ANNOYED AT ME NOW, SO I NEED TO PATCH THINGS UP A BIT.
AH...
I SEE.
IS THAT... SO?
BUT ISN'T THERE A CHANCE...
...THAT HER COLD ATTITUDE IS REALLY AN EXPRESSION OF **LOVE**? YOU KNOW...
NAH. THAT'S JUST A FANTASY.
WHOA...

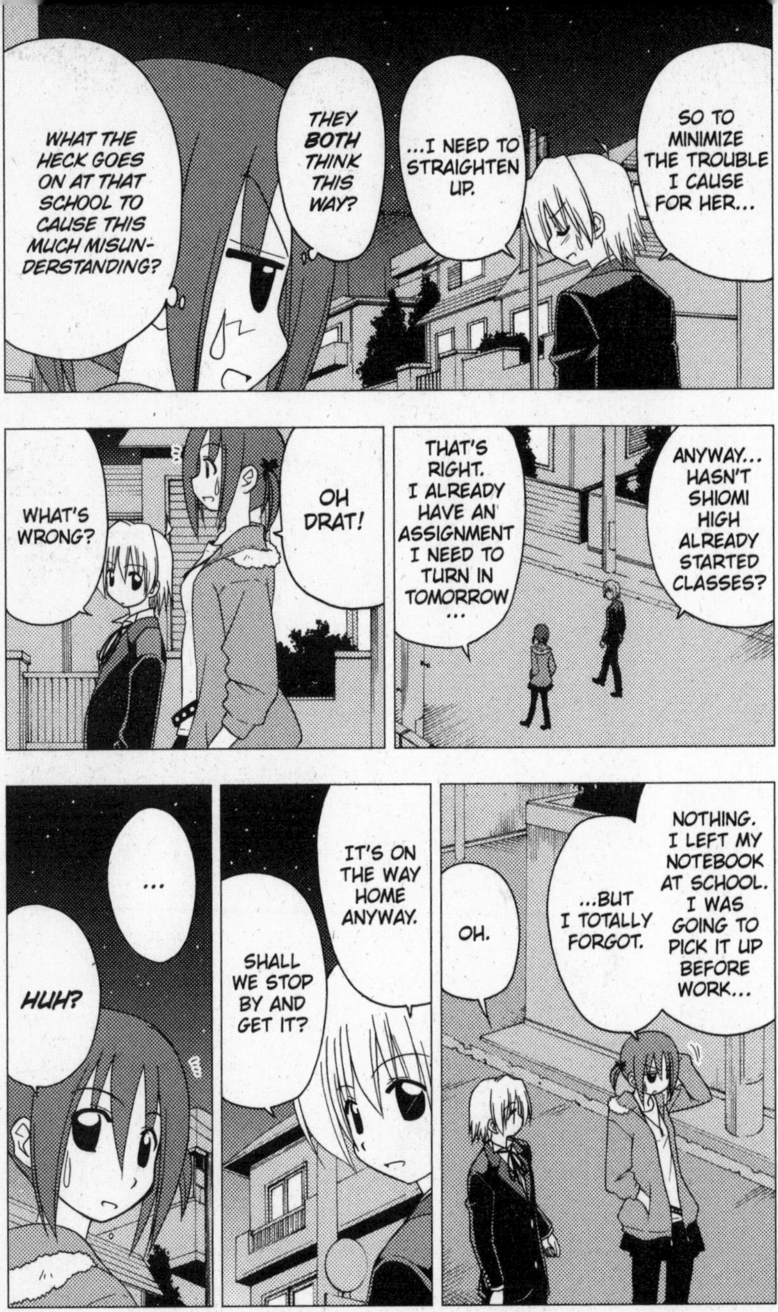
SO TO MINIMIZE THE TROUBLE I CAUSE FOR HER...
...I NEED TO STRAIGHTEN UP.
THEY BOTH THINK THIS WAY?
WHAT THE HECK GOES ON AT THAT SCHOOL TO CAUSE THIS MUCH MISUN-DERSTANDING?
ANYWAY... HASN'T SHIOMI HIGH ALREADY STARTED CLASSES?
THAT'S RIGHT. I ALREADY HAVE AN ASSIGNMENT I NEED TO TURN IN TOMORROW...
OH DRAT!
WHAT'S WRONG?
NOTHING. I LEFT MY NOTEBOOK AT SCHOOL. I WAS GOING TO PICK IT UP BEFORE WORK...
...BUT I TOTALLY FORGOT.
OH.
IT'S ON THE WAY HOME ANYWAY.
SHALL WE STOP BY AND GET IT?
...
HUH?

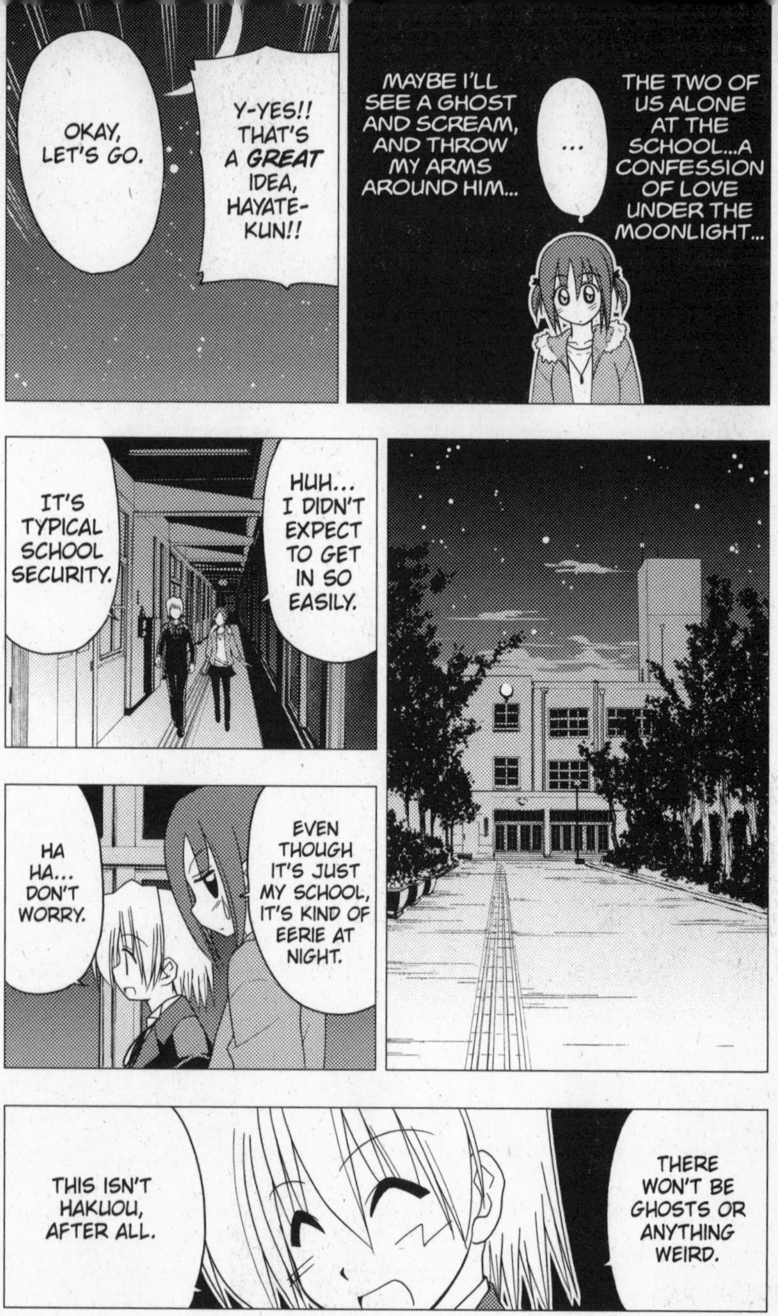
THE TWO OF US ALONE AT THE SCHOOL...A CONFESSION OF LOVE UNDER THE MOONLIGHT...
...
MAYBE I'LL SEE A GHOST AND SCREAM, AND THROW MY ARMS AROUND HIM...
Y-YES!! THAT'S A GREAT IDEA, HAYATE-KUN!!
OKAY, LET'S GO.
HUH... I DIDN'T EXPECT TO GET IN SO EASILY.
IT'S TYPICAL SCHOOL SECURITY.
EVEN THOUGH IT'S JUST MY SCHOOL, IT'S KIND OF EERIE AT NIGHT.
HA HA... DON'T WORRY.
THERE WON'T BE GHOSTS OR ANYTHING WEIRD.
THIS ISN'T HAKUOU, AFTER ALL.

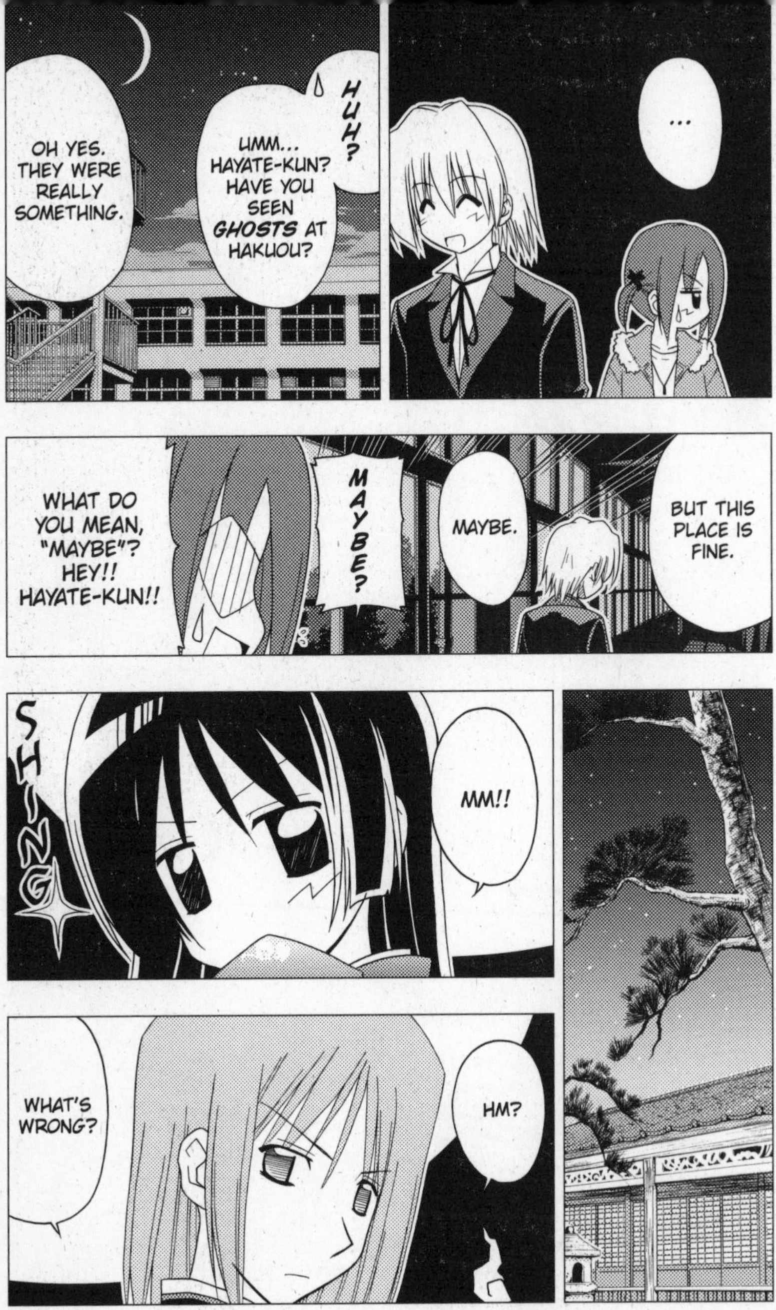
...
HUH?
UMM... HAYATE-KUN? HAVE YOU SEEN GHOSTS AT HAKUOU?
OH YES. THEY WERE REALLY SOMETHING.
BUT THIS PLACE IS FINE.
MAYBE.
MAYBE?
WHAT DO YOU MEAN, "MAYBE"? HEY!! HAYATE-KUN!!
MM!!
SHING
HM?
WHAT'S WRONG?

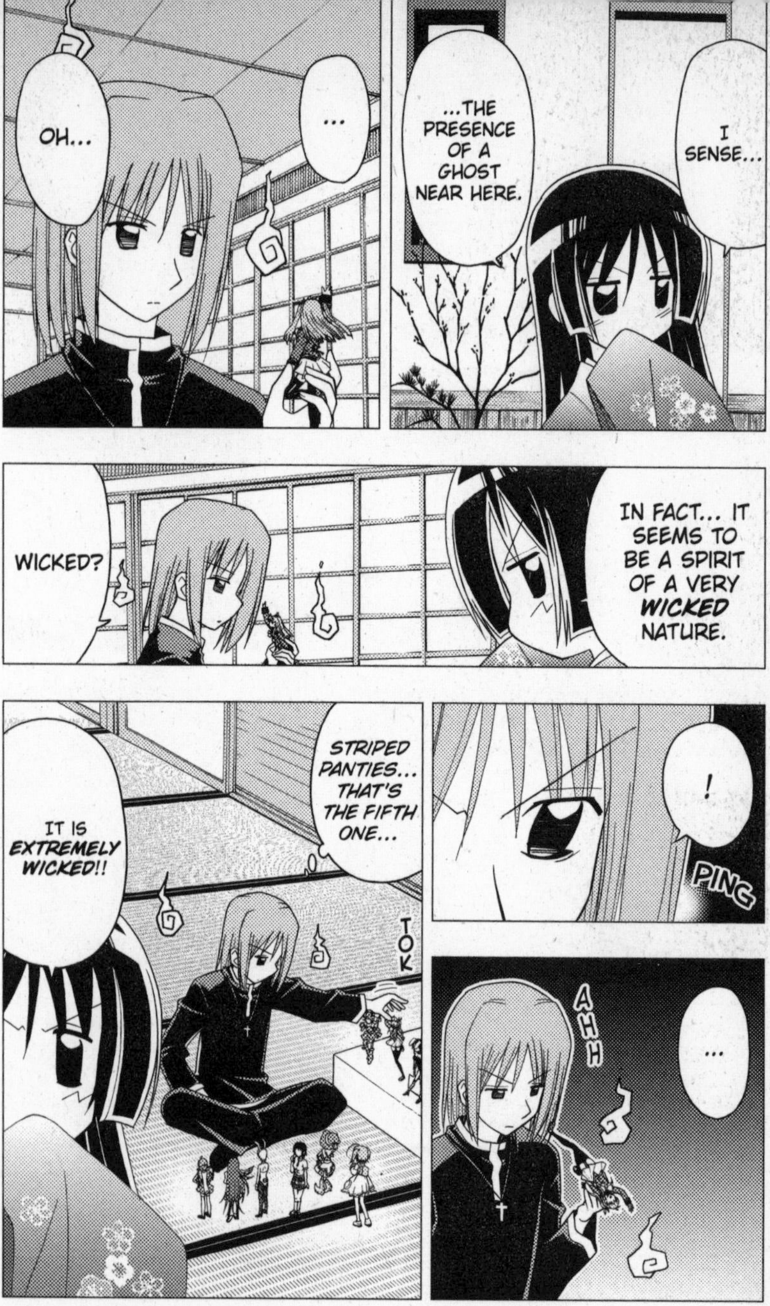
I SENSE...
...THE PRESENCE OF A GHOST NEAR HERE.
...
OH...
IN FACT... IT SEEMS TO BE A SPIRIT OF A VERY WICKED NATURE.
WICKED?
!
PING
AHH
...
STRIPED PANTIES... THAT'S THE FIFTH ONE...
TOK
IT IS EXTREMELY WICKED!!

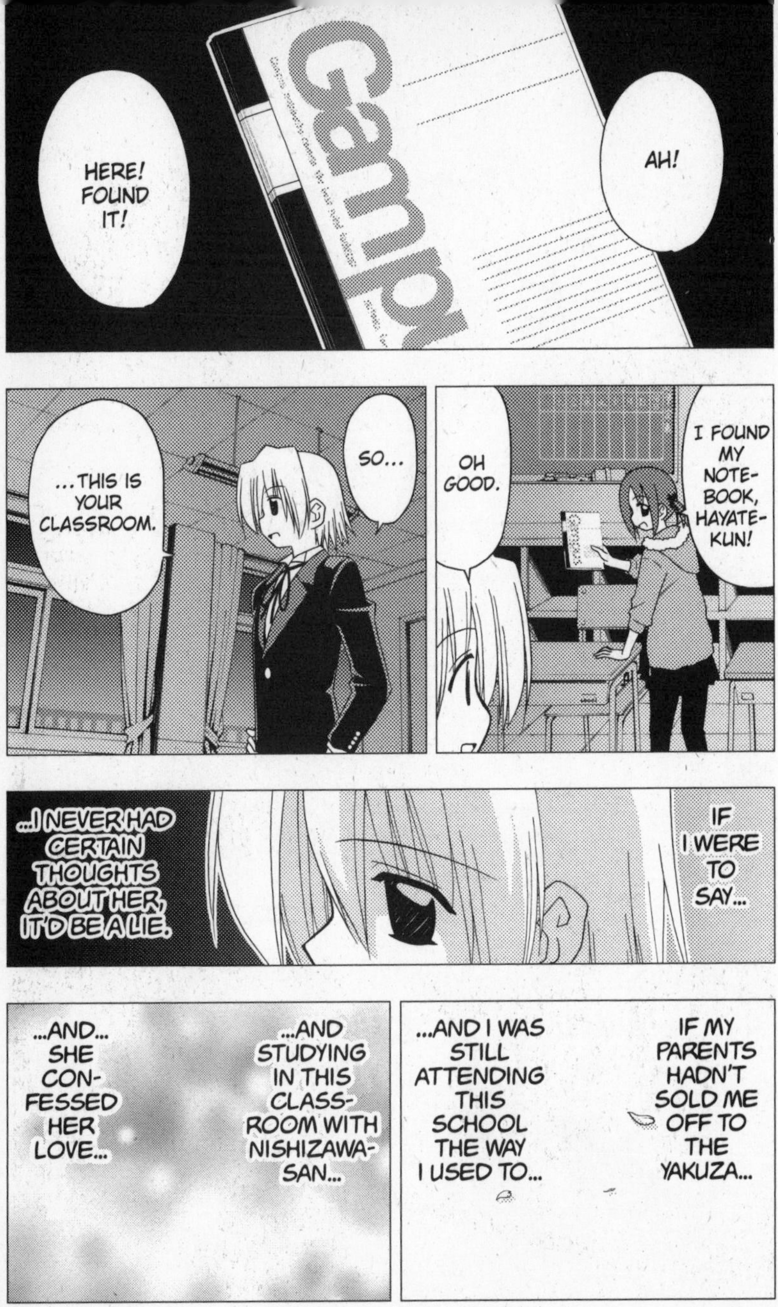
AH!
HERE! FOUND IT!
I FOUND MY NOTE-BOOK, HAYATE-KUN!
OH GOOD.
SO...
...THIS IS YOUR CLASSROOM.
IF I WERE TO SAY...
...I NEVER HAD CERTAIN THOUGHTS ABOUT HER, IT'D BE A LIE.
IF MY PARENTS HADN'T SOLD ME OFF TO THE YAKUZA...
...AND I WAS STILL ATTENDING THIS SCHOOL THE WAY I USED TO...
...AND STUDYING IN THIS CLASS-ROOM WITH NISHIZAWA-SAN...
...AND... SHE CON-FESSED HER LOVE...

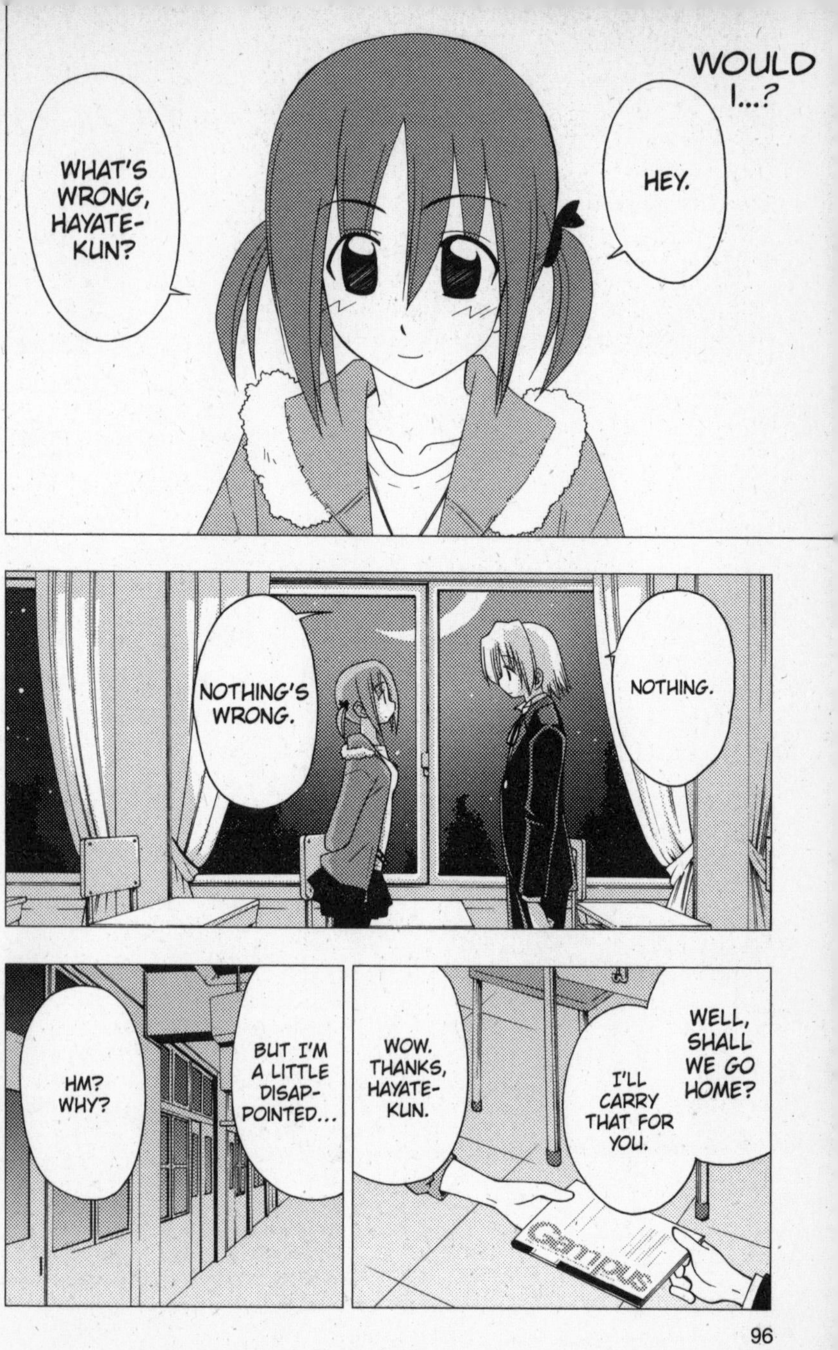
WOULD I...?
HEY.
WHAT'S WRONG, HAYATE-KUN?
NOTHING.
NOTHING'S WRONG.
WELL, SHALL WE GO HOME?
I'LL CARRY THAT FOR YOU.
Campus
WOW. THANKS, HAYATE-KUN.
BUT I'M A LITTLE DISAPPOINTED...
HM? WHY?

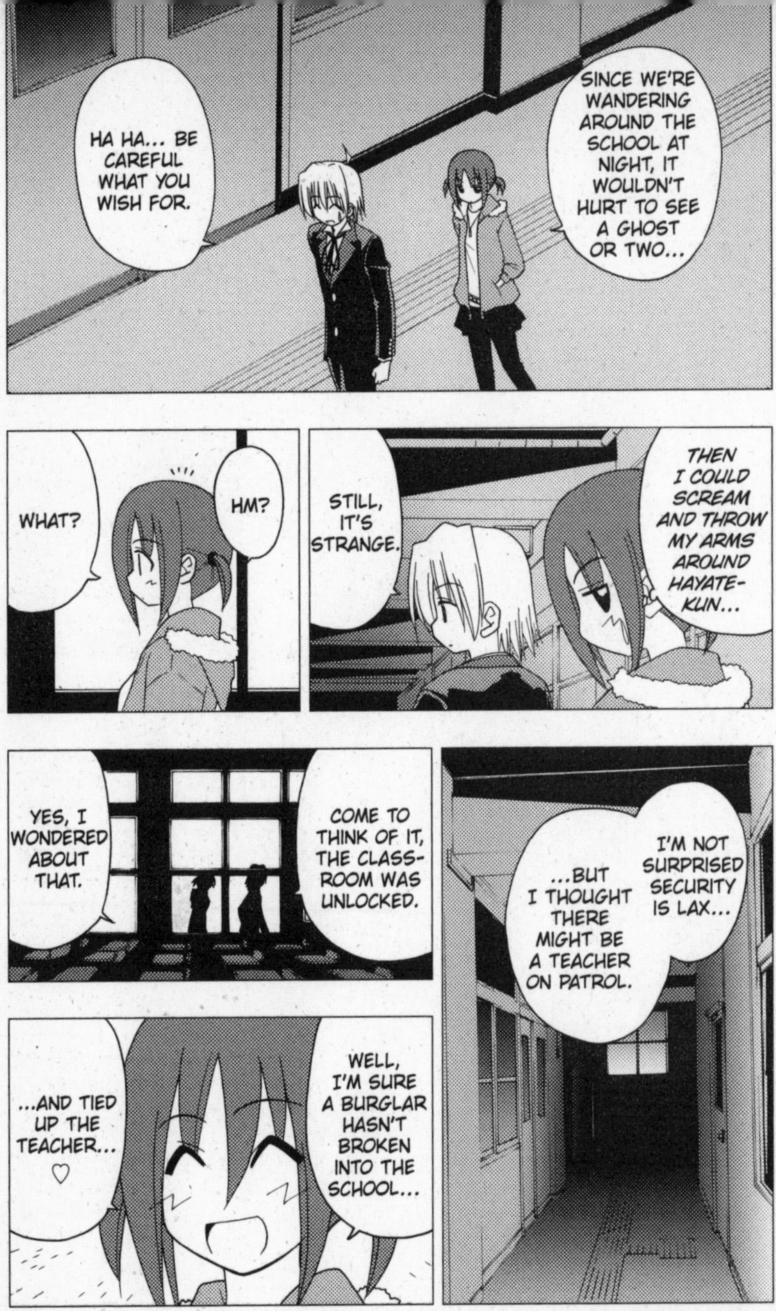
SINCE WE'RE WANDERING AROUND THE SCHOOL AT NIGHT, IT WOULDN'T HURT TO SEE A GHOST OR TWO...
HA HA... BE CAREFUL WHAT YOU WISH FOR.
THEN I COULD SCREAM AND THROW MY ARMS AROUND HAYATE-KUN...
STILL, IT'S STRANGE.
HM?
WHAT?
I'M NOT SURPRISED SECURITY IS LAX...
...BUT I THOUGHT THERE MIGHT BE A TEACHER ON PATROL.
COME TO THINK OF IT, THE CLASS-ROOM WAS UNLOCKED.
YES, I WONDERED ABOUT THAT.
WELL, I'M SURE A BURGLAR HASN'T BROKEN INTO THE SCHOOL...
...AND TIED UP THE TEACHER... ♡

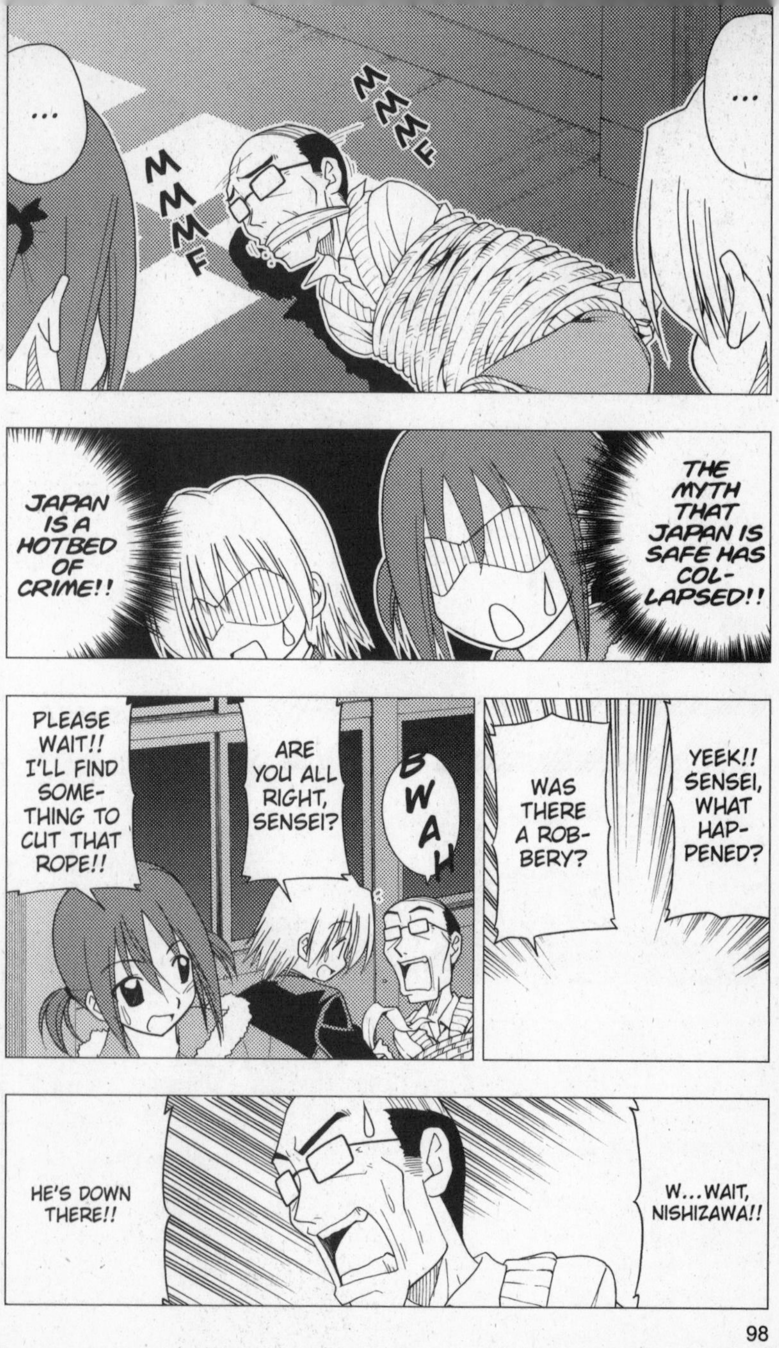
...
MMMF
MMMF
...
THE MYTH THAT JAPAN IS SAFE HAS COL-LAPSED!!
JAPAN IS A HOTBED OF CRIME!!
YEEK!! SENSEI, WHAT HAP-PENED?
WAS THERE A ROB-BERY?
BWAH
ARE YOU ALL RIGHT, SENSEI?
PLEASE WAIT!! I'LL FIND SOME-THING TO CUT THAT ROPE!!
W...WAIT, NISHIZAWA!!
HE'S DOWN THERE!!

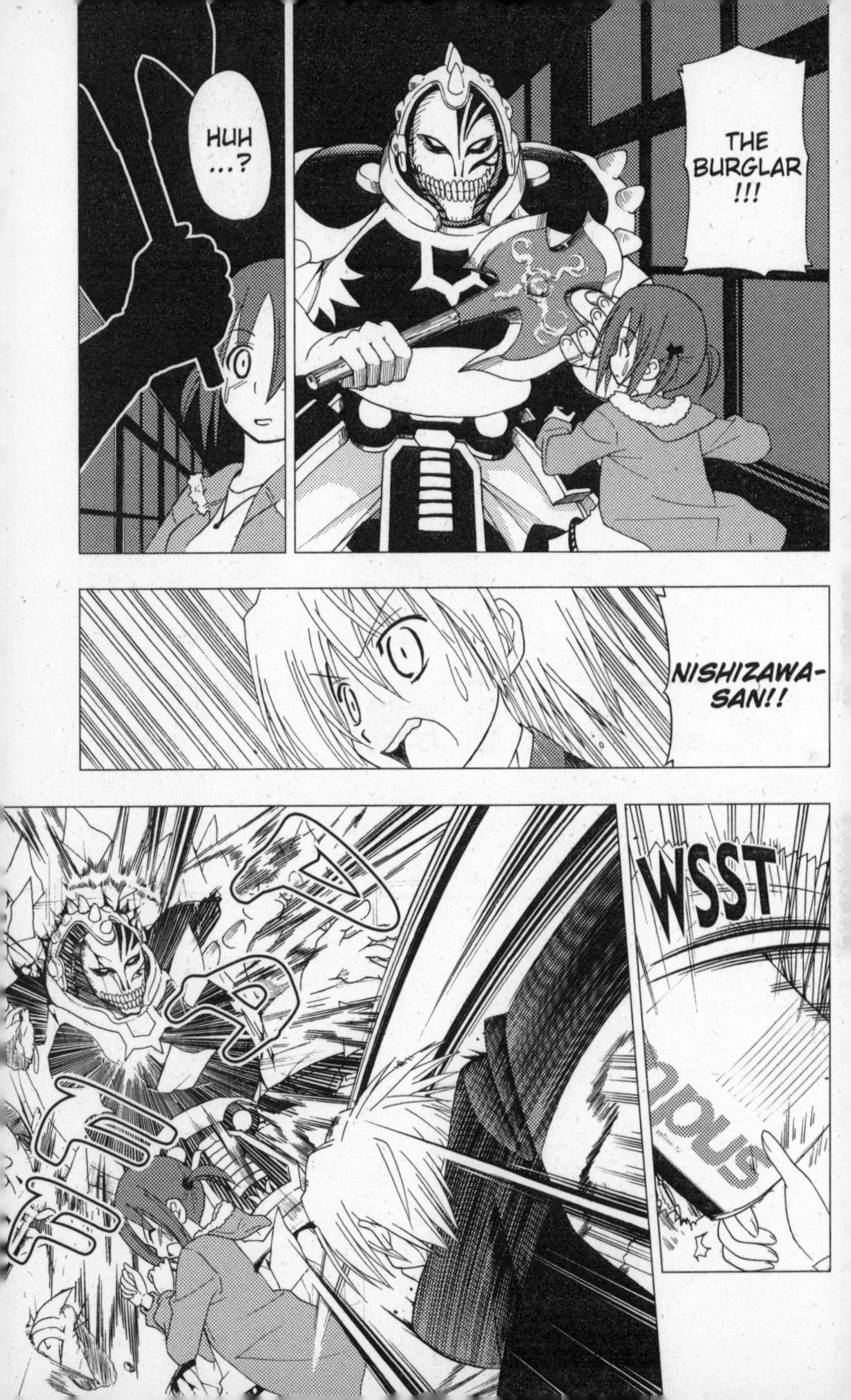
THE BURGLAR!!!
HUH ...?
NISHIZAWA-SAN!!
WSST

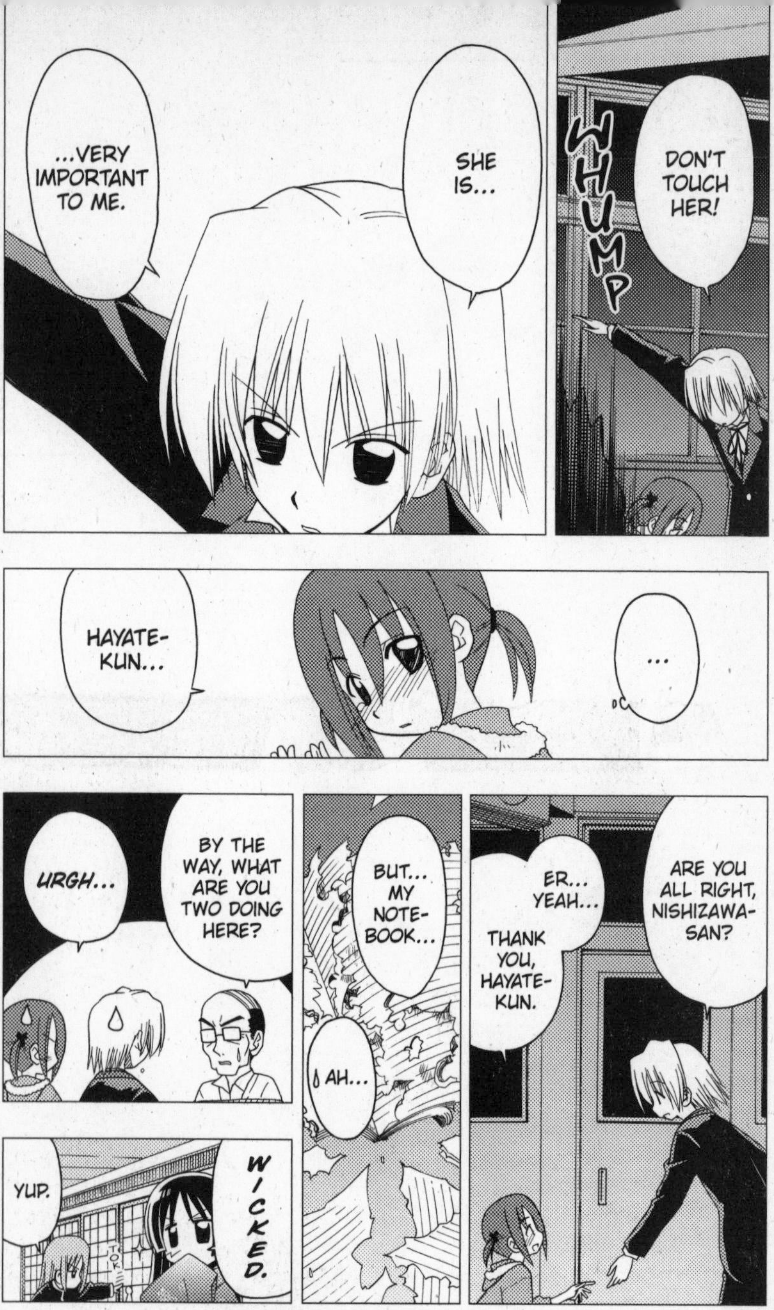
DON'T TOUCH HER!
WHUMP
SHE IS...
...VERY IMPORTANT TO ME.
...
HAYATE-KUN...
ARE YOU ALL RIGHT, NISHIZAWA-SAN?
ER... YEAH...
THANK YOU, HAYATE-KUN.
BUT... MY NOTEBOOK...
AH...
BY THE WAY, WHAT ARE YOU TWO DOING HERE?
URGH...
WICKED.
YUP.

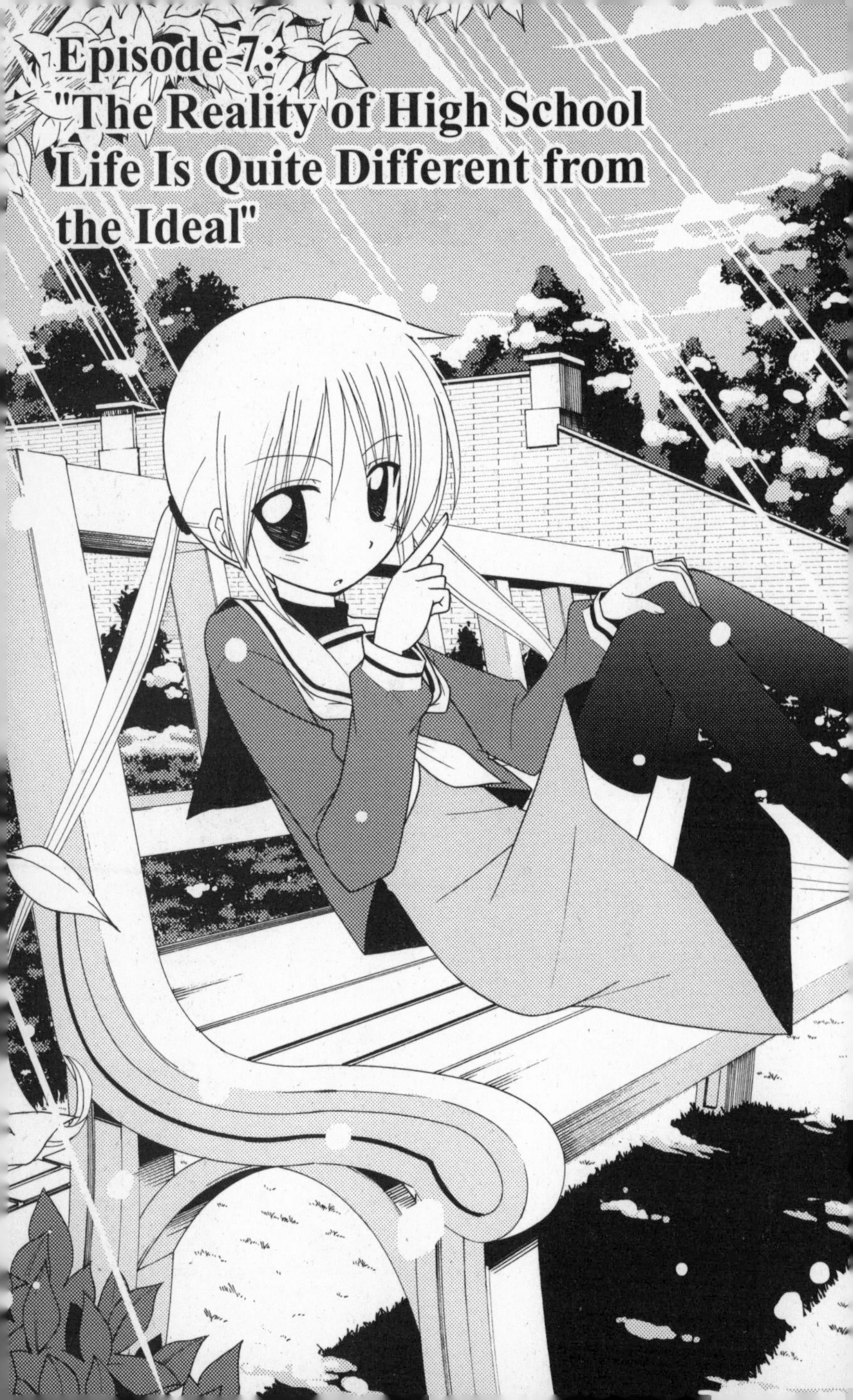
Episode 7:
"The Reality of High School Life Is Quite Different from the Ideal"

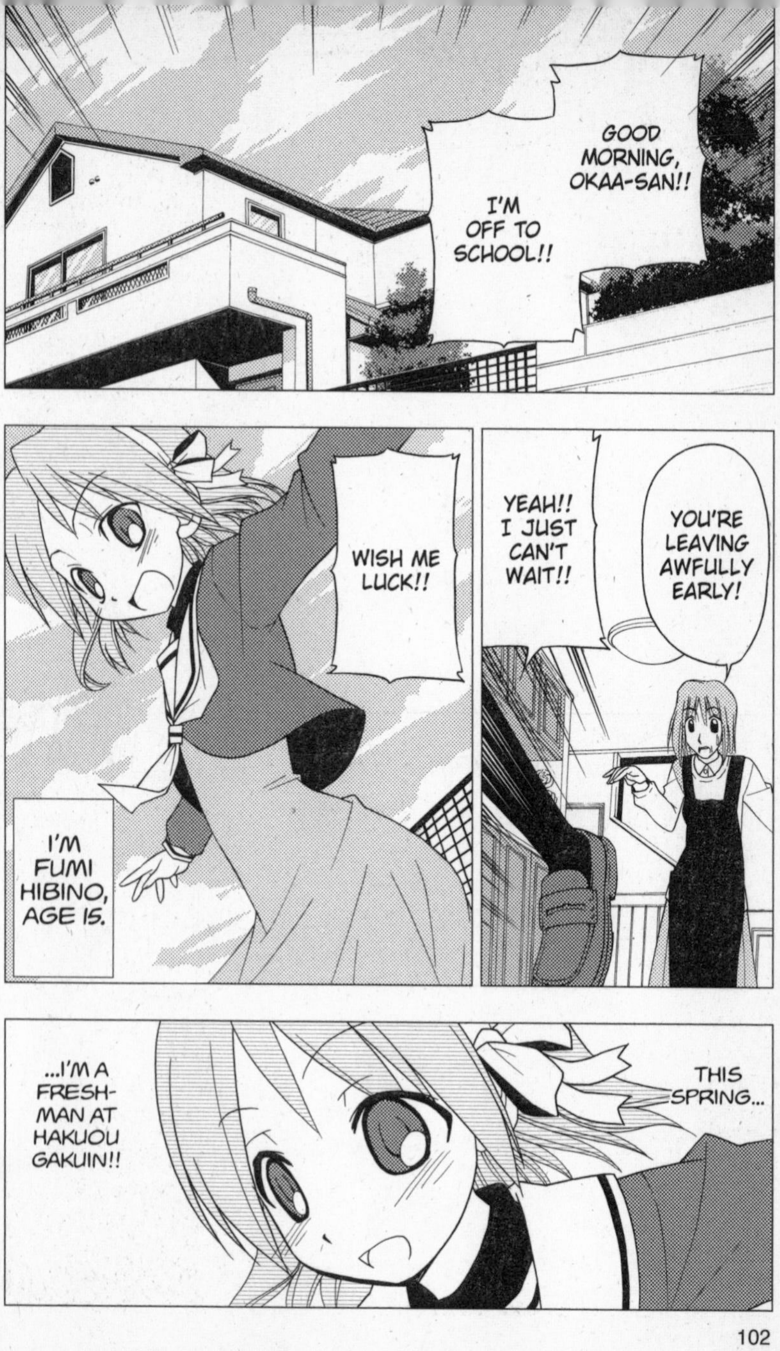
GOOD MORNING, OKAA-SAN!!
I'M OFF TO SCHOOL!!
YOU'RE LEAVING AWFULLY EARLY!
YEAH!! I JUST CAN'T WAIT!!
WISH ME LUCK!!
I'M FUMI HIBINO, AGE 15.
THIS SPRING...
...I'M A FRESHMAN AT HAKUOU GAKUIN!!

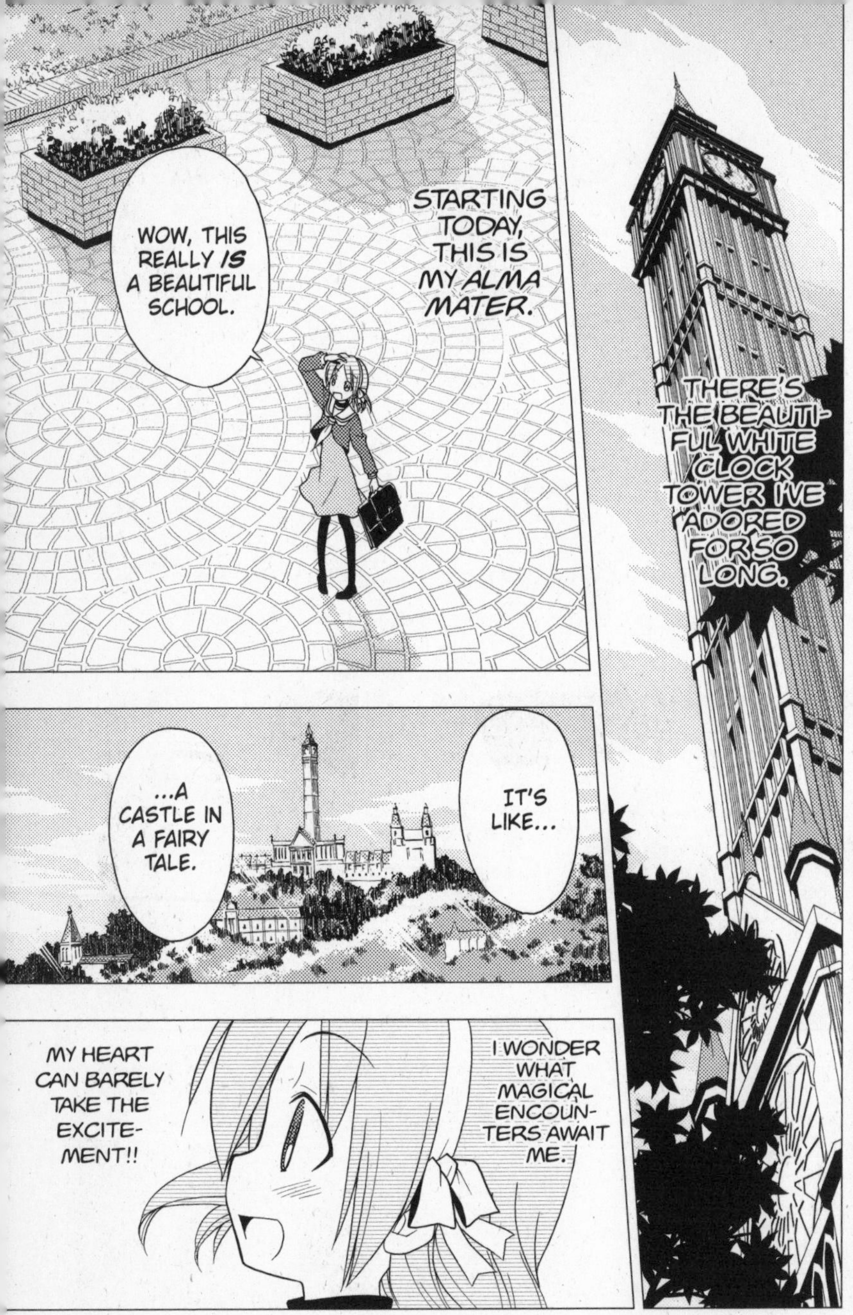
THERE'S THE BEAUTIFUL WHITE CLOCK TOWER I'VE ADORED FOR SO LONG.
STARTING TODAY, THIS IS MY ALMA MATER.
WOW, THIS REALLY *IS* A BEAUTIFUL SCHOOL.
IT'S LIKE...
...A CASTLE IN A FAIRY TALE.
I WONDER WHAT MAGICAL ENCOUNTERS AWAIT ME.
MY HEART CAN BARELY TAKE THE EXCITEMENT!!

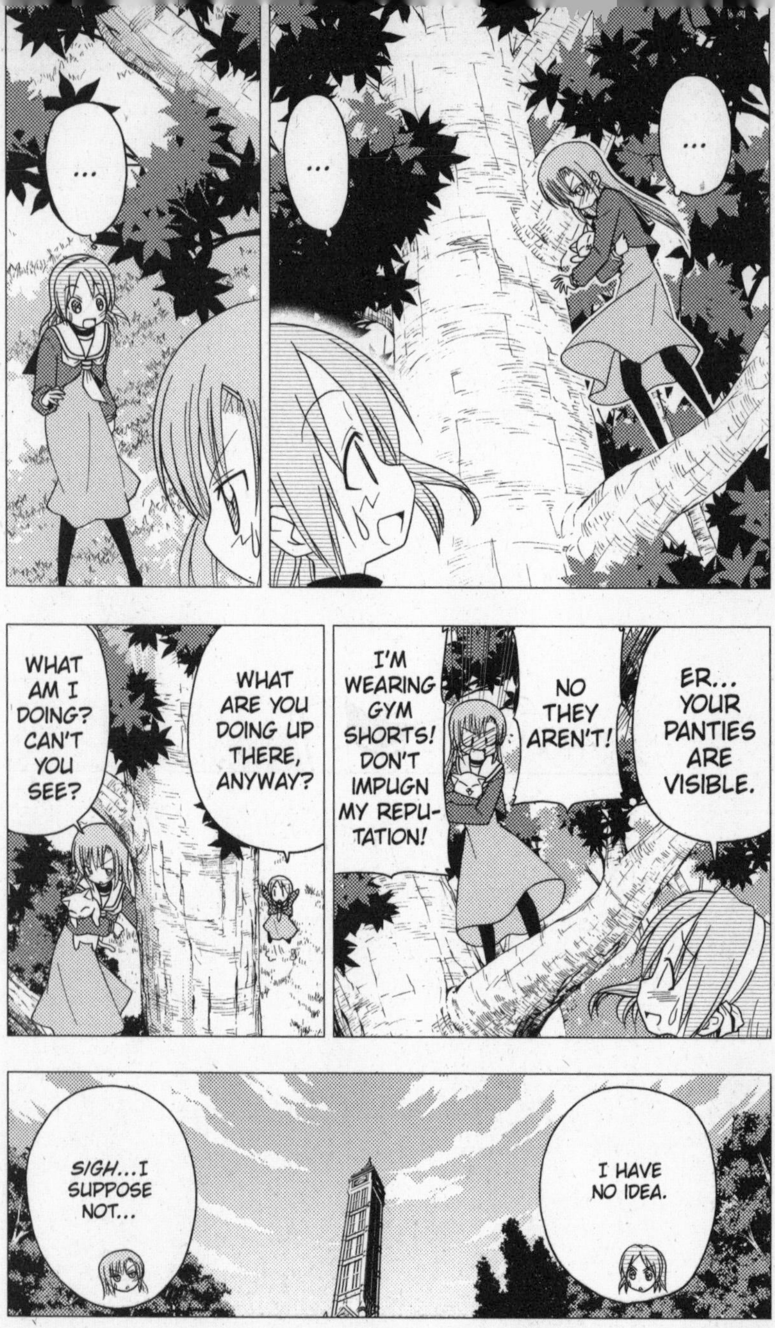
...
...
...
ER... YOUR PANTIES ARE VISIBLE.
NO THEY AREN'T!
I'M WEARING GYM SHORTS! DON'T IMPUGN MY REPUTATION!
WHAT ARE YOU DOING UP THERE, ANYWAY?
WHAT AM I DOING? CAN'T YOU SEE?
I HAVE NO IDEA.
SIGH...I SUPPOSE NOT...

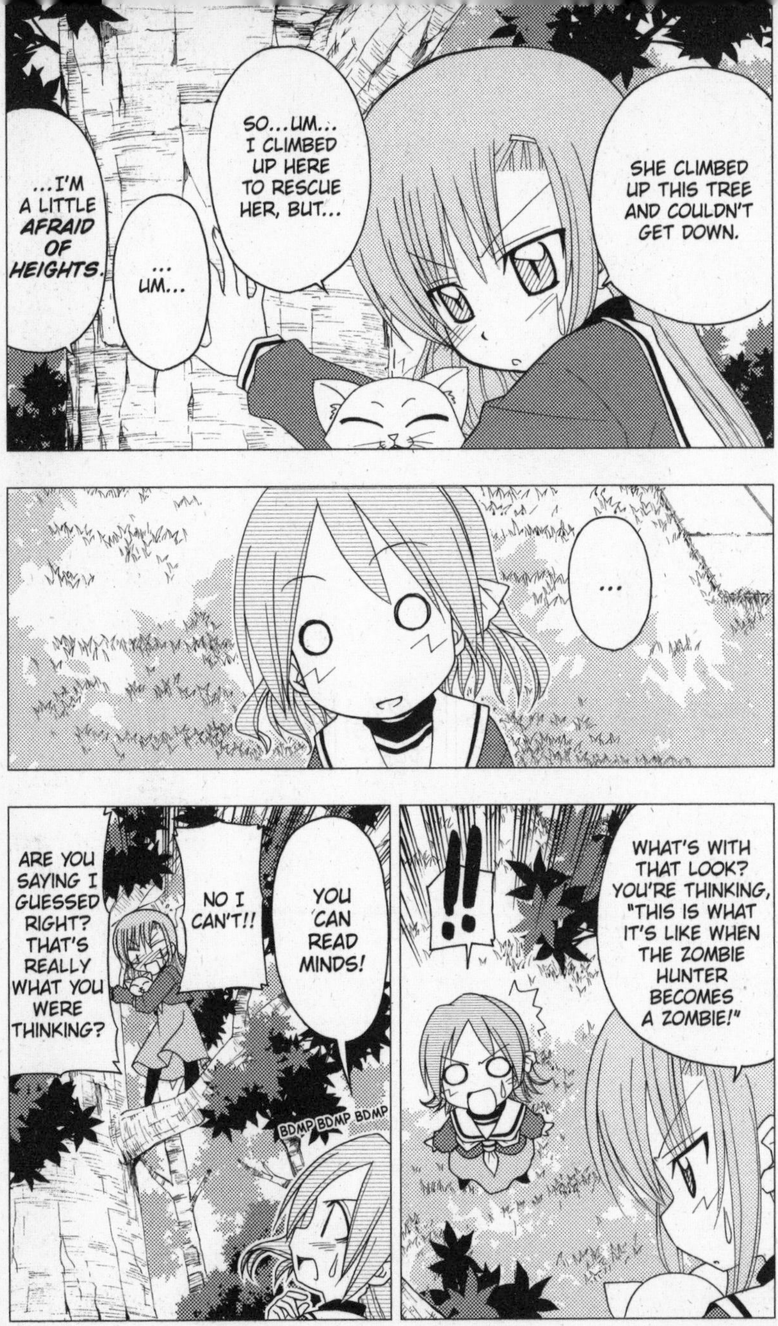
SHE CLIMBED UP THIS TREE AND COULDN'T GET DOWN.
SO...UM... I CLIMBED UP HERE TO RESCUE HER, BUT...
... UM...
...I'M A LITTLE *AFRAID* OF *HEIGHTS*.
...
WHAT'S WITH THAT LOOK? YOU'RE THINKING, "THIS IS WHAT IT'S LIKE WHEN THE ZOMBIE HUNTER BECOMES A ZOMBIE!"
!!
YOU CAN READ MINDS!
NO I CAN'T!!
ARE YOU SAYING I GUESSED RIGHT? THAT'S REALLY WHAT YOU WERE THINKING?
BDMP BDMP BDMP

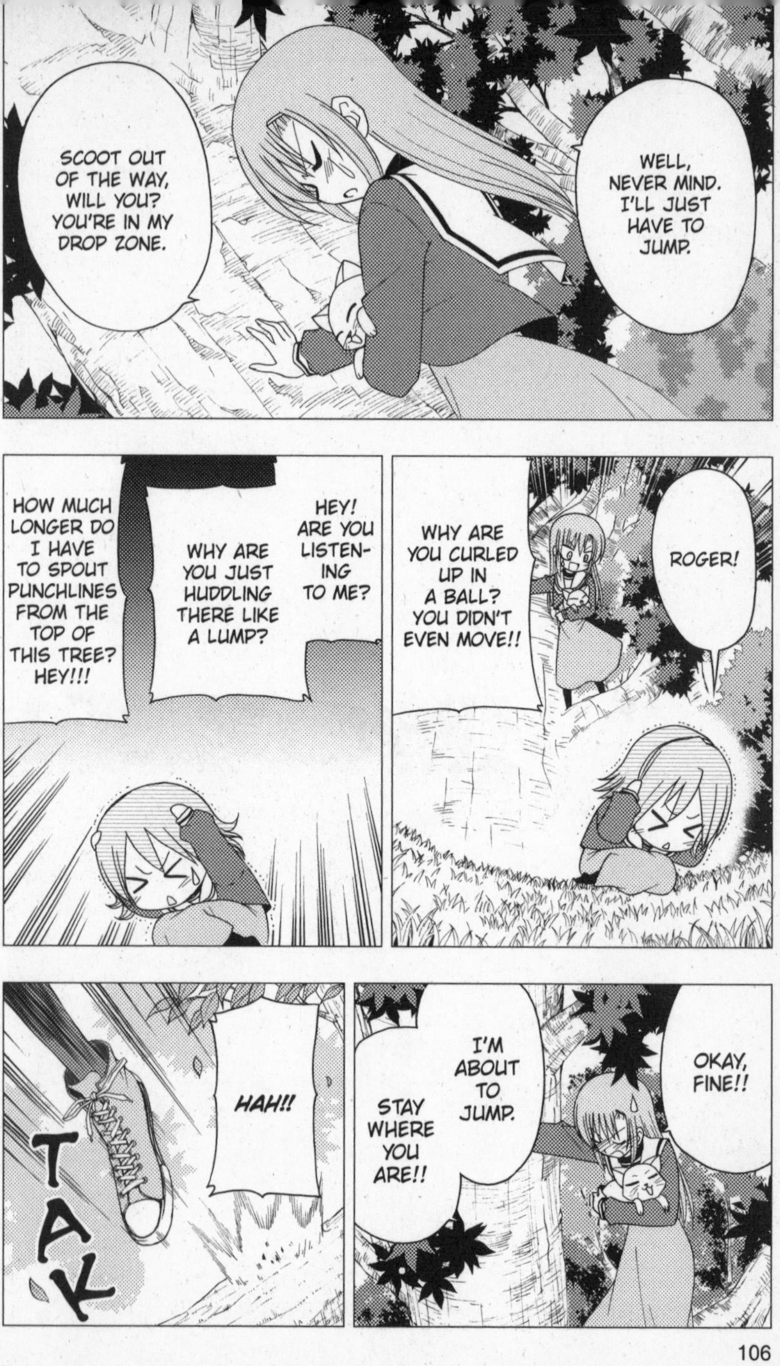
WELL, NEVER MIND. I'LL JUST HAVE TO JUMP.
SCOOT OUT OF THE WAY, WILL YOU? YOU'RE IN MY DROP ZONE.
ROGER!
WHY ARE YOU CURLED UP IN A BALL? YOU DIDN'T EVEN MOVE!!
HEY! ARE YOU LISTEN-ING TO ME?
WHY ARE YOU JUST HUDDLING THERE LIKE A LUMP?
HOW MUCH LONGER DO I HAVE TO SPOUT PUNCHLINES FROM THE TOP OF THIS TREE? HEY!!!
OKAY, FINE!!
I'M ABOUT TO JUMP.
STAY WHERE YOU ARE!!
HAH!!
TAK

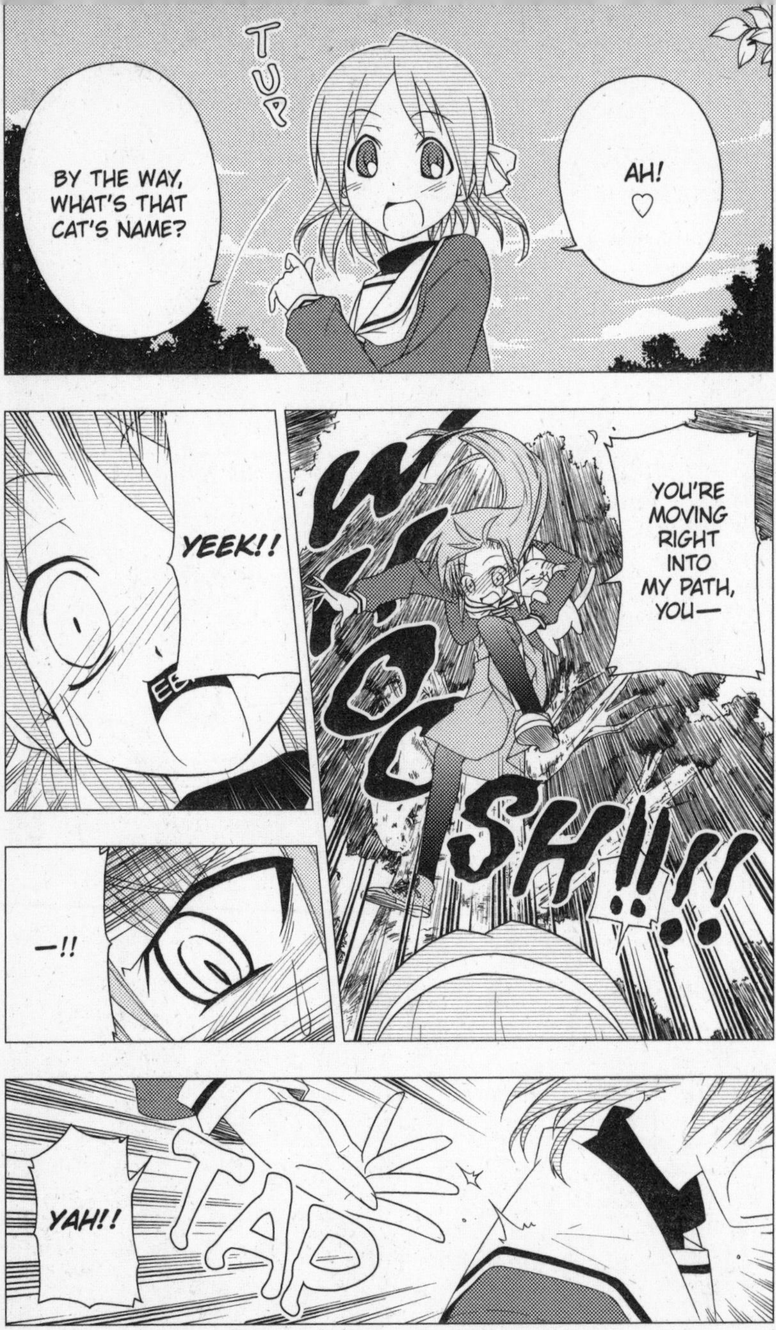
AH! ♡
TUP
BY THE WAY, WHAT'S THAT CAT'S NAME?
YOU'RE MOVING RIGHT INTO MY PATH, YOU—
WHOOSH!!!!
YEEK!!
—!!
TAP
YAH!!

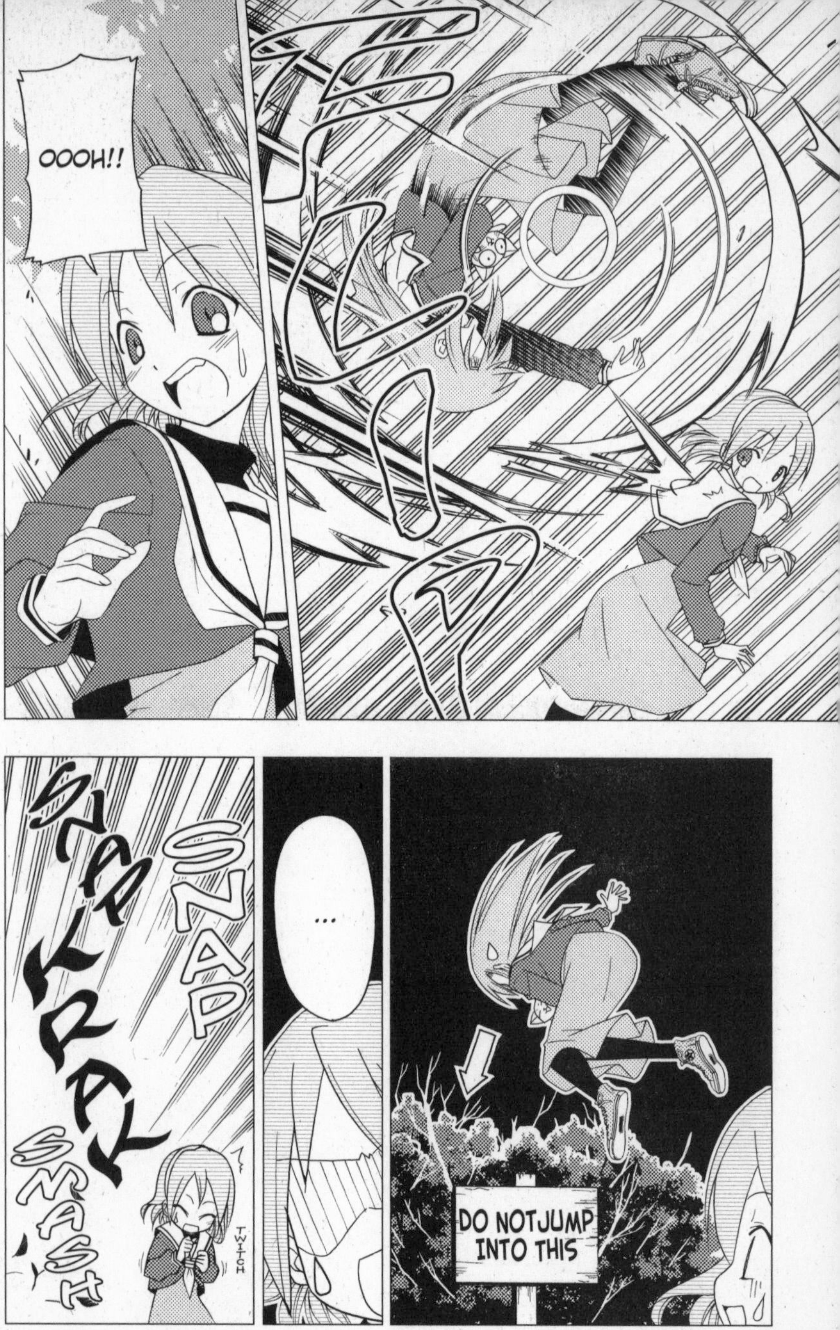
OOOH!!
DO NOTJUMP INTO THIS
...
SNAP
SNAP KRAK
SMASH
TWITCH

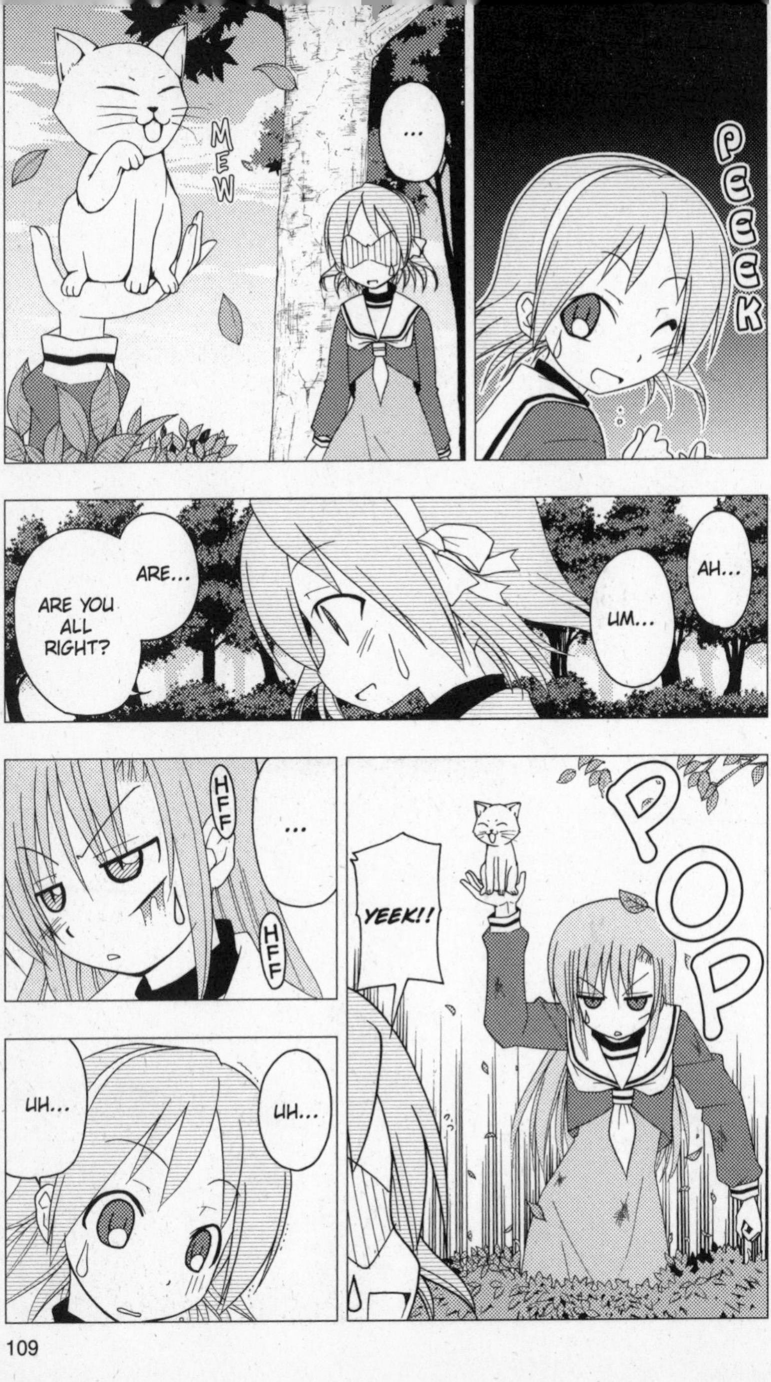
PEEEK
...
MEW
AH...
UM...
ARE...
ARE YOU ALL RIGHT?
POP
YEEK!!
...
HFF
HFF
UH...
UH...

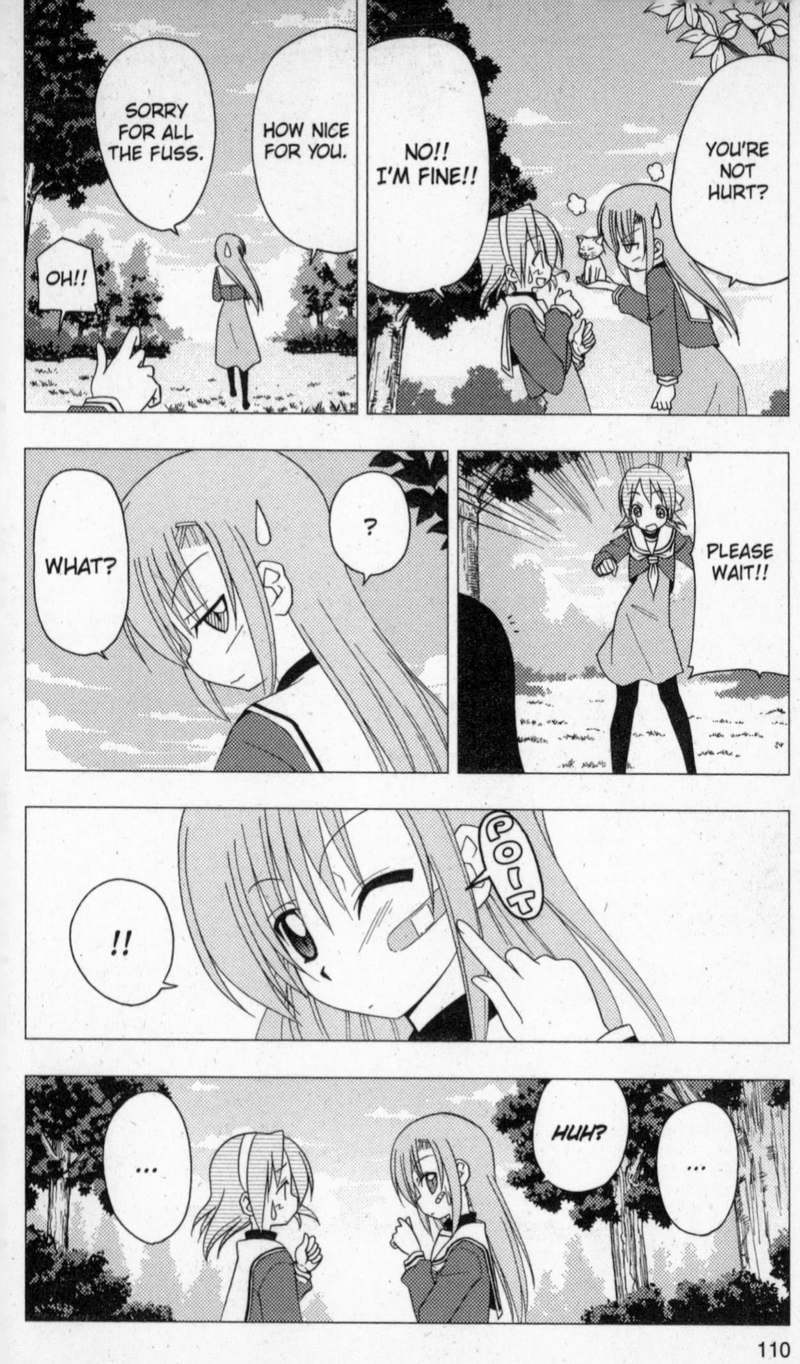
YOU'RE NOT HURT?
NO!! I'M FINE!!
HOW NICE FOR YOU.
SORRY FOR ALL THE FUSS.
OH!!
PLEASE WAIT!!
?
WHAT?
POIT
!!
...
HUH?
...

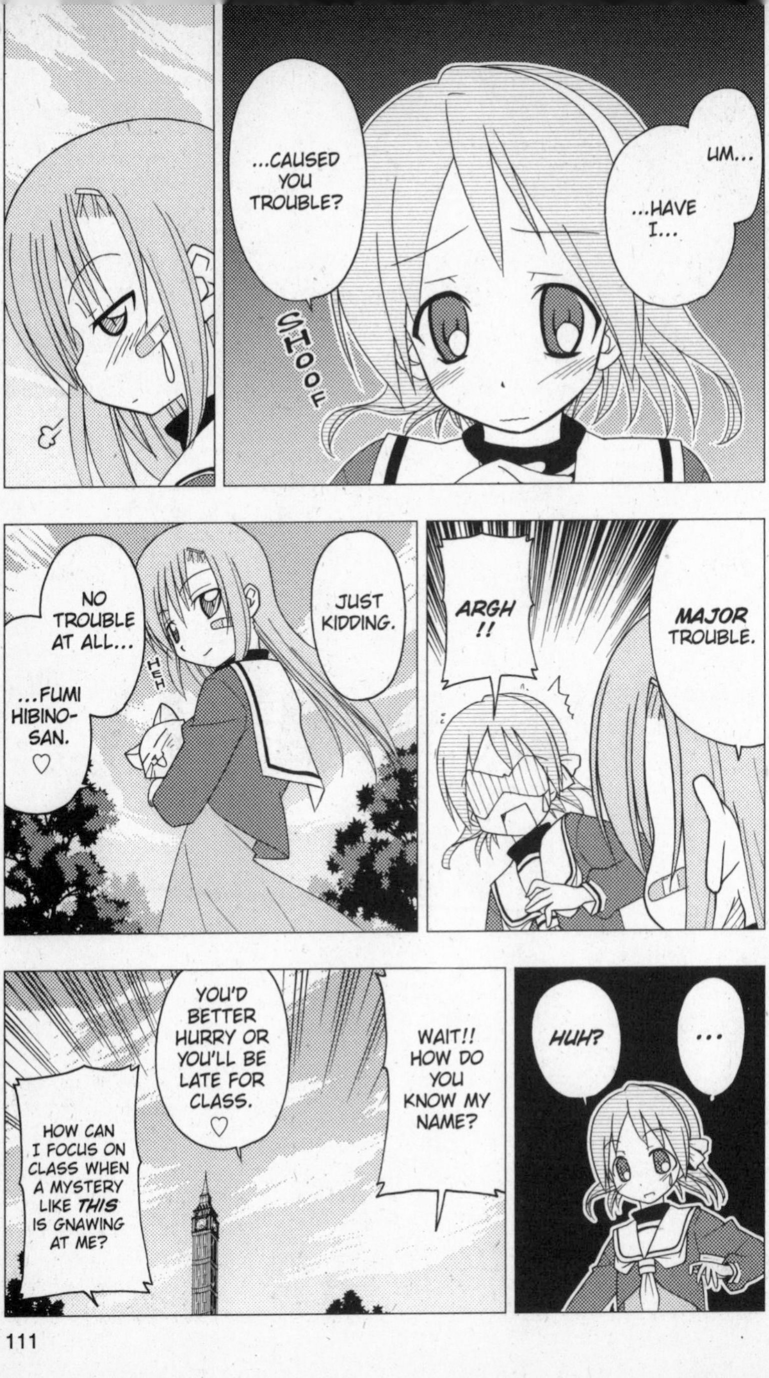
UM... ...HAVE I...
...CAUSED YOU TROUBLE?
SHOOF
MAJOR TROUBLE.
ARGH!!
JUST KIDDING.
NO TROUBLE AT ALL... ...FUMI HIBINO-SAN. ♡
HEH
...
HUH?
WAIT!! HOW DO YOU KNOW MY NAME?
YOU'D BETTER HURRY OR YOU'LL BE LATE FOR CLASS. ♡
HOW CAN I FOCUS ON CLASS WHEN A MYSTERY LIKE THIS IS GNAWING AT ME?

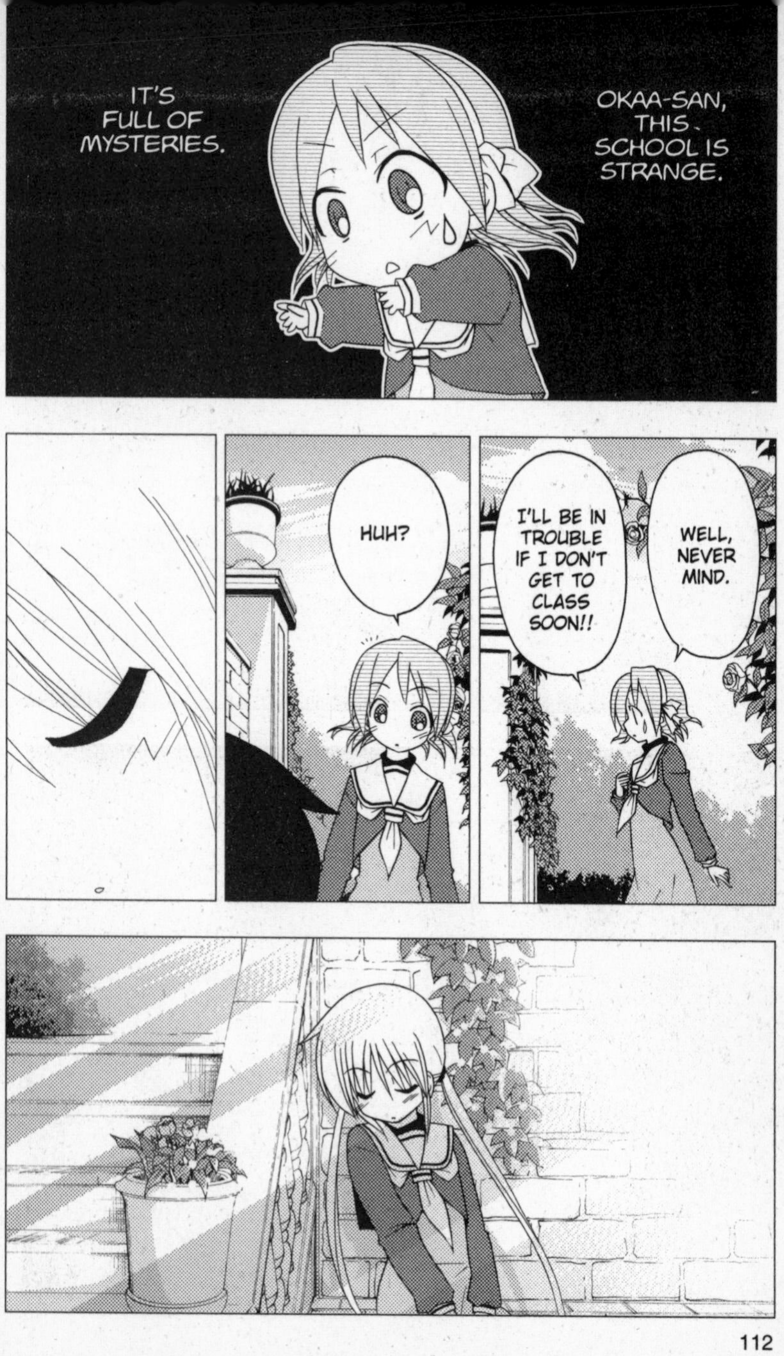
OKAA-SAN, THIS SCHOOL IS STRANGE.
IT'S FULL OF MYSTERIES.
WELL, NEVER MIND.
I'LL BE IN TROUBLE IF I DON'T GET TO CLASS SOON!!
HUH?

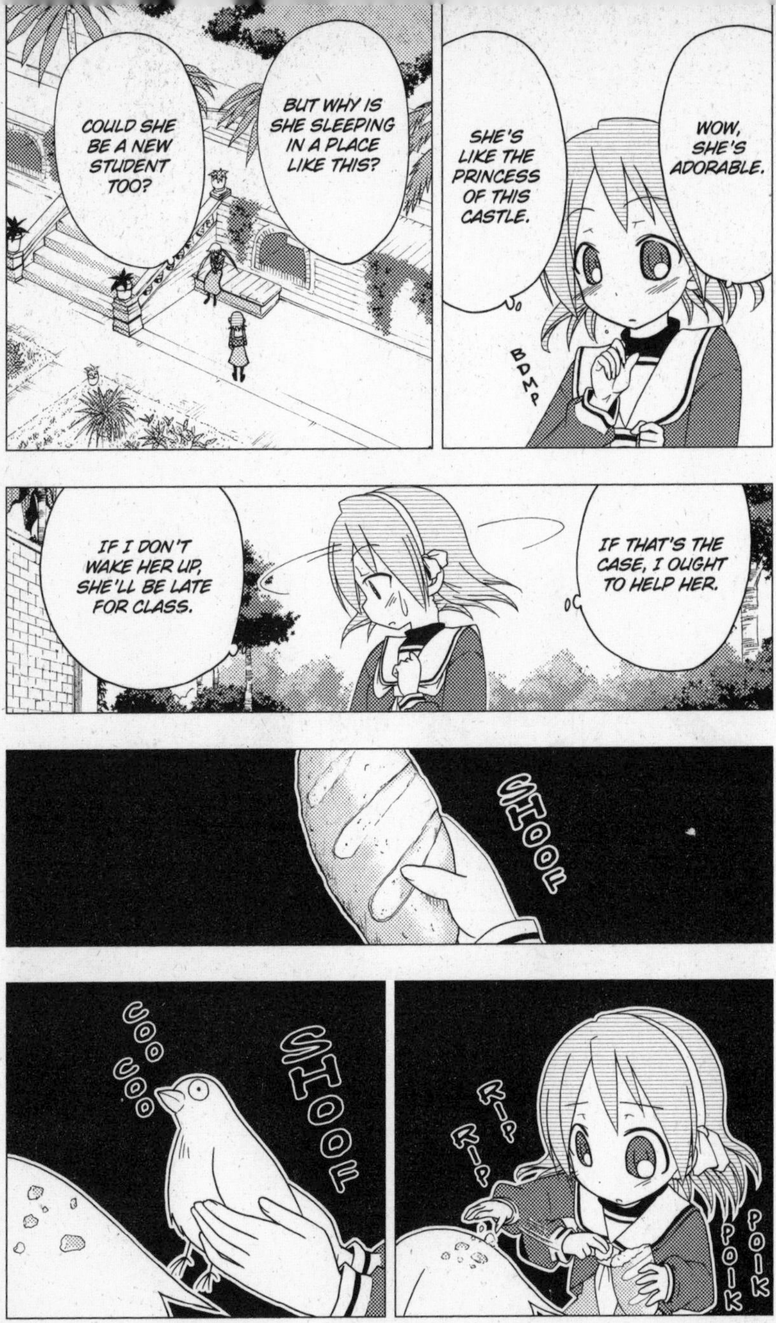
WOW, SHE'S ADORABLE.
SHE'S LIKE THE PRINCESS OF THIS CASTLE.
BDMP
BUT WHY IS SHE SLEEPING IN A PLACE LIKE THIS?
COULD SHE BE A NEW STUDENT TOO?
IF THAT'S THE CASE, I OUGHT TO HELP HER.
IF I DON'T WAKE HER UP, SHE'LL BE LATE FOR CLASS.
SHOOF
POIK POIK
RIP RIP
SHOOF
COO COO

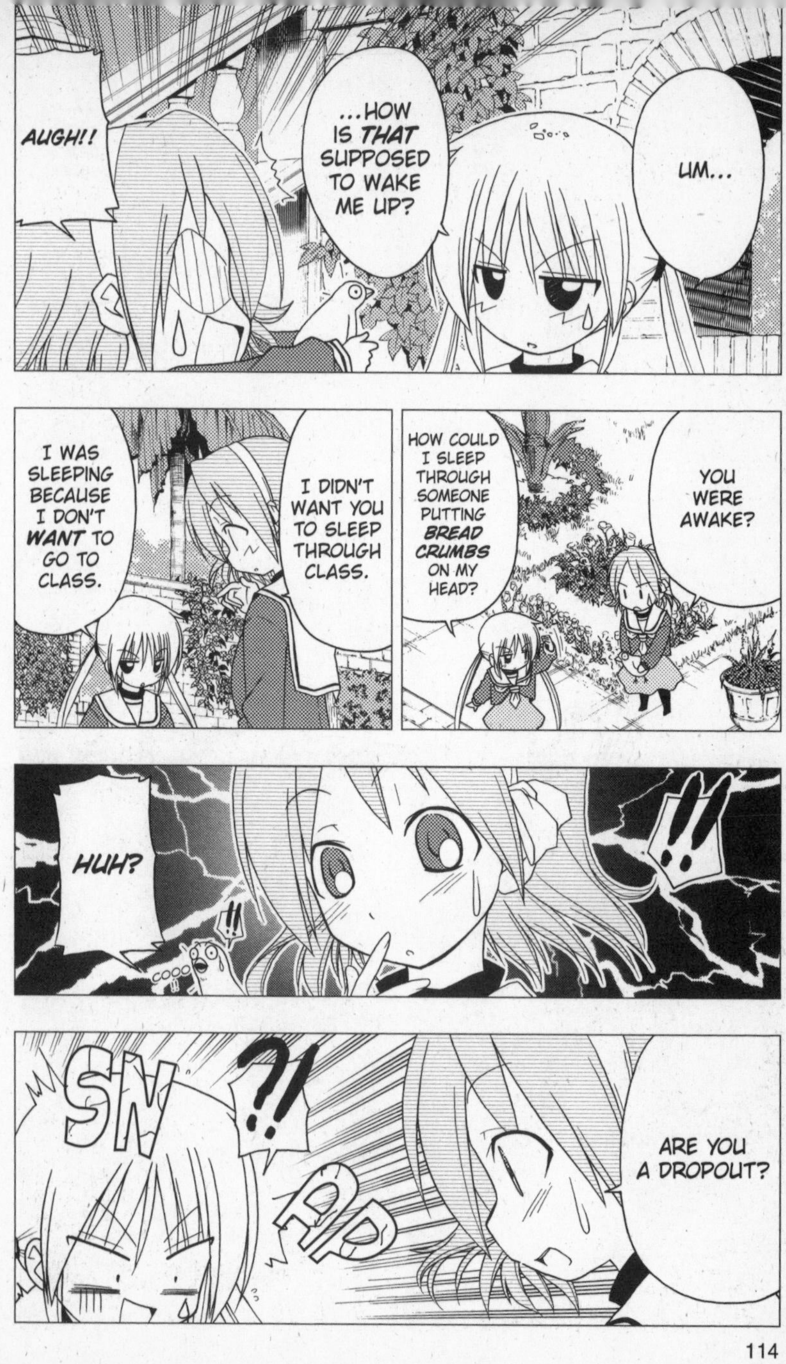
UM...
...HOW IS *THAT* SUPPOSED TO WAKE ME UP?
AUGH!!
YOU WERE AWAKE?
HOW COULD I SLEEP THROUGH SOMEONE PUTTING *BREAD CRUMBS* ON MY HEAD?
I DIDN'T WANT YOU TO SLEEP THROUGH CLASS.
I WAS SLEEPING BECAUSE I DON'T *WANT* TO GO TO CLASS.
!!
HUH?
!!
COOO
ARE YOU A DROPOUT?
SNAP
?!

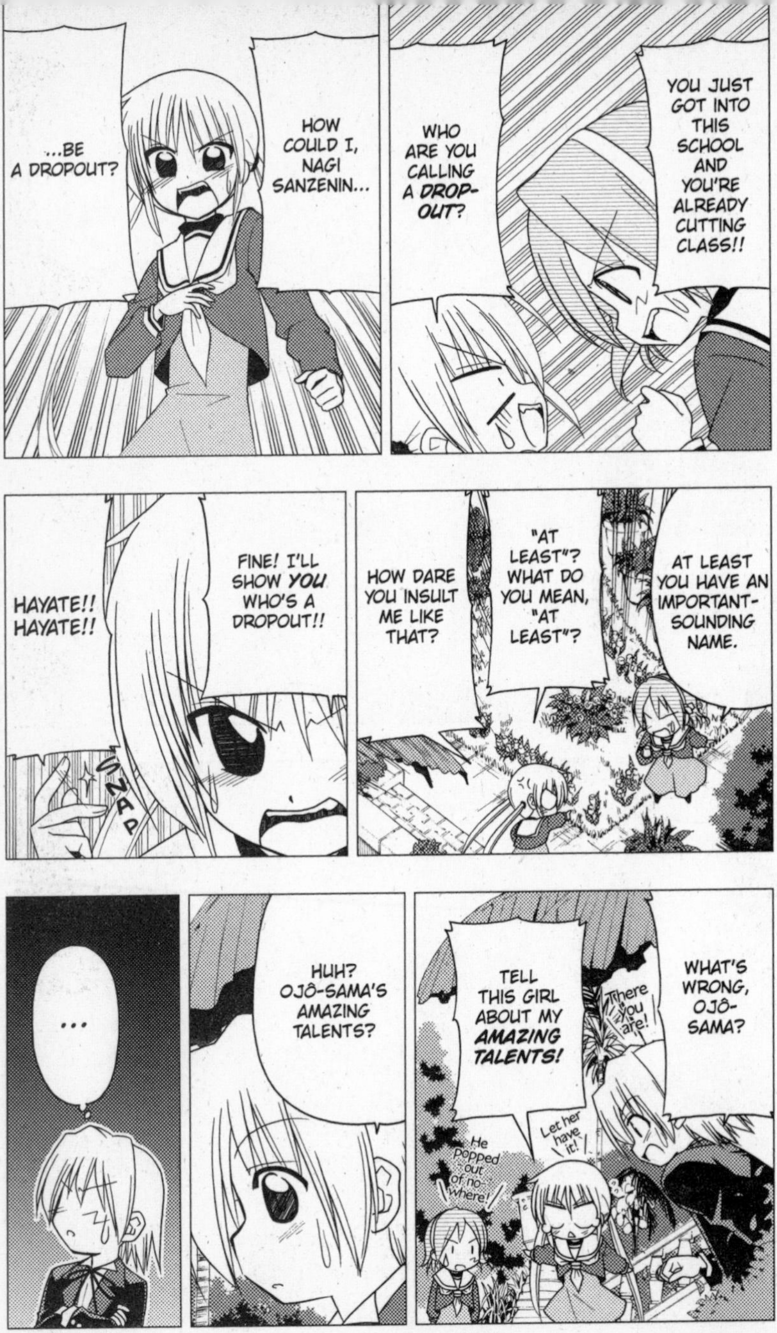
YOU JUST GOT INTO THIS SCHOOL AND YOU'RE ALREADY CUTTING CLASS!!
WHO ARE YOU CALLING A DROP-OUT?
HOW COULD I, NAGI SANZENIN...
...BE A DROPOUT?
AT LEAST YOU HAVE AN IMPORTANT-SOUNDING NAME.
"AT LEAST"? WHAT DO YOU MEAN, "AT LEAST"?
HOW DARE YOU INSULT ME LIKE THAT?
FINE! I'LL SHOW YOU WHO'S A DROPOUT!!
HAYATE!! HAYATE!!
SNAP
WHAT'S WRONG, OJÔ-SAMA?
There you are!
TELL THIS GIRL ABOUT MY AMAZING TALENTS!
Let her have it!
He popped out of nowhere!
HUH? OJÔ-SAMA'S AMAZING TALENTS?
...

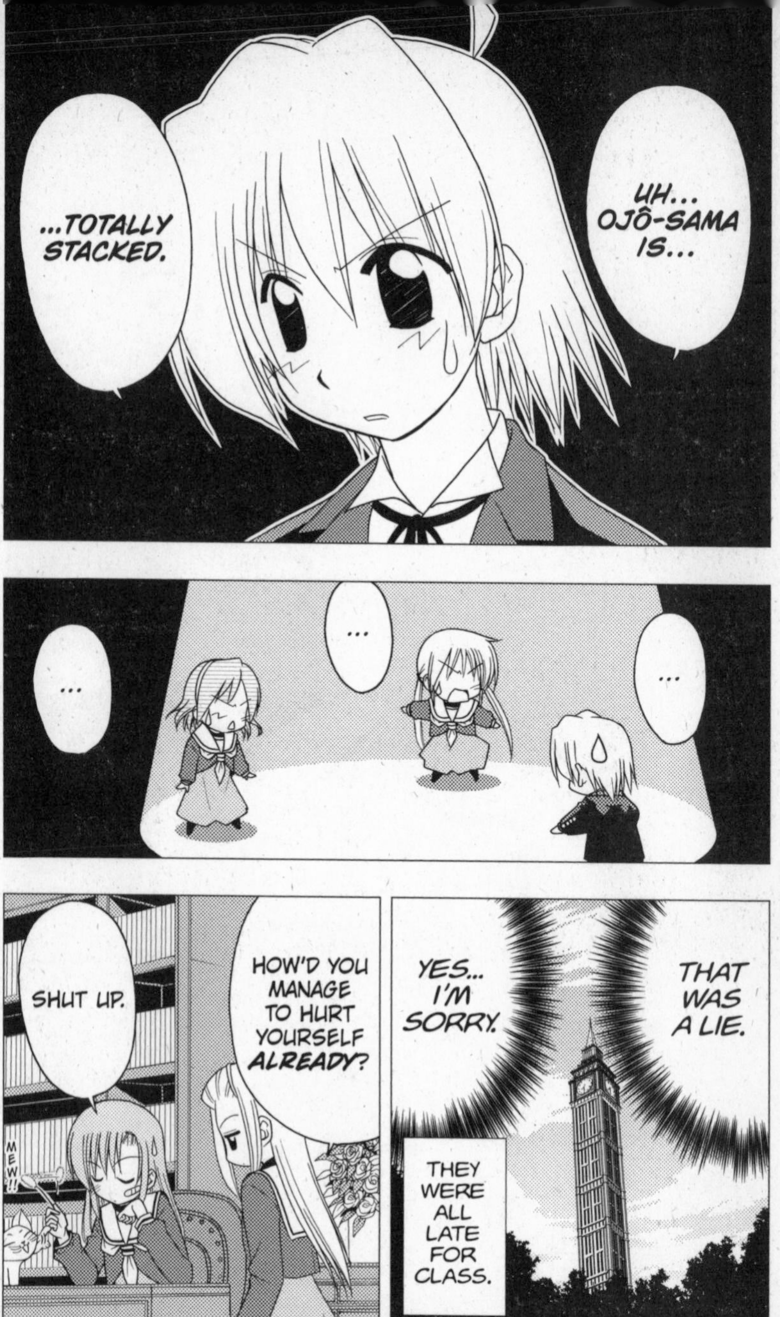
UH... OJÔ-SAMA IS...
...TOTALLY STACKED.
...
...
...
THAT WAS A LIE.
YES... I'M SORRY.
THEY WERE ALL LATE FOR CLASS.
HOW'D YOU MANAGE TO HURT YOURSELF ALREADY?
SHUT UP.
MEW!!

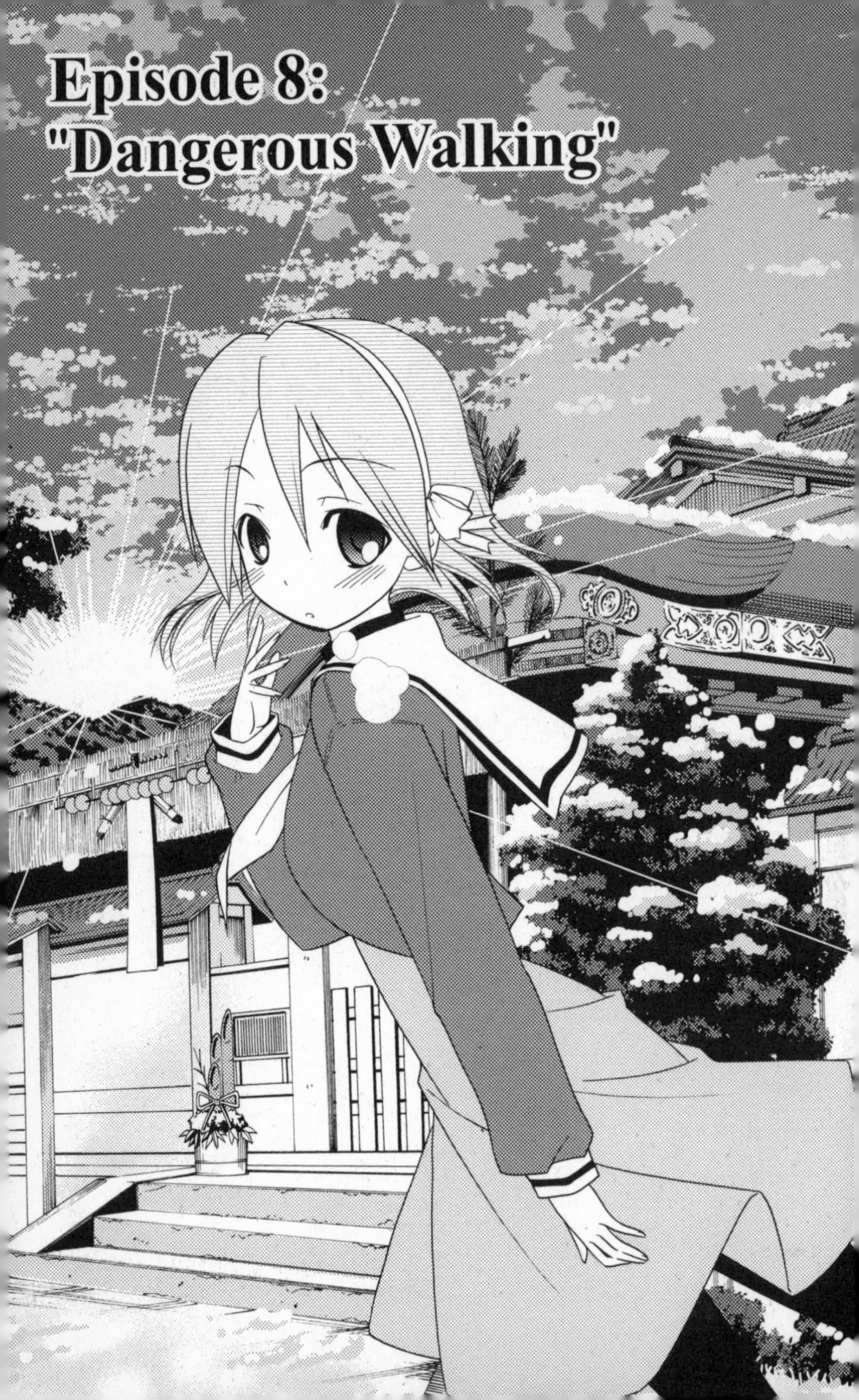
Episode 8:
"Dangerous Walking"

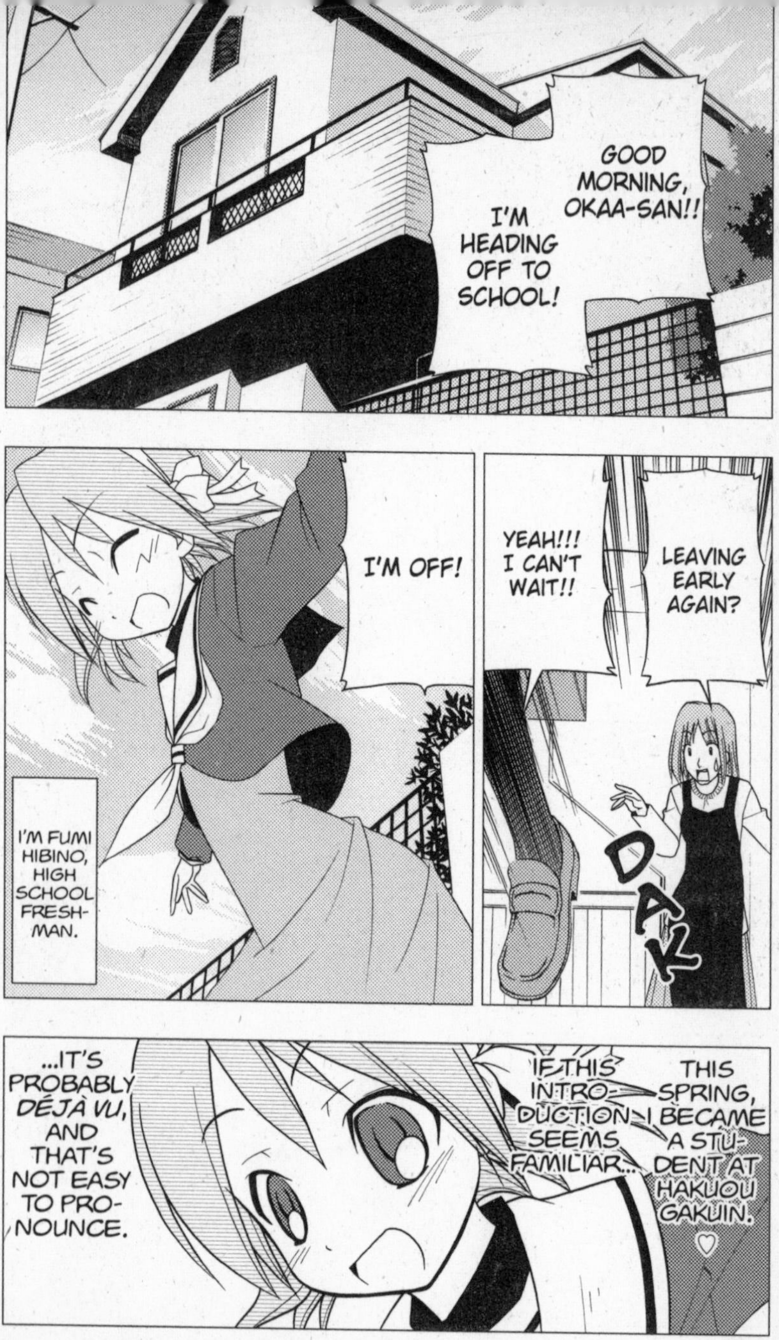
GOOD MORNING, OKAA-SAN!!
I'M HEADING OFF TO SCHOOL!
LEAVING EARLY AGAIN?
YEAH!!! I CAN'T WAIT!!
DAK
I'M OFF!
I'M FUMI HIBINO, HIGH SCHOOL FRESH-MAN.
THIS SPRING, I BECAME A STU-DENT AT HAKUOU GAKUIN. ♡
IF THIS INTRO-DUCTION SEEMS FAMILIAR...
...IT'S PROBABLY *DÉJÀ VU*, AND THAT'S NOT EASY TO PRO-NOUNCE.

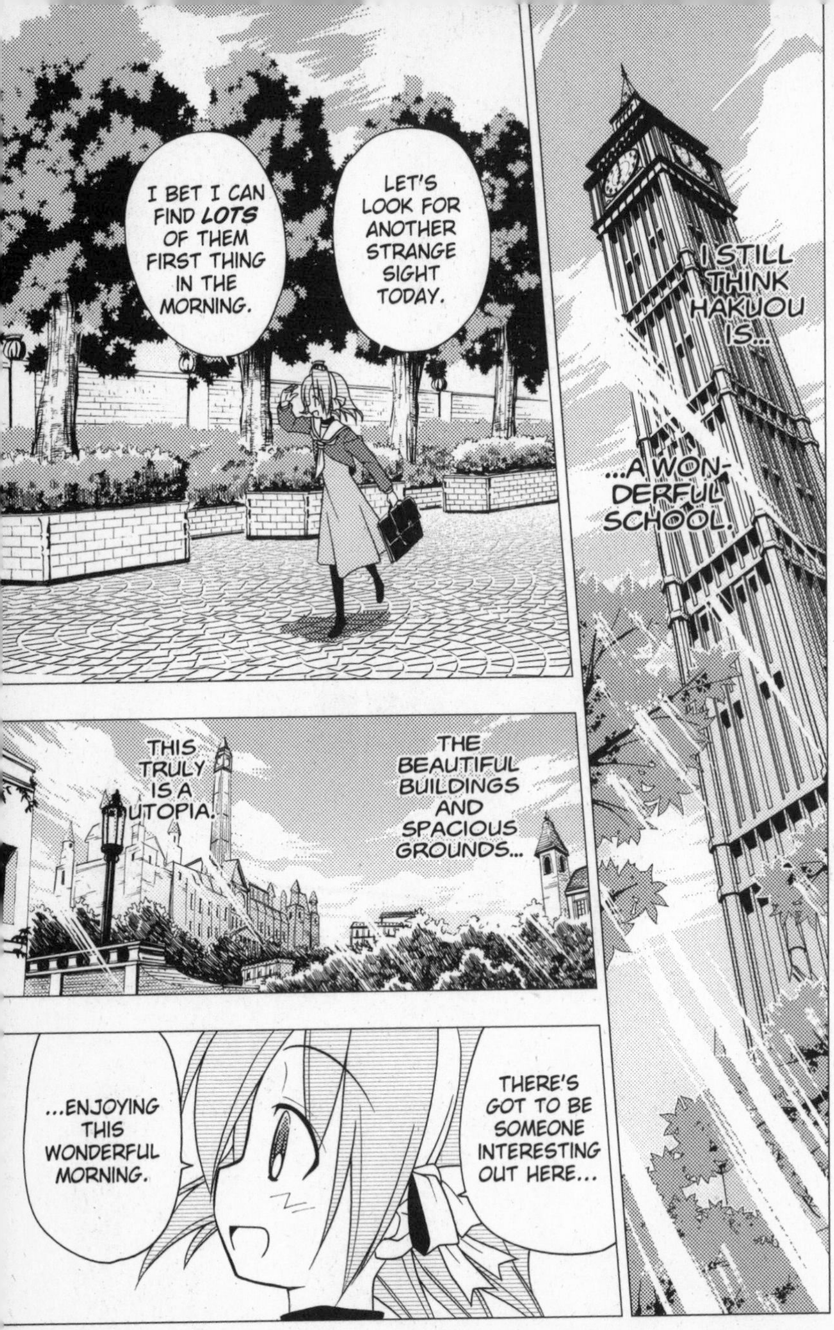
I STILL THINK HAKUOU IS...
...A WONDERFUL SCHOOL.
LET'S LOOK FOR ANOTHER STRANGE SIGHT TODAY.
I BET I CAN FIND LOTS OF THEM FIRST THING IN THE MORNING.
THE BEAUTIFUL BUILDINGS AND SPACIOUS GROUNDS...
THIS TRULY IS A UTOPIA.
THERE'S GOT TO BE SOMEONE INTERESTING OUT HERE...
...ENJOYING THIS WONDERFUL MORNING.

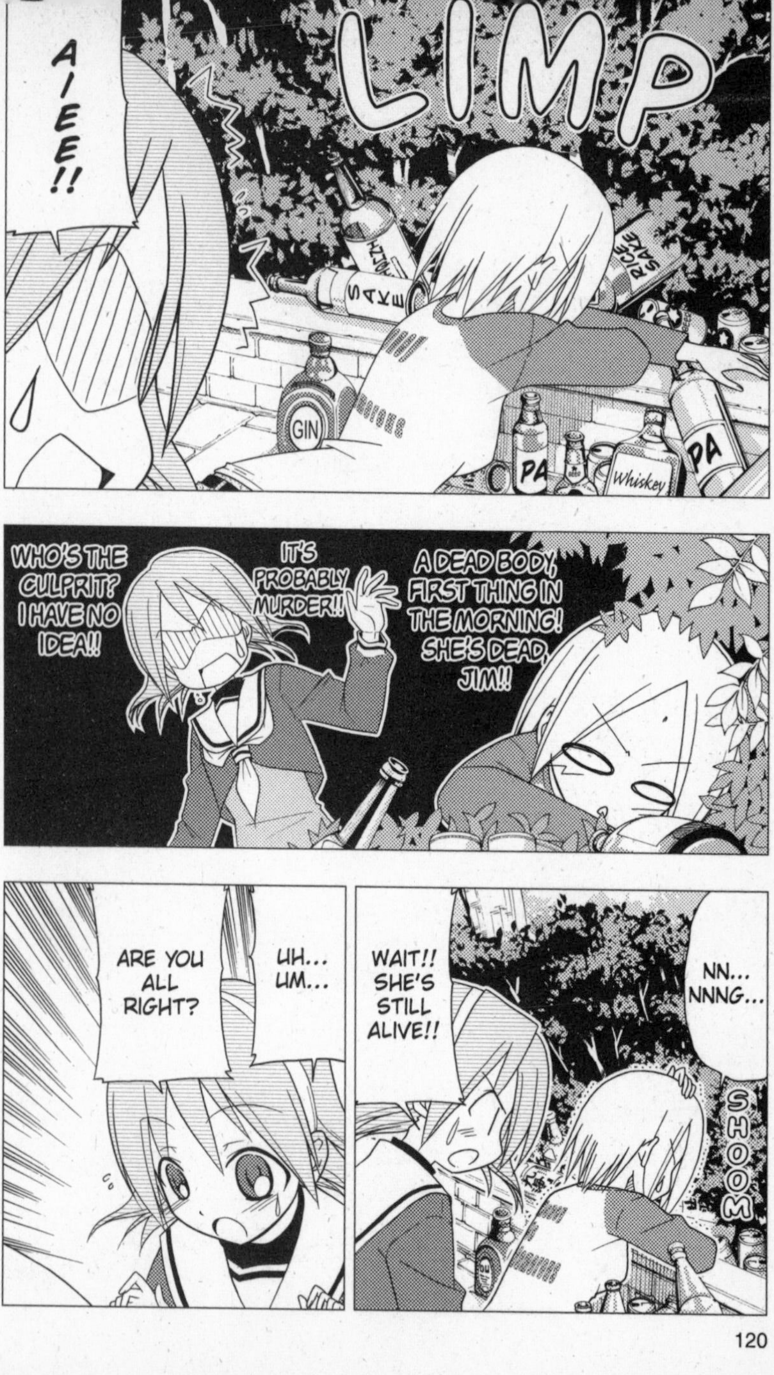
LIMP
AIEEE!!
RICE SAKE
SAKE
GIN
PA
Whiskey
PA
A DEAD BODY, FIRST THING IN THE MORNING! SHE'S DEAD, JIM!!
IT'S PROBABLY MURDER!!
WHO'S THE CULPRIT? I HAVE NO IDEA!!
NN... NNNG...
SHOOM
WAIT!! SHE'S STILL ALIVE!!
UH... UM...
ARE YOU ALL RIGHT?

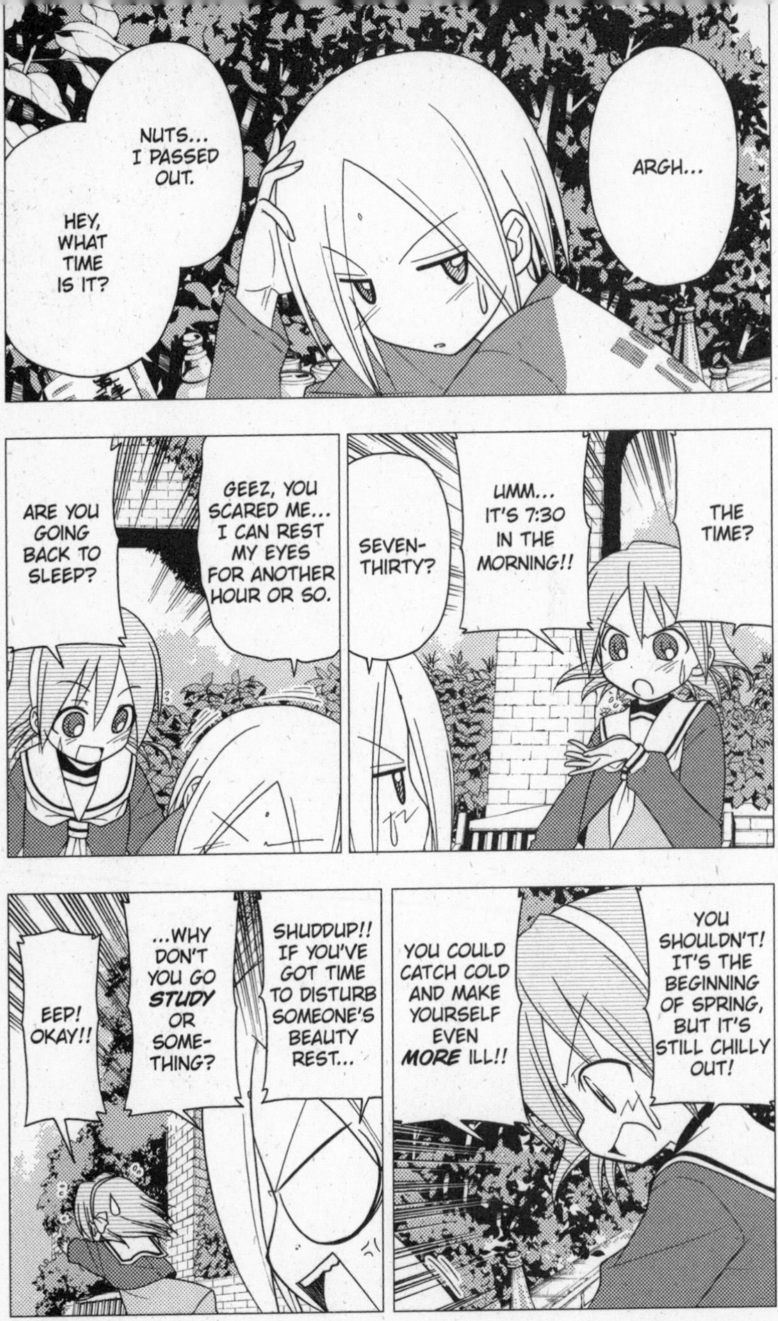
ARGH...
NUTS... I PASSED OUT.
HEY, WHAT TIME IS IT?
THE TIME?
UMM... IT'S 7:30 IN THE MORNING!!
SEVEN-THIRTY?
GEEZ, YOU SCARED ME... I CAN REST MY EYES FOR ANOTHER HOUR OR SO.
ARE YOU GOING BACK TO SLEEP?
YOU SHOULDN'T! IT'S THE BEGINNING OF SPRING, BUT IT'S STILL CHILLY OUT!
YOU COULD CATCH COLD AND MAKE YOURSELF EVEN MORE ILL!!
SHUDDUP!! IF YOU'VE GOT TIME TO DISTURB SOMEONE'S BEAUTY REST...
...WHY DON'T YOU GO STUDY OR SOMETHING?
EEP! OKAY!!

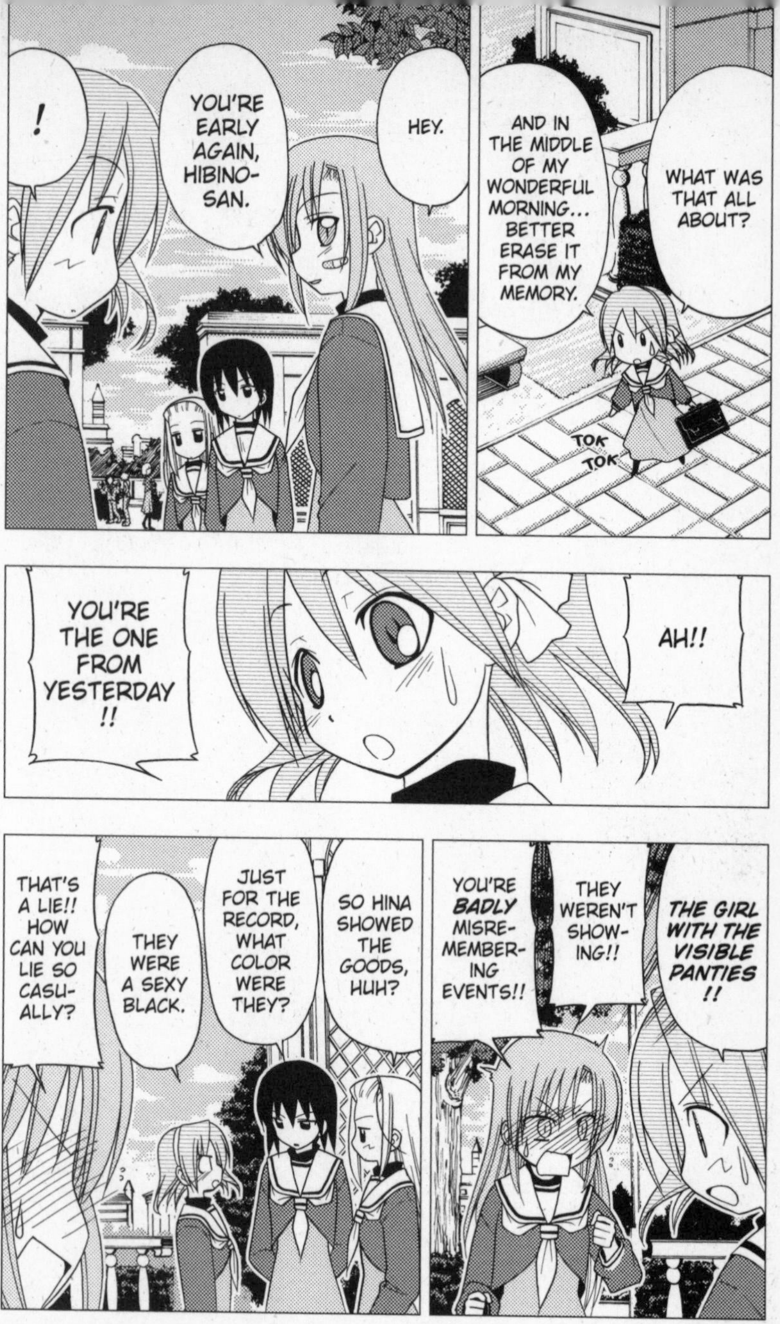
WHAT WAS THAT ALL ABOUT?
AND IN THE MIDDLE OF MY WONDERFUL MORNING... BETTER ERASE IT FROM MY MEMORY.
TOK TOK
HEY.
YOU'RE EARLY AGAIN, HIBINO-SAN.
!
AH!!
YOU'RE THE ONE FROM YESTERDAY!!
THE GIRL WITH THE VISIBLE PANTIES!!
THEY WEREN'T SHOWING!!
YOU'RE *BADLY* MISREMEMBERING EVENTS!!
SO HINA SHOWED THE GOODS, HUH?
JUST FOR THE RECORD, WHAT COLOR WERE THEY?
THEY WERE A SEXY BLACK.
THAT'S A LIE!! HOW CAN YOU LIE SO CASUALLY?

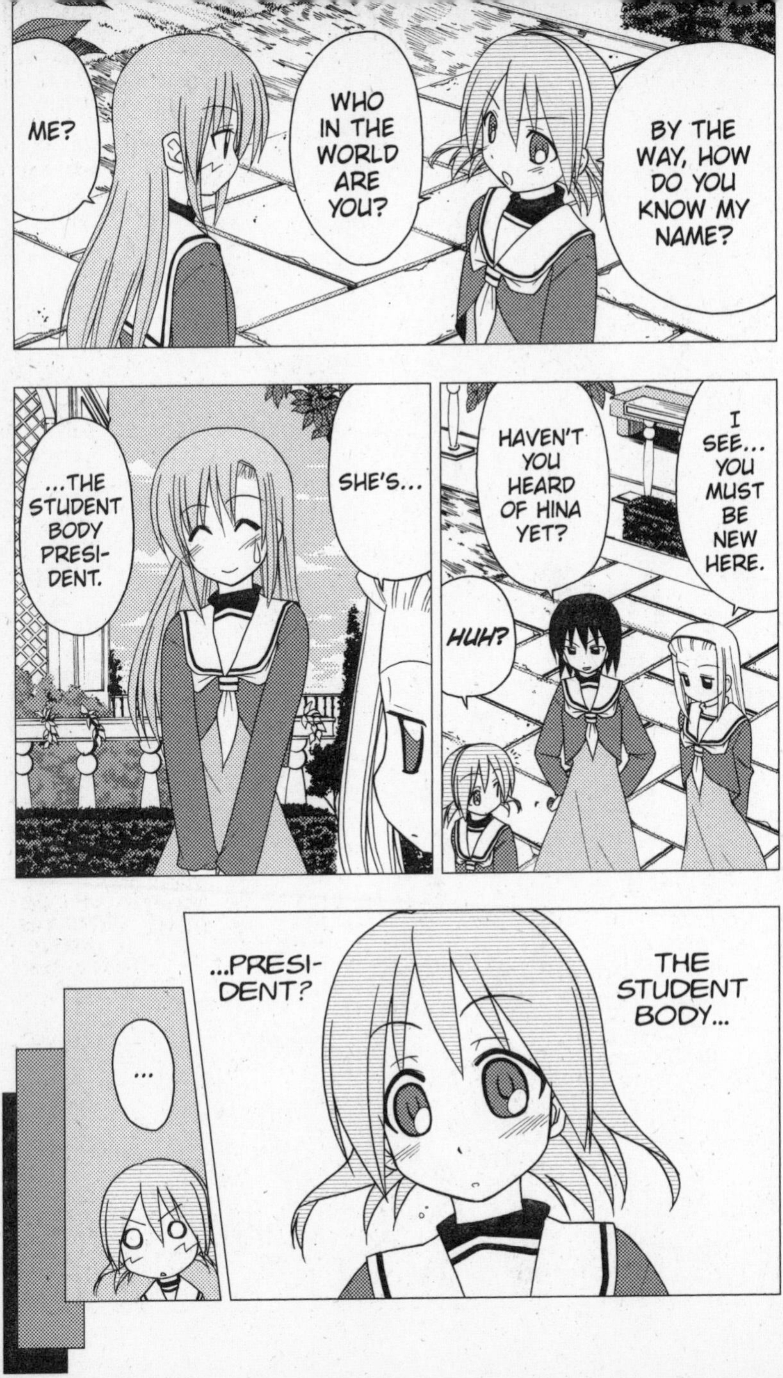
BY THE WAY, HOW DO YOU KNOW MY NAME?
WHO IN THE WORLD ARE YOU?
ME?
I SEE... YOU MUST BE NEW HERE.
HAVEN'T YOU HEARD OF HINA YET?
HUH?
SHE'S...
...THE STUDENT BODY PRESIDENT.
THE STUDENT BODY...
...PRESIDENT?
...

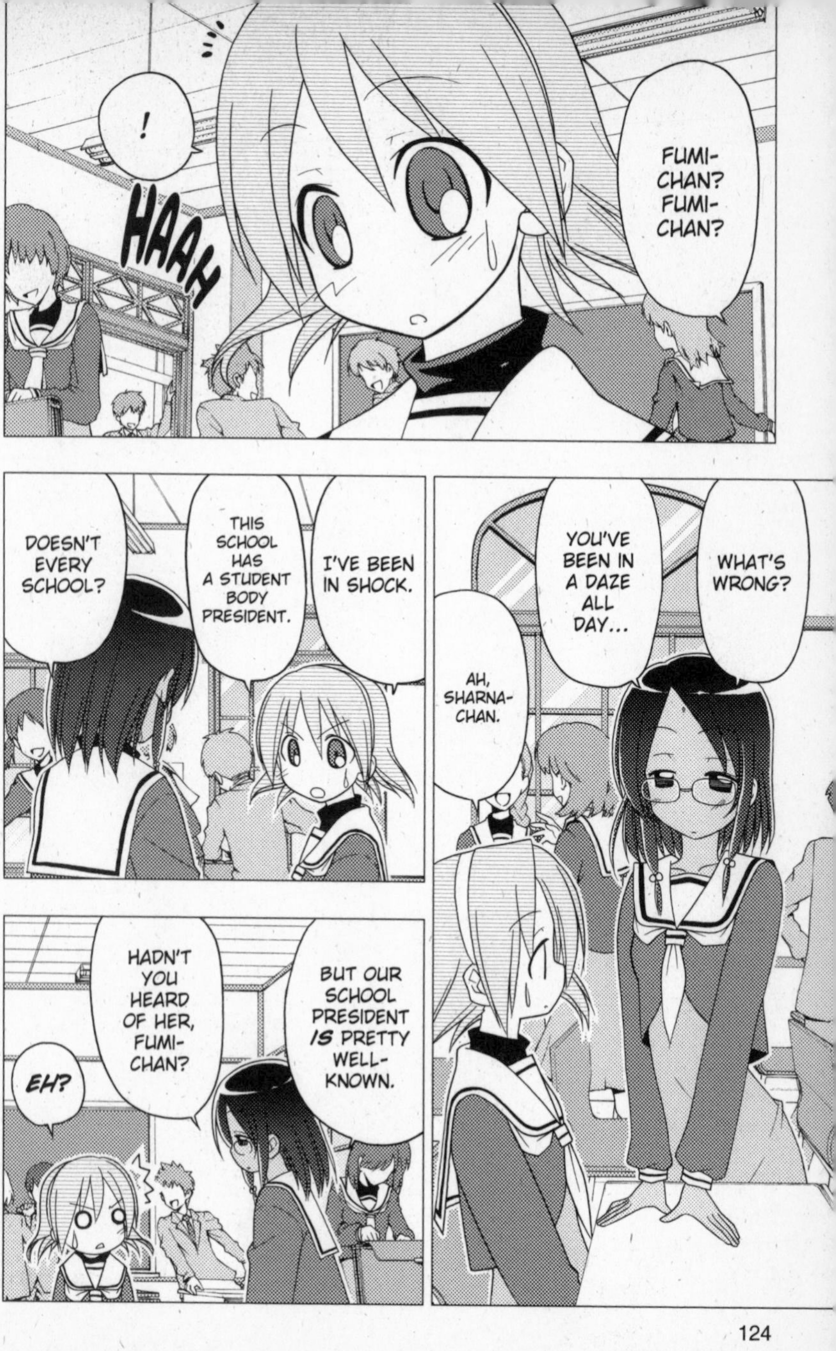
FUMI-CHAN? FUMI-CHAN?
!
HAAH
WHAT'S WRONG?
YOU'VE BEEN IN A DAZE ALL DAY...
AH, SHARNA-CHAN.
I'VE BEEN IN SHOCK.
THIS SCHOOL HAS A STUDENT BODY PRESIDENT.
DOESN'T EVERY SCHOOL?
BUT OUR SCHOOL PRESIDENT *IS* PRETTY WELL-KNOWN.
HADN'T YOU HEARD OF HER, FUMI-CHAN?
EH?

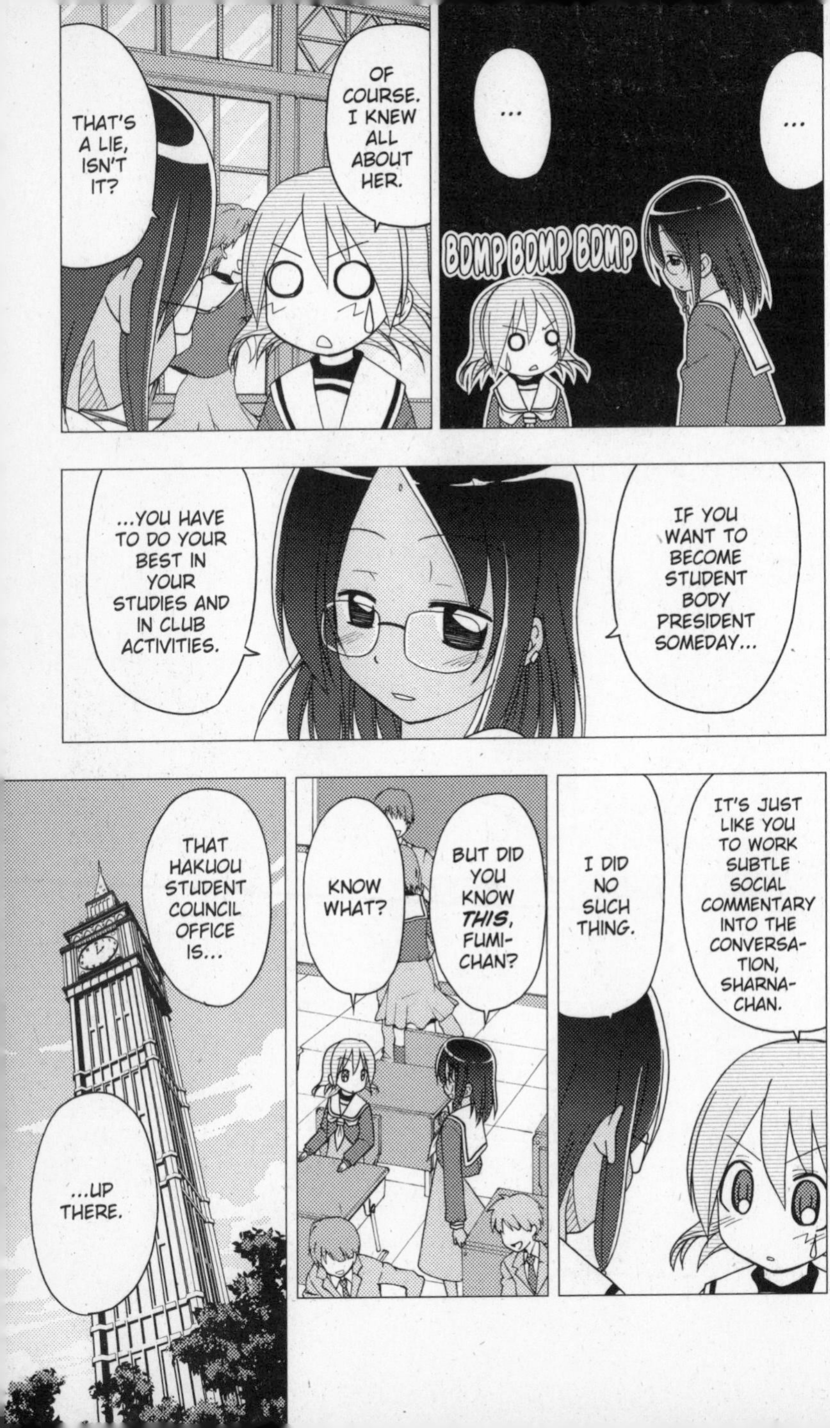
...
...
BDMP BDMP BDMP
OF COURSE. I KNEW ALL ABOUT HER.
THAT'S A LIE, ISN'T IT?
IF YOU WANT TO BECOME STUDENT BODY PRESIDENT SOMEDAY...
...YOU HAVE TO DO YOUR BEST IN YOUR STUDIES AND IN CLUB ACTIVITIES.
IT'S JUST LIKE YOU TO WORK SUBTLE SOCIAL COMMENTARY INTO THE CONVERSA-TION, SHARNA-CHAN.
I DID NO SUCH THING.
BUT DID YOU KNOW *THIS*, FUMI-CHAN?
KNOW WHAT?
THAT HAKUOU STUDENT COUNCIL OFFICE IS...
...UP THERE.

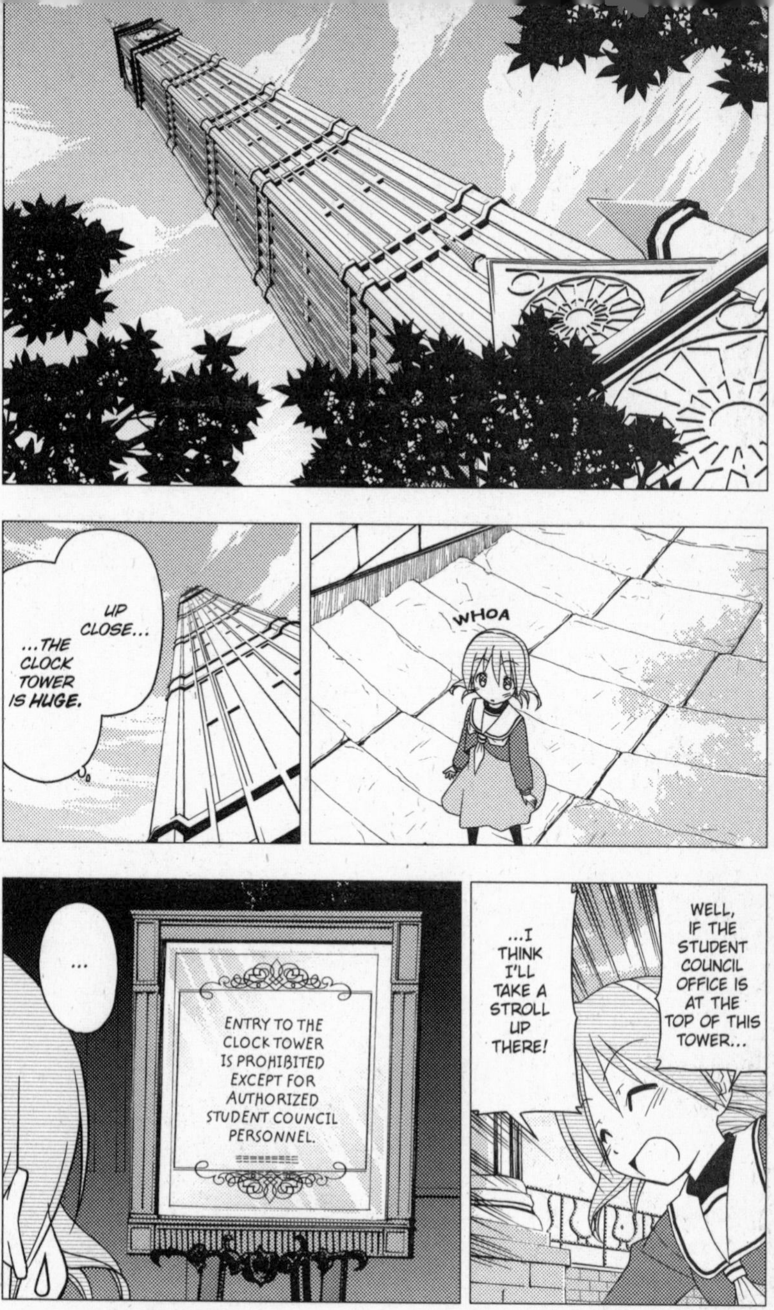
WHOA
UP CLOSE...
...THE CLOCK TOWER IS HUGE.
WELL, IF THE STUDENT COUNCIL OFFICE IS AT THE TOP OF THIS TOWER...
...I THINK I'LL TAKE A STROLL UP THERE!
ENTRY TO THE CLOCK TOWER IS PROHIBITED EXCEPT FOR AUTHORIZED STUDENT COUNCIL PERSONNEL.
...

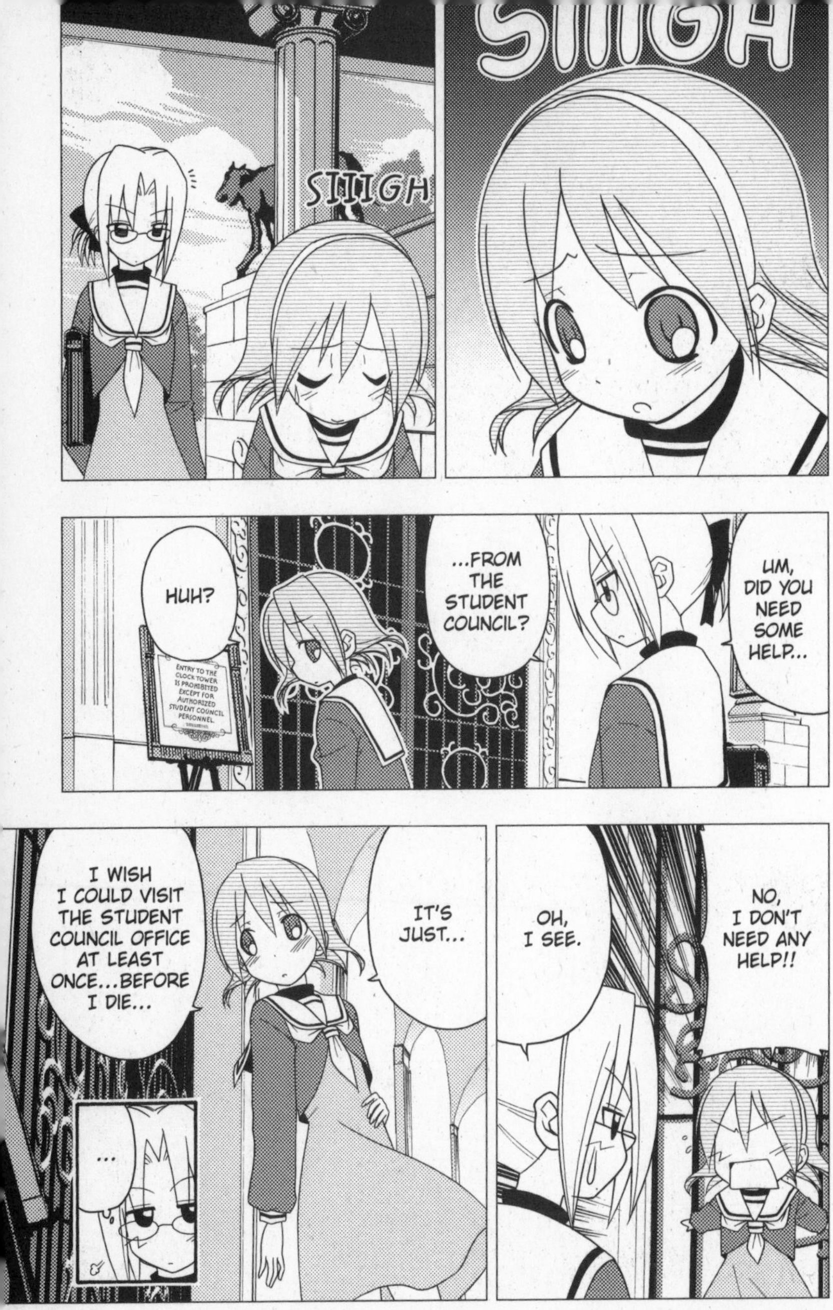
SIIIGH
SIIIGH
UM, DID YOU NEED SOME HELP...
...FROM THE STUDENT COUNCIL?
HUH?
ENTRY TO THE CLOCK TOWER IS PROHIBITED EXCEPT FOR AUTHORIZED STUDENT COUNCIL PERSONNEL.
NO, I DON'T NEED ANY HELP!!
OH, I SEE.
IT'S JUST...
I WISH I COULD VISIT THE STUDENT COUNCIL OFFICE AT LEAST ONCE...BEFORE I DIE...
...

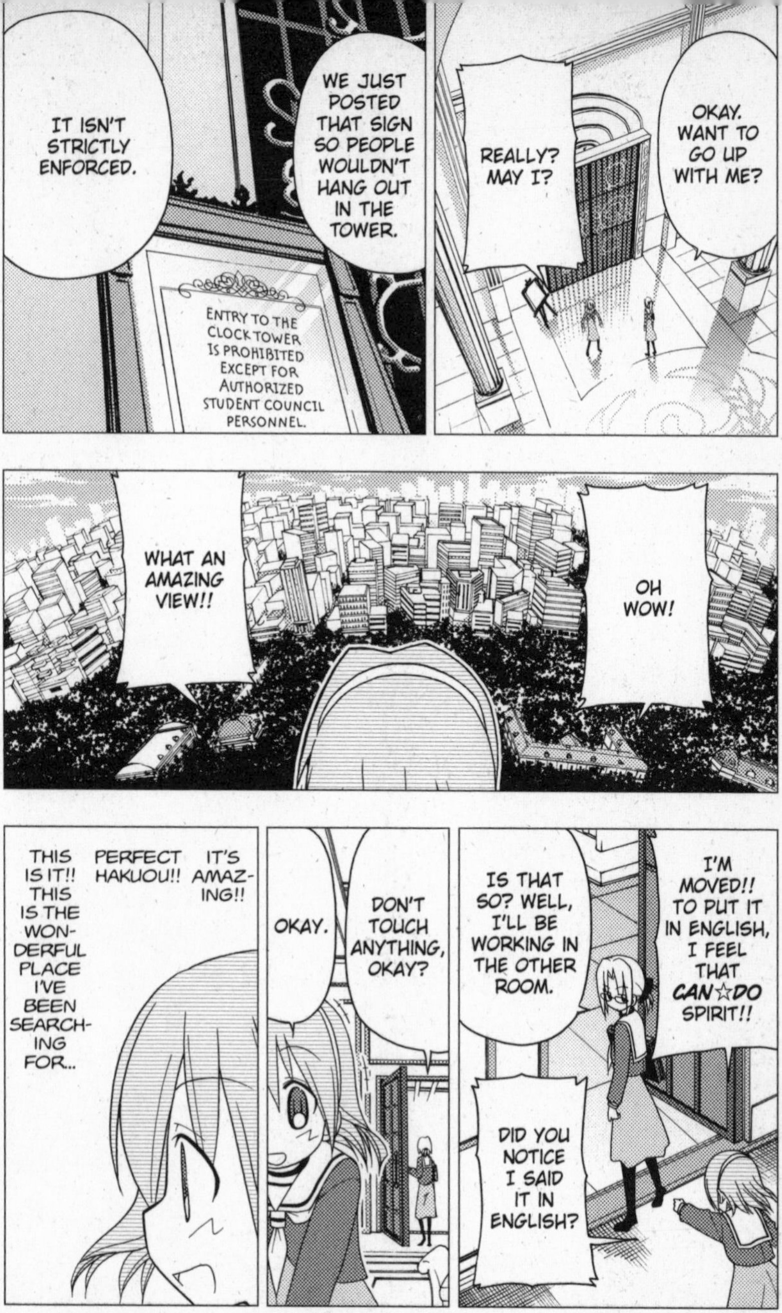
OKAY. WANT TO GO UP WITH ME?
REALLY? MAY I?
WE JUST POSTED THAT SIGN SO PEOPLE WOULDN'T HANG OUT IN THE TOWER.
IT ISN'T STRICTLY ENFORCED.
ENTRY TO THE CLOCK TOWER IS PROHIBITED EXCEPT FOR AUTHORIZED STUDENT COUNCIL PERSONNEL.
OH WOW!
WHAT AN AMAZING VIEW!!
I'M MOVED!! TO PUT IT IN ENGLISH, I FEEL THAT **CAN☆DO** SPIRIT!!
IS THAT SO? WELL, I'LL BE WORKING IN THE OTHER ROOM.
DID YOU NOTICE I SAID IT IN ENGLISH?
DON'T TOUCH ANYTHING, OKAY?
OKAY.
IT'S AMAZ-ING!!
PERFECT HAKUOU!!
THIS IS IT!! THIS IS THE WON-DERFUL PLACE I'VE BEEN SEARCH-ING FOR...

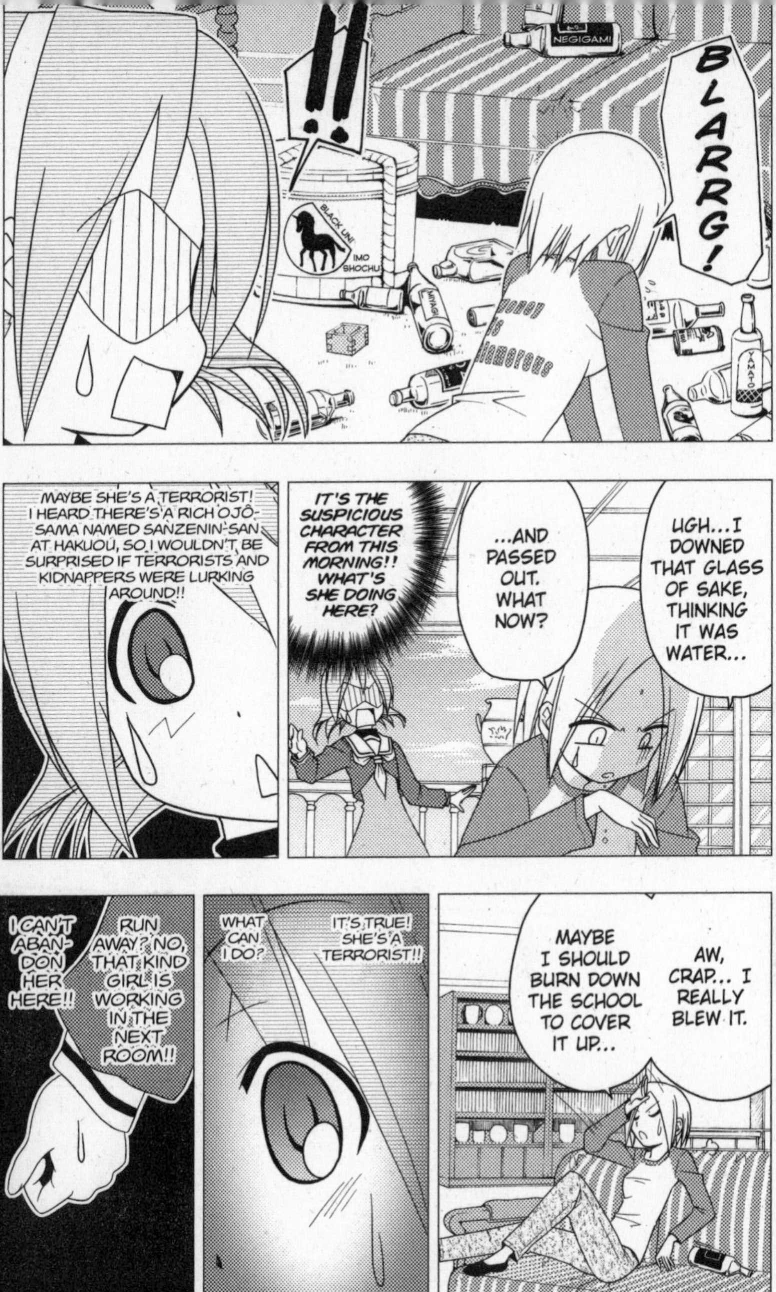
BLARRG!
NEGIGAMI
!!
BLACK UNI
IMO SHOCHU
MIYAGI
YAMATO
UGH... I DOWNED THAT GLASS OF SAKE, THINKING IT WAS WATER...
...AND PASSED OUT. WHAT NOW?
IT'S THE SUSPICIOUS CHARACTER FROM THIS MORNING!! WHAT'S SHE DOING HERE?
MAYBE SHE'S A TERRORIST! I HEARD THERE'S A RICH OJÔ-SAMA NAMED SANZENIN-SAN AT HAKUOU, SO I WOULDN'T BE SURPRISED IF TERRORISTS AND KIDNAPPERS WERE LURKING AROUND!!
AW, CRAP... I REALLY BLEW IT.
MAYBE I SHOULD BURN DOWN THE SCHOOL TO COVER IT UP...
IT'S TRUE! SHE'S A TERRORIST!!
WHAT CAN I DO?
RUN AWAY? NO, THAT KIND GIRL IS WORKING IN THE NEXT ROOM!!
I CAN'T ABANDON HER HERE!!

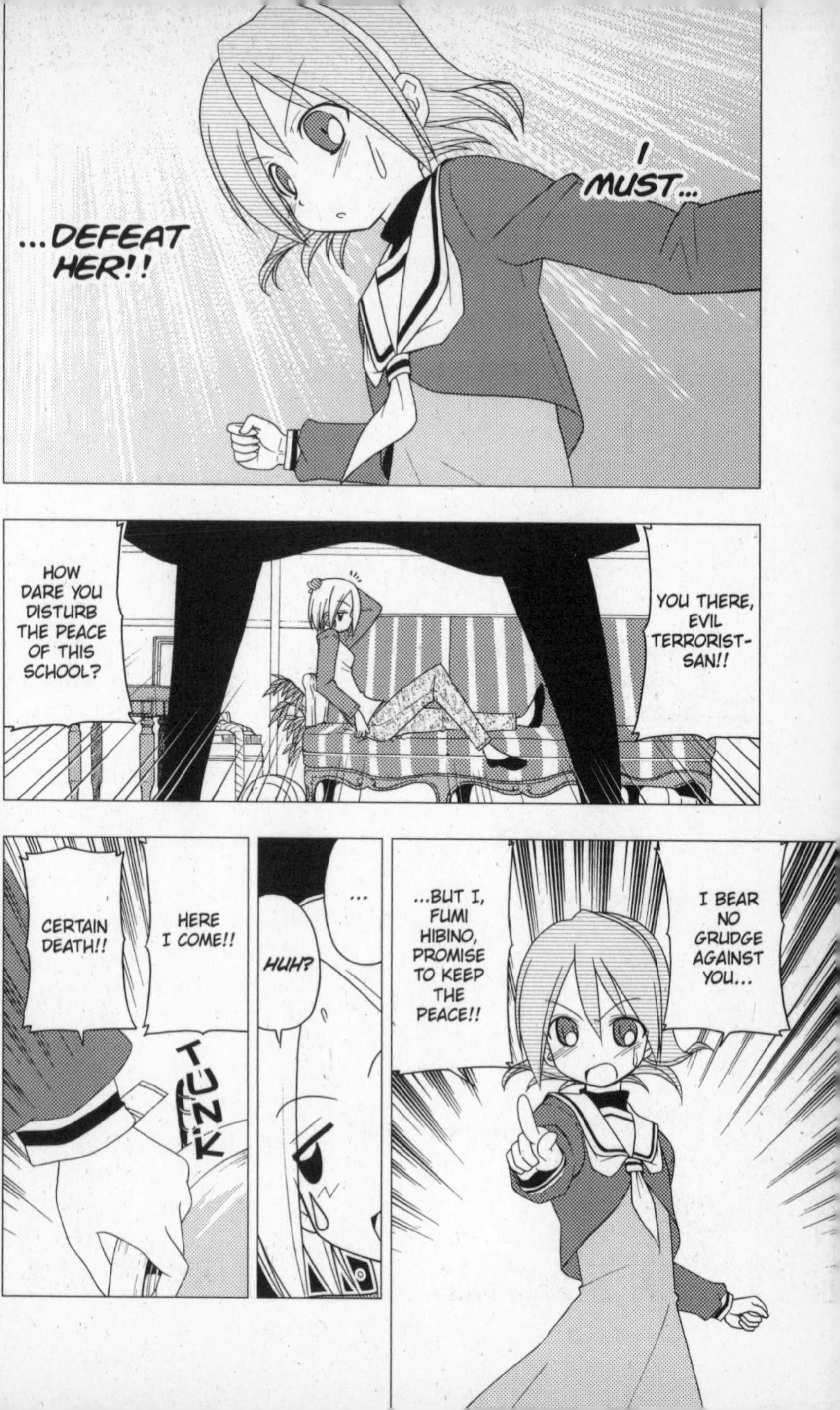
I MUST...
...DEFEAT HER!!
YOU THERE, EVIL TERRORIST-SAN!!
HOW DARE YOU DISTURB THE PEACE OF THIS SCHOOL?
I BEAR NO GRUDGE AGAINST YOU...
...BUT I, FUMI HIBINO, PROMISE TO KEEP THE PEACE!!
...
HUH?
HERE I COME!!
CERTAIN DEATH!!
TUNK

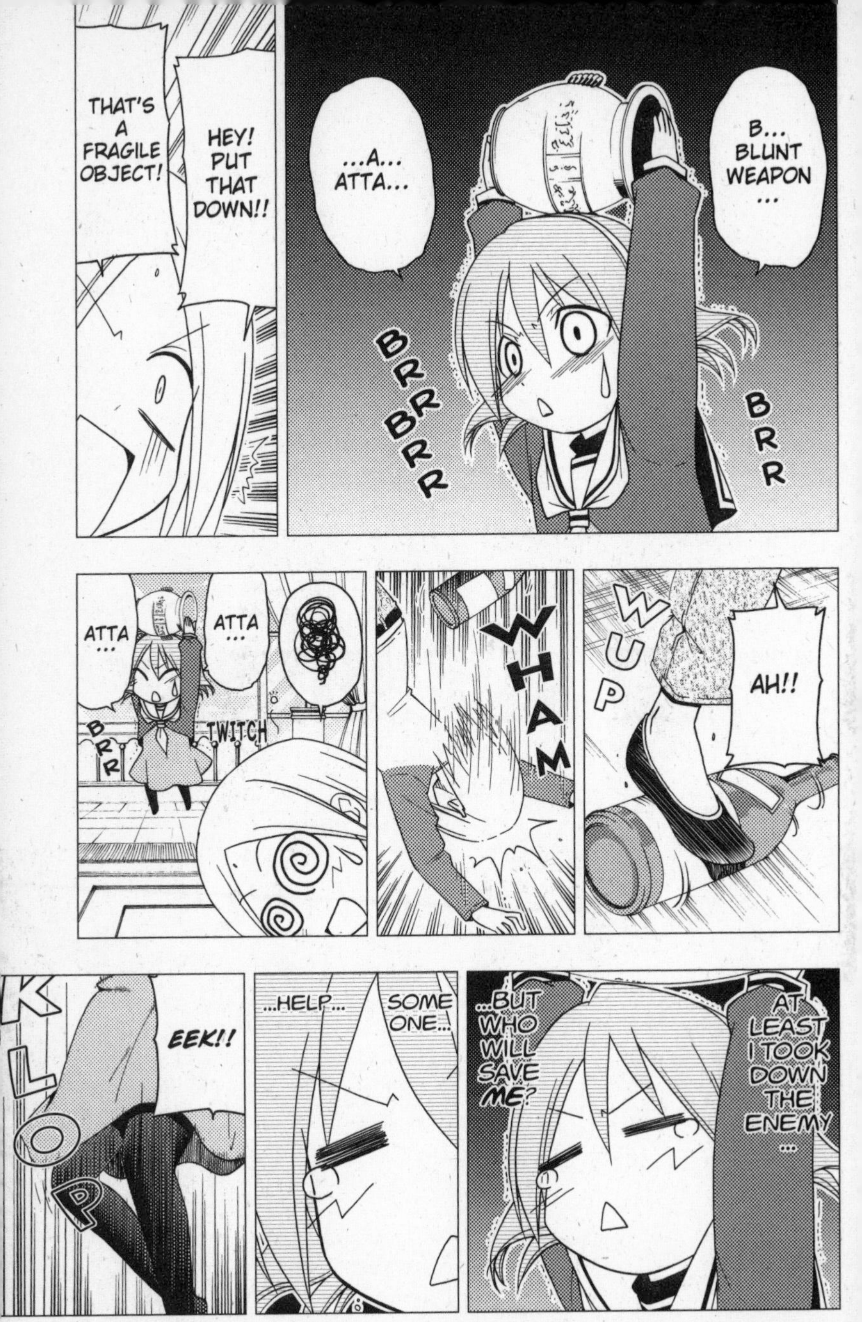
B... BLUNT WEAPON ...
...A... ATTA...
BRR
BRRRRR
HEY! PUT THAT DOWN!!
THAT'S A FRAGILE OBJECT!
WUP
AH!!
WHAM
ATTA ...
ATTA ...
BRR
TWITCH
AT LEAST I TOOK DOWN THE ENEMY ...
...BUT WHO WILL SAVE ME?
SOME ONE...
...HELP...
EEK!!
KLLOP

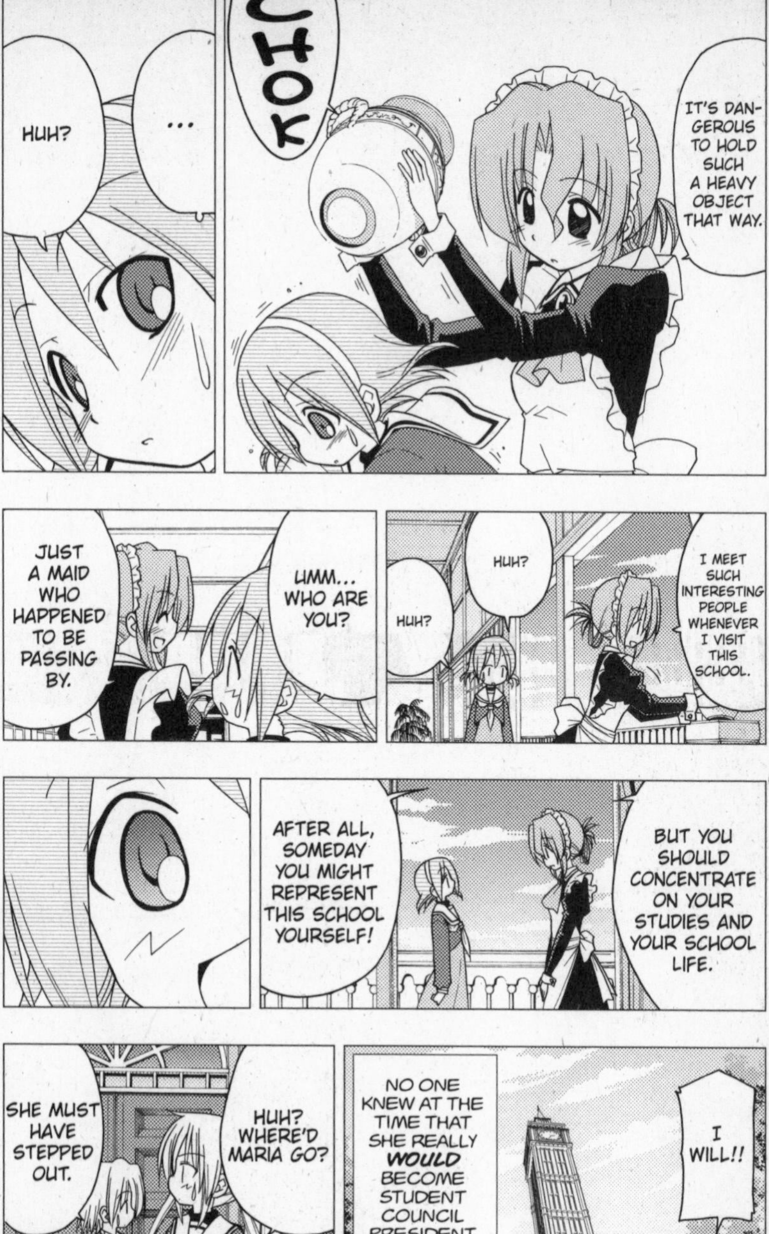
IT'S DANGEROUS TO HOLD SUCH A HEAVY OBJECT THAT WAY.
CHOK
...
HUH?
I MEET SUCH INTERESTING PEOPLE WHENEVER I VISIT THIS SCHOOL.
HUH?
HUH?
UMM... WHO ARE YOU?
JUST A MAID WHO HAPPENED TO BE PASSING BY.
BUT YOU SHOULD CONCENTRATE ON YOUR STUDIES AND YOUR SCHOOL LIFE.
AFTER ALL, SOMEDAY YOU MIGHT REPRESENT THIS SCHOOL YOURSELF!
I WILL!!
NO ONE KNEW AT THE TIME THAT SHE REALLY ***WOULD*** BECOME STUDENT COUNCIL PRESIDENT SOMEDAY...
HUH? WHERE'D MARIA GO?
SHE MUST HAVE STEPPED OUT.

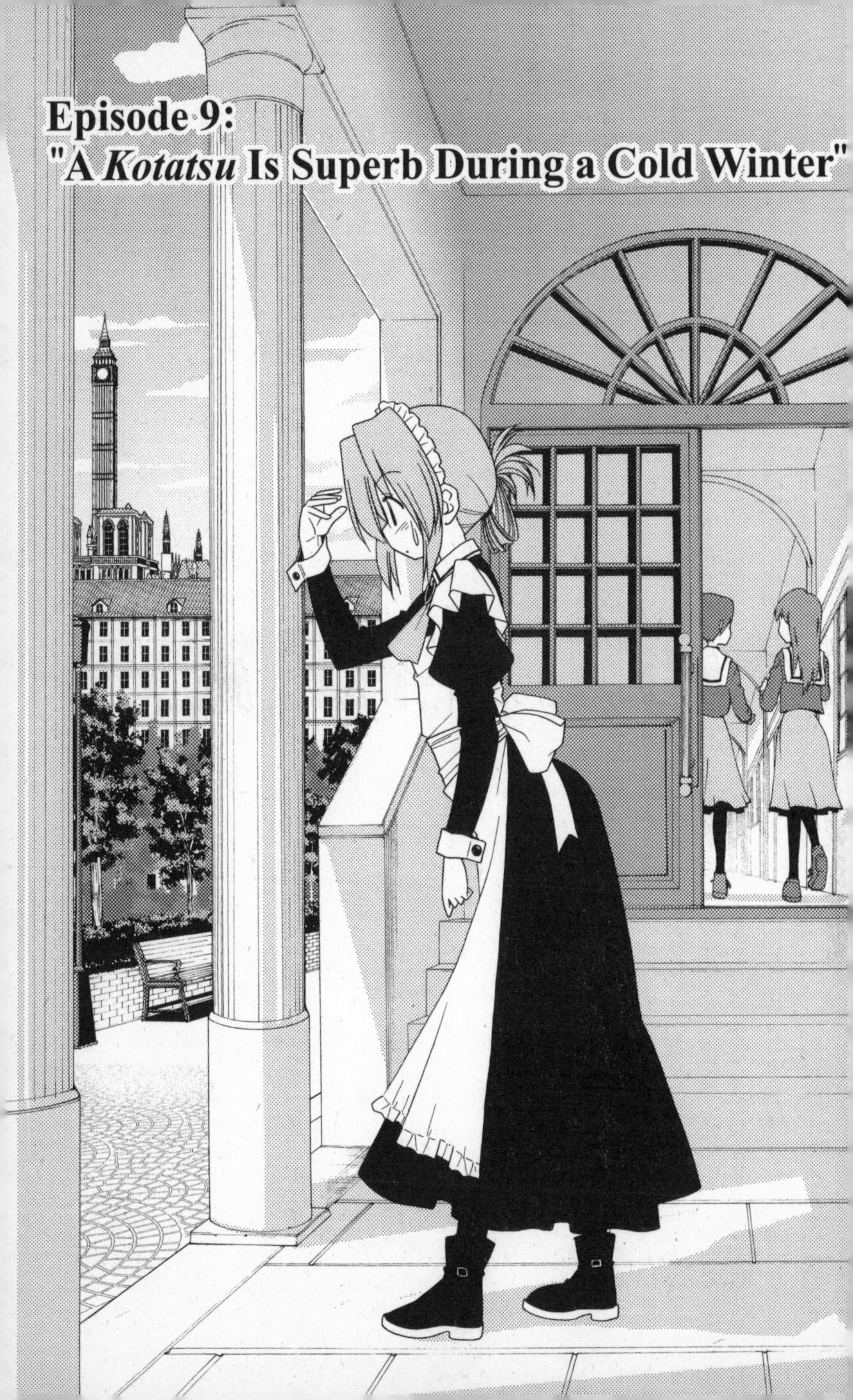
Episode 9:
"A *Kotatsu* Is Superb During a Cold Winter"

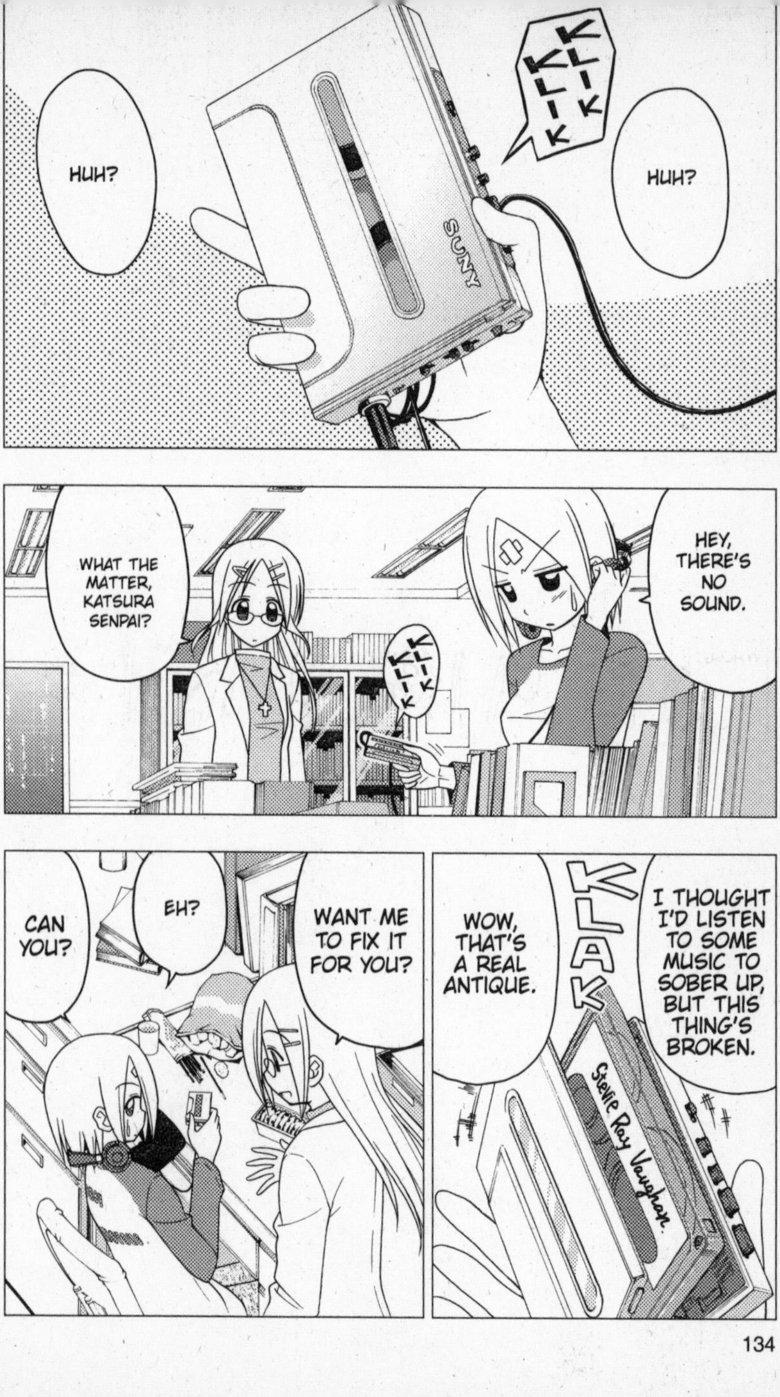
KLIK KLIK
HUH?
HUH?
HEY, THERE'S NO SOUND.
KLIK KLIK
WHAT THE MATTER, KATSURA SENPAI?
I THOUGHT I'D LISTEN TO SOME MUSIC TO SOBER UP, BUT THIS THING'S BROKEN.
KLAK
WOW, THAT'S A REAL ANTIQUE.
Stevie Ray Vaughan.
WANT ME TO FIX IT FOR YOU?
EH?
CAN YOU?

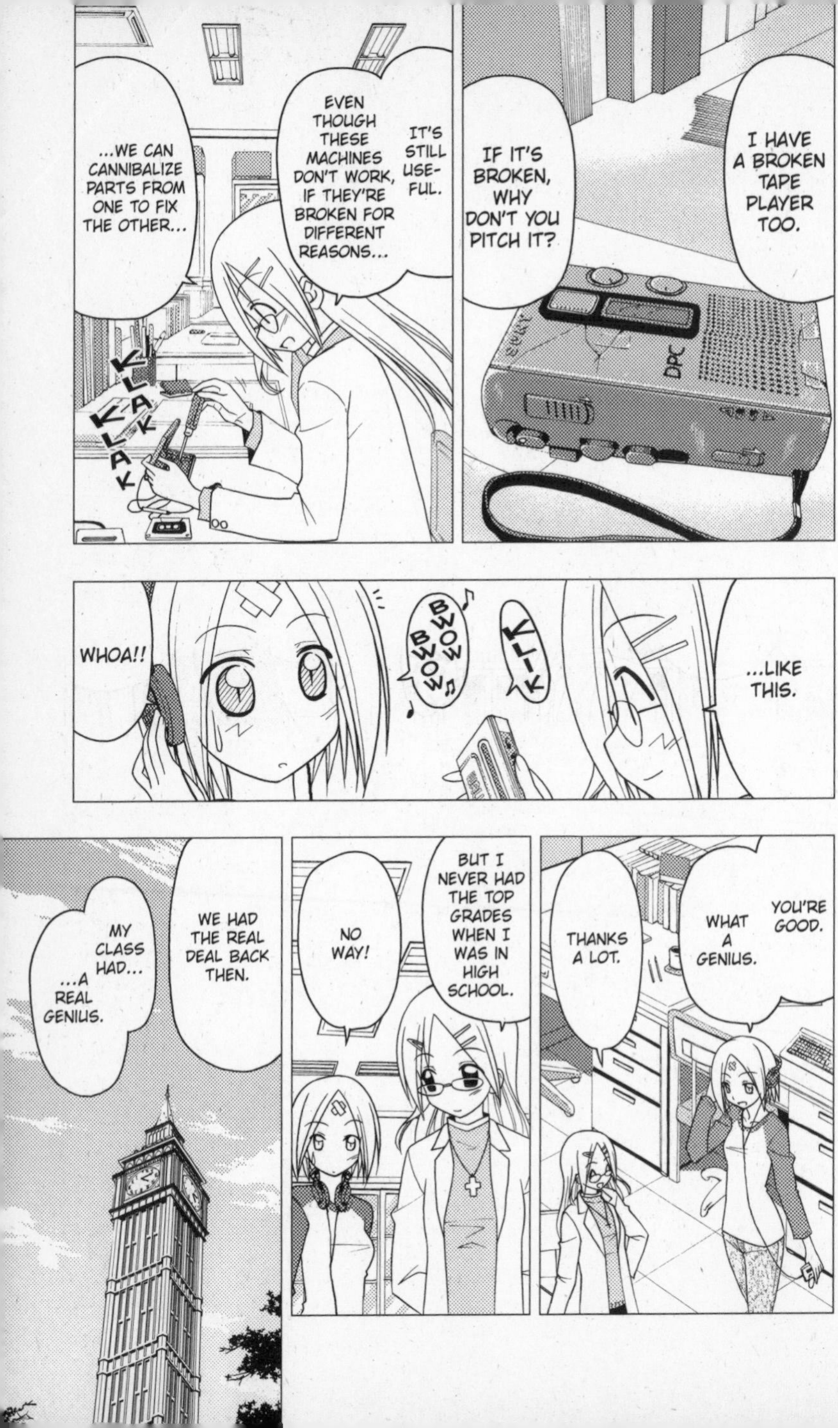
I HAVE A BROKEN TAPE PLAYER TOO.
IF IT'S BROKEN, WHY DON'T YOU PITCH IT?
IT'S STILL USE-FUL.
EVEN THOUGH THESE MACHINES DON'T WORK, IF THEY'RE BROKEN FOR DIFFERENT REASONS...
...WE CAN CANNIBALIZE PARTS FROM ONE TO FIX THE OTHER...
KLAK KLAK
KLAK
...LIKE THIS.
KLIK
BWOW BWOW
WHOA!!
YOU'RE GOOD.
WHAT A GENIUS.
THANKS A LOT.
BUT I NEVER HAD THE TOP GRADES WHEN I WAS IN HIGH SCHOOL.
NO WAY!
WE HAD THE REAL DEAL BACK THEN.
MY CLASS HAD...
...A REAL GENIUS.

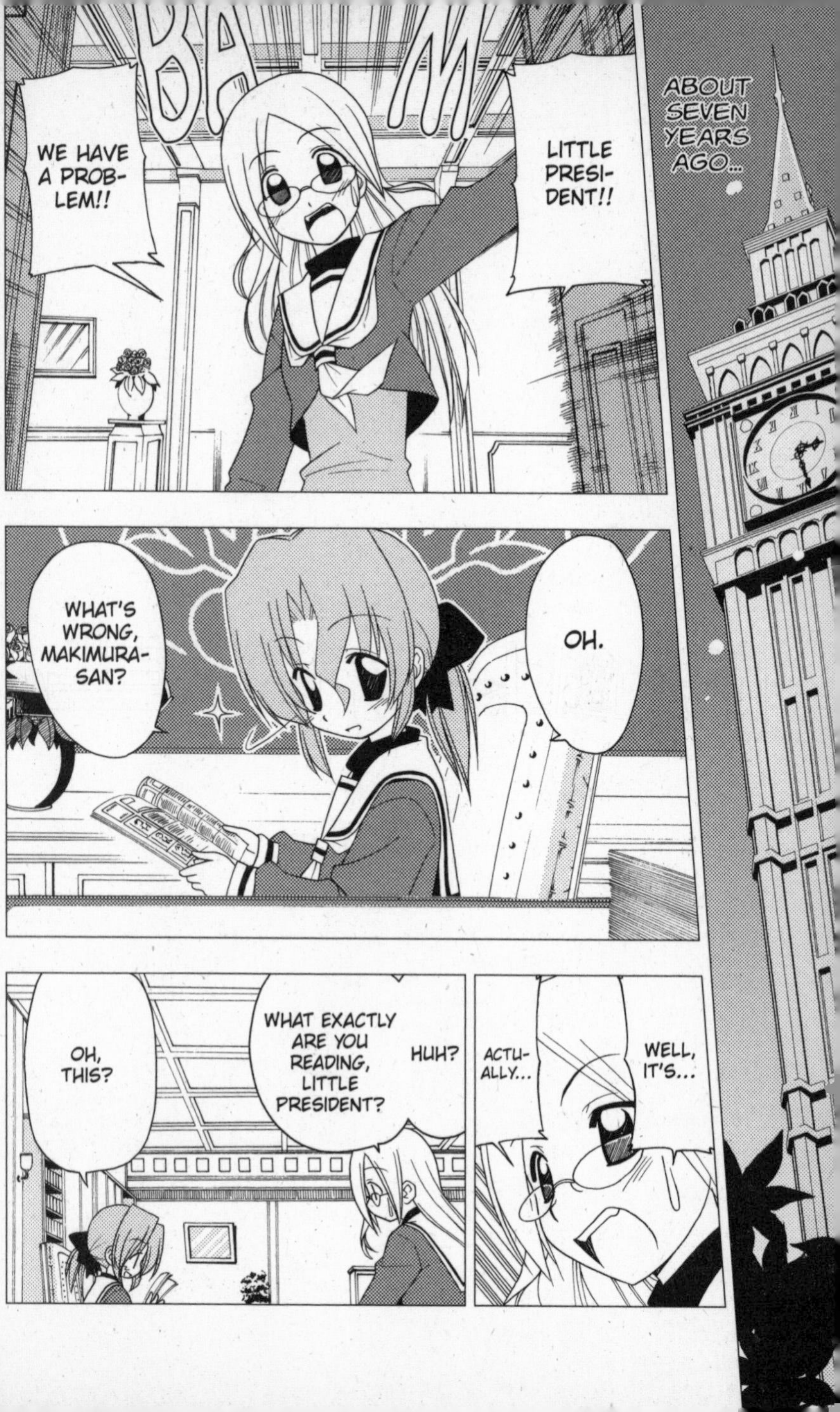
ABOUT SEVEN YEARS AGO...
BAM
LITTLE PRESIDENT!!
WE HAVE A PROBLEM!!
OH.
WHAT'S WRONG, MAKIMURA-SAN?
WELL, IT'S...
ACTUALLY...
HUH?
WHAT EXACTLY ARE YOU READING, LITTLE PRESIDENT?
OH, THIS?

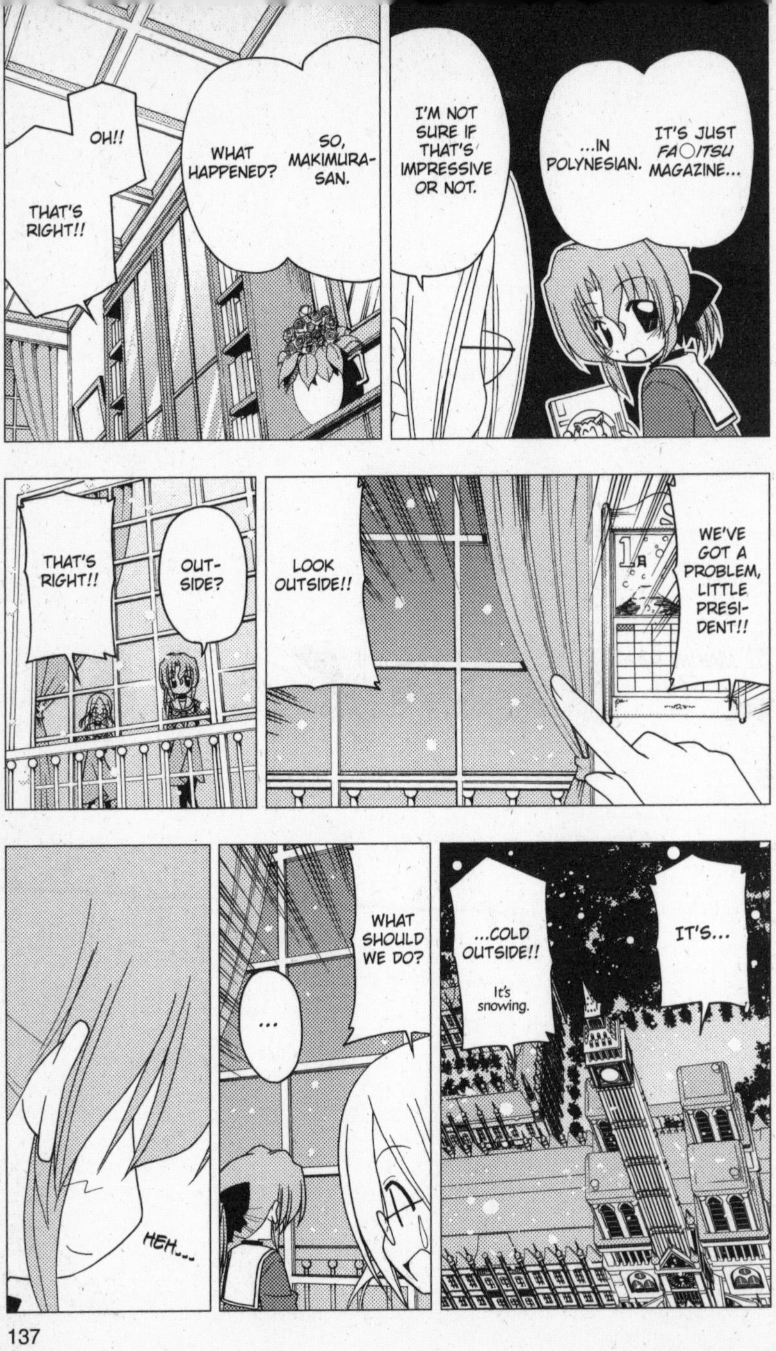
IT'S JUST FA◯ITSU MAGAZINE...
...IN POLYNESIAN.
I'M NOT SURE IF THAT'S IMPRESSIVE OR NOT.
SO, MAKIMURA-SAN.
WHAT HAPPENED?
OH!!
THAT'S RIGHT!!
WE'VE GOT A PROBLEM, LITTLE PRESIDENT!!
LOOK OUTSIDE!!
OUT-SIDE?
THAT'S RIGHT!!
IT'S...
...COLD OUTSIDE!!
It's snowing.
WHAT SHOULD WE DO?
...
HEH...

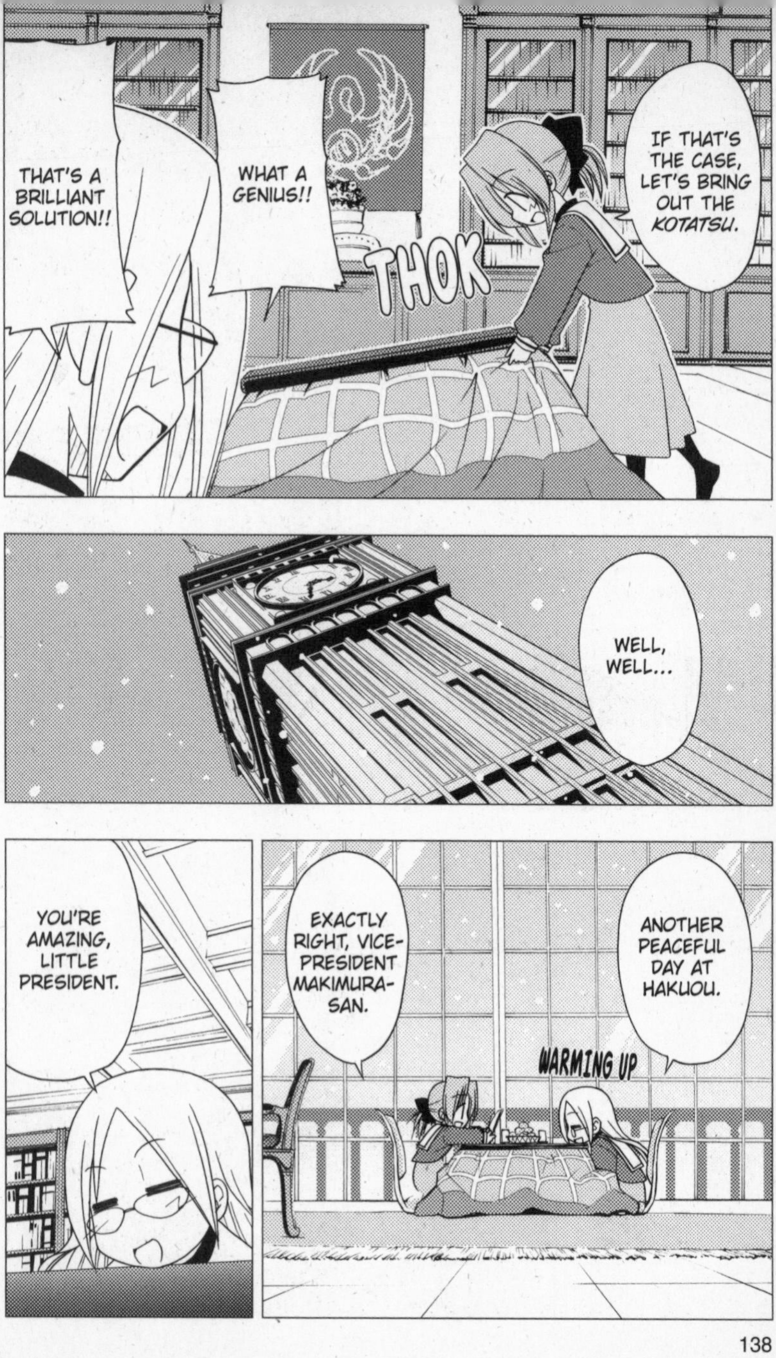
IF THAT'S THE CASE, LET'S BRING OUT THE *KOTATSU*.
THOK
WHAT A GENIUS!!
THAT'S A BRILLIANT SOLUTION!!
WELL, WELL...
ANOTHER PEACEFUL DAY AT HAKUOU.
WARMING UP
EXACTLY RIGHT, VICE-PRESIDENT MAKIMURA-SAN.
YOU'RE AMAZING, LITTLE PRESIDENT.

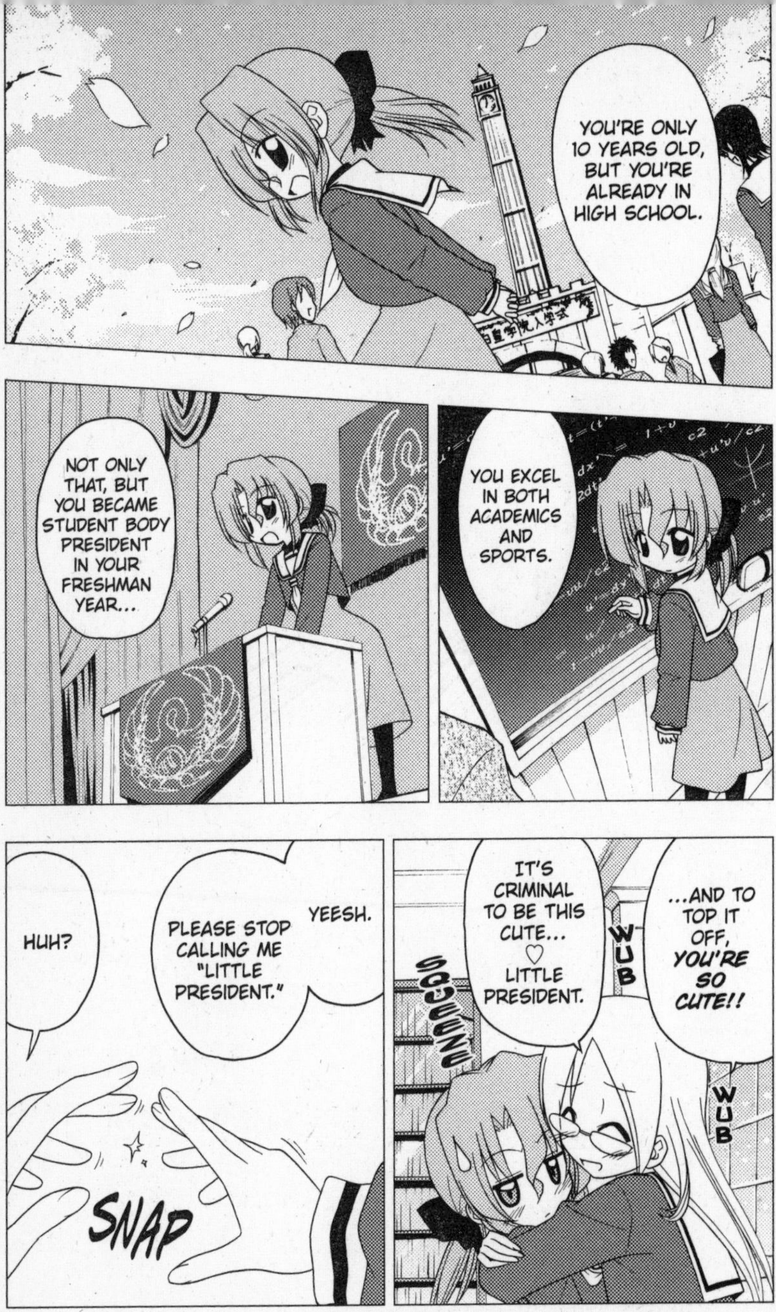
YOU'RE ONLY 10 YEARS OLD, BUT YOU'RE ALREADY IN HIGH SCHOOL.
YOU EXCEL IN BOTH ACADEMICS AND SPORTS.
NOT ONLY THAT, BUT YOU BECAME STUDENT BODY PRESIDENT IN YOUR FRESHMAN YEAR...
...AND TO TOP IT OFF, *YOU'RE SO CUTE!!*
WUB
WUB
IT'S CRIMINAL TO BE THIS CUTE... ♡ LITTLE PRESIDENT.
SQUEEZE
YEESH.
PLEASE STOP CALLING ME "LITTLE PRESIDENT."
HUH?
SNAP

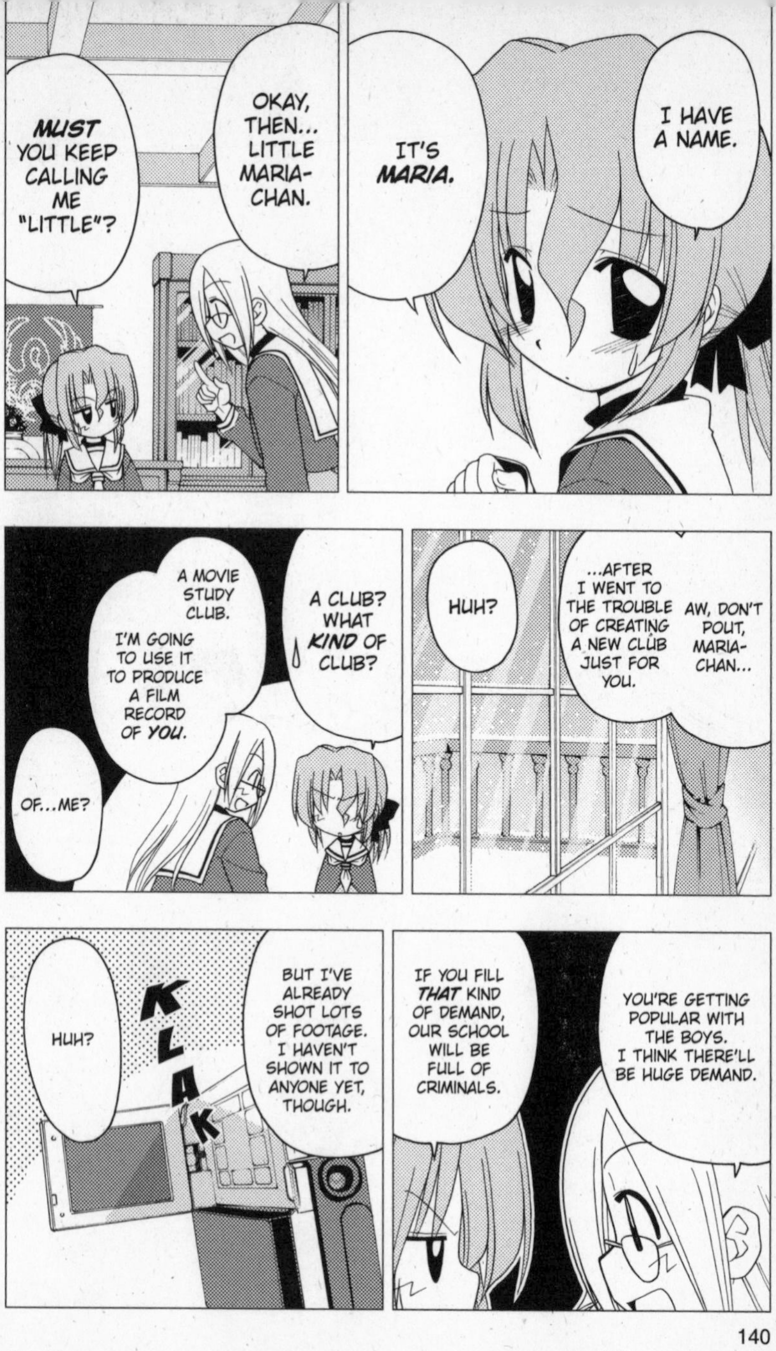
I HAVE A NAME.
IT'S MARIA.
OKAY, THEN... LITTLE MARIA-CHAN.
MUST YOU KEEP CALLING ME "LITTLE"?
AW, DON'T POUT, MARIA-CHAN...
...AFTER I WENT TO THE TROUBLE OF CREATING A NEW CLUB JUST FOR YOU.
HUH?
A CLUB? WHAT KIND OF CLUB?
A MOVIE STUDY CLUB.
I'M GOING TO USE IT TO PRODUCE A FILM RECORD OF YOU.
OF...ME?
YOU'RE GETTING POPULAR WITH THE BOYS. I THINK THERE'LL BE HUGE DEMAND.
IF YOU FILL THAT KIND OF DEMAND, OUR SCHOOL WILL BE FULL OF CRIMINALS.
BUT I'VE ALREADY SHOT LOTS OF FOOTAGE. I HAVEN'T SHOWN IT TO ANYONE YET, THOUGH.
KLAK
HUH?

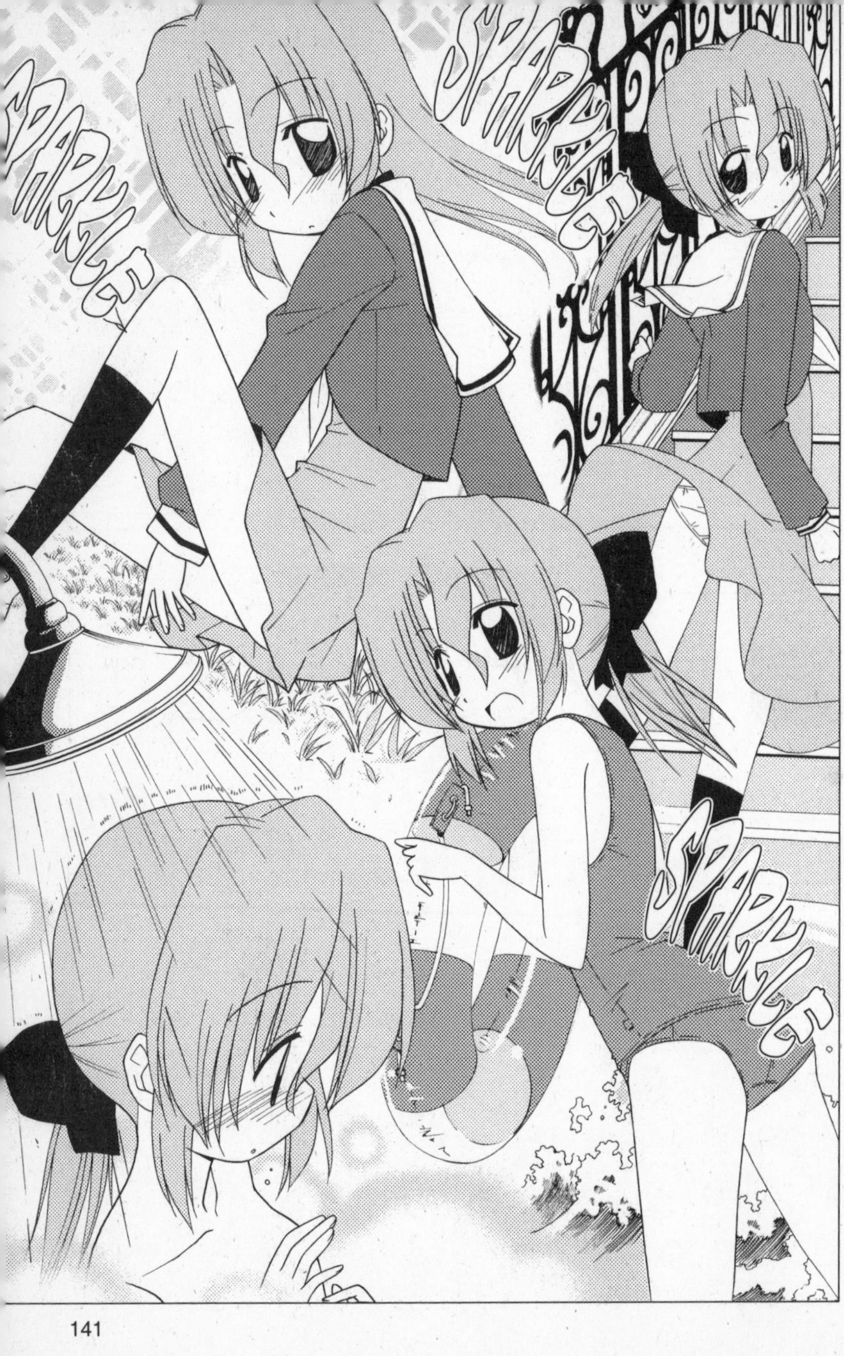
SPARKLE
SPARKLE
SPARKLE

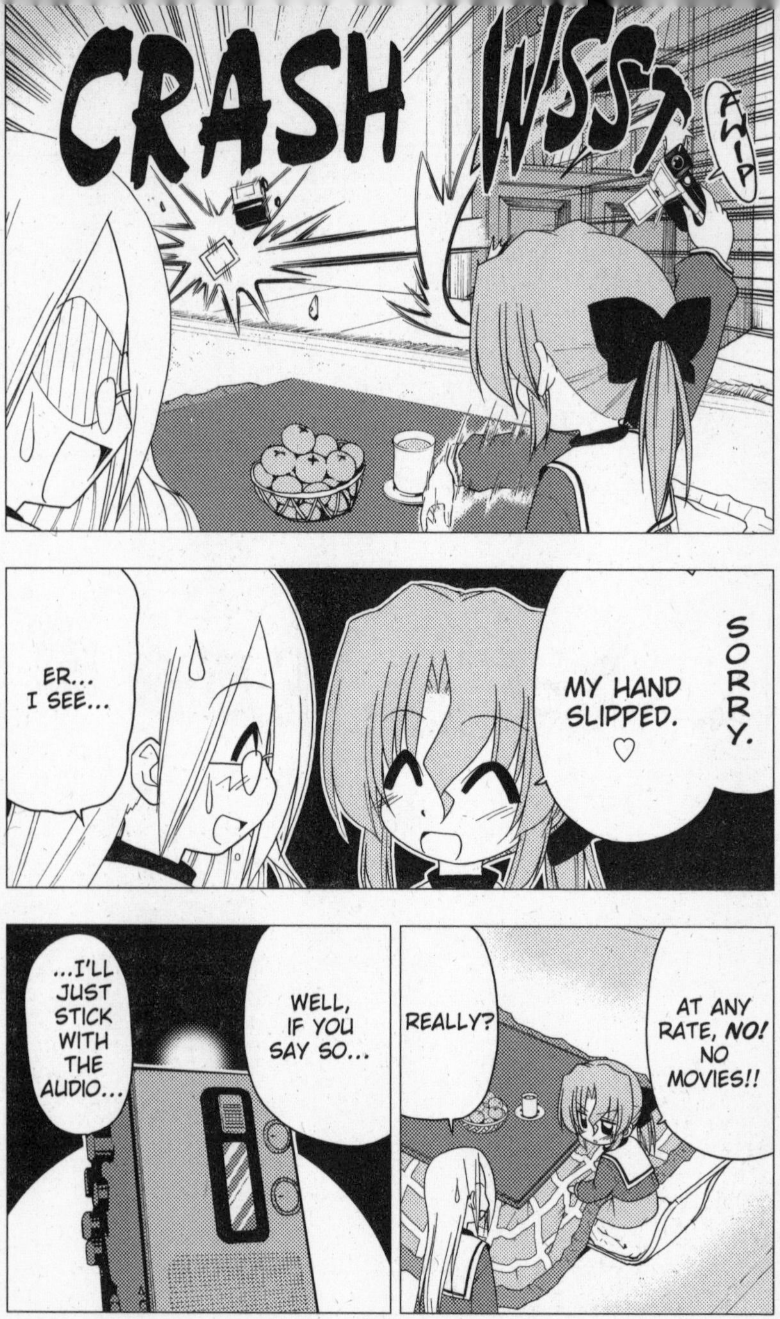
FWIP
WSST
CRASH
SORRY.
MY HAND SLIPPED. ♡
ER... I SEE...
AT ANY RATE, *NO!* NO MOVIES!!
REALLY?
WELL, IF YOU SAY SO...
...I'LL JUST STICK WITH THE AUDIO...

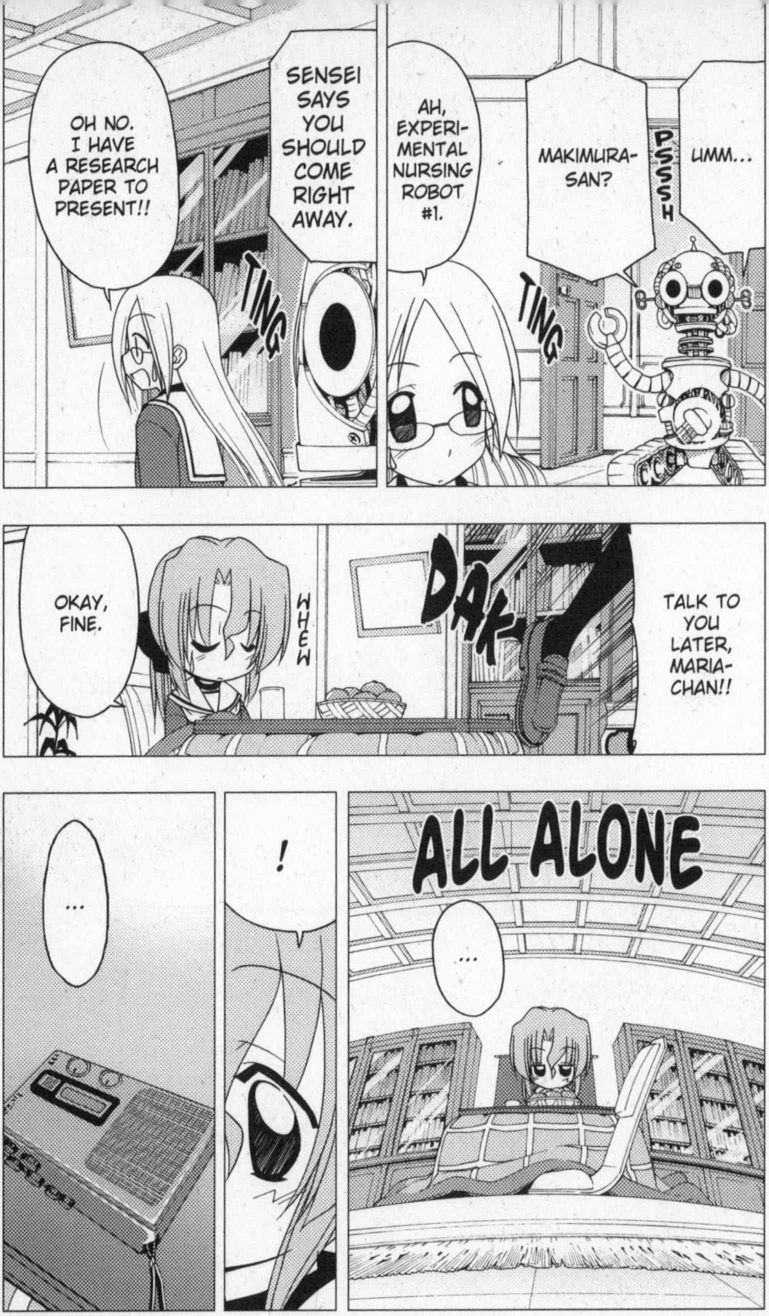
UMM...
PSSSH
MAKIMURA-SAN?
AH, EXPERIMENTAL NURSING ROBOT #1.
TING
SENSEI SAYS YOU SHOULD COME RIGHT AWAY.
TING
OH NO. I HAVE A RESEARCH PAPER TO PRESENT!!
TALK TO YOU LATER, MARIA-CHAN!!
DAK
WHEW
OKAY, FINE.
ALL ALONE
...
!
...

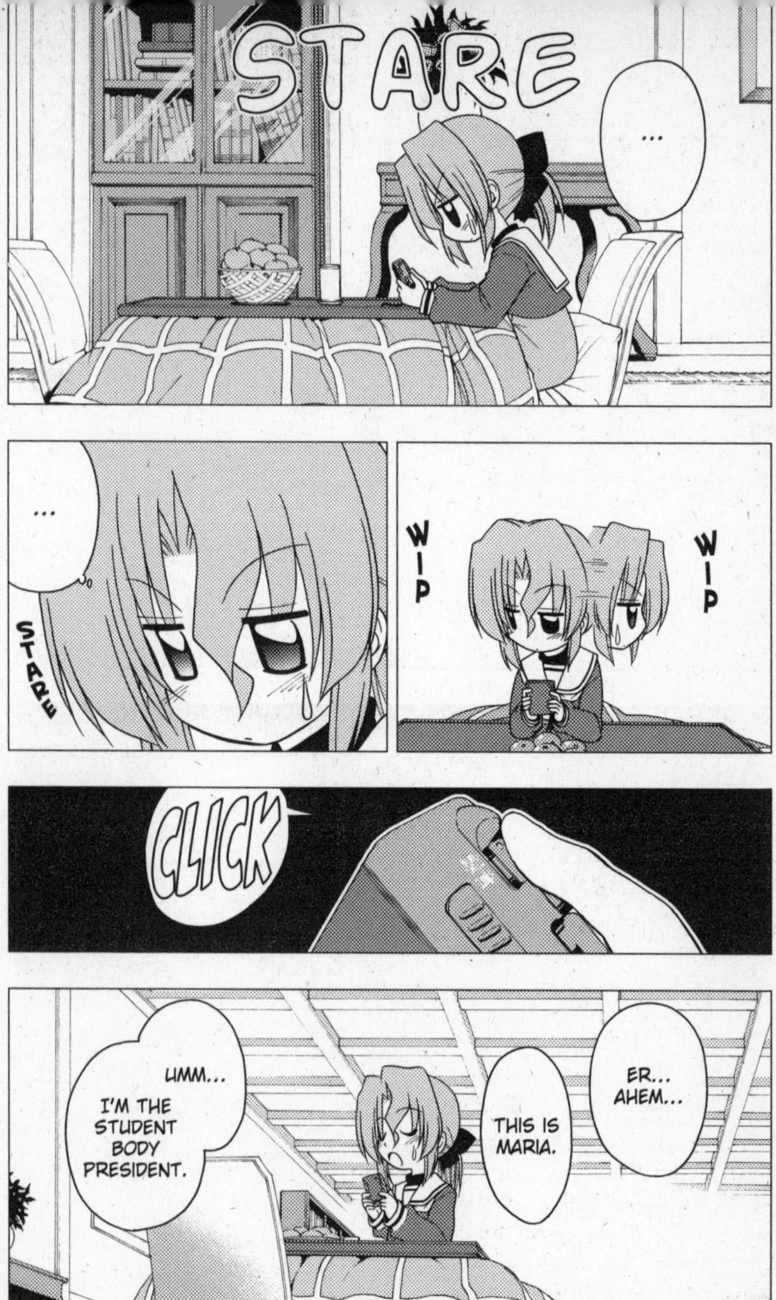
STARE
...
WIP
WIP
...
STARE
CLICK
ER... AHEM...
THIS IS MARIA.
UMM... I'M THE STUDENT BODY PRESIDENT.

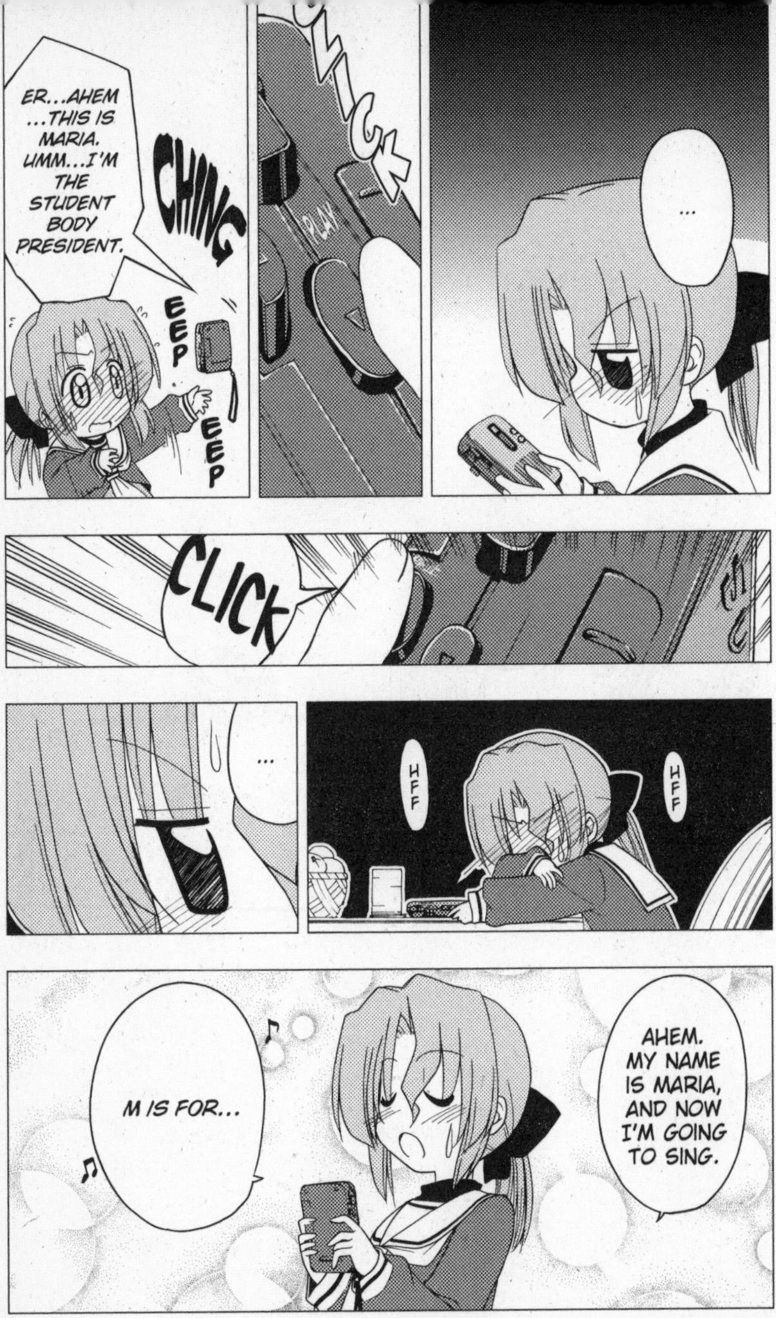
...
PLAY
ER...AHEM ...THIS IS MARIA. UMM...I'M THE STUDENT BODY PRESIDENT.
CHING
EEP EEP
EEP EEP
CLICK
HFF
HFF
...
AHEM. MY NAME IS MARIA, AND NOW I'M GOING TO SING.
M IS FOR...

AH, MARIA-CHAN, I JUST REMEM-BERED...

HFF

HFF

...

BY THE WAY...

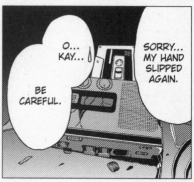

O... KAY...

BE CAREFUL.

SORRY... MY HAND SLIPPED AGAIN.

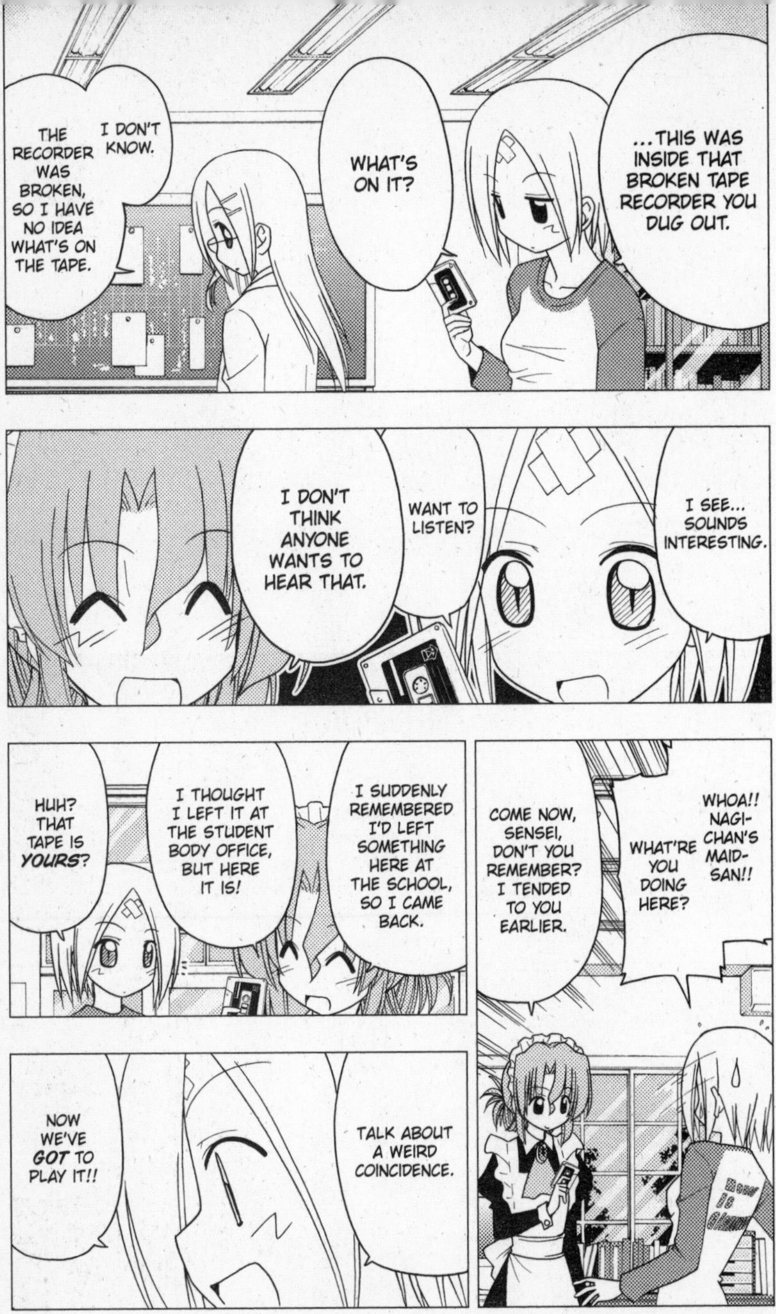
...THIS WAS INSIDE THAT BROKEN TAPE RECORDER YOU DUG OUT.
WHAT'S ON IT?
I DON'T KNOW.
THE RECORDER WAS BROKEN, SO I HAVE NO IDEA WHAT'S ON THE TAPE.
I SEE... SOUNDS INTERESTING.
WANT TO LISTEN?
I DON'T THINK ANYONE WANTS TO HEAR THAT.
WHOA!! NAGI-CHAN'S MAID-SAN!!
WHAT'RE YOU DOING HERE?
COME NOW, SENSEI, DON'T YOU REMEMBER? I TENDED TO YOU EARLIER.
I SUDDENLY REMEMBERED I'D LEFT SOMETHING HERE AT THE SCHOOL, SO I CAME BACK.
I THOUGHT I LEFT IT AT THE STUDENT BODY OFFICE, BUT HERE IT IS!
HUH? THAT TAPE IS *YOURS*?
TALK ABOUT A WEIRD COINCIDENCE.
NOW WE'VE *GOT* TO PLAY IT!!

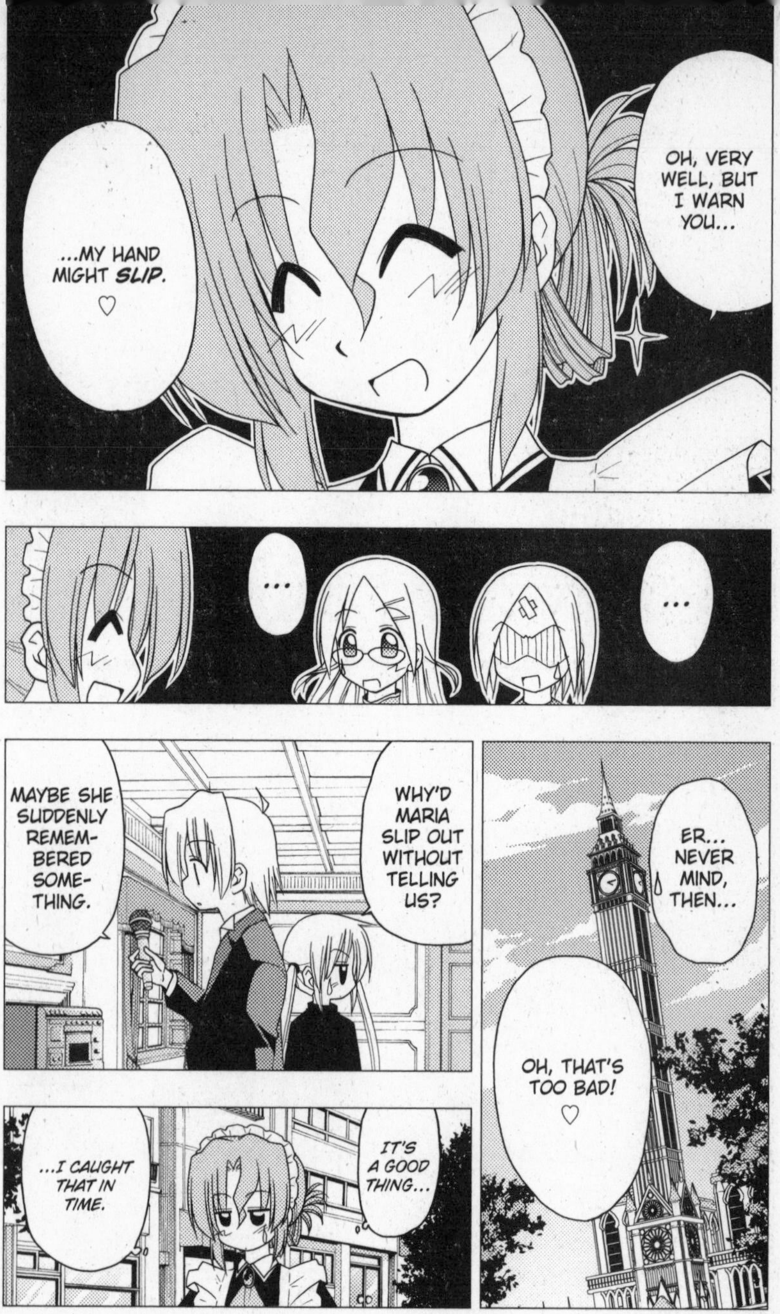

OH, VERY WELL, BUT I WARN YOU...
...MY HAND MIGHT **SLIP**. ♡
...
...
ER... NEVER MIND, THEN...
OH, THAT'S TOO BAD! ♡
WHY'D MARIA SLIP OUT WITHOUT TELLING US?
MAYBE SHE SUDDENLY REMEM-BERED SOME-THING.
IT'S A GOOD THING...
...I CAUGHT THAT IN TIME.

Episode 10: "Sure, All My *Otoshidama* Is Gone, but the Memories Will Never Fade"

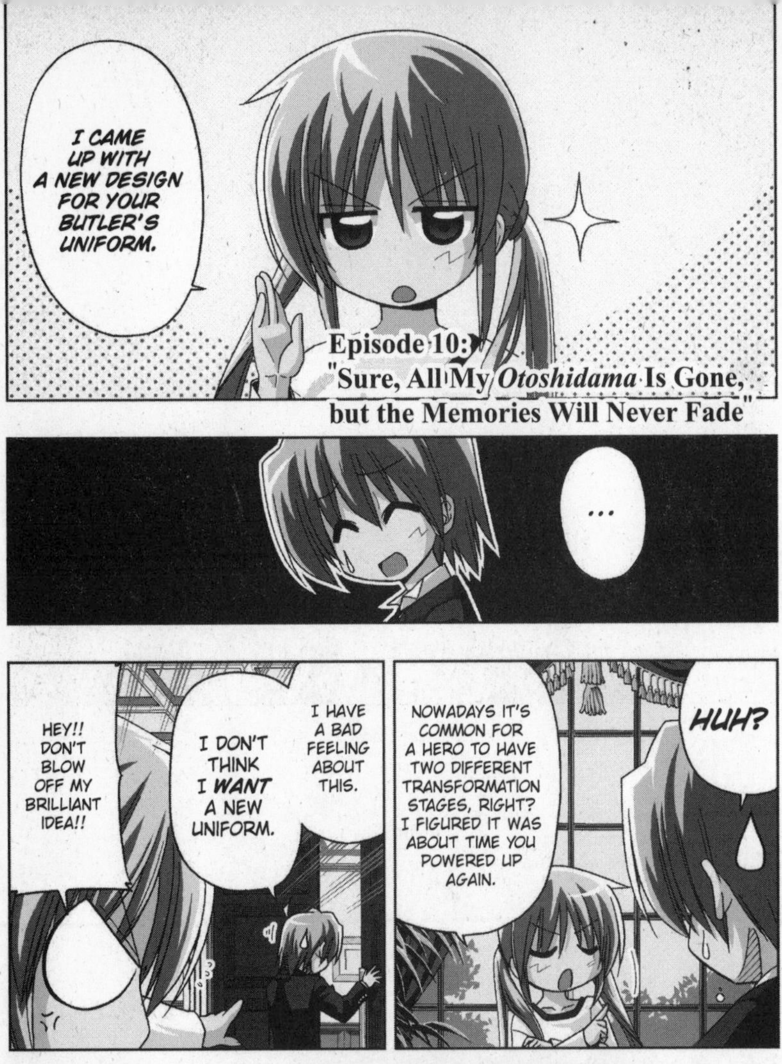
I CAME UP WITH A NEW DESIGN FOR YOUR BUTLER'S UNIFORM.
...
HUH?
NOWADAYS IT'S COMMON FOR A HERO TO HAVE TWO DIFFERENT TRANSFORMATION STAGES, RIGHT? I FIGURED IT WAS ABOUT TIME YOU POWERED UP AGAIN.
I HAVE A BAD FEELING ABOUT THIS.
I DON'T THINK I *WANT* A NEW UNIFORM.
HEY!! DON'T BLOW OFF MY BRILLIANT IDEA!!
IT'S GOING TO BE A MAID UNIFORM OR A SAILOR SUIT WITH A MINISKIRT OR SOMETHING, ISN'T IT?
NO, I'M SERIOUS! ALTHOUGH THOSE *ARE* GOOD IDEAS...
KYAAA!!

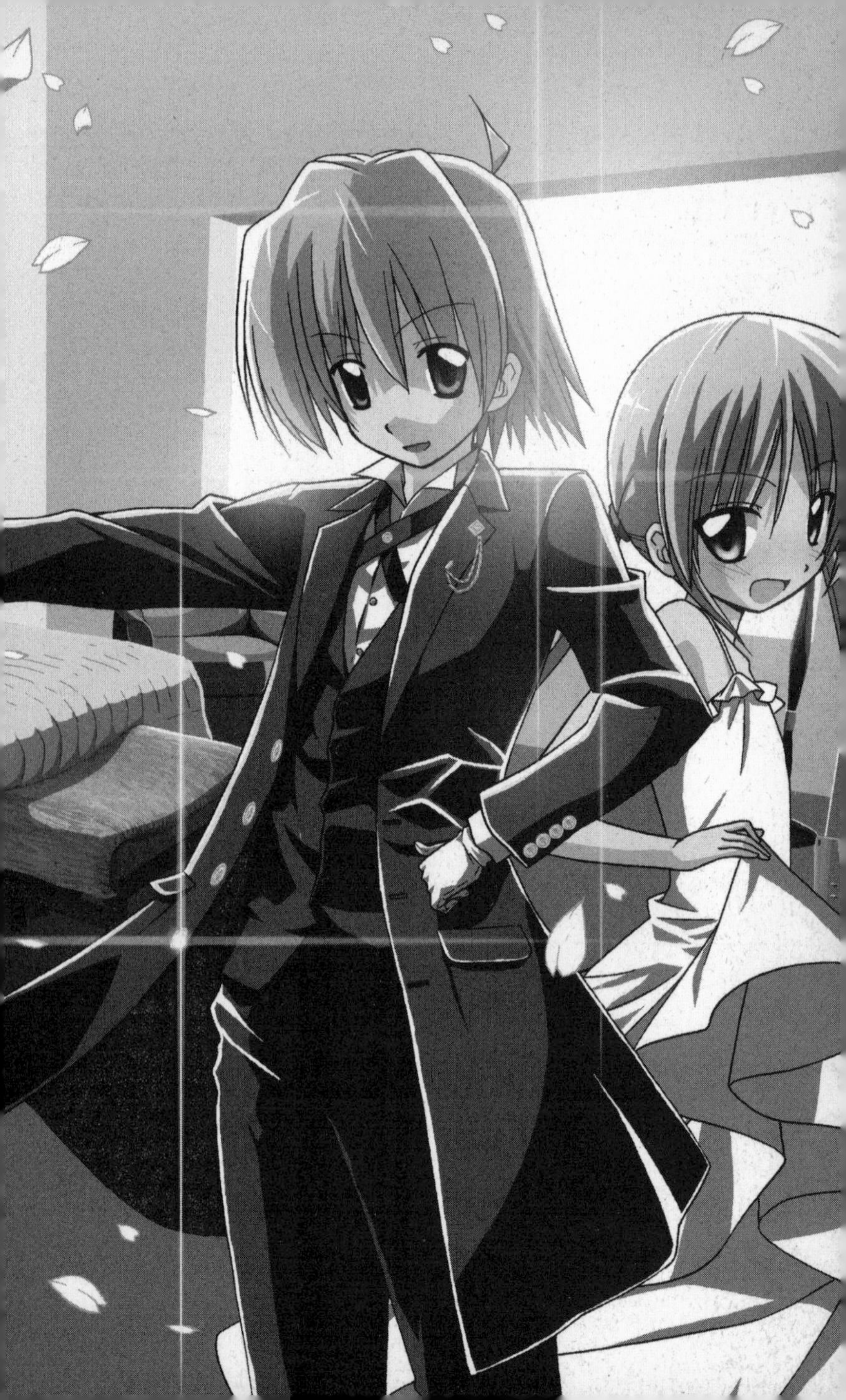

Episode 10:
"Sure, All My *Otoshidama* Is Gone, but the Memories Will Never Fade"

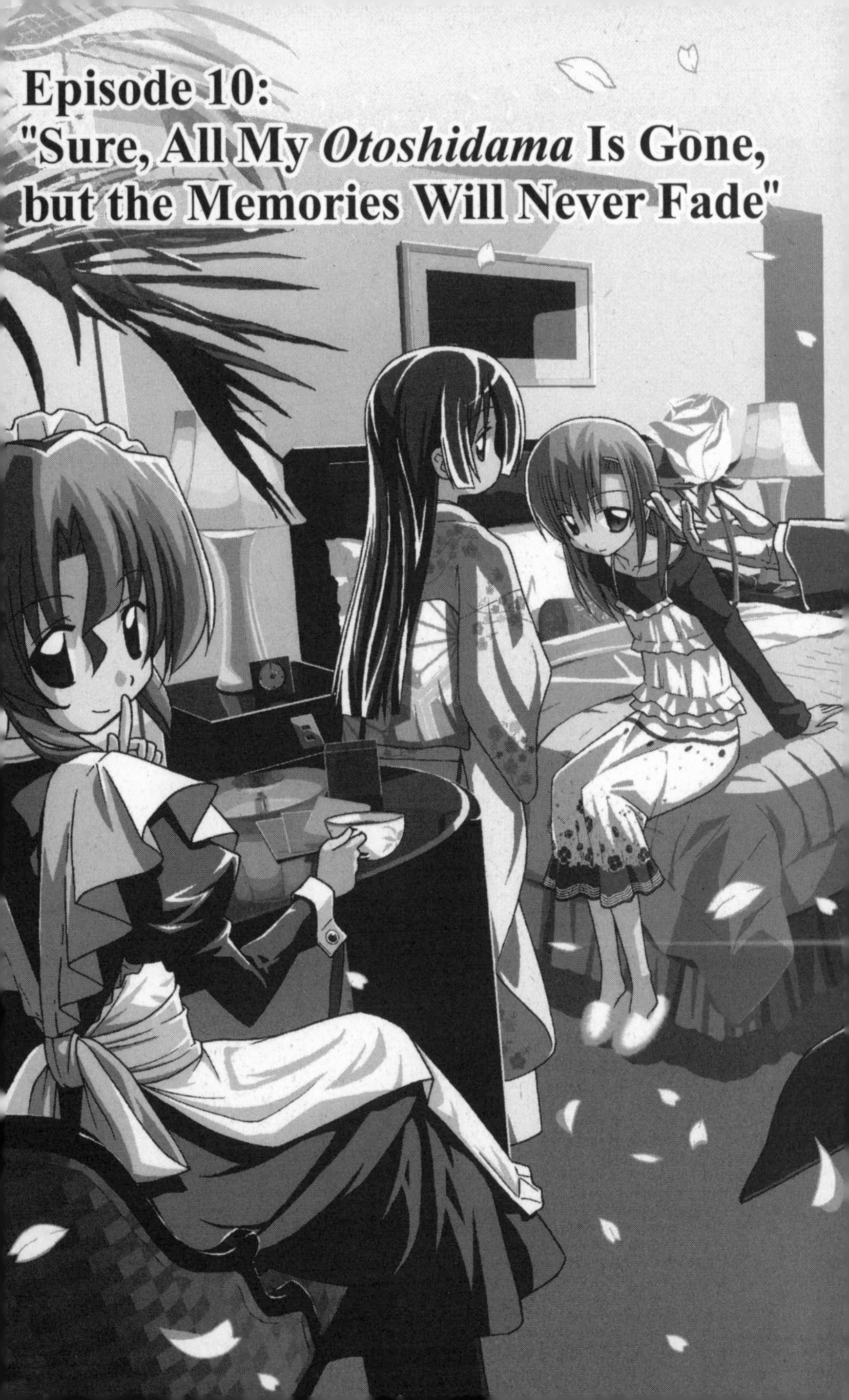

ハヤテのごとく!
Hayate the combat butler

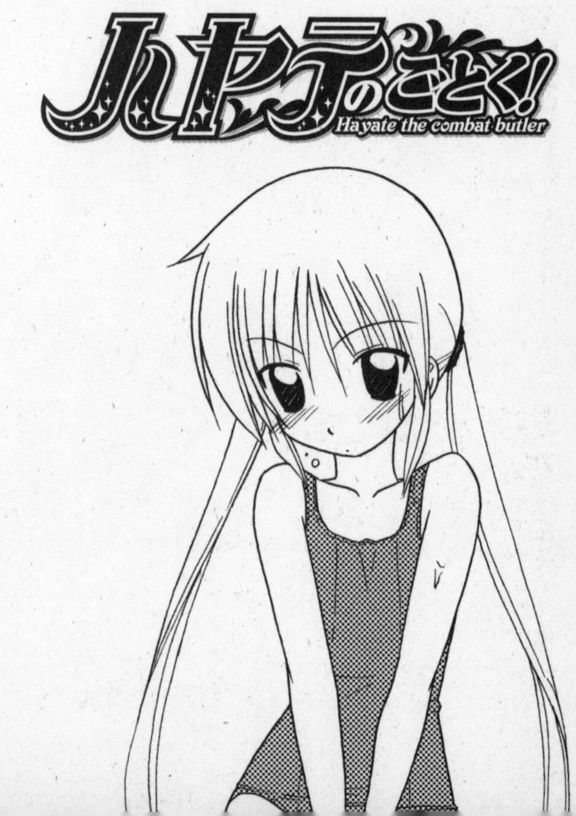

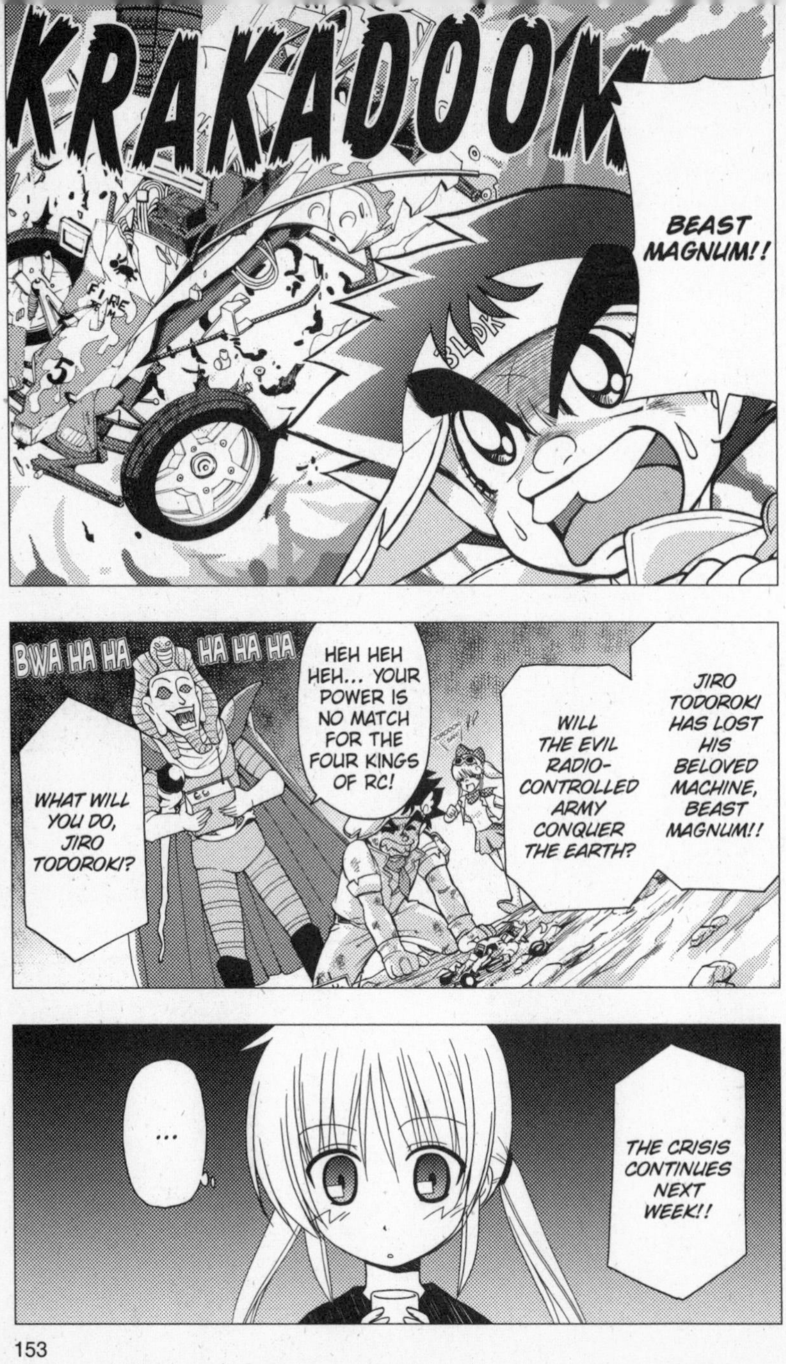
KRAKADOOOM
BEAST MAGNUM!!
JIRO TODOROKI HAS LOST HIS BELOVED MACHINE, BEAST MAGNUM!!
WILL THE EVIL RADIO-CONTROLLED ARMY CONQUER THE EARTH?
HEH HEH HEH... YOUR POWER IS NO MATCH FOR THE FOUR KINGS OF RC!
HA HA HA
BWA HA HA
WHAT WILL YOU DO, JIRO TODOROKI?
THE CRISIS CONTINUES NEXT WEEK!!
...

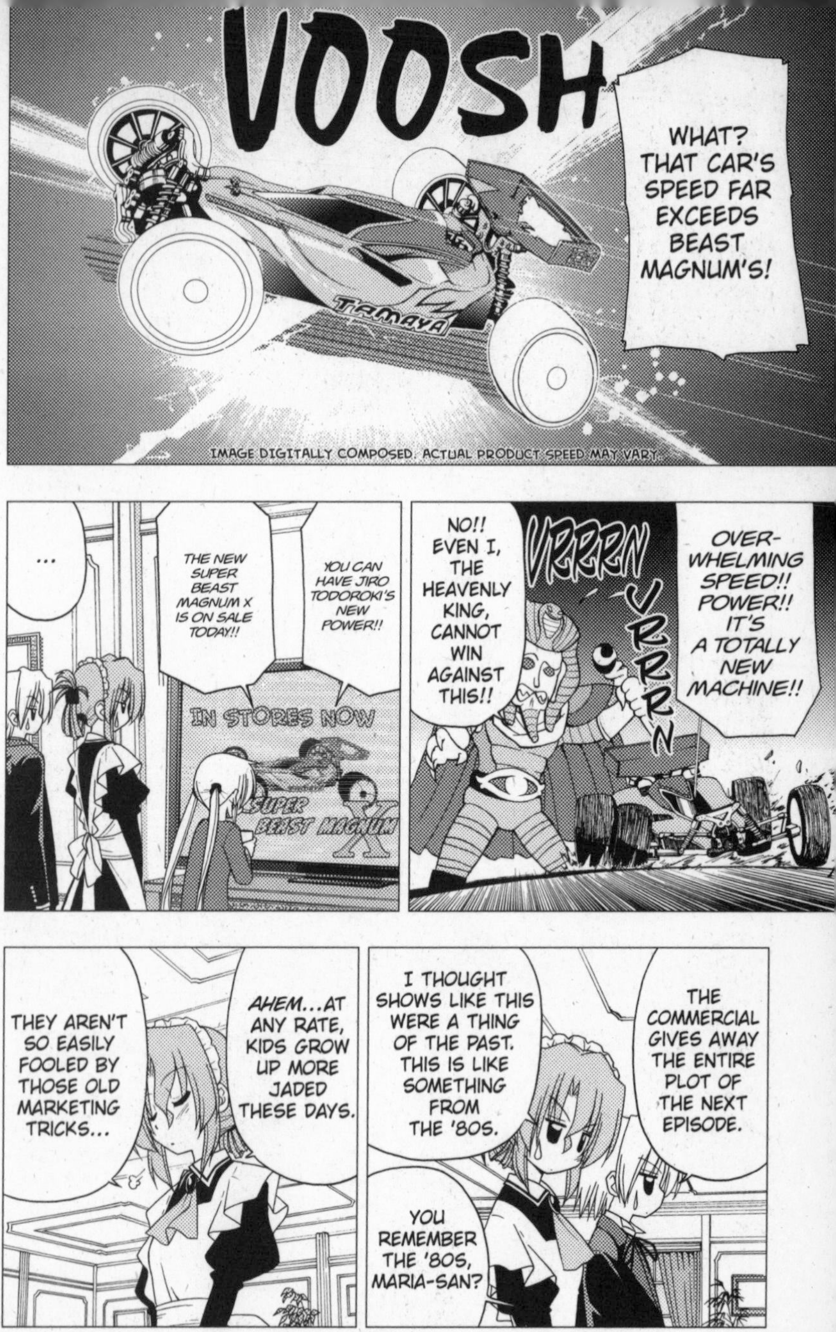
VOOSH
WHAT? THAT CAR'S SPEED FAR EXCEEDS BEAST MAGNUM'S!
TAMAYA
IMAGE DIGITALLY COMPOSED. ACTUAL PRODUCT SPEED MAY VARY.
OVER-WHELMING SPEED!! POWER!! IT'S A TOTALLY NEW MACHINE!!
VRRRN
VRRRN
NO!! EVEN I, THE HEAVENLY KING, CANNOT WIN AGAINST THIS!!
YOU CAN HAVE JIRO TODOROKI'S NEW POWER!!
THE NEW SUPER BEAST MAGNUM X IS ON SALE TODAY!!
IN STORES NOW
SUPER BEAST MAGNUM X
...
THE COMMERCIAL GIVES AWAY THE ENTIRE PLOT OF THE NEXT EPISODE.
I THOUGHT SHOWS LIKE THIS WERE A THING OF THE PAST. THIS IS LIKE SOMETHING FROM THE '80S.
YOU REMEMBER THE '80S, MARIA-SAN?
AHEM...AT ANY RATE, KIDS GROW UP MORE JADED THESE DAYS.
THEY AREN'T SO EASILY FOOLED BY THOSE OLD MARKETING TRICKS...

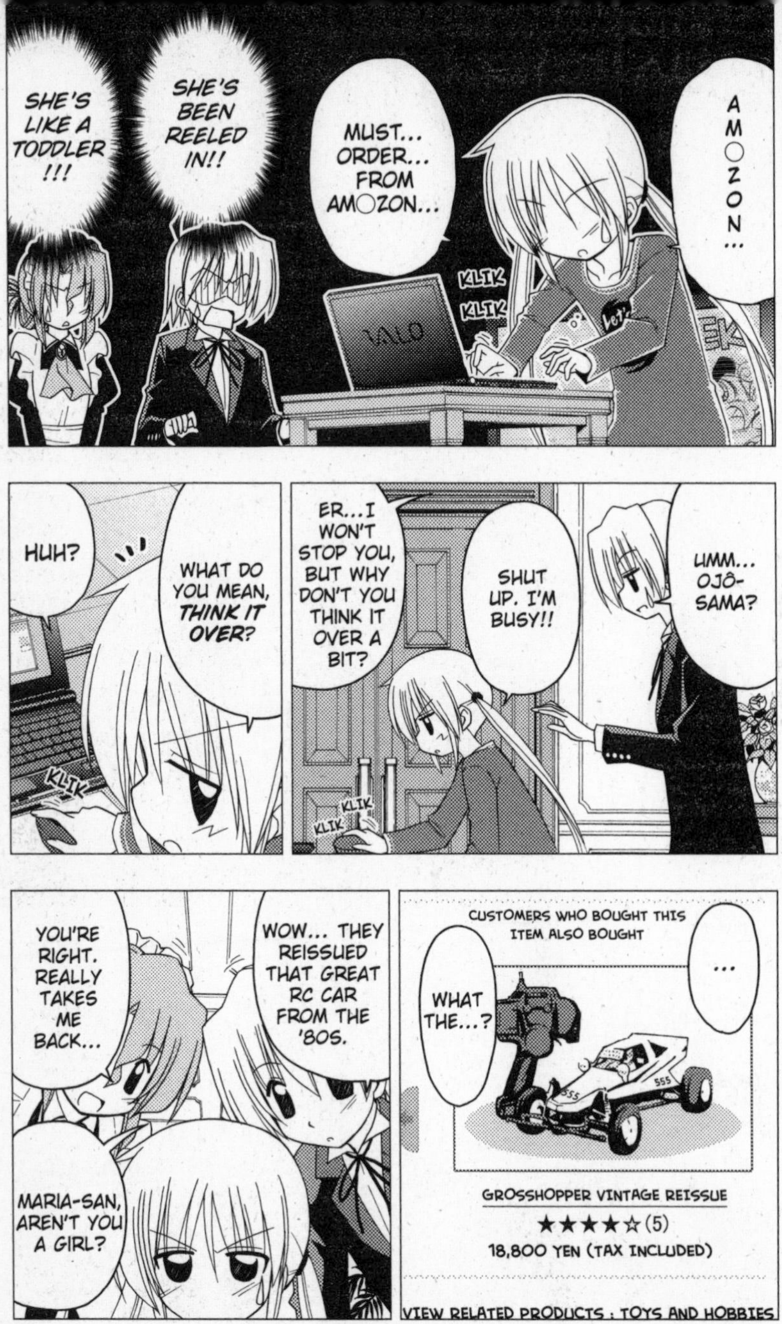
AM○ZON...
MUST... ORDER... FROM AM○ZON...
KLIK KLIK
SHE'S BEEN REELED IN!!
SHE'S LIKE A TODDLER!!!
UMM... OJÔ-SAMA?
SHUT UP. I'M BUSY!!
ER...I WON'T STOP YOU, BUT WHY DON'T YOU THINK IT OVER A BIT?
KLIK KLIK
WHAT DO YOU MEAN, THINK IT OVER?
HUH?
KLIK
CUSTOMERS WHO BOUGHT THIS ITEM ALSO BOUGHT
...
WHAT THE...?
GROSSHOPPER VINTAGE REISSUE
★★★★☆ (5)
18,800 YEN (TAX INCLUDED)
VIEW RELATED PRODUCTS : TOYS AND HOBBIES
WOW... THEY REISSUED THAT GREAT RC CAR FROM THE '80S.
YOU'RE RIGHT. REALLY TAKES ME BACK...
MARIA-SAN, AREN'T YOU A GIRL?

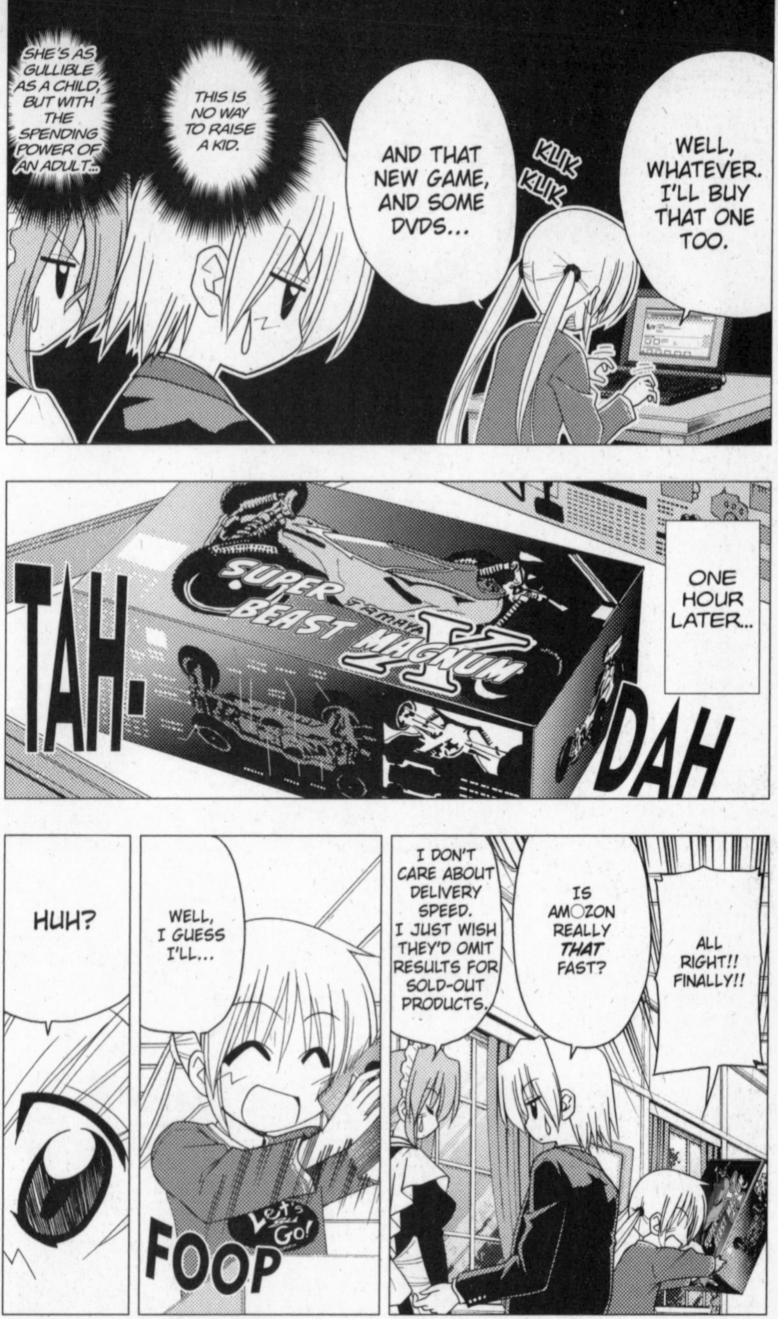

WELL, WHATEVER. I'LL BUY THAT ONE TOO.
KLIK KLIK
AND THAT NEW GAME, AND SOME DVDS...
THIS IS NO WAY TO RAISE A KID.
SHE'S AS GULLIBLE AS A CHILD, BUT WITH THE SPENDING POWER OF AN ADULT...
ONE HOUR LATER...
TAH-
DAH
SUPER BEAST MAGNUM X
TAMAYA
ALL RIGHT!! FINALLY!!
IS AM○ZON REALLY *THAT* FAST?
I DON'T CARE ABOUT DELIVERY SPEED. I JUST WISH THEY'D OMIT RESULTS FOR SOLD-OUT PRODUCTS.
WELL, I GUESS I'LL...
Let's Go!
FOOP
HUH?

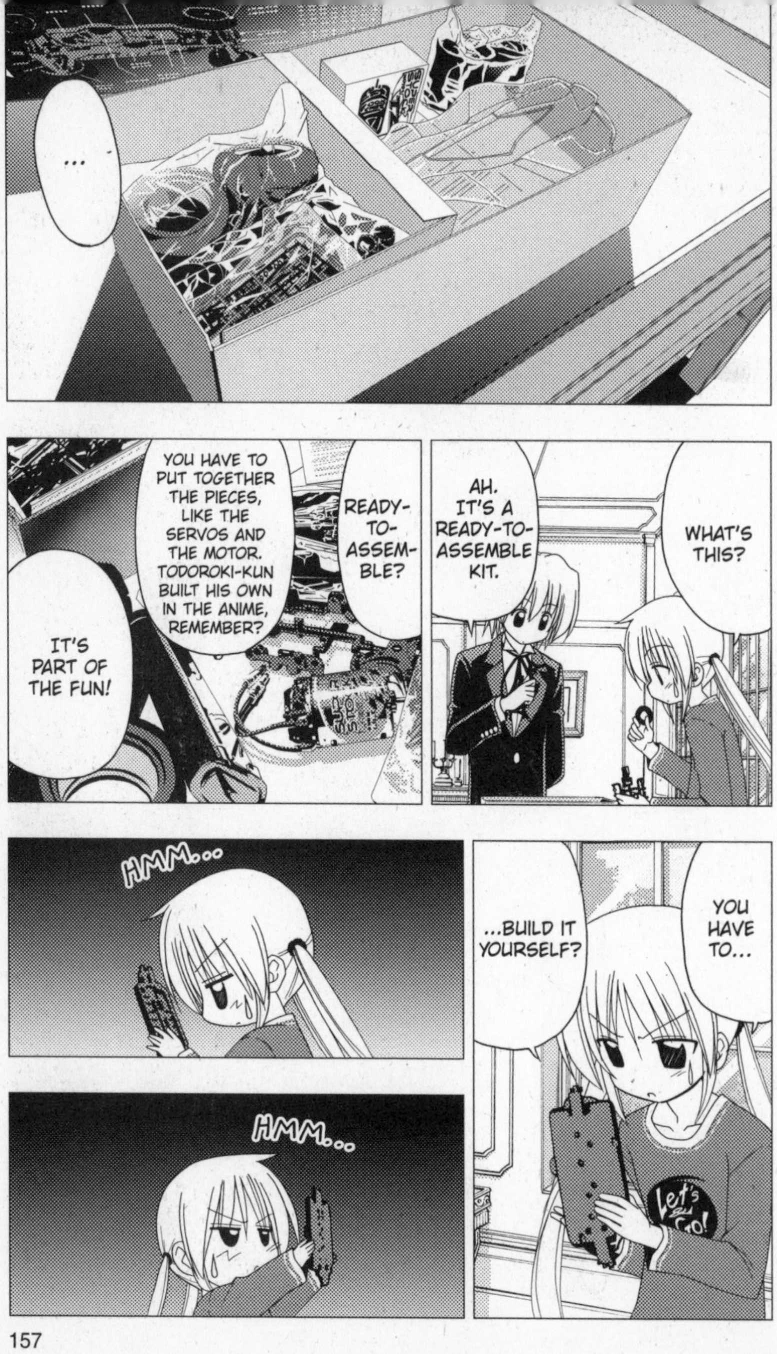
...
WHAT'S THIS?
AH. IT'S A READY-TO-ASSEMBLE KIT.
READY-TO-ASSEMBLE?
YOU HAVE TO PUT TOGETHER THE PIECES, LIKE THE SERVOS AND THE MOTOR. TODOROKI-KUN BUILT HIS OWN IN THE ANIME, REMEMBER?
IT'S PART OF THE FUN!
YOU HAVE TO...
...BUILD IT YOURSELF?
HMM...
HMM...

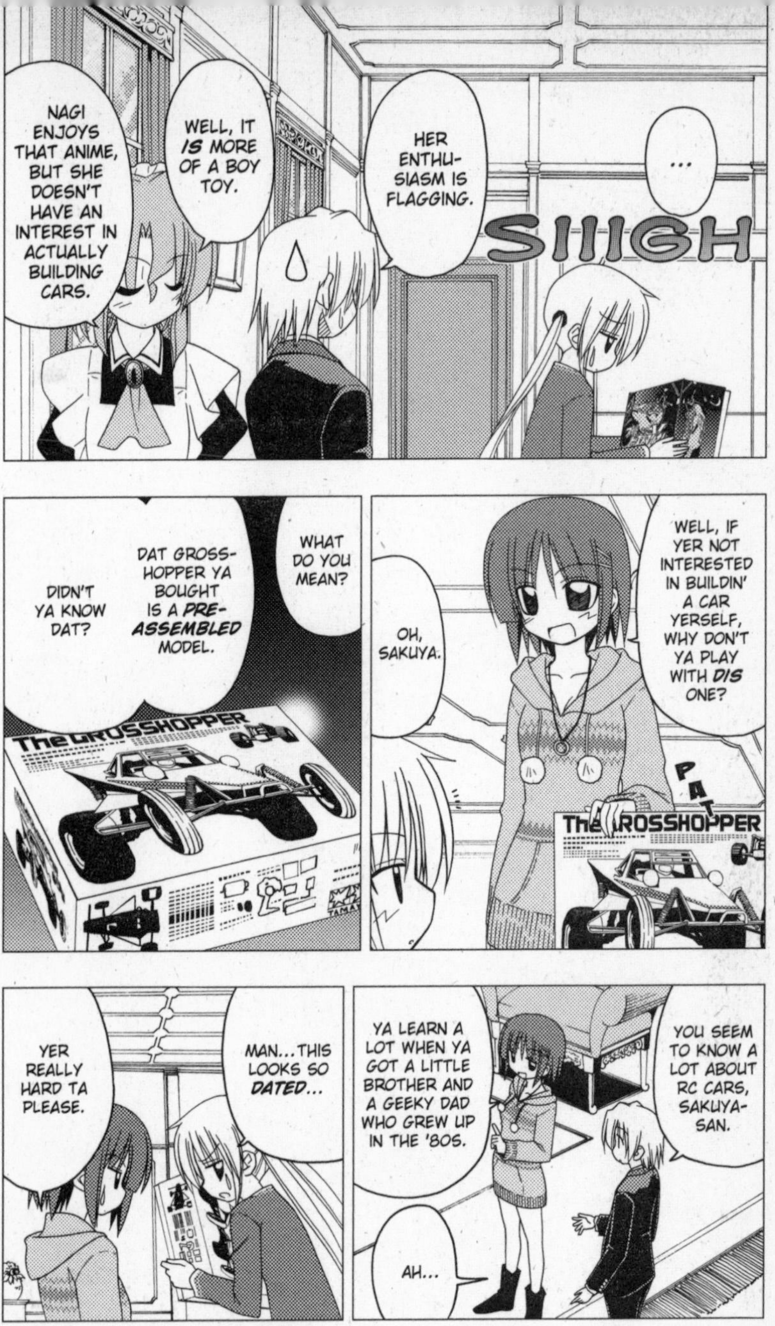
...
SIIIGH
HER ENTHUSIASM IS FLAGGING.
WELL, IT *IS* MORE OF A BOY TOY.
NAGI ENJOYS THAT ANIME, BUT SHE DOESN'T HAVE AN INTEREST IN ACTUALLY BUILDING CARS.
WELL, IF YER NOT INTERESTED IN BUILDIN' A CAR YERSELF, WHY DON'T YA PLAY WITH *DIS* ONE?
PAT
The GROSSHOPPER
OH, SAKUYA.
WHAT DO YOU MEAN?
DAT GROSSHOPPER YA BOUGHT IS A ***PRE-ASSEMBLED*** MODEL.
DIDN'T YA KNOW DAT?
The GROSSHOPPER
YOU SEEM TO KNOW A LOT ABOUT RC CARS, SAKUYA-SAN.
YA LEARN A LOT WHEN YA GOT A LITTLE BROTHER AND A GEEKY DAD WHO GREW UP IN THE '80S.
AH...
MAN...THIS LOOKS SO ***DATED***...
YER REALLY HARD TA PLEASE.

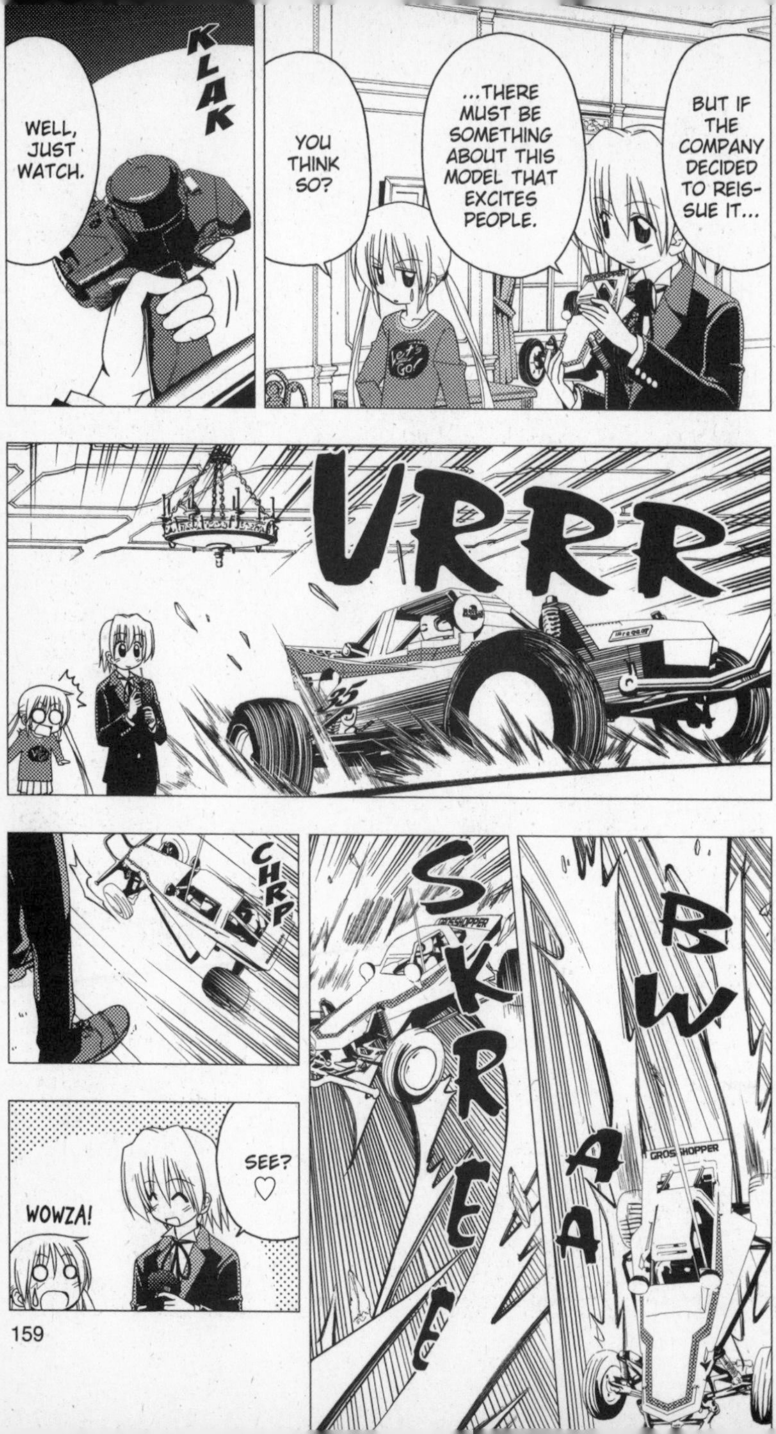
BUT IF THE COMPANY DECIDED TO REIS-SUE IT...
...THERE MUST BE SOMETHING ABOUT THIS MODEL THAT EXCITES PEOPLE.
YOU THINK SO?
KLAK
WELL, JUST WATCH.
URRR
BWAA
SKREE
CHRP
SEE? ♡
WOWZA!

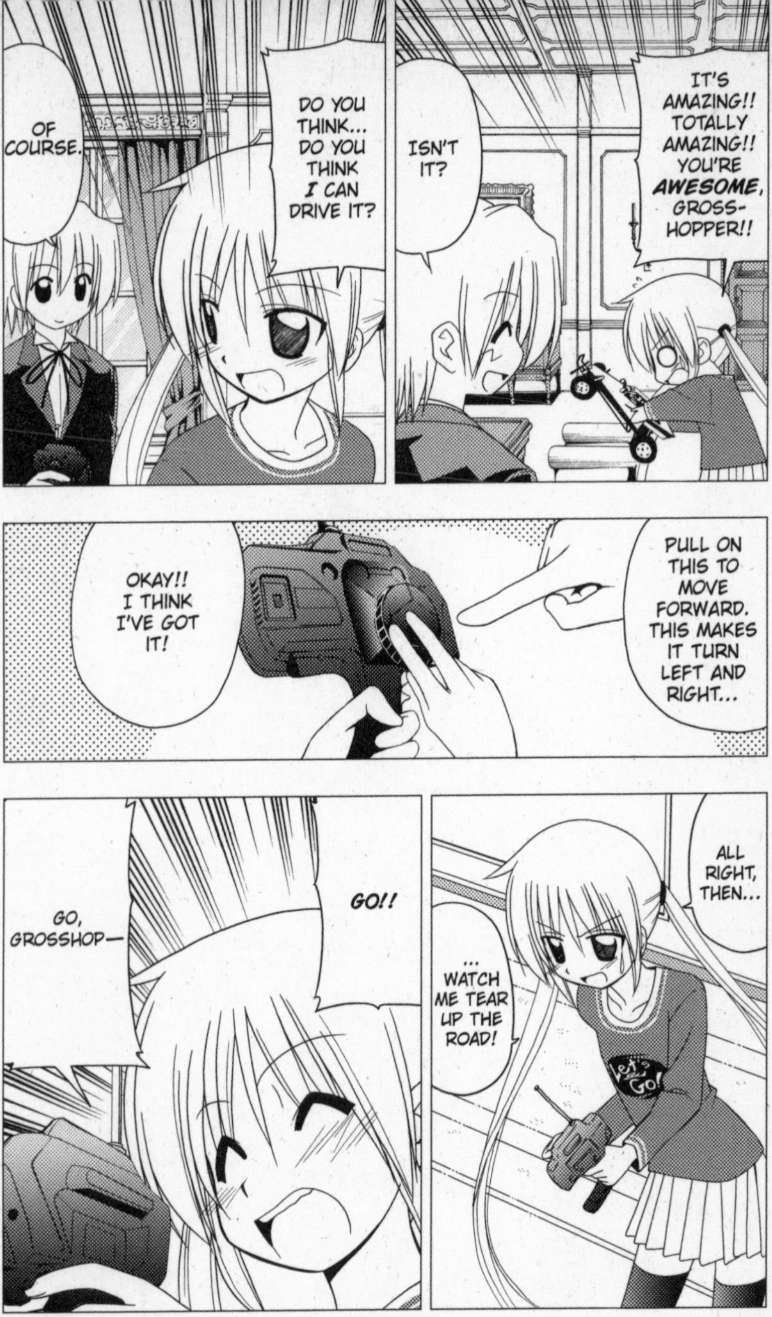
IT'S AMAZING!! TOTALLY AMAZING!! YOU'RE **AWESOME**, GROSS-HOPPER!!
ISN'T IT?
DO YOU THINK... DO YOU THINK *I* CAN DRIVE IT?
OF COURSE.
PULL ON THIS TO MOVE FORWARD. THIS MAKES IT TURN LEFT AND RIGHT...
OKAY!! I THINK I'VE GOT IT!
ALL RIGHT, THEN...
... WATCH ME TEAR UP THE ROAD!
Let's Go!
GO!!
GO, GROSSHOP—

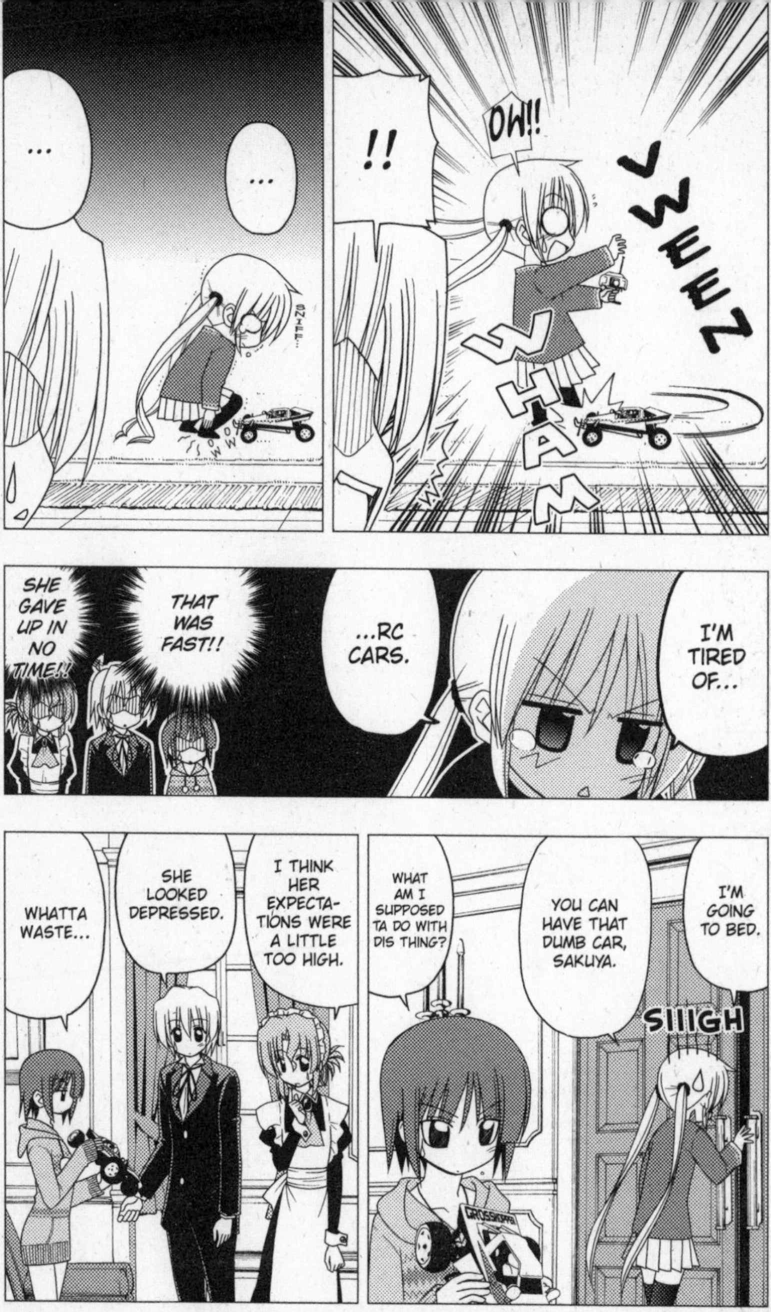

!!
OW!!
VWEEN
WHAM
...
...
SNIFF...
OWW...
I'M TIRED OF...
...RC CARS.
THAT WAS FAST!!
SHE GAVE UP IN NO TIME!!
I'M GOING TO BED.
SIIIGH
YOU CAN HAVE THAT DUMB CAR, SAKUYA.
WHAT AM I SUPPOSED TA DO WITH DIS THING?
I THINK HER EXPECTA-TIONS WERE A LITTLE TOO HIGH.
SHE LOOKED DEPRESSED.
WHATTA WASTE...

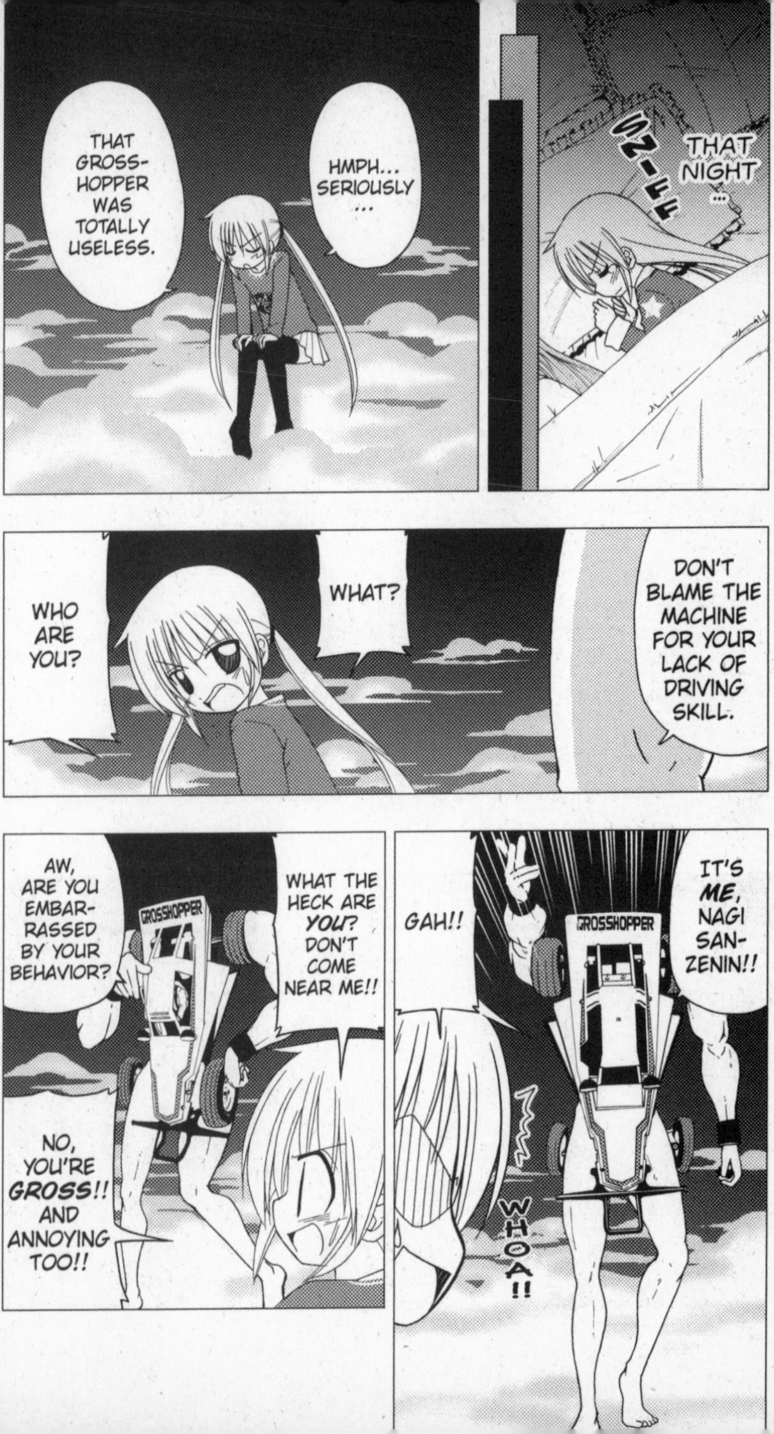
THAT NIGHT...
SNIFF
HMPH... SERIOUSLY...
THAT GROSS-HOPPER WAS TOTALLY USELESS.
DON'T BLAME THE MACHINE FOR YOUR LACK OF DRIVING SKILL.
WHAT?
WHO ARE YOU?
IT'S *ME*, NAGI SAN-ZENIN!!
GROSSHOPPER
GAH!!
WHOA!!
WHAT THE HECK ARE *YOU*? DON'T COME NEAR ME!!
AW, ARE YOU EMBAR-RASSED BY YOUR BEHAVIOR?
GROSSHOPPER
NO, YOU'RE ***GROSS***!! AND ANNOYING TOO!!

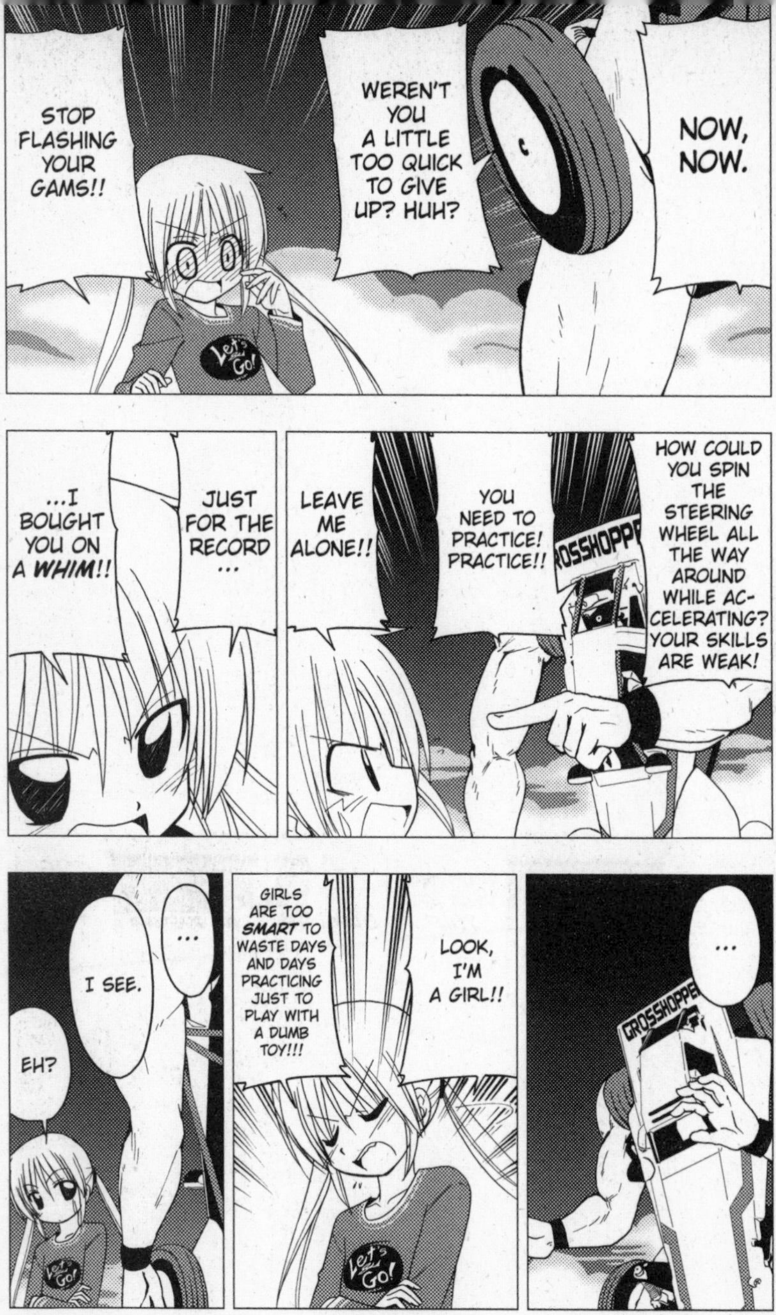
NOW, NOW.
WEREN'T YOU A LITTLE TOO QUICK TO GIVE UP? HUH?
STOP FLASHING YOUR GAMS!!
HOW COULD YOU SPIN THE STEERING WHEEL ALL THE WAY AROUND WHILE AC-CELERATING? YOUR SKILLS ARE WEAK!
GROSSHOPPE
YOU NEED TO PRACTICE! PRACTICE!!
LEAVE ME ALONE!!
JUST FOR THE RECORD ...
...I BOUGHT YOU ON A WHIM!!
...
GROSSHOPPE
LOOK, I'M A GIRL!!
GIRLS ARE TOO SMART TO WASTE DAYS AND DAYS PRACTICING JUST TO PLAY WITH A DUMB TOY!!!
Let's Go!
...
I SEE.
EH?
Let's Go!

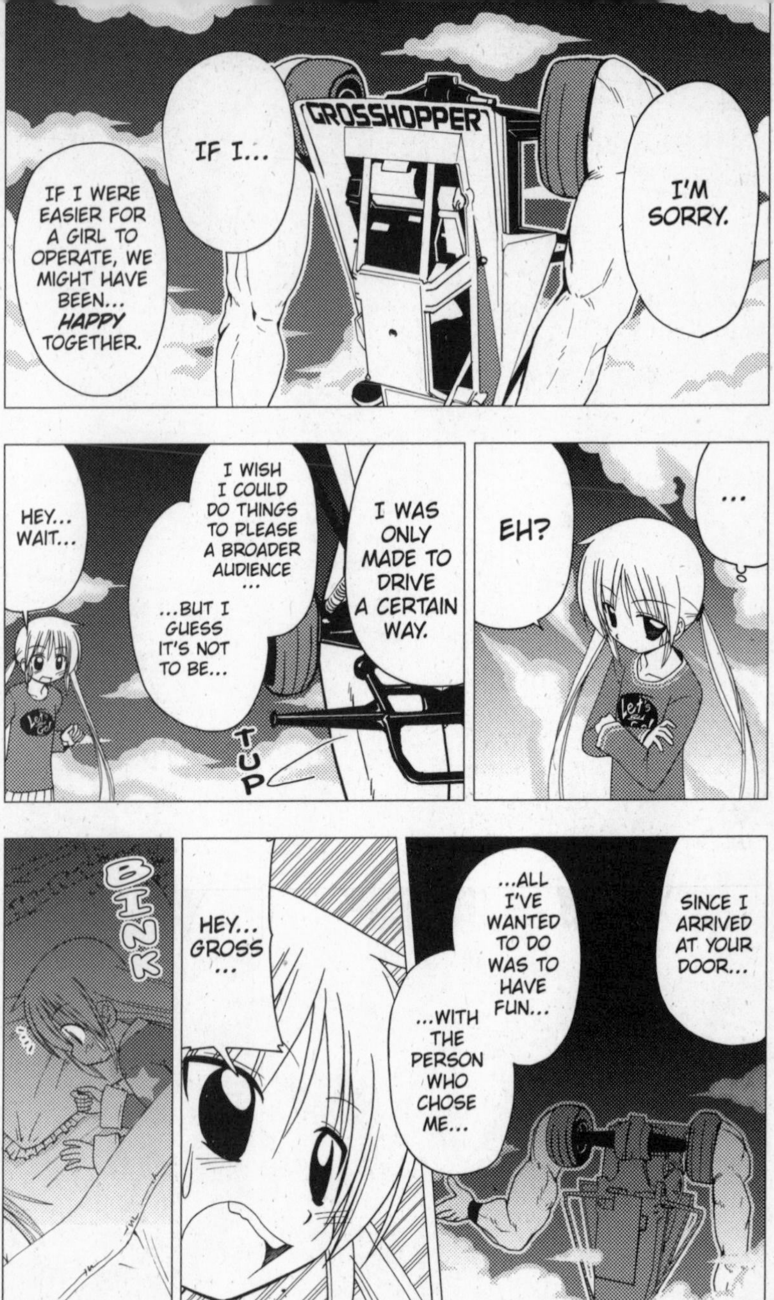
GROSSHOPPER
I'M SORRY.
IF I...
IF I WERE EASIER FOR A GIRL TO OPERATE, WE MIGHT HAVE BEEN... *HAPPY* TOGETHER.
...
EH?
I WAS ONLY MADE TO DRIVE A CERTAIN WAY.
I WISH I COULD DO THINGS TO PLEASE A BROADER AUDIENCE...
...BUT I GUESS IT'S NOT TO BE...
HEY... WAIT...
TUP
SINCE I ARRIVED AT YOUR DOOR...
...ALL I'VE WANTED TO DO WAS TO HAVE FUN...
...WITH THE PERSON WHO CHOSE ME...
HEY... GROSS...
BINK

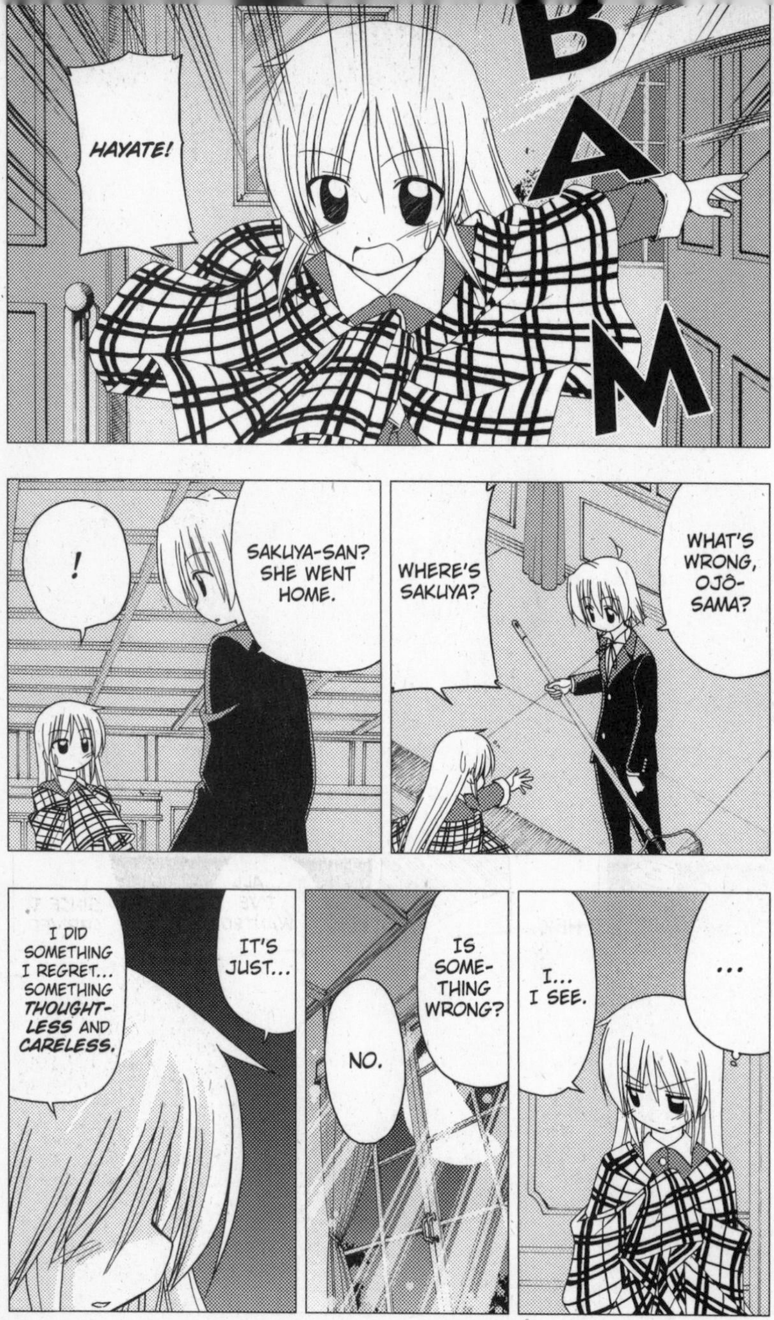
BAM
HAYATE!
WHAT'S WRONG, OJÔ-SAMA?
WHERE'S SAKUYA?
SAKUYA-SAN? SHE WENT HOME.
!
...
I... I SEE.
IS SOME-THING WRONG?
NO.
IT'S JUST...
I DID SOMETHING I REGRET... SOMETHING THOUGHT-LESS AND CARELESS.

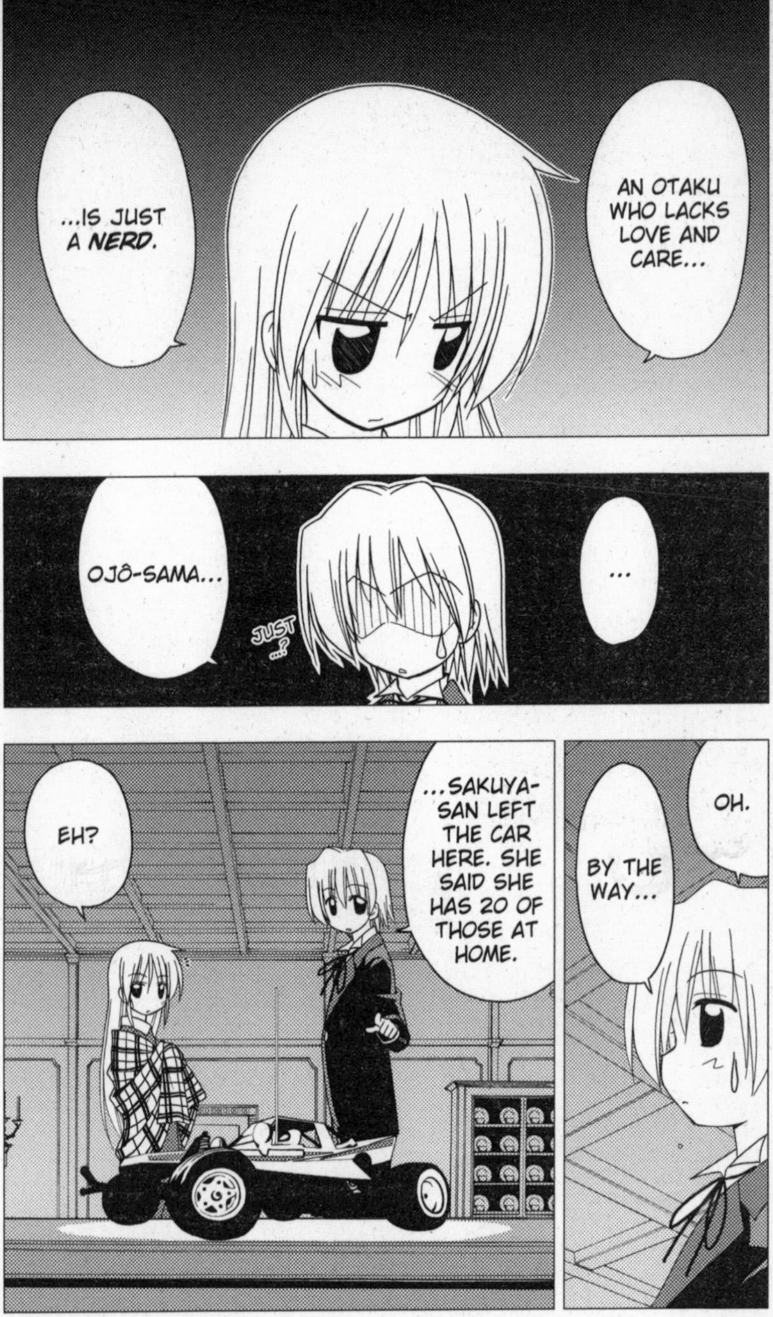
AN OTAKU WHO LACKS LOVE AND CARE...
...IS JUST A NERD.
...
OJÔ-SAMA...
JUST ...?
OH.
BY THE WAY...
...SAKUYA-SAN LEFT THE CAR HERE. SHE SAID SHE HAS 20 OF THOSE AT HOME.
EH?

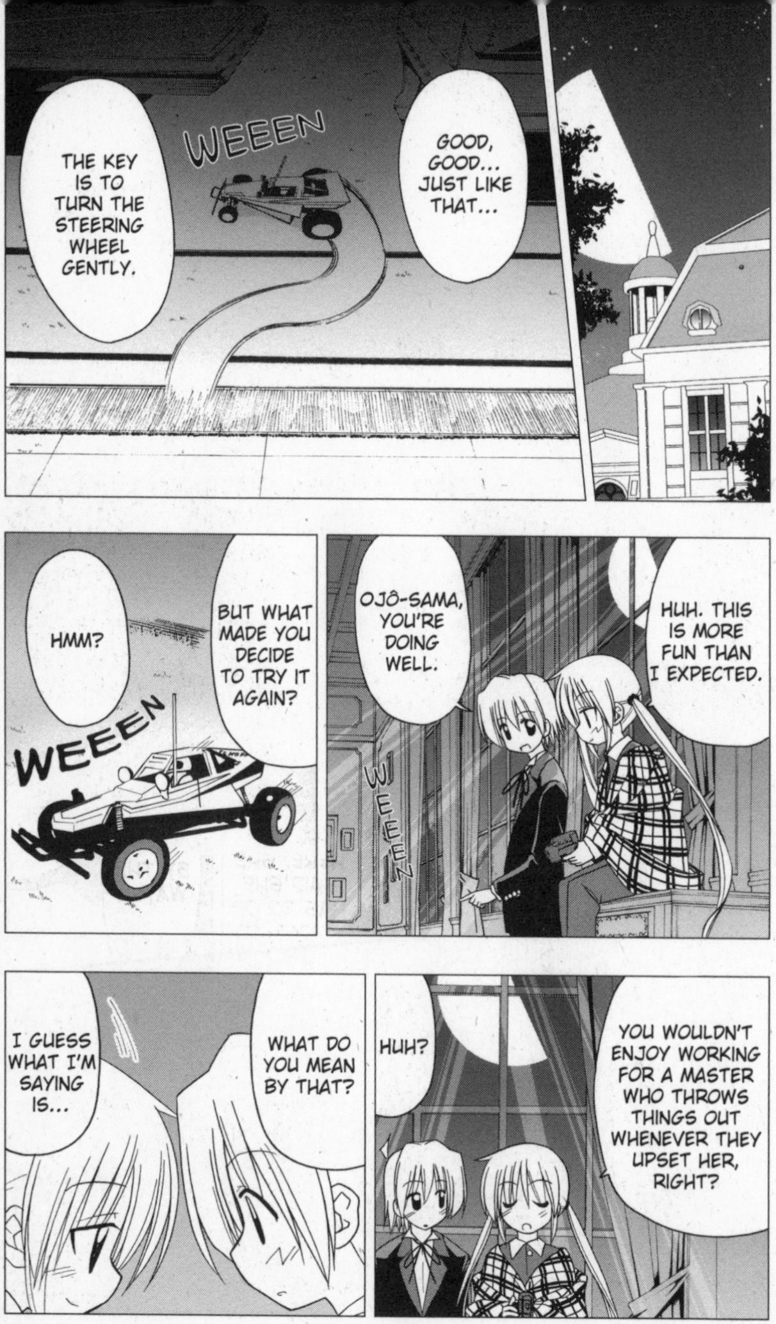
GOOD, GOOD... JUST LIKE THAT...
WEEEN
THE KEY IS TO TURN THE STEERING WHEEL GENTLY.
HUH. THIS IS MORE FUN THAN I EXPECTED.
OJÔ-SAMA, YOU'RE DOING WELL.
WEEEN
BUT WHAT MADE YOU DECIDE TO TRY IT AGAIN?
HMM?
WEEEN
YOU WOULDN'T ENJOY WORKING FOR A MASTER WHO THROWS THINGS OUT WHENEVER THEY UPSET HER, RIGHT?
HUH?
WHAT DO YOU MEAN BY THAT?
I GUESS WHAT I'M SAYING IS...

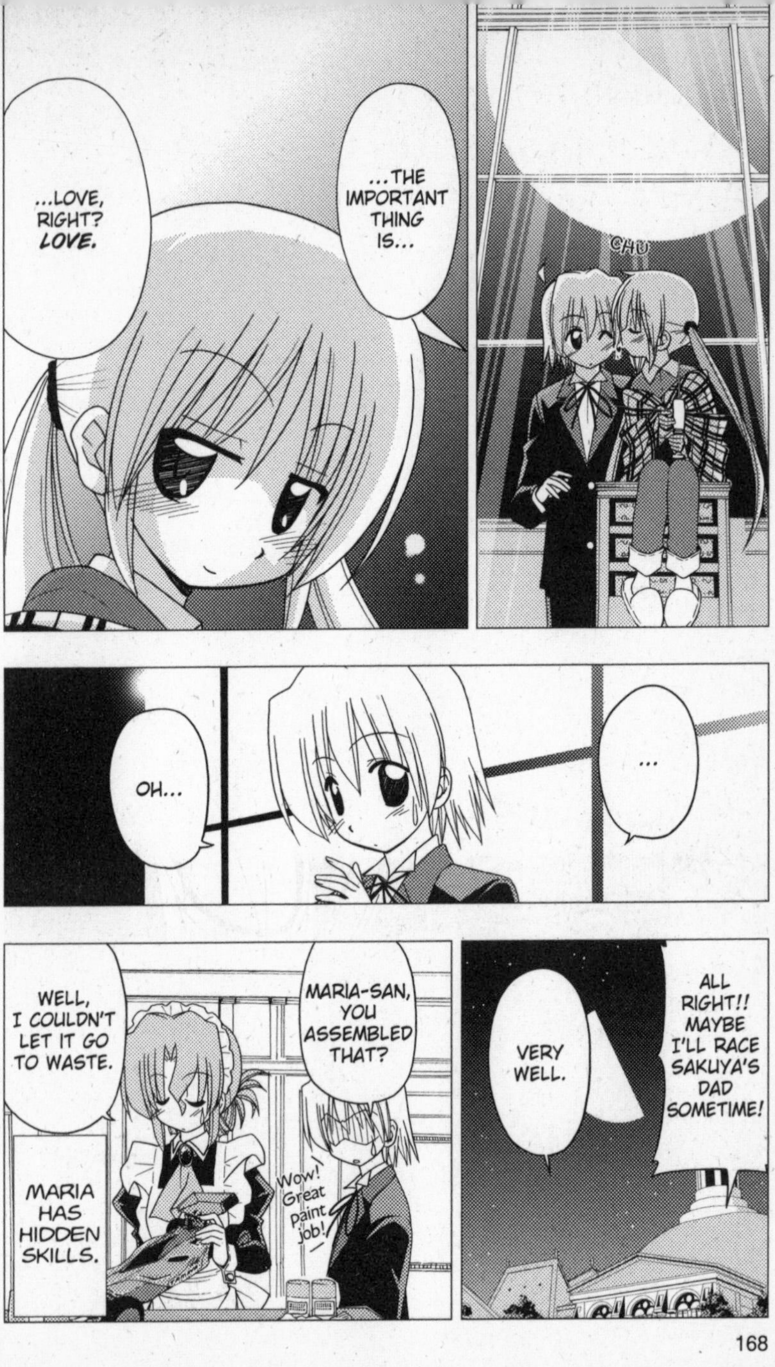
CHU
...THE IMPORTANT THING IS...
...LOVE, RIGHT? *LOVE.*
...
OH...
ALL RIGHT!! MAYBE I'LL RACE SAKUYA'S DAD SOMETIME!
VERY WELL.
MARIA-SAN, YOU ASSEMBLED THAT?
WELL, I COULDN'T LET IT GO TO WASTE.
Wow! Great paint job!
MARIA HAS HIDDEN SKILLS.

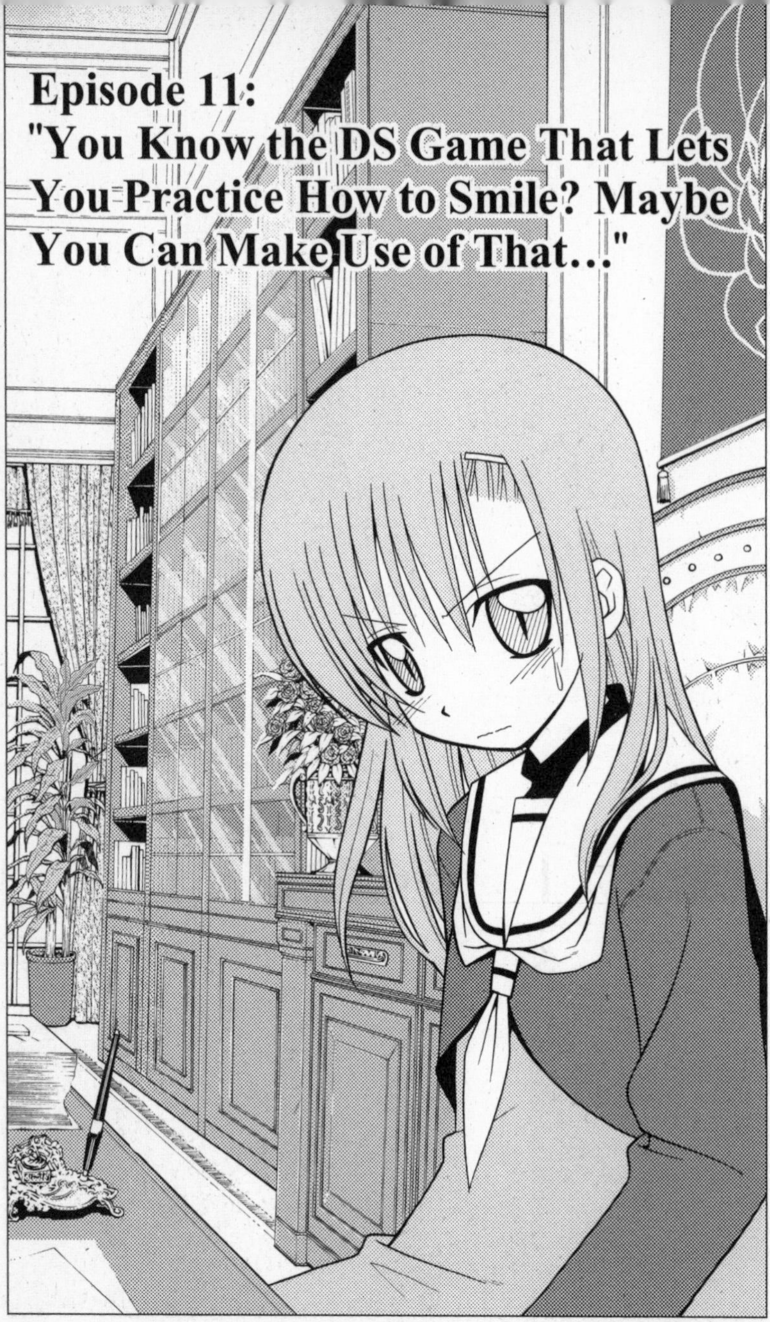
Episode 11:
"You Know the DS Game That Lets You Practice How to Smile? Maybe You Can Make Use of That..."

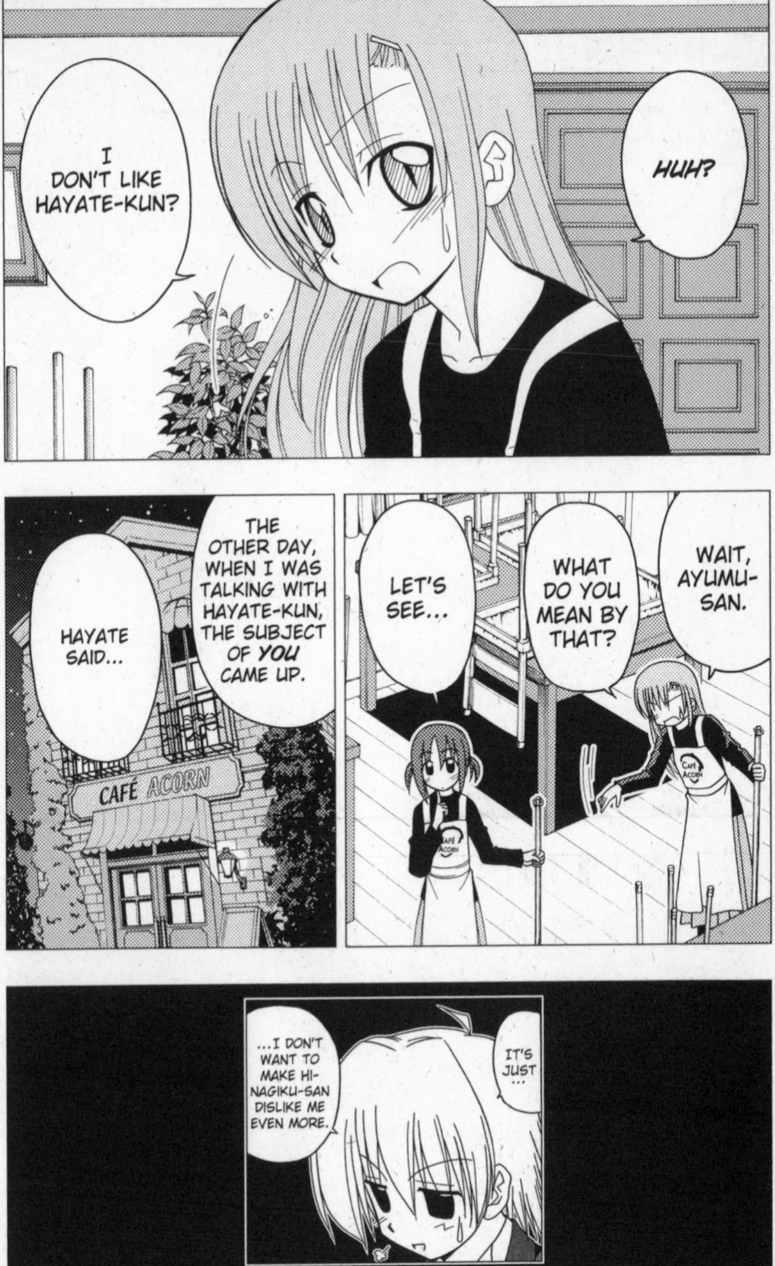
HUH?
I DON'T LIKE HAYATE-KUN?
WAIT, AYUMU-SAN.
WHAT DO YOU MEAN BY THAT?
LET'S SEE...
THE OTHER DAY, WHEN I WAS TALKING WITH HAYATE-KUN, THE SUBJECT OF *YOU* CAME UP.
HAYATE SAID...
CAFÉ ACORN
IT'S JUST...
...I DON'T WANT TO MAKE HINAGIKU-SAN DISLIKE ME EVEN MORE.

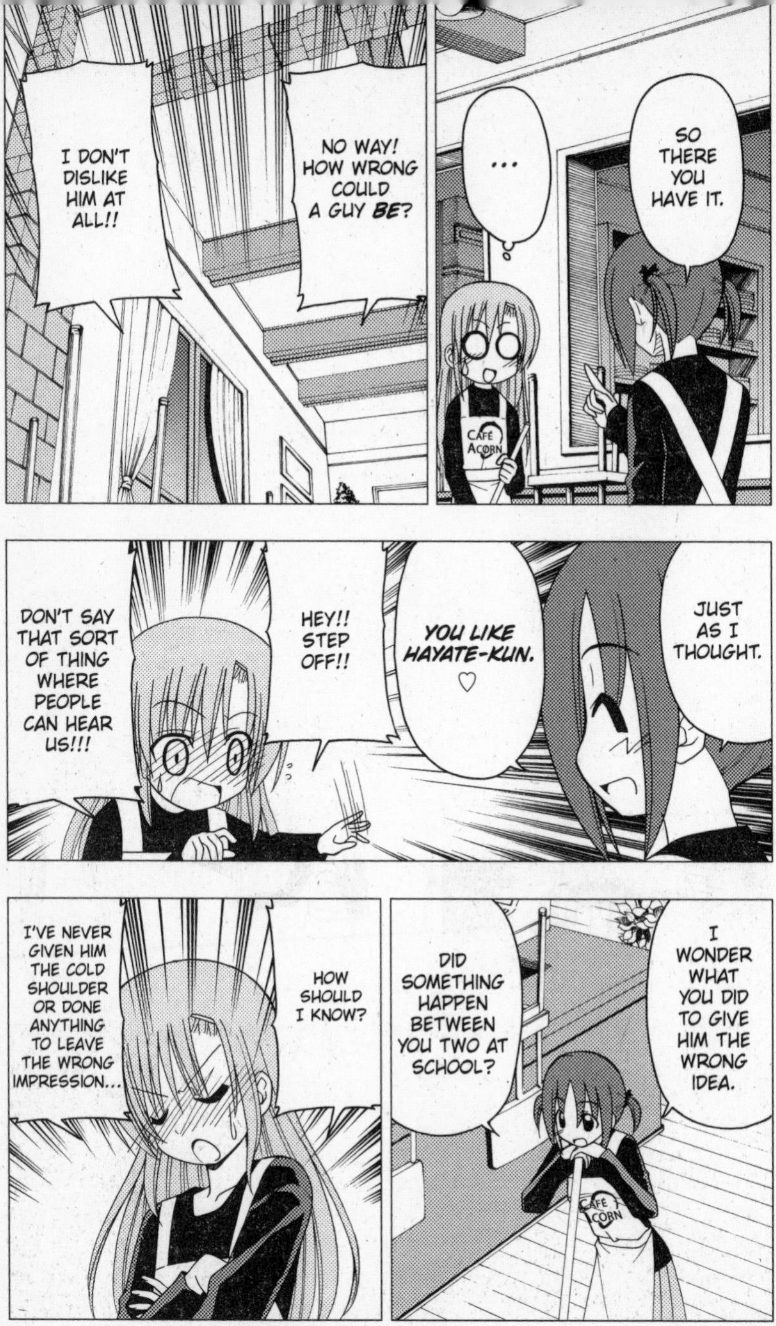
SO THERE YOU HAVE IT.
...
CAFÉ ACORN
NO WAY! HOW WRONG COULD A GUY *BE*?
I DON'T DISLIKE HIM AT ALL!!
JUST AS I THOUGHT.
YOU LIKE HAYATE-KUN. ♡
HEY!! STEP OFF!!
DON'T SAY THAT SORT OF THING WHERE PEOPLE CAN HEAR US!!!
I WONDER WHAT YOU DID TO GIVE HIM THE WRONG IDEA.
DID SOMETHING HAPPEN BETWEEN YOU TWO AT SCHOOL?
HOW SHOULD I KNOW?
I'VE NEVER GIVEN HIM THE COLD SHOULDER OR DONE ANYTHING TO LEAVE THE WRONG IMPRESSION...

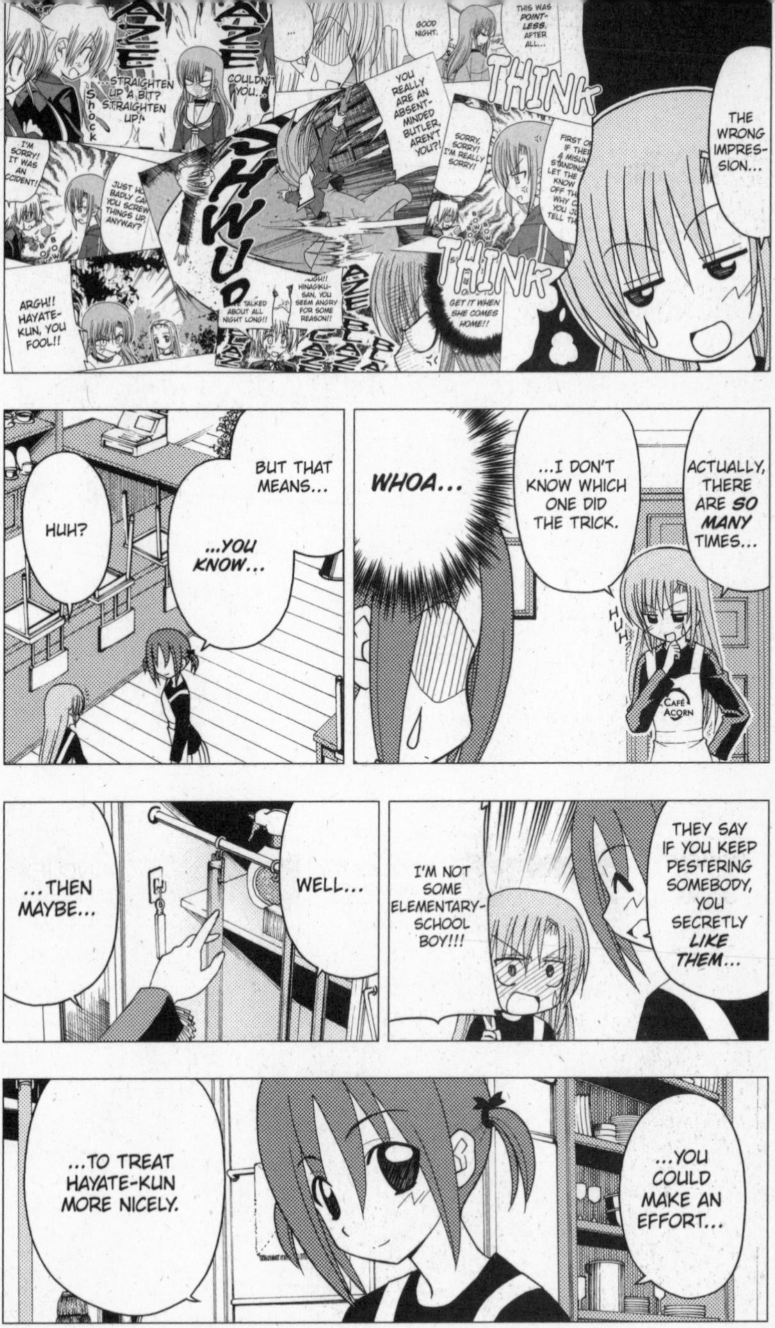
THE WRONG IMPRESSION...
THIS WAS POINTLESS, AFTER ALL...
THINK
GOOD NIGHT.
...
YOU REALLY ARE AN ABSENT-MINDED BUTLER, AREN'T YOU?!
SORRY, SORRY! I'M REALLY SORRY!
COULDN'T YOU...
...STRAIGHTEN UP A BIT? STRAIGHTEN UP!
Shock
SHWUD
THINK
GET IT WHEN SHE COMES HOME!!
ARGH!! HAYATE-KUN, YOU FOOL!!
ACTUALLY, THERE ARE SO MANY TIMES...
...I DON'T KNOW WHICH ONE DID THE TRICK.
WHOA...
BUT THAT MEANS...
...YOU KNOW...
HUH?
THEY SAY IF YOU KEEP PESTERING SOMEBODY, YOU SECRETLY LIKE THEM...
I'M NOT SOME ELEMENTARY-SCHOOL BOY!!!
WELL...
...THEN MAYBE...
...YOU COULD MAKE AN EFFORT...
...TO TREAT HAYATE-KUN MORE NICELY.

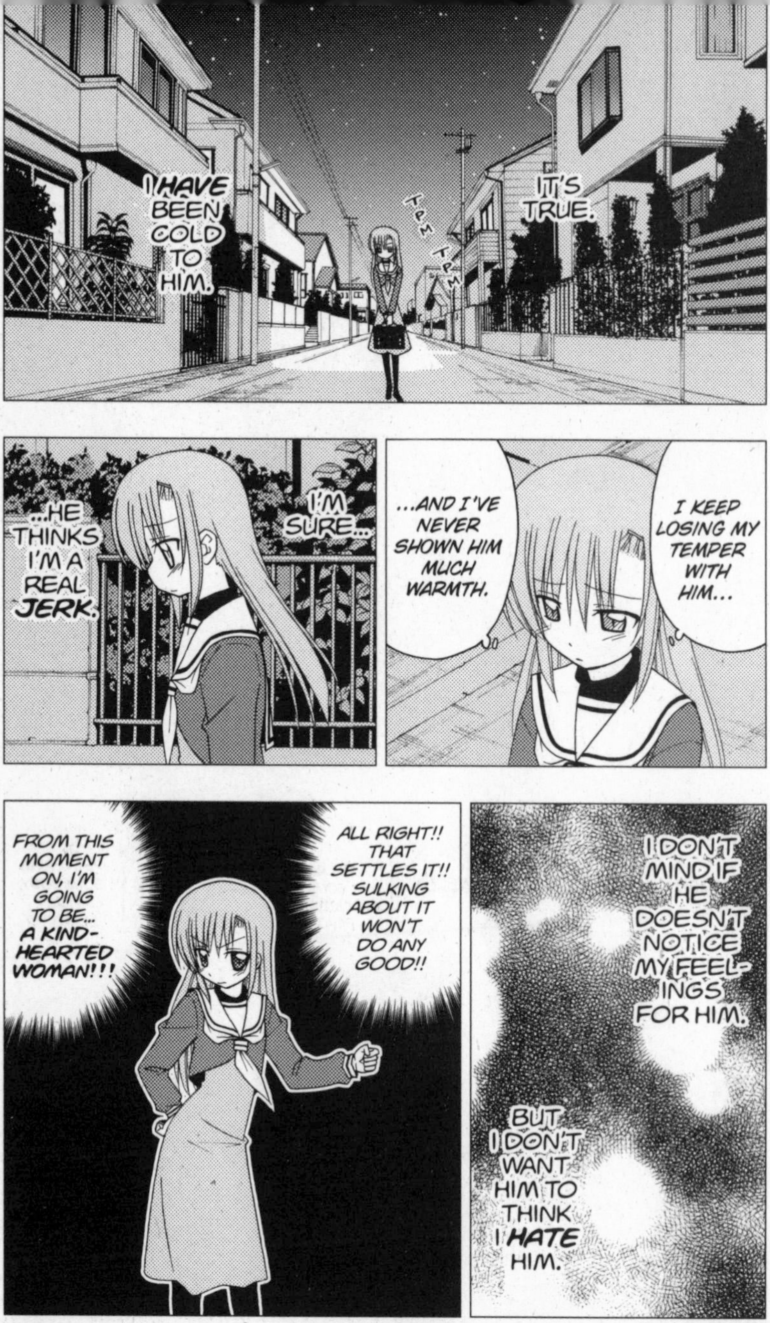
IT'S TRUE.
TPM TPM
I HAVE BEEN COLD TO HIM.
I KEEP LOSING MY TEMPER WITH HIM...
...AND I'VE NEVER SHOWN HIM MUCH WARMTH.
I'M SURE...
...HE THINKS I'M A REAL JERK.
I DON'T MIND IF HE DOESN'T NOTICE MY FEELINGS FOR HIM.
BUT I DON'T WANT HIM TO THINK I HATE HIM.
ALL RIGHT!! THAT SETTLES IT!! SULKING ABOUT IT WON'T DO ANY GOOD!!
FROM THIS MOMENT ON, I'M GOING TO BE... A KIND-HEARTED WOMAN!!!

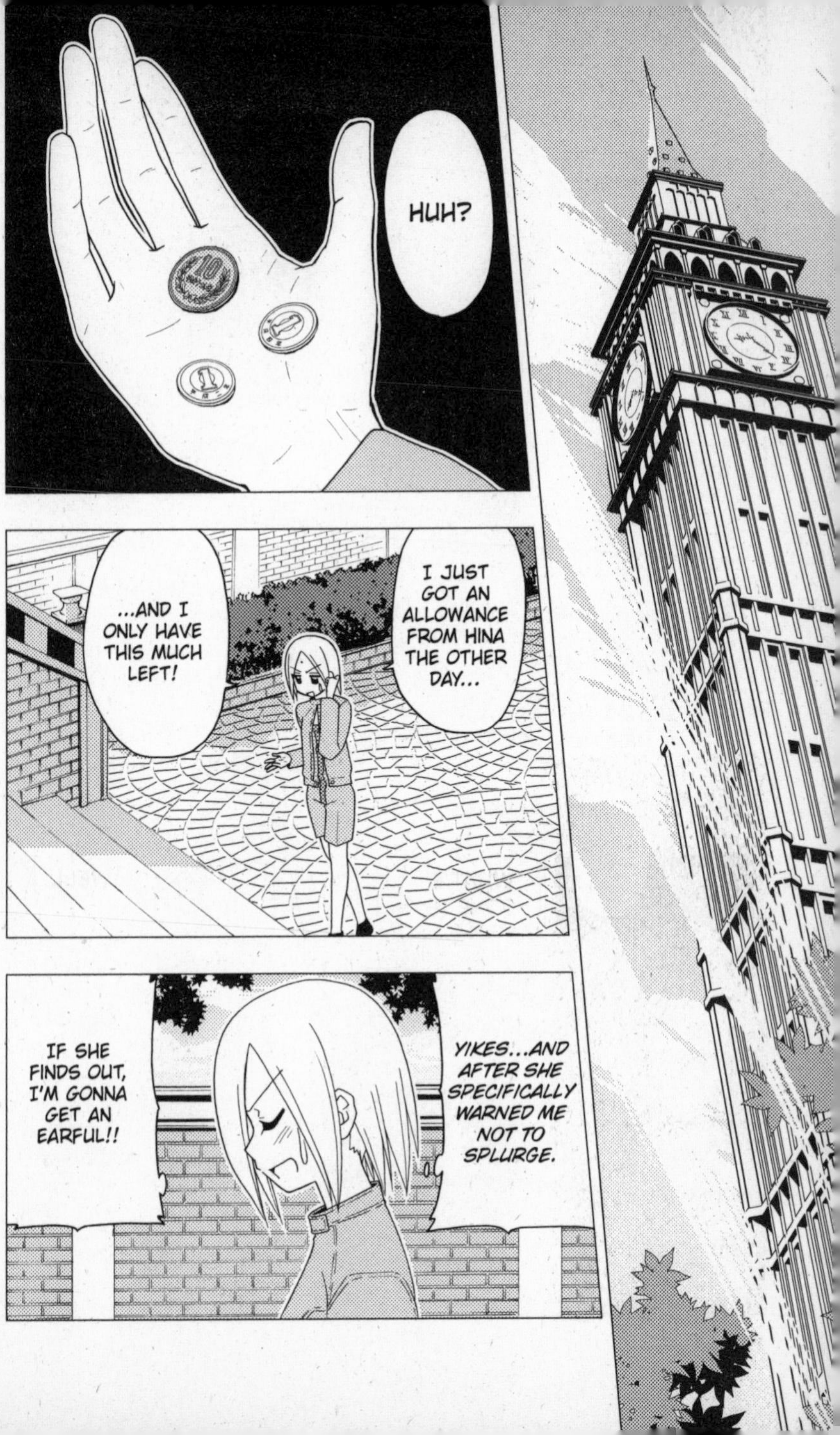
HUH?
I JUST GOT AN ALLOWANCE FROM HINA THE OTHER DAY...
...AND I ONLY HAVE THIS MUCH LEFT!
YIKES...AND AFTER SHE SPECIFICALLY WARNED ME NOT TO SPLURGE.
IF SHE FINDS OUT, I'M GONNA GET AN EARFUL!!

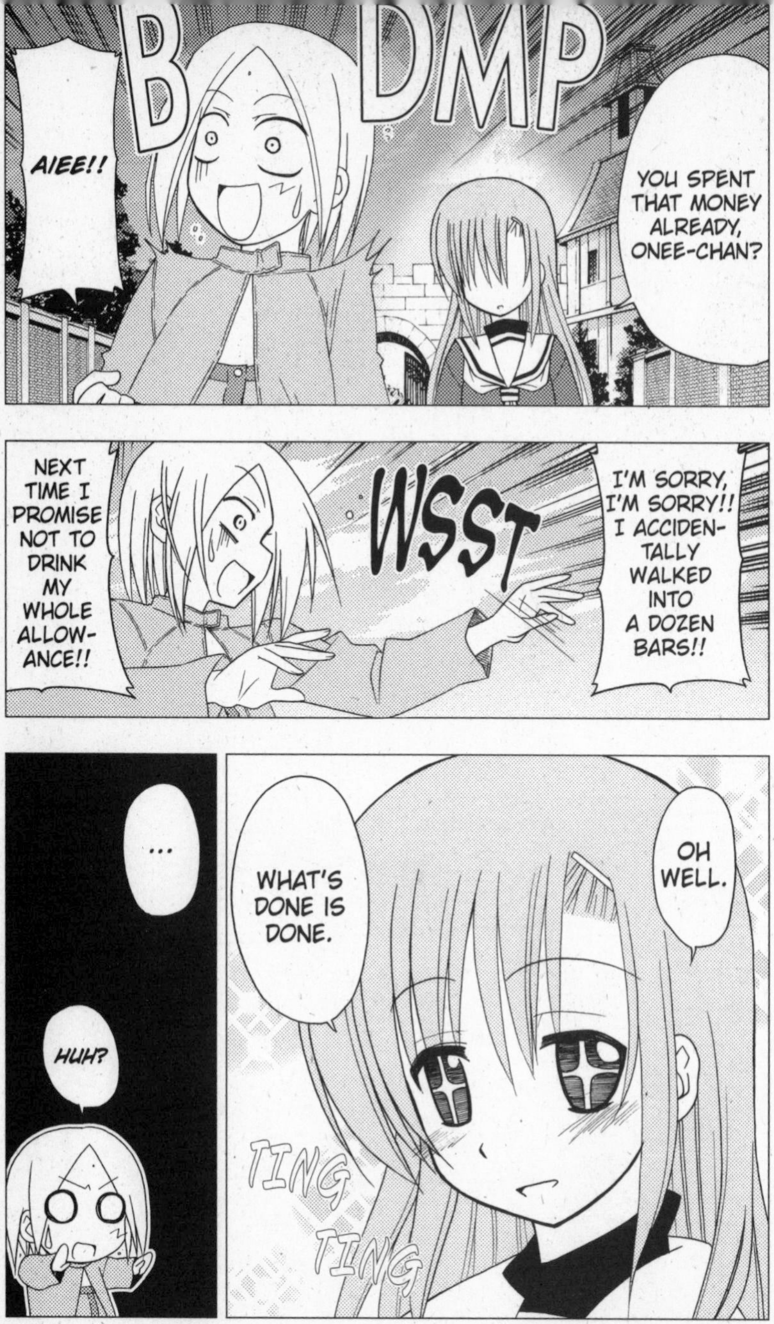
YOU SPENT THAT MONEY ALREADY, ONEE-CHAN?
BDMP
AIEE!!
I'M SORRY, I'M SORRY!! I ACCIDENTALLY WALKED INTO A DOZEN BARS!!
WSST
NEXT TIME I PROMISE NOT TO DRINK MY WHOLE ALLOWANCE!!
OH WELL.
WHAT'S DONE IS DONE.
TING TING
...
HUH?

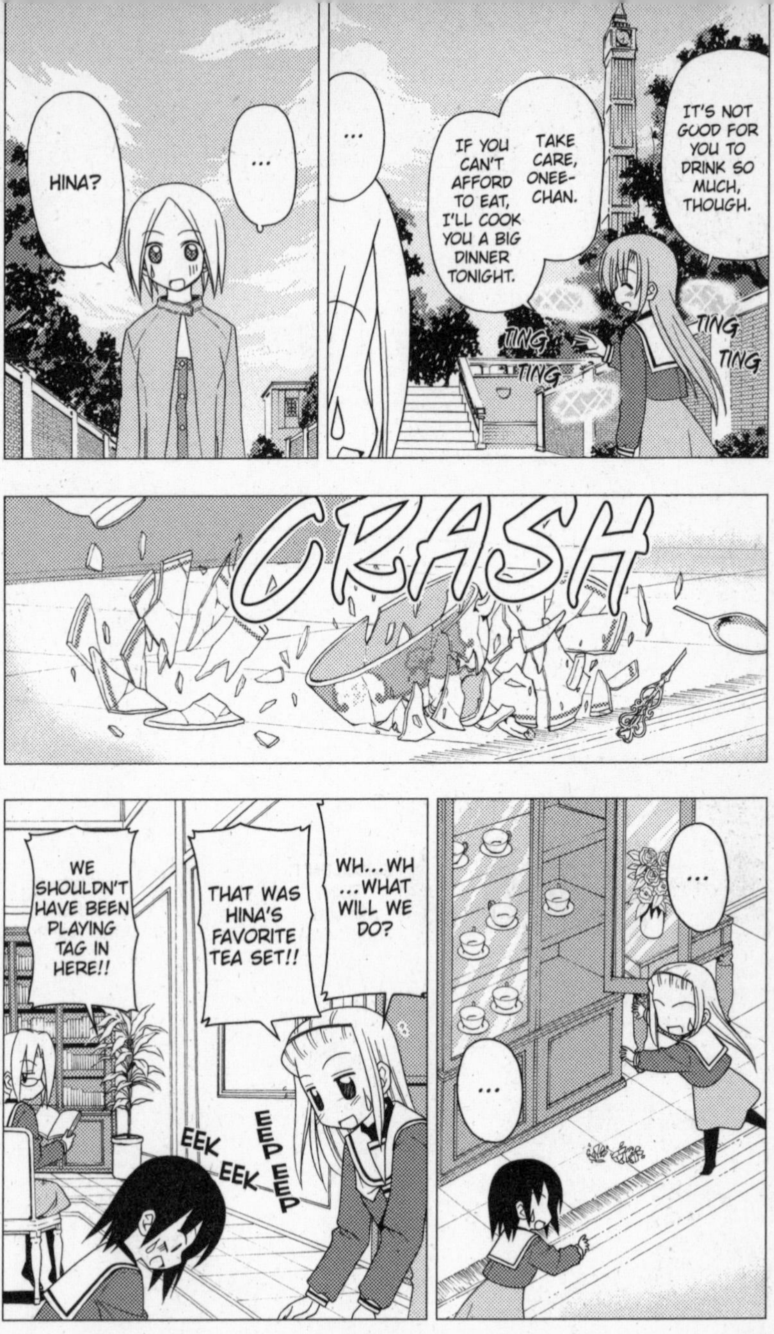
IT'S NOT GOOD FOR YOU TO DRINK SO MUCH, THOUGH.
TAKE CARE, ONEE-CHAN.
IF YOU CAN'T AFFORD TO EAT, I'LL COOK YOU A BIG DINNER TONIGHT.
...
TING TING
TING TING
...
HINA?
CRASH
...
...
WH...WH ...WHAT WILL WE DO?
THAT WAS HINA'S FAVORITE TEA SET!!
WE SHOULDN'T HAVE BEEN PLAYING TAG IN HERE!!
EEP EEP
EEK EEK

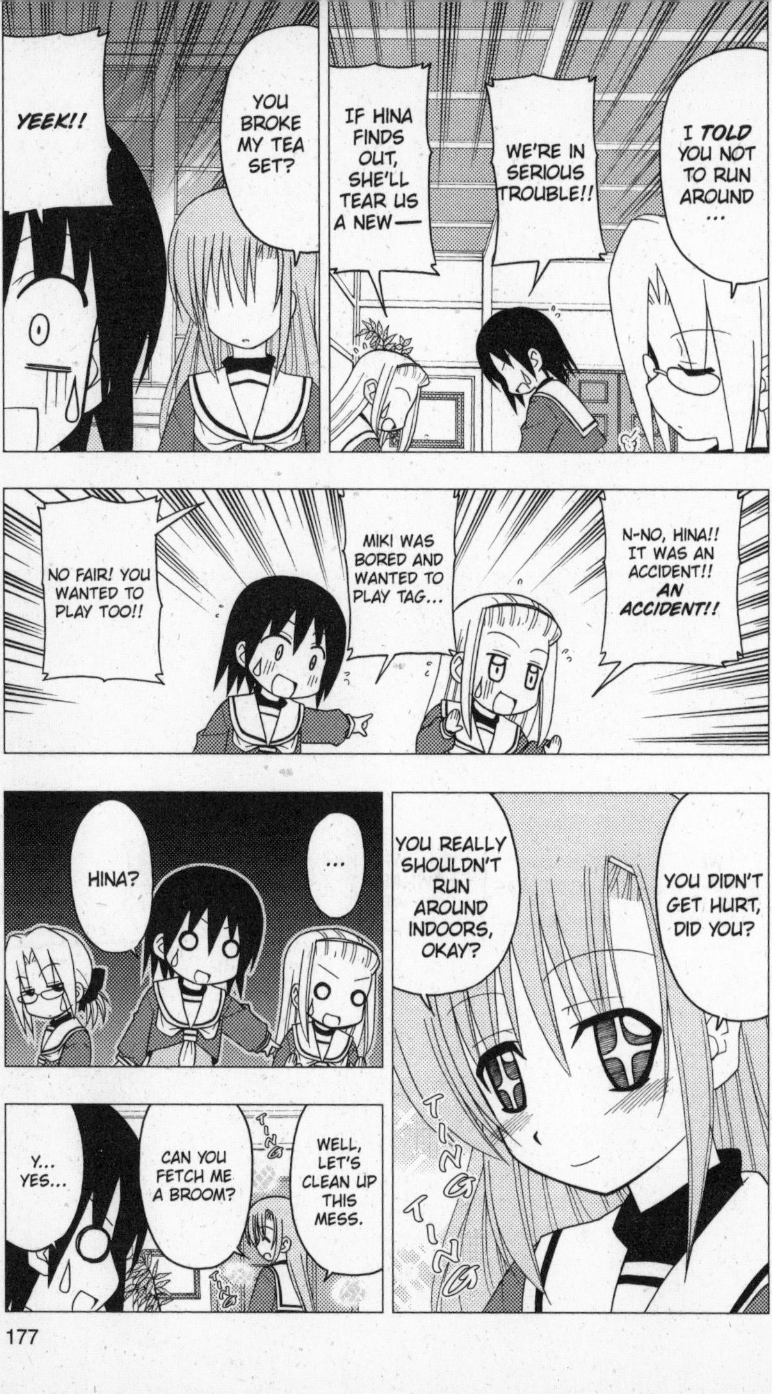
I *TOLD* YOU NOT TO RUN AROUND...
WE'RE IN SERIOUS TROUBLE!!
IF HINA FINDS OUT, SHE'LL TEAR US A NEW—
YOU BROKE MY TEA SET?
YEEK!!
N-NO, HINA!! IT WAS AN ACCIDENT!! *AN ACCIDENT!!*
MIKI WAS BORED AND WANTED TO PLAY TAG...
NO FAIR! YOU WANTED TO PLAY TOO!!
YOU DIDN'T GET HURT, DID YOU?
YOU REALLY SHOULDN'T RUN AROUND INDOORS, OKAY?
...
HINA?
WELL, LET'S CLEAN UP THIS MESS.
CAN YOU FETCH ME A BROOM?
Y... YES...

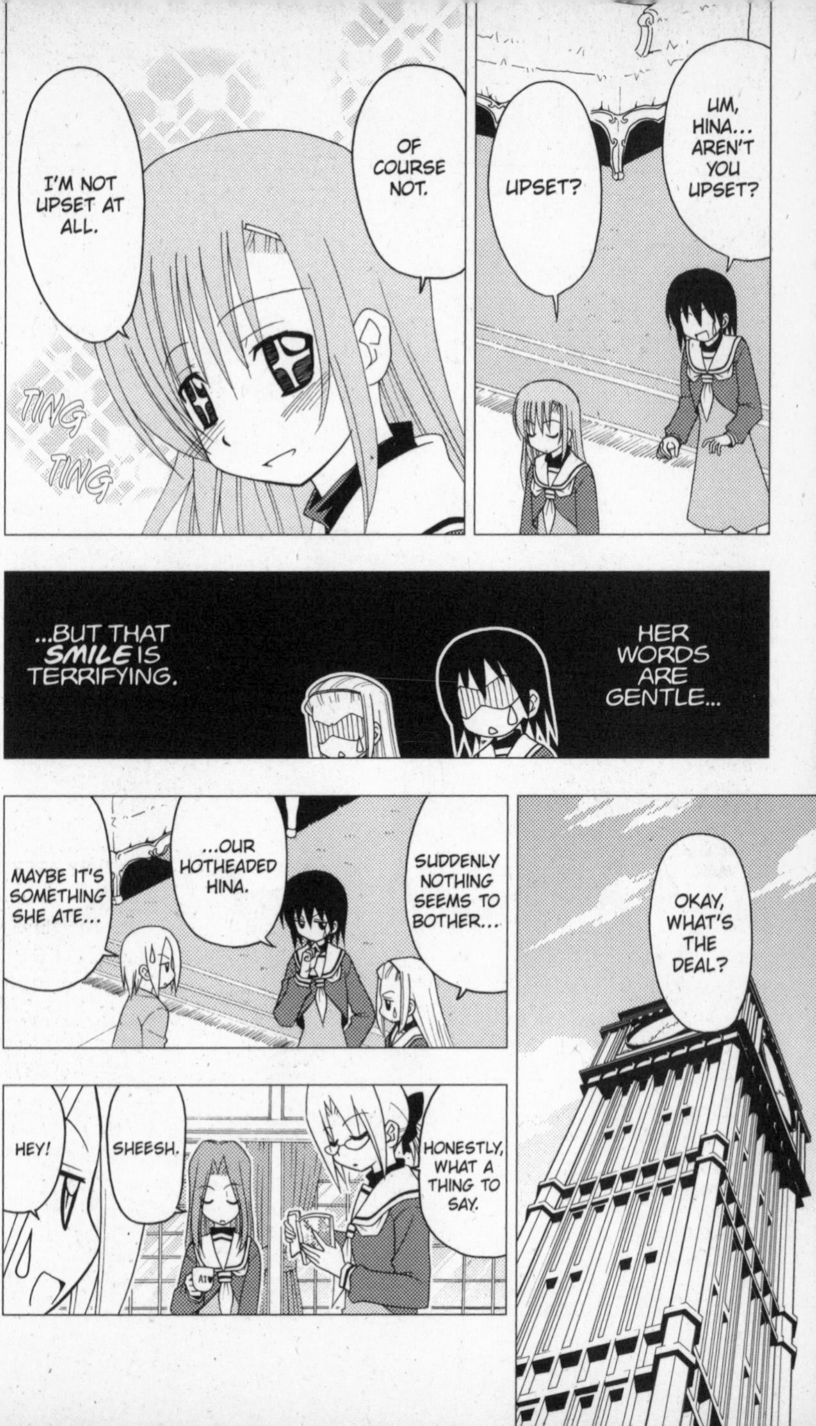
UM, HINA... AREN'T YOU UPSET?
UPSET?
OF COURSE NOT.
I'M NOT UPSET AT ALL.
TING
TING
HER WORDS ARE GENTLE...
...BUT THAT SMILE IS TERRIFYING.
OKAY, WHAT'S THE DEAL?
SUDDENLY NOTHING SEEMS TO BOTHER...
...OUR HOTHEADED HINA.
MAYBE IT'S SOMETHING SHE ATE...
HONESTLY, WHAT A THING TO SAY.
SHEESH.
HEY!

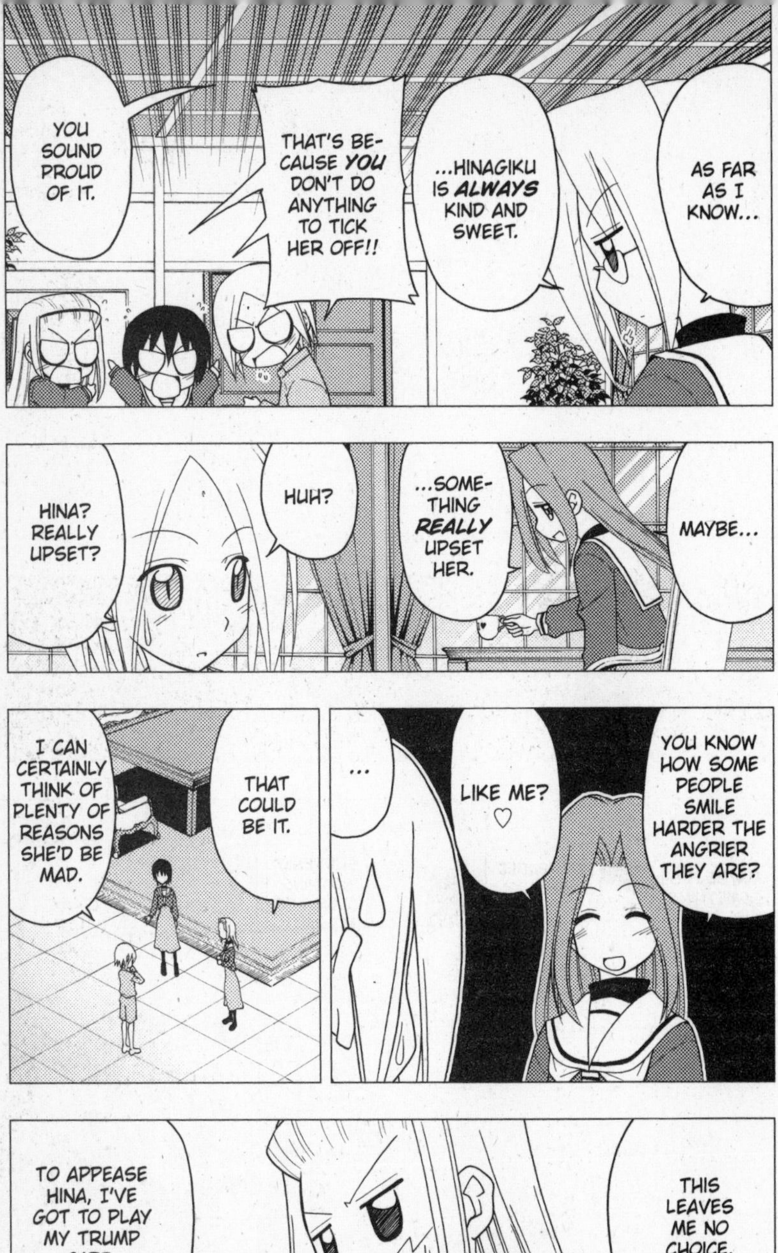
AS FAR AS I KNOW...
...HINAGIKU IS *ALWAYS* KIND AND SWEET.
THAT'S BE-CAUSE *YOU* DON'T DO ANYTHING TO TICK HER OFF!!
YOU SOUND PROUD OF IT.
MAYBE...
...SOME-THING *REALLY* UPSET HER.
HUH?
HINA? REALLY UPSET?
YOU KNOW HOW SOME PEOPLE SMILE HARDER THE ANGRIER THEY ARE?
LIKE ME? ♡
...
THAT COULD BE IT.
I CAN CERTAINLY THINK OF PLENTY OF REASONS SHE'D BE MAD.
THIS LEAVES ME NO CHOICE.
TO APPEASE HINA, I'VE GOT TO PLAY MY TRUMP CARD.

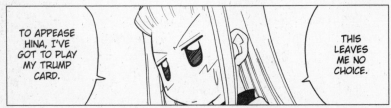

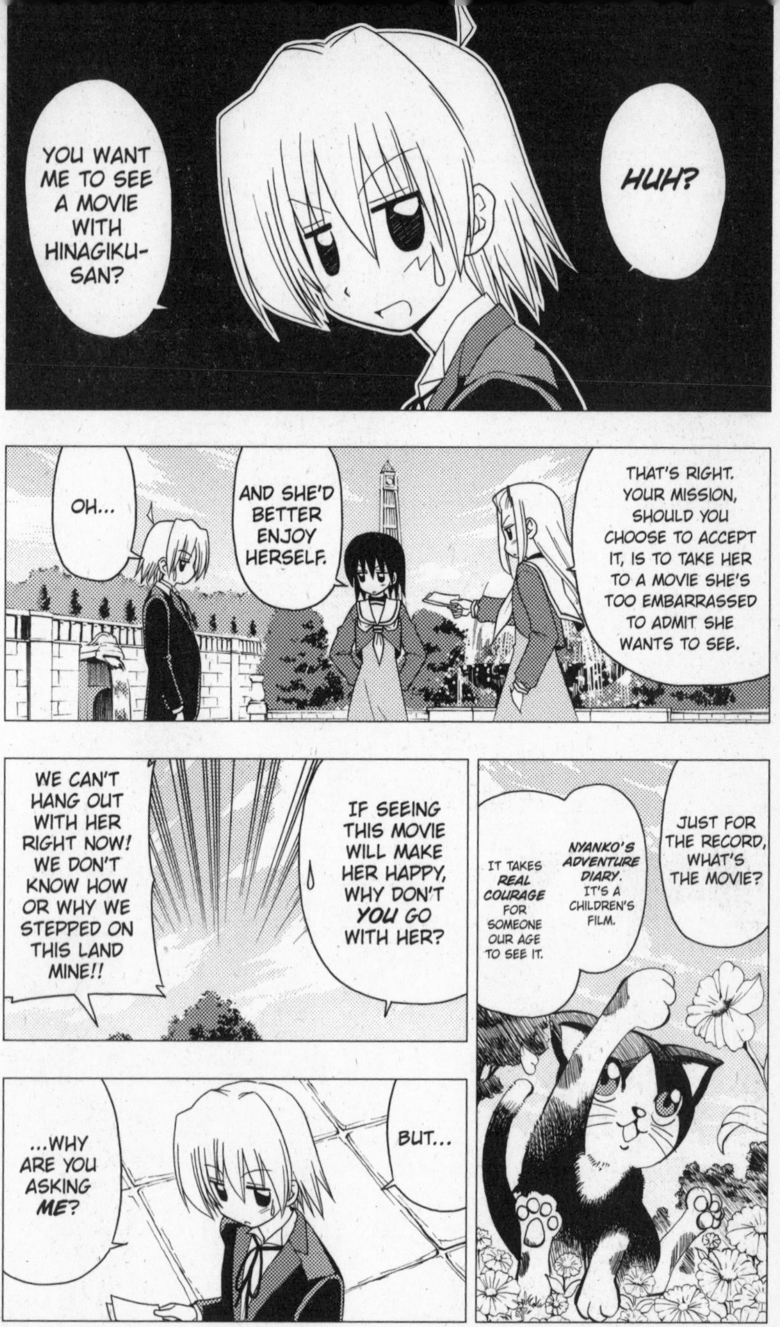
HUH?
YOU WANT ME TO SEE A MOVIE WITH HINAGIKU-SAN?
THAT'S RIGHT. YOUR MISSION, SHOULD YOU CHOOSE TO ACCEPT IT, IS TO TAKE HER TO A MOVIE SHE'S TOO EMBARRASSED TO ADMIT SHE WANTS TO SEE.
AND SHE'D BETTER ENJOY HERSELF.
OH...
JUST FOR THE RECORD, WHAT'S THE MOVIE?
NYANKO'S ADVENTURE DIARY. IT'S A CHILDREN'S FILM.
IT TAKES **REAL COURAGE** FOR SOMEONE OUR AGE TO SEE IT.
IF SEEING THIS MOVIE WILL MAKE HER HAPPY, WHY DON'T ***YOU*** GO WITH HER?
WE CAN'T HANG OUT WITH HER RIGHT NOW! WE DON'T KNOW HOW OR WHY WE STEPPED ON THIS LAND MINE!!
BUT...
...WHY ARE YOU ASKING ***ME***?

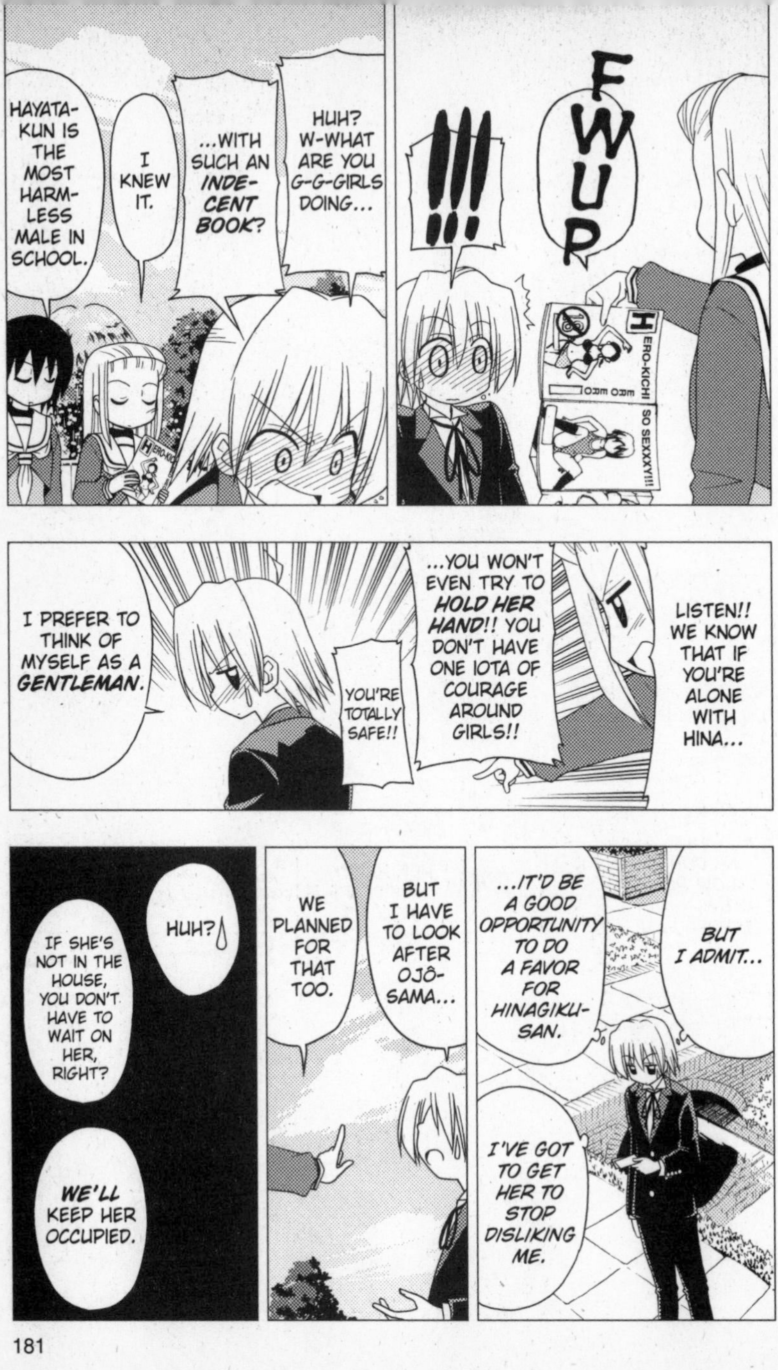
FWUP
!!!
HERO-KICHI
SO SEXXXY!!!
HUH? W-WHAT ARE YOU G-G-GIRLS DOING...
...WITH SUCH AN INDECENT BOOK?
I KNEW IT.
HAYATA-KUN IS THE MOST HARMLESS MALE IN SCHOOL.
LISTEN!! WE KNOW THAT IF YOU'RE ALONE WITH HINA...
...YOU WON'T EVEN TRY TO HOLD HER HAND!! YOU DON'T HAVE ONE IOTA OF COURAGE AROUND GIRLS!!
YOU'RE TOTALLY SAFE!!
I PREFER TO THINK OF MYSELF AS A GENTLEMAN.
BUT I ADMIT...
...IT'D BE A GOOD OPPORTUNITY TO DO A FAVOR FOR HINAGIKU-SAN.
I'VE GOT TO GET HER TO STOP DISLIKING ME.
BUT I HAVE TO LOOK AFTER OJÔ-SAMA...
WE PLANNED FOR THAT TOO.
HUH?
IF SHE'S NOT IN THE HOUSE, YOU DON'T HAVE TO WAIT ON HER, RIGHT?
WE'LL KEEP HER OCCUPIED.

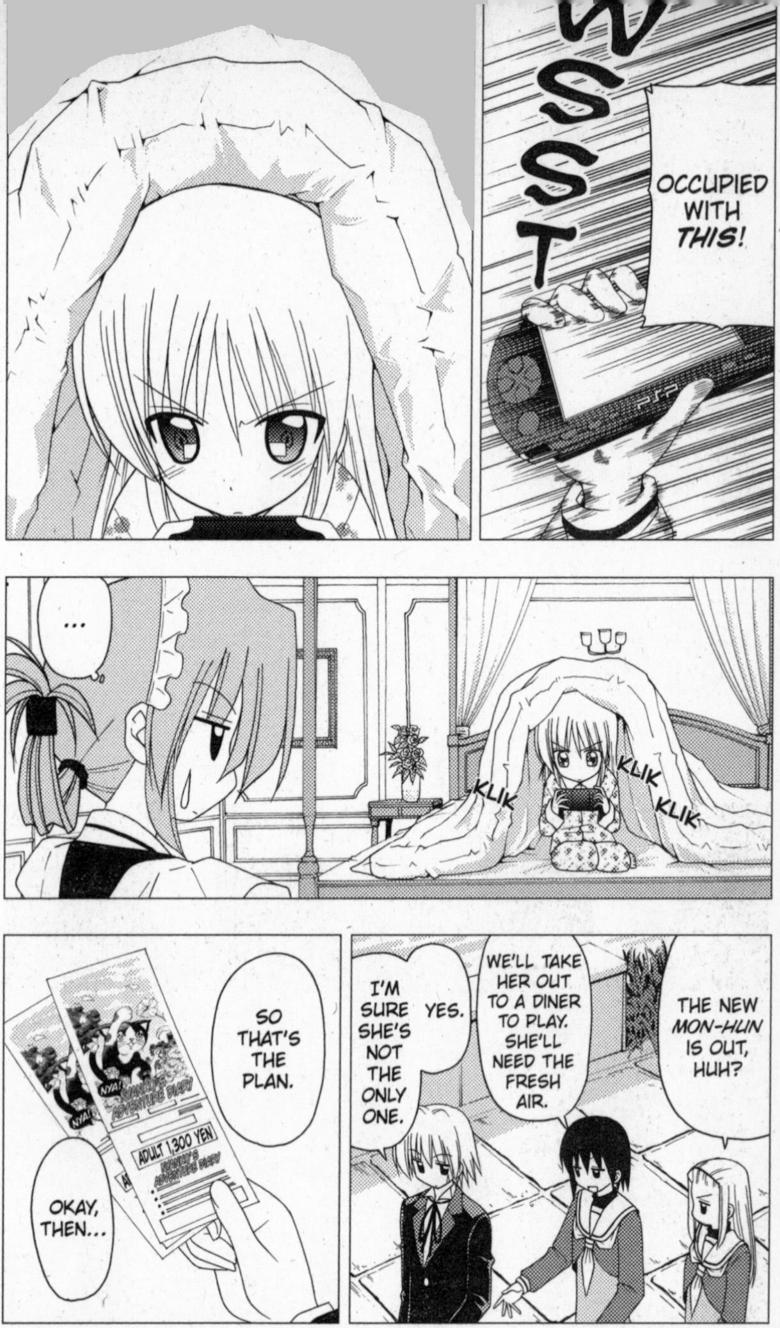

WSST
OCCUPIED WITH *THIS*!
...
KLIK
KLIK
KLIK
THE NEW *MON-HUN* IS OUT, HUH?
WE'LL TAKE HER OUT TO A DINER TO PLAY. SHE'LL NEED THE FRESH AIR.
YES.
I'M SURE SHE'S NOT THE ONLY ONE.
SO THAT'S THE PLAN.
NYA!
NYANKO'S ADVENTURE DIARY
ADULT 1,300 YEN
NYANKO'S ADVENTURE DIARY
OKAY, THEN...

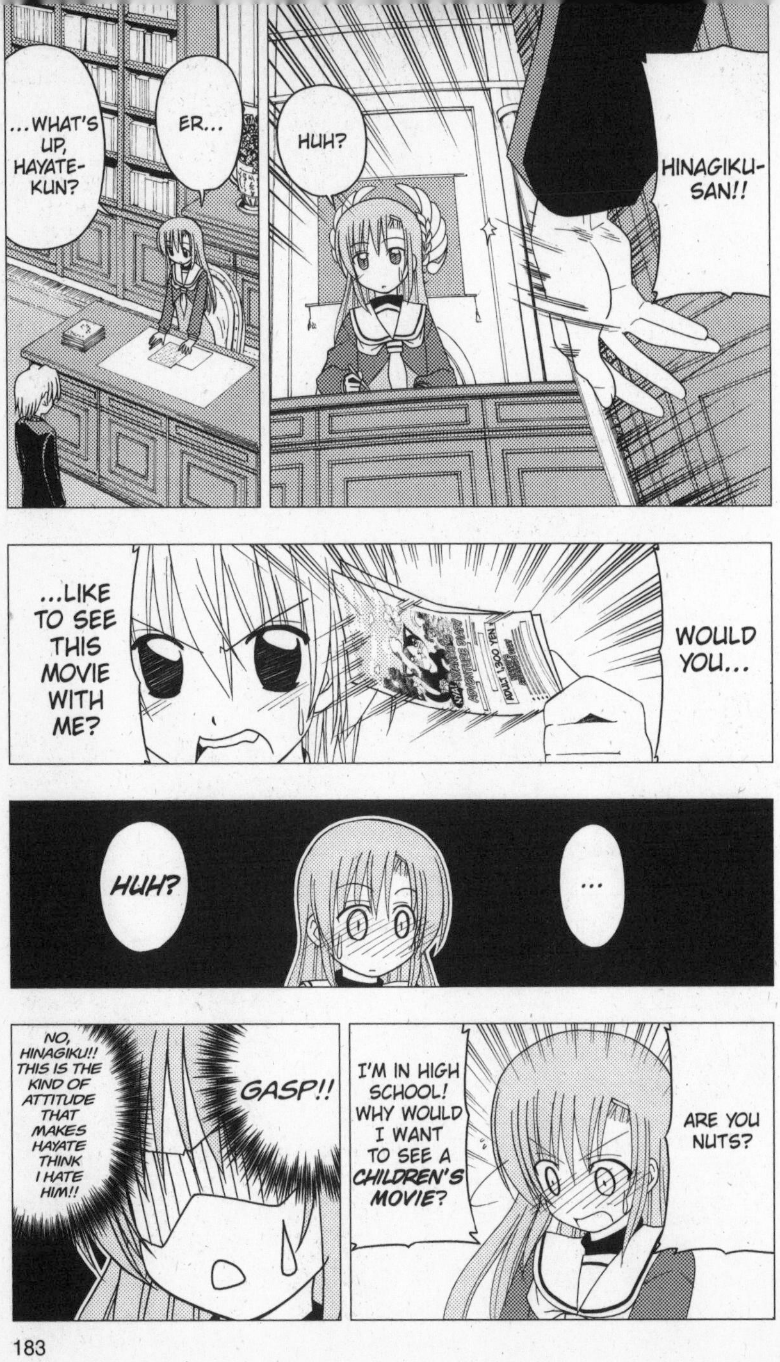
HINAGIKU-SAN!!
HUH?
ER...
...WHAT'S UP, HAYATE-KUN?
WOULD YOU...
...LIKE TO SEE THIS MOVIE WITH ME?
ADULT 1,300 YEN
...
HUH?
ARE YOU NUTS?
I'M IN HIGH SCHOOL! WHY WOULD I WANT TO SEE A CHILDREN'S MOVIE?
GASP!!
NO, HINAGIKU!! THIS IS THE KIND OF ATTITUDE THAT MAKES HAYATE THINK I HATE HIM!!

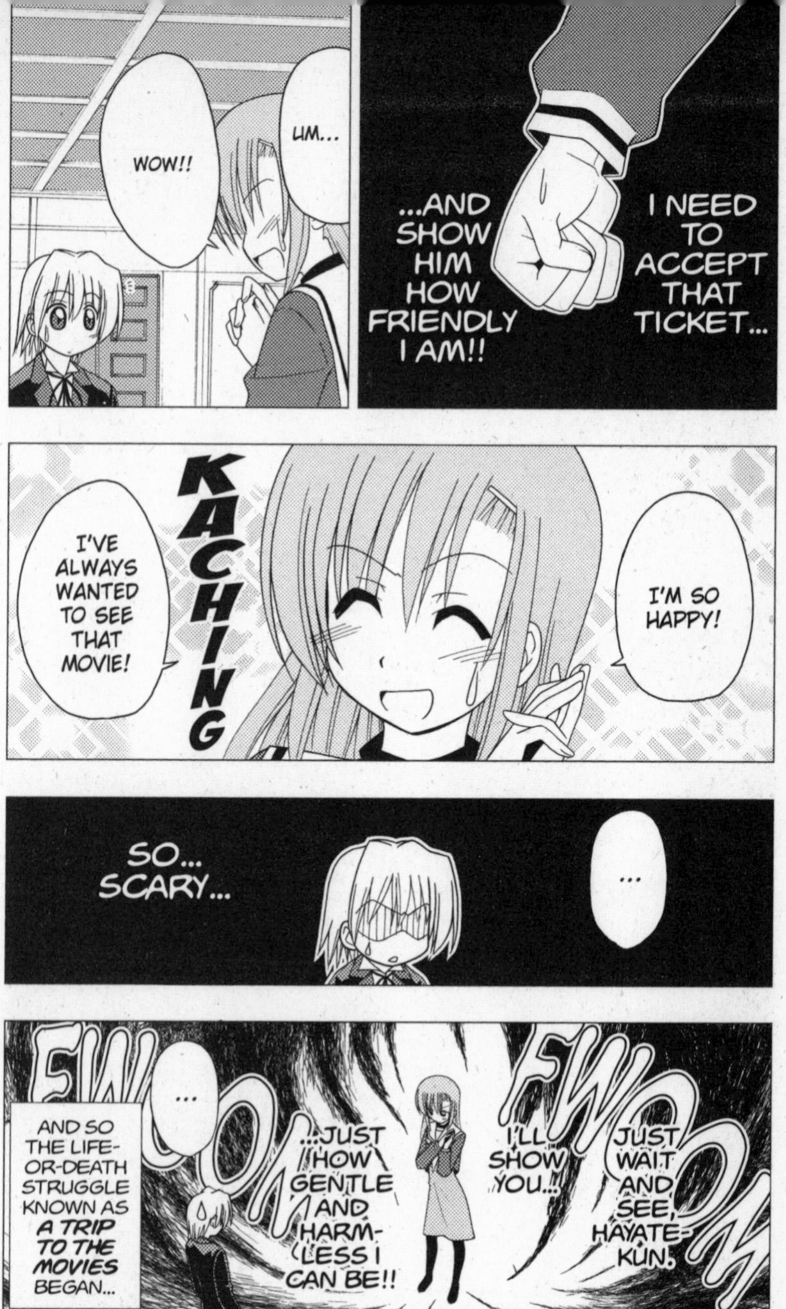
I NEED TO ACCEPT THAT TICKET...
...AND SHOW HIM HOW FRIENDLY I AM!!
UM...
WOW!!
I'M SO HAPPY!
KACHING
I'VE ALWAYS WANTED TO SEE THAT MOVIE!
...
SO... SCARY...
FWOOM
JUST WAIT AND SEE, HAYATE-KUN.
I'LL SHOW YOU...
...JUST HOW GENTLE AND HARM-LESS I CAN BE!!
FWOOM
...
AND SO THE LIFE-OR-DEATH STRUGGLE KNOWN AS ***A TRIP TO THE MOVIES*** BEGAN...

TO BE CONTINUED

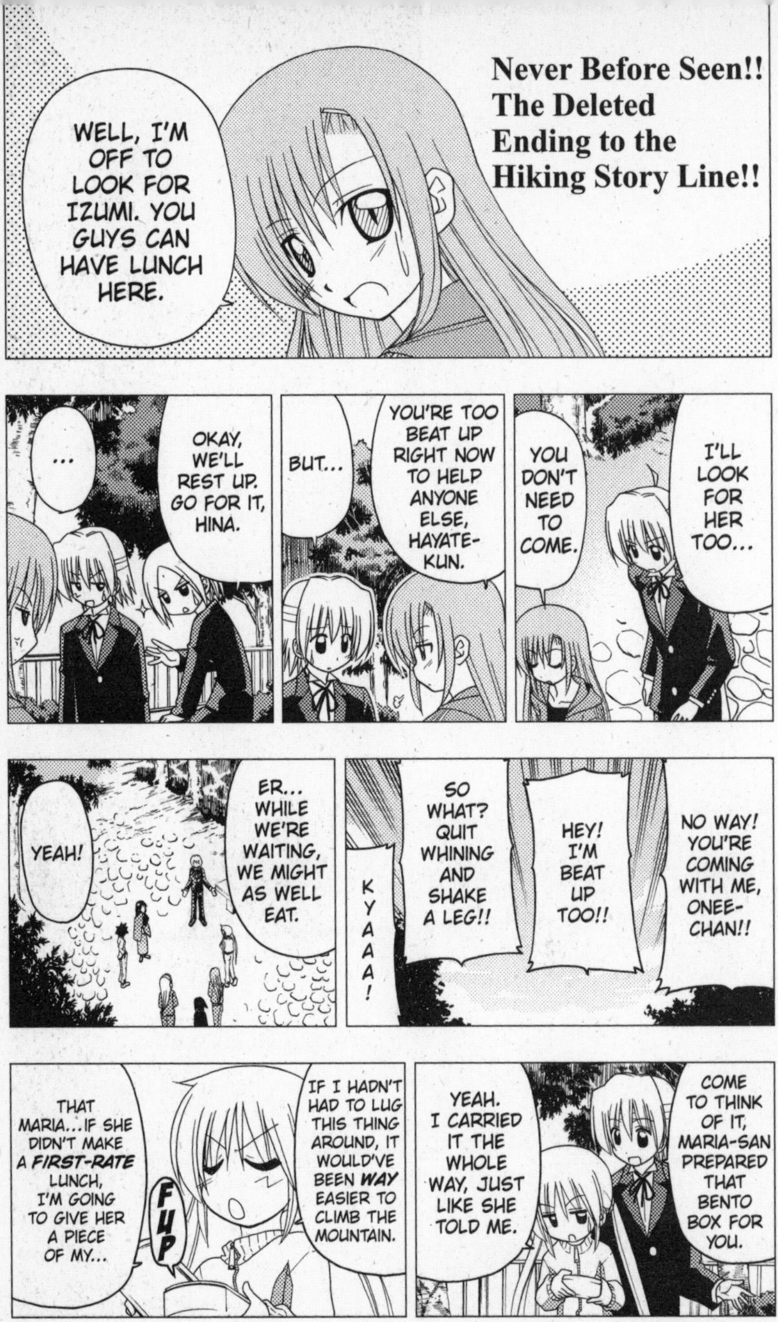
Never Before Seen!! The Deleted Ending to the Hiking Story Line!!
WELL, I'M OFF TO LOOK FOR IZUMI. YOU GUYS CAN HAVE LUNCH HERE.
I'LL LOOK FOR HER TOO...
YOU DON'T NEED TO COME.
YOU'RE TOO BEAT UP RIGHT NOW TO HELP ANYONE ELSE, HAYATE-KUN.
BUT...
OKAY, WE'LL REST UP. GO FOR IT, HINA.
...
NO WAY! YOU'RE COMING WITH ME, ONEE-CHAN!!
HEY! I'M BEAT UP TOO!!
SO WHAT? QUIT WHINING AND SHAKE A LEG!!
KYAAAA!
ER... WHILE WE'RE WAITING, WE MIGHT AS WELL EAT.
YEAH!
COME TO THINK OF IT, MARIA-SAN PREPARED THAT BENTO BOX FOR YOU.
YEAH. I CARRIED IT THE WHOLE WAY, JUST LIKE SHE TOLD ME.
IF I HADN'T HAD TO LUG THIS THING AROUND, IT WOULD'VE BEEN *WAY* EASIER TO CLIMB THE MOUNTAIN.
FUP
THAT MARIA...IF SHE DIDN'T MAKE A *FIRST-RATE* LUNCH, I'M GOING TO GIVE HER A PIECE OF MY...

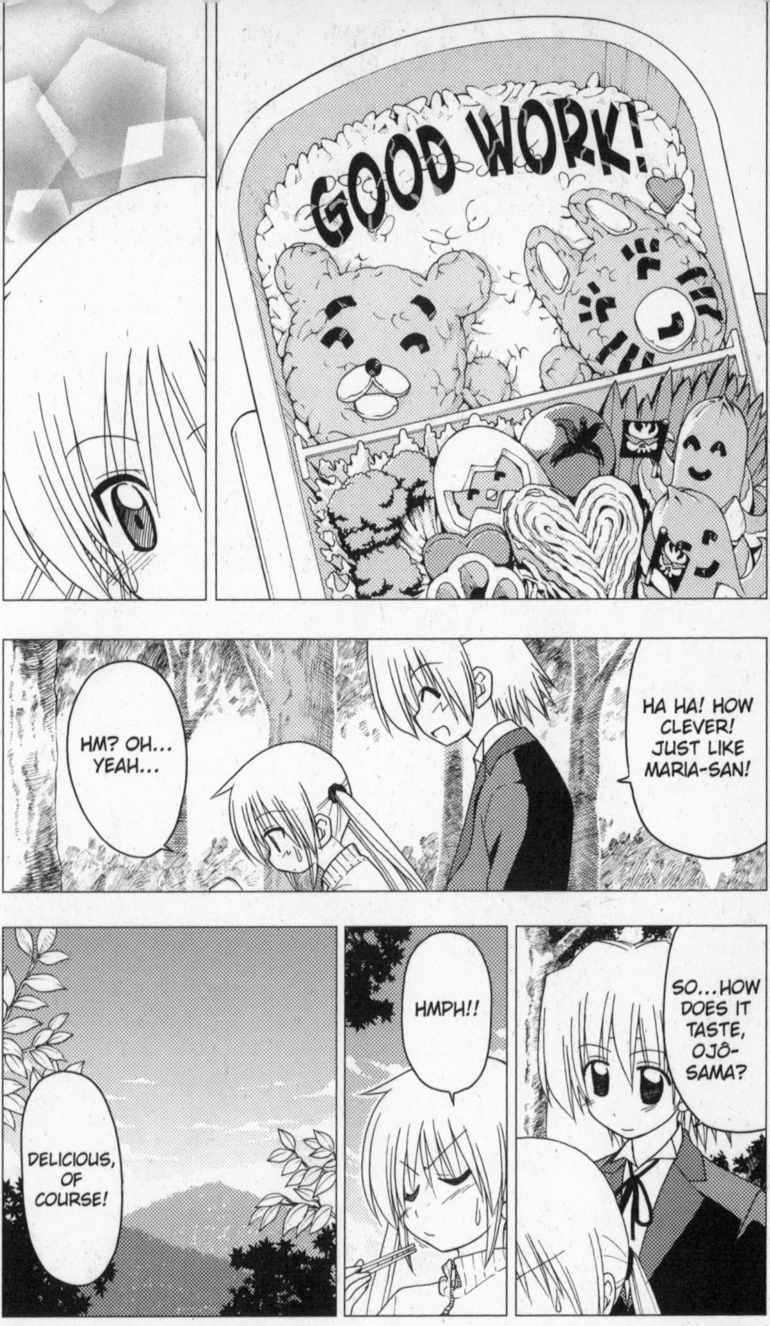
GOOD WORK!
HA HA! HOW CLEVER! JUST LIKE MARIA-SAN!
HM? OH... YEAH...
SO...HOW DOES IT TASTE, OJÔ-SAMA?
HMPH!!
DELICIOUS, OF COURSE!

HAYATE THE COMBAT BUTLER

BONUS PAGE

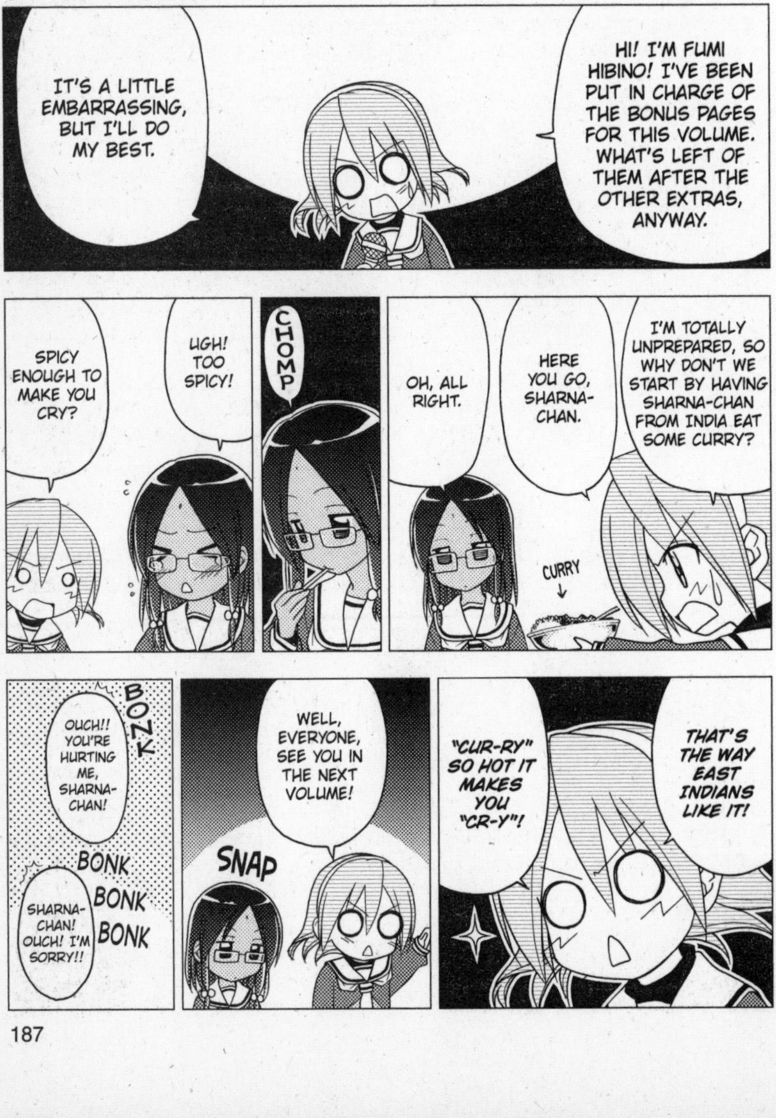
HI! I'M FUMI HIBINO! I'VE BEEN PUT IN CHARGE OF THE BONUS PAGES FOR THIS VOLUME. WHAT'S LEFT OF THEM AFTER THE OTHER EXTRAS, ANYWAY.
IT'S A LITTLE EMBARRASSING, BUT I'LL DO MY BEST.
I'M TOTALLY UNPREPARED, SO WHY DON'T WE START BY HAVING SHARNA-CHAN FROM INDIA EAT SOME CURRY?
HERE YOU GO, SHARNA-CHAN.
OH, ALL RIGHT.
CURRY
CHOMP
UGH! TOO SPICY!
SPICY ENOUGH TO MAKE YOU CRY?
THAT'S THE WAY EAST INDIANS LIKE IT!
"CUR-RY" SO HOT IT MAKES YOU "CR-Y"!
WELL, EVERYONE, SEE YOU IN THE NEXT VOLUME!
SNAP
BONK
OUCH!! YOU'RE HURTING ME, SHARNA-CHAN!
BONK
BONK
BONK
SHARNA-CHAN! OUCH! I'M SORRY!!

THIS YEAR THE *HAYATE* MANGA RAN ALONGSIDE THE FIRST SEASON OF THE ANIME. IT GOT ME ALL WOBBLY AND EXHAUSTED, BUT, THANKS TO YOUR SUPPORT, THE PRODUCERS HAVE GREENLIT A SECOND SEASON.

THANK YOU ALL SO VERY MUCH. I SINCERELY HOPE YOU'LL KEEP READING AND WATCHING!

SO HOW DID YOU LIKE *HAYATE THE COMBAT BUTLER* VOLUME 15? SINCE ALL THE STORY LINES IN VOLUME 14 TOOK UP MULTIPLE CHAPTERS, I TRIED TO DO MOST OF THE STORY LINES IN THIS VOLUME AS ONE-SHOTS. MAYBE GOING FROM ONE EXTREME TO ANOTHER COULD BE THIS MANGA'S TRADEMARK. I WANTED TO FINISH HINAGIKU'S STORY IN THIS VOLUME, BUT, TRY AS I MIGHT, IT SPILLED OVER AGAIN…SORRY. BUT IT'LL PAY OFF IN THE NEXT VOLUME!☆

THE BONUS STORY IS A DELETED ENDING THAT WAS ORIGINALLY PLANNED FOR THE FIRST STORY LINE IN THIS VOLUME. I REVEALED THE COMPLETE DETAILS ABOUT WHAT HAPPENED ON THE JAPANESE *SHONEN SUNDAY* WEBSITE.

TO MAKE A LONG STORY SHORT, SHIINA-SENSEI'S MANGA, *ZETTAI KAREN CHILDREN*, FEATURED A STORY LINE ABOUT A SCHOOL TRIP AT THE SAME TIME AS MY STORY LINE, AND THERE WAS A SCENE WITH A MESSAGE INSIDE A BENTO BOX. IT WAS, UNBELIEVABLY, THE EXACT SAME PUNCHLINE. I GUESS YOU COULD SEE IT AS GREAT MINDS THINKING ALIKE, BUT IN THE END I DECIDED TO SCRAP MY ENDING.

BUT THE INCIDENT CREATED AN OPPORTUNITY FOR THE *HAYATE* CHARACTERS TO MAKE A GUEST APPEARANCE IN *ZETTAI KAREN CHILDREN*, WHICH WAS FUN.☆ I'D LOVE IT IF HAYATE COULD APPEAR IN THE *ZETTAI* ANIME.☆

IN ANY CASE, I'LL KEEP TRYING TO LIVE UP TO YOUR EXPECTATIONS, SO PLEASE CHECK OUT THE NEXT VOLUME! IN VOLUME 16 I'LL BE REVEALING SECRETS ABOUT IZUMI'S FAMILY THAT NO ONE HAS EVEN IMAGINED! WELL, SEE YOU THEN!

BUH-BYE!☆

HAYATE THE COMBAT BUTLER

BAD END (7)

THIS IS WHAT HAPPENS IF YOU ROTATE THE STICK TOO SLOWLY !!!

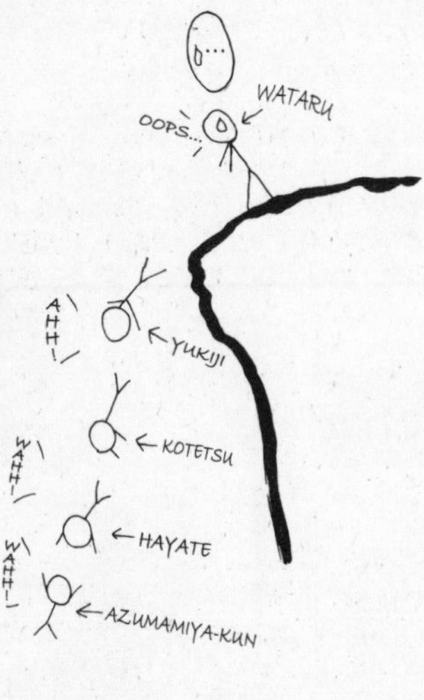
WATARU
OOPS...
AHH!
← YUKIJI
WAHH!
← KOTETSU
WAHH!
← HAYATE
← AZUMAMIYA-KUN

IMPOSSIBLE!!!

An Idea from a Genius

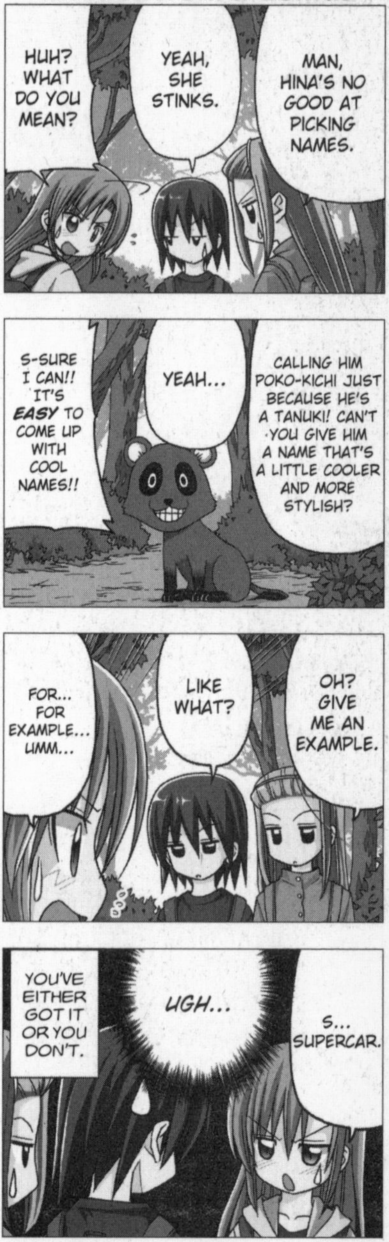
MAN, HINA'S NO GOOD AT PICKING NAMES.
YEAH, SHE STINKS.
HUH? WHAT DO YOU MEAN?
CALLING HIM POKO-KICHI JUST BECAUSE HE'S A TANUKI! CAN'T YOU GIVE HIM A NAME THAT'S A LITTLE COOLER AND MORE STYLISH?
YEAH...
S-SURE I CAN!! IT'S *EASY* TO COME UP WITH COOL NAMES!!
OH? GIVE ME AN EXAMPLE.
LIKE WHAT?
FOR... FOR EXAMPLE... UMM...
S... SUPERCAR.
UGH...
YOU'VE EITHER GOT IT OR YOU DON'T.

An Education for a Genius

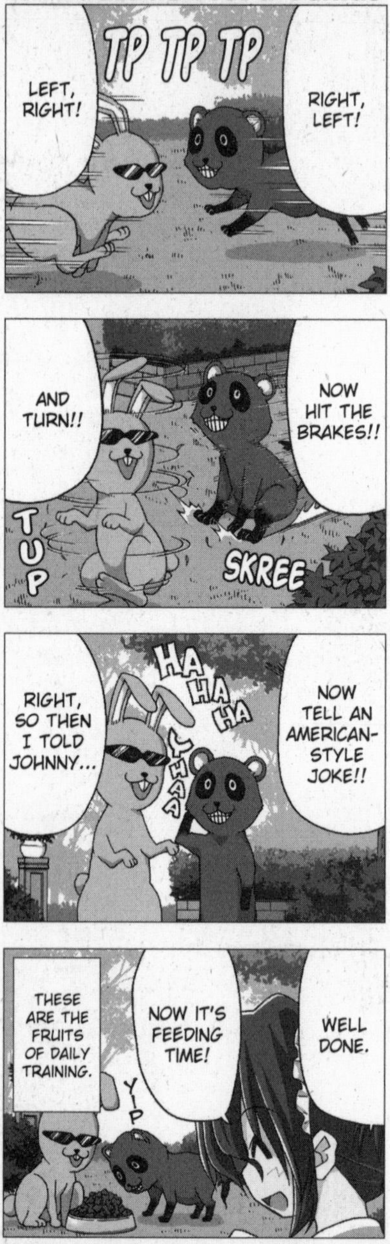
RIGHT, LEFT!
TP TP TP
LEFT, RIGHT!
NOW HIT THE BRAKES!!
SKREE
AND TURN!!
TUP
NOW TELL AN AMERICAN-STYLE JOKE!!
HA HA HA
YHAA
RIGHT, SO THEN I TOLD JOHNNY...
WELL DONE.
NOW IT'S FEEDING TIME!
YIP
THESE ARE THE FRUITS OF DAILY TRAINING.

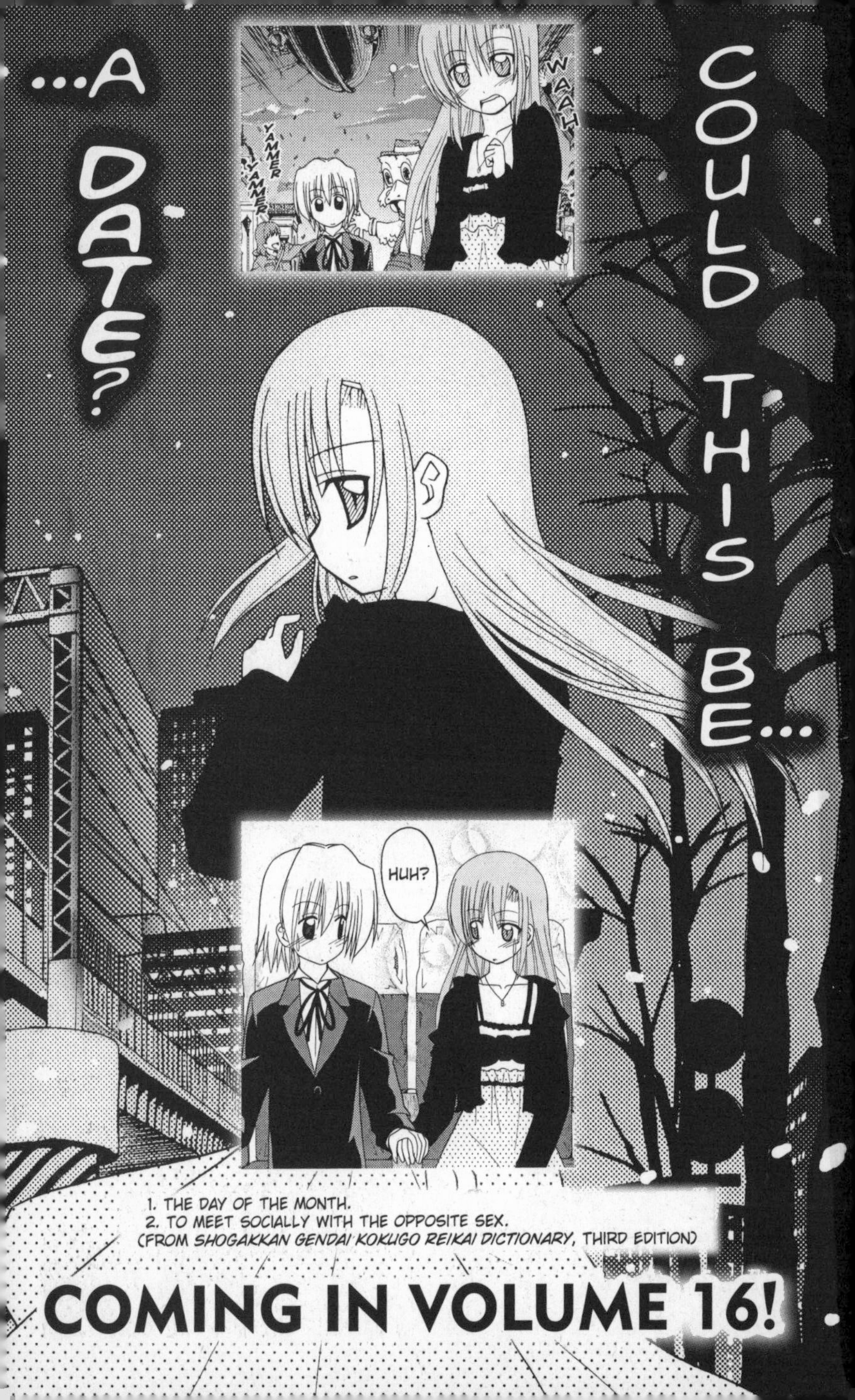
COULD THIS BE...
...A DATE?
WAAAH
YAMMER YAMMER
HUH?
1. THE DAY OF THE MONTH.
2. TO MEET SOCIALLY WITH THE OPPOSITE SEX.
(FROM SHOGAKKAN GENDAI KOKUGO REIKAI DICTIONARY, THIRD EDITION)
COMING IN VOLUME 16!

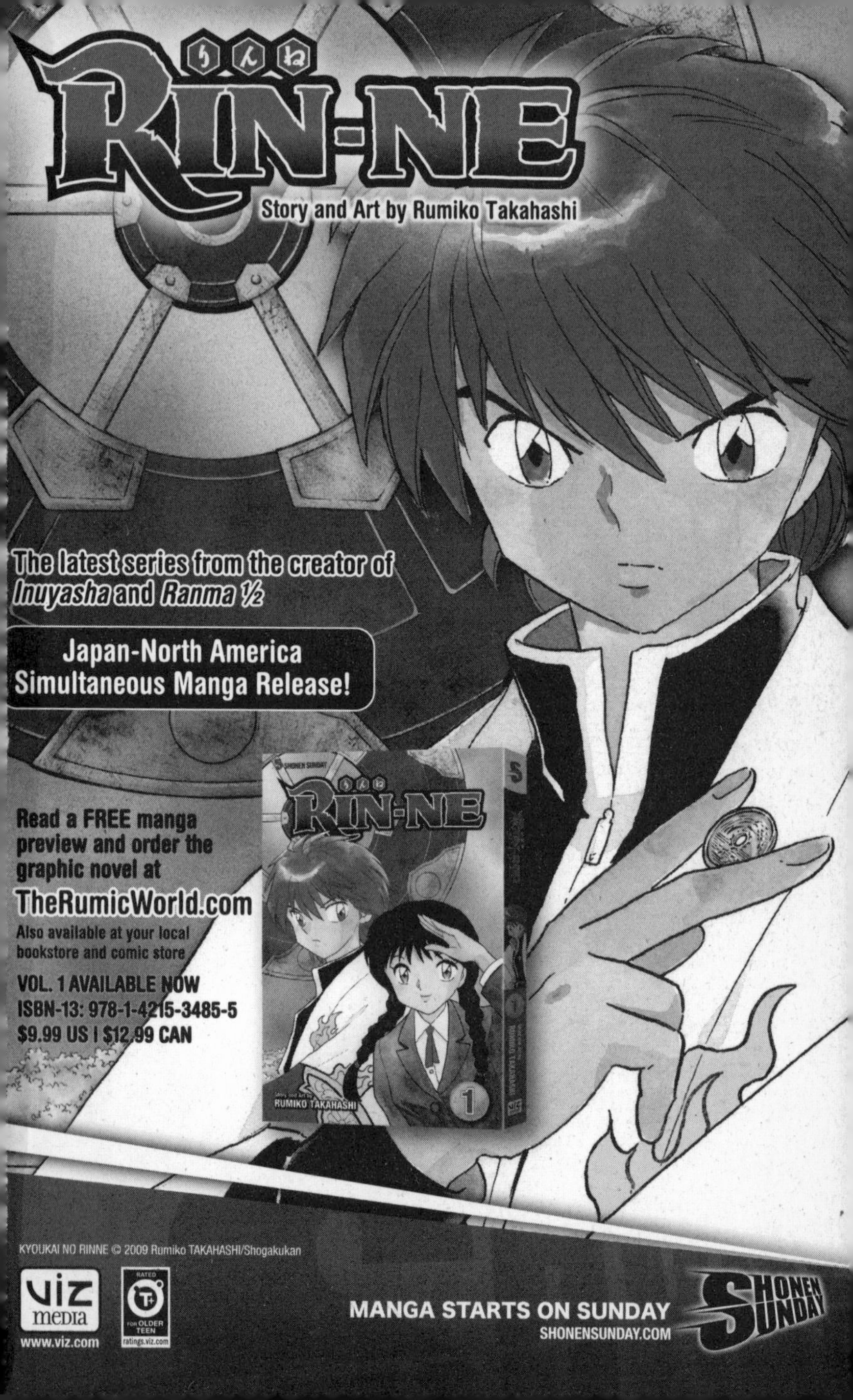
りんね
RIN-NE
Story and Art by Rumiko Takahashi
The latest series from the creator of *Inuyasha* and *Ranma ½*
Japan-North America Simultaneous Manga Release!
SHONEN SUNDAY
RIN-NE
Story and Art by RUMIKO TAKAHASHI
1
Read a FREE manga preview and order the graphic novel at
TheRumicWorld.com
Also available at your local bookstore and comic store
VOL. 1 AVAILABLE NOW
ISBN-13: 978-1-4215-3485-5
$9.99 US | $12.99 CAN
KYOUKAI NO RINNE © 2009 Rumiko TAKAHASHI/Shogakukan
viz media
www.viz.com
RATED T+ FOR OLDER TEEN
ratings.viz.com
MANGA STARTS ON SUNDAY
SHONENSUNDAY.COM
SHONEN SUNDAY